IS THE BBC IN CRISIS?

EDITED BY
JOHN MAIR, RICHARD TAIT
and
RICHARD LANCE KEEBLE

Published 2014 by Abramis academic publishing

www.abramis.co.uk

ISBN 978 1 84549 621 0

Printed and bound in the United Kingdom

Typeset in Garamond 11pt

Abramis is an imprint of arima publishing.

arima publishing
ASK House, Northgate Avenue
Bury St Edmunds, Suffolk IP32 6BB
t: (+44) 01284 700321

www.arimapublishing.com

Contents

Acknowledgements   viii

The editors   ix

Introduction: Wither the BBC
Michael Grade (Lord Grade of Yarmouth)   1

Section 1. Panorama: Setting the scene
John Mair   7

1. History repeating itself? Hutton, Savile and the future of the BBC
Richard Tait, CBE   12

2. The BBC's cultural mission and how it interweaves with democracy and the
economy
Sir Peter Bazalgette, Chair of Arts Council England   27

3. Turning up the temperature: The BBC and political pressure
Phil Harding, journalist and media consultant, BBC Controller Editorial Policy, 1996-2001
                                                                                   34

4. What Britons think of the BBC
Alice Enders, Senior Media Analyst at Enders Analysis   44

5. The BBC as spectacle: Those who live by camera die by it
John Mair   52

Section 2: Timewatch: From a historical perspective
Richard Tait   61

6. View from a journalistic bystander
Tara Conlan, freelance media writer for the Guardian *and* Observer   65

7. Reporting the crisis from inside the beast
Torin Douglas, MBE, BBC Media Correspondent 1989-2013   73

8. BBC licence fee negotiations – past and future
Raymond Snoddy, OBE, journalist and broadcaster, presenter BBC Newswatch, *2005-2013*
                                                                                   84

Section 3: Here is the news – and it's not all good!
John Mair 91

9. Thirteen days in the life of *Newsnight*
Vin Ray, writer, Founding Director BBC College of Journalism, BBC 96

10. 'A BBC anxious about making friends and ensuring survival has some very hard thinking to do'
Peter Preston, media columnist, the Observer, *Editor, the* Guardian, *1975-95* 108

. 11. How the BBC leans to the right
Professor Justin Lewis, Dean of Research in the Arts, Humanities and Social Sciences, Cardiff University 114

12. Facts, informed opinion and mere opinion
Julian Petley, Professor of Screen Media at Brunel University 121

13. BBC in crisis: 'The Westminster conspiracy'
David Edwards and David Cromwell, Editors of Media Lens 134

Section 4: Casualty: Crises – past and present
Richard Lance Keeble 145

14. BBC and the PR challenge
Richard Peel, Managing Director, RPPR, Head of Public Relations, BBC News 1987-98
150

15. The coming crisis
Jean Seaton, Professor of Media History at the University of Westminster 158

16. BBC Radio censorship rows: Lessons from history
Tim Crook, Visiting Professor of Broadcast Journalism at Birmingham City University 166

17. Crisis? What crisis? The real BBC catastrophe is yet to happen
Steven Barnett, Professor of Communications at Westminster University 176

18. The conventions of the BBC
Brian Winston holds the Lincoln Professorship at the University of Lincoln 183

Section 5: The Money Programme: The BBC 'Officer Class' fill their boots
John Mair   193

19. How BBC executives lost the public service ethos
Nicholas Jones, for 30 years a BBC correspondent   198

20. Sweet partings
Suzanne Franks, Professor of Journalism at City University London   205

Section 6: Songs of Praise: The Reithian 'Holy Trinity' in danger
Richard Lance Keeble   211

21. Who cares about BBC education?
Fiona Chesterton, BBC Controller Adult Learning, 1998-2004   215

22. Grasping the Thistle: Is the BBC still relevant to Scotland?
Atholl Duncan, BBC Scotland Head of News and Current Affairs, 2006-2011 223

23. A clear case of journalistic under-performance: The house that Birt (and Hall) built
Professor David Lloyd, Commissioning Editor, News and Current Affairs, Channel Four 1986-2003   231

24. Still hideously white?
Farrukh Dhondy, writer and Multicultural Commissioning Editor of Channel 4 1984-1997
                                                                           239

Section 7: The nation's Trust: Trust in the Trust?
Richard Tait   247

25. A question of Trust
David Liddiment, BBC Trustee 2006-2014, former Network Controller ITV 1997-2002
                                                                           253

26. Need for clarity at the Corporation on who is responsible for what
Sir Howard Davies, Director of the London School of Economics and Political Science 2003-2011   260

27. A crisis of independence
Tim Suter, CEO Perspective Associates, Ofcom Partner 2003-2007, Head of Broadcasting Policy DCMS 2002-2003   268

28. The licence fee and the question of BBC funding
David Elstein, Chief Executive of Channel 5 1996-2000, Head of Programming at BSkyB,
Director of Programmes at Thames TV 1986-1993   274

29. When The Jacuzzi Stopped
Bernard Clark, originator of BBC Watchdog and independent producer for 30 years   285

30. The best is yet to come
Andrew Scadding, BBC Head of Corporate Affairs   291

Acknowledgements

This is the eleventh in the Abramis series of journalism/academic texts created by Professor Richard Lance Keeble and John Mair in 2008. Thanks for this volume go to, primarily, the authors and contributors who have been unstinting in creating their chapters, who have given their work *pro-bono* (as have the editors on all the books) and who suffer a torrent of emails from the editors reminding them of looming deadlines. Most respond well. We have thirty high level contributors in this volume. They have delivered. Commissioning well and chivvying, not so well, works.

We also need to thank warmly Richard and Pete Franklin, of Abramis, who support and publish the series in double-quick time with great aplomb and little fuss. And Peter Hnatuskha for designing another simple but stunning cover.

Lastly, our families who have lived this and other 'hackademic' projects for too long. They are the real heroes…

John Mair, Oxford
Richard Tait, London
Richard Lance Keeble, Withcall, Lincolnshire
February 2014

The editors

John Mair has taught journalism at the Universities of Coventry, Kent, Northampton, Brunel, Edinburgh Napier, Guyana and the Communication University of China. He has now edited twelve 'hackademic' volumes over the last five years on subjects ranging from trust in TV, the health of investigative journalism, reporting the 'Arab Spring' to three volumes on the Leveson Inquiry. He and Richard Lance Keeble invented the sub-genre. John also invented the Coventry Conversations which attracted 350 media movers and shakers to Coventry University while the podcasts of those have been downloaded five million times worldwide. Since then, he has launched the Northampton Chronicles, MediaMondays at Napier and most recently the Harrow Conversations at Westminster. In a previous life, he was an award-winning producer/director for the BBC, ITV and Channel Four and a secondary school teacher.

Richard Tait, CBE, is Professor of Journalism, School of Journalism, Media and Cultural Studies, Cardiff University. He was Director of the Cardiff Centre for Journalism from 2002 to 2012. He began his journalism career in business magazines and then joined the BBC where he became Editor of *The Money Programme*, *Newsnight* and the 1987 General Election Results Programme. He moved to ITN in 1987 as Editor of Channel 4 News and became Editor-in-Chief in 1995. From 2002 to 2004 he wrote a column on media policy for the *Financial Times* Creative Business section. In 2004, he joined the BBC board as a governor and from 2006 to 2010 was Trustee and Chair of the Editorial Standards Committee. He is a Fellow of the Society of Editors and the Royal Television Society and Treasurer of the International News Safety Institute.

Richard Lance Keeble has been Professor of Journalism at the University of Lincoln since 2003. Before that he was the Executive Editor of the *Teacher*, the weekly newspaper of the National Union of Teachers and he lectured at City University London for 19 years. He has written and edited 28 publications on a wide range of subjects including peace journalism, literary journalism, journalism ethics, practical reporting skills, George Orwell, the coverage of US/UK militarism and the links between the intelligence services and Fleet Street. He is also joint editor of *Ethical Space: The International Journal of Communication Ethics* and the winner of a National Teacher Fellowship in 2011 – the highest prize for teachers in higher education. He is chair of both the George Orwell Society and Louth Male Voice Choir.

Introduction:
Wither the BBC

**The BBC should – and can – survive, writes Michael Grade,
but only if it makes a radical break with its past**

There are three established UK institutions you would not invent today if you
had a blank sheet of paper and were 'creating' a new Great Britain: an hereditary
monarchy, an unelected second legislature (the House of Lords) and, yes, the
British Broadcasting Corporation.)The arguments against these 'anachronisms'
are more powerful and more easily articulated than the arguments in favour of
their continued existence. Yet, somehow, their emotional grip on the hearts and
minds of the British people seems likely to hold sway for generations to come.
They help to define the curious, often mystical aura of Great Britain – they are
what make us 'different', core brand values, if you like jargon.

How well I remember the late Lady Thatcher defending our monarchy with
the words: 'My mother used to say that without our monarchy we would be just
like (pause for contemptuous emphasis) Belgium!'

My remit here, as the last Chairman of the old BBC governors, is the BBC:
some anachronism – three and a half billion pounds of public intervention in a
dynamic and ever growing media market. How can the BBC argue its case to
survive against such odds? Intellectual logic, both economic and social (how
better could we spend £3.5 billion?) are against them. On the other hand,
political sentiment will usually follow the public mood – and this is where the
BBC scores heaviest. The electorate is emotionally attached to 'Auntie' in a way
that politicians can only envy. The public backlash to the fallout from the
Hutton Inquiry, when Blair, Campbell et al, brought the Corporation to its knees,
I believe, really surprised and scared the Labour government. It demonstrated
beyond doubt the overwhelming public support for '*its*' BBC. I count myself as a
firm believer in the idea of the BBC.

Thinking the unthinkable

But can the BBC survive long term? Will my grandchildren still value the kind of public service content that we have valued from the BBC all these years? Can they continue to hold out against the market forces that threaten to make them irrelevant? Can they justify the licence fee, or regressive poll tax as it is defined by its enemies? Will they be forced into an irrelevant, elitist ghetto of market failure, filling in the tiny niche taste voids left by the private sector?

Not in its present form is my verdict. The BBC has an assured place in the modern history of Britain, and yet in one very damaging respect it is a slave to its history. When it started out and then developed, there were no studios. It had to design, build, own and operate its own. There were no electronics companies, so it had to design and create its own cameras, TV lighting, and other operating systems. There were no independent programme makers so it made its own. I could go on and on. It is in the DNA of the BBC that 'we can and must do everything ourselves'. It still seems to believe in owning real estate, studios, post-production and, yes, programme making – it is as if the private sector did not exist. It goes on expanding in areas that require huge resources, yet more management, more HR departments, more spectrum, more channels, more, more, more.

The recent wave of remuneration horrors serves as a red light warning that in the process of expansion the BBC has forgotten the value *of* money. Not surprising given the size of the cheque (£3.5 billion remember) that arrives every year. Where there is no bottom line, no profit and loss account, no need to 'earn' revenue, territory becomes the yardstick. More licence fee, more services on line or over the air.

In the great Hollywood gangster movie *Little Caesar*, in a quiet moment away from the murder and mayhem, Edward G. Robinson, in the title role, is asked by a sidekick what he really wants. Without hesitation he responds simply: 'I want more.' He would have made a classic director-general. This cannot and must not continue if the BBC is to retain public support.

The BBC under its impressive new Director-General Tony Hall and with the board of Trustees must be radical in the upcoming charter renewal debate. The future of the BBC lies in a root and branch reversal of its default territorial agenda. It must think the unthinkable.

Blueprint for survival

Here are my starters for ten: merge channels BBC 2 and 4 – and surrender the spectrum and invest heavily in one, properly funded channel. Does any viewer understand the difference between 2 and 4 today? I certainly don't. With one such channel to fund maybe we will have a channel that can afford challenging UK drama every week of the year.

Outsource *all* production processes and facilities (studios, post production, film and TV) to a private sector more than capable of absorbing the work (I declare my interest here as chairman of Pinewood and Shepperton studios). This will free up capital expenditure, resource management, headcount, investment capital and much more besides. The BBC must finally accept that it just doesn't need to own and operate any of these facilities services any longer. It seems to have survived when its transmitters were privatised against its wishes.

The independent production sector now provides a huge proportion of BBC TV and radio programming, outside of news. It supports Channel 4's entire output. What is the justification for the BBC continuing to run BBC in-house production any longer in areas such as drama, documentaries, light entertainment, comedy etc etc? No point at all. Any producer who comes up through the BBC in-house ranks and makes a name for his or herself, soon leaves to start their own production company or join an existing one.

This may come as a shock to BBC thinking, but it no longer enjoys a monopoly of creativity. When David Attenborough now plies his genius with independent Atlantic Films, you *know* the game is up. It is time for the BBC to become a publisher/broadcaster along Channel 4 lines. Some monies freed up should be mandated for industry training. 'In house' production should remain exclusively for news and, maybe, just maybe, for current affairs strands such as *Panorama*.

The above shopping list would be a start; a signal that the BBC at last understands that less is actually more. Fewer departments, fewer managers with six figure salaries, fewer demands on cash and a smaller target for its enemies. In essence a simpler, much more manageable institution. Perhaps the LSE or some such organisation could model these ideas to see how much lower the licence fee could be set.

Preserving the core mission

None of my above contribution to the debate would in any way dilute or risk the BBC's core mission which is to transform the public's money into programmes and services that at one time or another, on one service or another, radio or TV or on line, they can each value.

(The BBC has an indispensable role to play in journalism, not just internationally through the World Service, but throughout the four nations and the regions) I was and remain a committed supporter of the BBC's journey out of London. The precarious state of regional printed news throughout the UK will ultimately leave a democratic deficit which only the BBC, with its public funding, is placed to fill. Regional news and news of and for the four nations is a key purpose of the BBC and will benefit greatly from investment, which it can only find with radical solutions – *not* an ever greater licence fee, their usual solution.

In addition, encouraging creative talent throughout Britain is another key purpose. In the old federal days of 16 ITV companies, Granada in the north west, Yorkshire, Central in the Midlands etc were hotbeds of local talent, places where writers, directors, performers and producers only needed a cheap bus ride to get a chance to express their talent. ITV today, like the BBC then, is pretty much a London consolidation. The opportunity for the BBC to travel in the opposite direction is one they should continue to embrace.

A word about BBC Worldwide in my scenario: it should continue its core role of exploiting the intellectual property funded by the licence fee, through international distribution (exports) and ancillary activities. The terms of trade between the BBC and independent producers in a publisher broadcaster model should ensure a full commercial return for the BBC in the further exploitation of programmes and formats. Worldwide exists to be a profit centre, based on its international success with BBC programme brands. That should continue. It should avoid speculative commercial expansion, it should avoid acquisitions. It should be run with a culture of ruthless profit maximisation. If it can achieve a commercial return running BBC channels around the world, good luck. Break even and losses should not be acceptable.

Sharing the licence fee?

Should the BBC fail to rise to the challenge of a radical future there is one option which would solve a number of problems – competitive funding for the licence fee. Let me explain. Online advertising is now overtaking traditional spend. This threatens all advertising-supported TV channels, from ITV and Channels 4 and 5 to the smallest digital offerings. If, and only if the BBC is still in *Little Caesar* mode and reluctant to embrace the modern way of doing things, I would take the most important and most threatened public service channel, namely Channel 4, out of the advertising market entirely. It is going to struggle more and more to maintain its special minority remit in the face of increased competition and reducing ad spend.

It should then be funded out of the total licence fee. It should retain its sovereignty – the last thing it needs is the suffocating embrace of the institutionalised BBC – but in a series of, say, tri-annual settlements, be put into competition with the BBC for a share of the licence fee, based on quality criteria to be designed by, say Ofcom. At a stroke, Channel 4's future would be assured, all of the private sector channels which are ad-supported, would receive a boost which would ensure sustained investment in original programmes (and improve the advertiser proposition) and, most important, the BBC would learn about the value of money. It would create a culture of transparency no governance system could replicate where the licence fee monopoly is maintained.

Governance (again)

... And so (yawn, yawn) to governance. Oh dear, yet again the debate about the future of the BBC will be dominated by everyone's pet governance model. I lived through the last debate as chairman of the governors and was in at the birth of the Trust, the creation, whose midwife was Tessa Jowell. It certainly isn't perfect, but it sure is better than what went before.

Let us be clear, there is no such thing as a perfect model of governance – neither in the public nor the private sectors. I give you just two examples of FTSE 100 companies who ticked every code compliant governance box:

Marconi and Royal Bank of Scotland. I rest my case. Governance structures are *no* substitute for individual judgement. That is the lesson of the BBC's travails over the years and so many private sector companies, too. Governance structural flaws do not cause disasters, it is poor human judgement.

Let the debate be about the shape and role of the BBC, then we can decide the best governance structure to implement it – and, of course, appoint the right people with sound judgement and wisdom who will overcome the inevitable flaws in whatever governance system is in place.

Note on the contributor
Michael Grade (Lord Grade of Yarmouth) is chairman of Pinewood and Shepperton Film Studios. He began his career as a newspaper journalist, became Director of Programmes at LWT from 1977 to 1981; Director of Programmes, BBC television from 1986 to 1987; Chief Executive of Channel 4 from 1988-1997; Chairman of the BBC from 2004 to 2006 and Executive Chairman and Chief Executive of ITV from 2007 to 2009.

Section 1:
Panorama: Setting the scene

John Mair

As *anni horribili* go 2012 and 2013 were pretty dire for the BBC. It has not got much better. 2014 started with at least two huge potential crises brewing: Dame Janet Smith was due to report on the sexual activities of Jimmy Savile (and others) in the BBC and the Public Accounts Committee was due to investigate further the Digital Media Initiative disaster which wasted £100 million – the licence fees of a city the size of Glasgow. Things can only get better before the two Lords Hall and Patten start to negotiate the next licence fee settlement and the royal charter which both start in 2017.

By then the Corporation will be up to 20 per cent smaller as a result of the last licence fee settlement in October 2010 when the then-Director-General Mark Thompson was effectively mugged over a lightning fast one-week period and told to accept the Secretary of State Jeremy Hunt and Chancellor George Osborne's strict terms or lump it! It meant real cuts in the Corporation's income and *de facto* 'top slicing' that reduced the amount to pay for the World Service, local television, S4C and more. The climate will be no better for negotiation in 2015/2016 especially if a majority Conservative government wins the 2015 election.

This book aims quite simply to set the agenda for discussion of the future of Britain's biggest and most trusted public service broadcaster. The BBC faces a plethora of problems but, at the moment, respect and positive brand image round the world are not one of them. As with the previous journalistic/academic volumes edited by John Mair and Richard Lance Keeble, it aims to bring together practitioners, active and passive, with media academics to take a 360-degree but thorough examination of the subject. *Is the BBC in Crisis?* is no exception.

By way of an introduction to the issues swirling around the BBC and its role, some seasoned practitioners set the scene – the panorama, in effect, for the whole book. Professor Richard Tait (one of the joint editors of this book) is amongst the most distinguished broadcast journalists and executives of this generation. He has edited *The Money Programme*, *Newsnight*, BBC general elections coverage, Channel Four News and was Editor-in-Chief of Independent Television News. In addition, he has served as both a BBC governor and a Trustee and was Director of the Centre for Journalism at Cardiff University. His feet in three camps – programme maker, television executive and academic – gives him a unique viewpoint on crises past and present. In his chapter, 'History repeating itself? Hutton, Savile and the future of the BBC', he looks to the future:

> The debate about the BBC's future as we approach discussions on the next charter is likely to raise some fundamental issues – the BBC's monopoly of the licence fee, its overall market impact, the scale and role of its journalism.

Tait examines in clinical detail two BBC crises nearly a decade apart – Gilligan/Hutton in 2003/4 and Savile/*Newsnight* in 2012/13. He concludes that the parallels between them are too close for comfort and sounds a warning for the new Director-General, Lord Hall, and the current BBC Trust Chair Lord Patten:

> The current executive and Trust have a comparatively short time to make the case for their vision of the future and their preferred structure of governance and regulation in a sceptical, if not openly hostile, political and commercial environment. The self-inflicted wounds of the last two years will not make that task any easier. The BBC must hope that the politicians remember at least one lesson from history – that hasty changes to the charter in response to a short-term crisis are not the best way to ensure the BBC remains the strong and independent organisation it must be to serve its audiences as they expect and deserve.

Optimism on the future of the Corporation

Professor Tait is an optimist on the future of the Corporation as is Sir Peter Bazalgette, Chair of Arts Council England. In 'The BBC's cultural mission and how it interweaves with democracy and the economy', Sir Peter, once a BBC producer before becoming a highly successful independent producer (*inter alia*, he brought *Big Brother* to British television!) argues for an outward-looking BBC sharing its cultural and economic capital with the nation:

> The BBC represents a massive market and social intervention. Historically this has been justified by the delivery of three things: trusted and reliable news and information, substantial output of original programming and a sustained investment in creative talent. In this way, the BBC has made a critical democratic, cultural and economic contribution to the life of our

country. I do not think these principles have changed. But the means of performing this role are changing and need to do so. In future, the Corporation should act less unilaterally and more as a partner.

Any BBC charter renewal, in his view, will come about through the BBC morphing from its traditional 'Auntie is always right' position to one of the ever-benevolent cultural uncle or grandfather to other cultural bodies.

> The BBC has no monopoly over our culture but it is probably the most significant player. In broadcasting, others, such as Channel 4 and ITV, are real contributors too. But when we ponder how and whether to renew the BBC's charter we start from where we are. Over ninety years Britain has built up considerable cultural capital in this one institution and it would be rash to squander it. This doesn't mean, however, that it should not change. For me, the most important shift is that if the BBC is to remain the sole recipient of the licence fee it needs to share it much more widely. It must move from the unilateral to the bilateral, from the *dirigiste* to the collaborative, from Reithian aloofness to a spirit of partnership. This is already happening.

The survival of the BBC relatively intact depends on the political temperature and political will after the May 2015 general election. Phil Harding has been at the receiving end of the whims of politicians for decades, firstly as Editor of the flagship Radio Four programme, *Today*, from 1987 to 1993 and then as Chief Political Adviser to the BBC from 1996 to 1997. In 'Turning up the temperature: The BBC and political pressure', he argues for a new and more direct public-BBC relationship bypassing the often unhelpful mediation of politicians. That way bullying can be avoided. Unless it does so, the Corporation might become the frog which was boiled to death slowly:

> The BBC will always be at the heart of political rows; it's almost part of its job. But … the political pressures on the BBC are mounting insidiously. It's been lots of small things: increasing pressure from MPs, the increasing numbers of appearances before select committees, the increasing acceptance that parts of the licence fee will be used for bits of national infrastructure, increasing scrutiny from the NAO (National Audit Office), increasingly strident criticism from the press and the linking of editorial pressure with corporate pressure. It's been a bit like the story of the frog in the boiling water. The changes have been subtle and have taken place over a long period of time so that no one has really noticed how hot the water has become.

How the BBC has become the story itself

John Mair is an editor of this and all the previous 'hackademic' volumes. He is a former BBC, ITV and Channel Four producer and director and a teacher of journalism. In 'The BBC as television spectacle', he argues that the BBC rather than reporting the story has itself become the story. From one appearance in front of parliamentary committees in 2004 to sixteen in 2013, the BBC has become the spectacle with its executives knowing the committee rooms of Parliament's Portcullis House as well as New Broadcasting House. BBC bosses are paraded in front of select committees like gladiators fed to lions in ancient Rome. The British press are far from disinterested spectators in this often gory scene. Worse, the BBC's own Parliamentary Channel and Democracy Live website are the platforms on which executives are shown eating constant crow live and recorded. They are televising their own career suicide notes and it is a spectacle with no light at the end of the tunnel.

> Old BBC hands when confronted with the current panoply of woes shrug their shoulders and say: 'It will blow over, it always does.' Alas, this time the issues and problems may be more deep-seated. And more troubles may be on their way: Mark Thompson (again) in February 2014 will be at the Public Accounts Committee trying (*ex post facto*) to justify the Digital Media Initiative fiasco developed under his watch but written off later at the cost of £100 million …. While in June 2014, the Dame Janet Smith report into the activities of Jimmy Savile (and others) within the BBC and the culture of the Corporation is due. That is literally a time bomb waiting to explode. How many more times will the new BBC brahmins be called back to the Portcullis House gladiatorial arena? When and how will the spectacle end? Probably not until 31 December 2016 and then most likely in tears.

Finally, how have all these traumas affected that precious flower – public (aka licence payers) trust and affection for the BBC? Alice Enders is an analyst for Britain's major broadcast consultant Enders Analysis. In 'What Britons think of the BBC', she reads the tea leaves and the Ofcom/BBC Trust opinion poll figures and concludes that, for the moment, the BBC is still, by and large, loved and trusted. A majority of UK adults still back the BBC's licence fee, judging it good value for money, but there is a worrying 43 per cent that do not. Three out of four Britons agree that 'the BBC makes high-quality programmes or online content'. Audiences also have a higher level of confidence in the BBC than other Public Service Broadcasters on most criteria assessed by Ofcom, especially on the questions that concern the quality of news programming. Popularity is still there too – the BBC's biggest cross-platform audience is for news, with BBC TV channels accounting for 274 billion minutes of TV news watched in the year to November 2013 (based on BARB/Infosys data), just over 70 per cent of the total viewed.

So, plenty of storms behind and plenty more ahead, the BBC now probably faces the most uncertain future of its 92-year existence. The world has changed, the BBC has changed some of the way with it but it has also delivered self-inflicted wounds on itself. The Corporation needs to change more – slimming down in numbers and range for starters-whilst continuing to deliver great programming. More transparency has meant more information for customers and elected representatives but much more jeopardy for the BBC Trust and executives and for the Corporation itself. The BBC that emerges post-2017 will be a very different beast.

History repeating itself? Hutton, Savile and the future of the BBC

Less than a decade after Hutton, the BBC's self-inflicted wounds over Savile have again made it vulnerable to political interference. Richard Tait argues that the similarities between the two crises are rather too close for comfort

In September 1974, I joined the BBC Television current affairs department as the lowest form of editorial life – a research assistant. At the end of my first day in the offices of *The Money Programme*, my new colleagues took me for a drink and told me I had made a terrible mistake – the programme was doomed, the editor (who had just hired me) was on the way out and as for the organisation I had joined, it was finished. It was the first, though not the last time in my career, that I heard the immortal phrase: 'What you have to understand, Richard, is that morale at the BBC is at an all time low.'

The BBC is never knowingly undersold in its own reaction to its crises – partly because its role in British public life puts it in an often hostile media spotlight like few other institutions, and partly because some of its own employees have an almost masochistic tendency to exaggerate (or, indeed, exacerbate) their own problems. However, when, nearly three decades later, I joined the BBC board of governors in the aftermath of the Hutton Report, I felt that this time the staff really were entitled to feel depressed. An item on the *Today* programme had led, indirectly, to the suicide of a government scientist, Dr. David Kelly, and directly to a bitter row with the Blair government. The subsequent condemnation of the BBC by a judge-led inquiry provoked in January 2004 the departures of Gavyn Davies, the BBC's respected Chairman, and Greg Dyke, who had achieved the almost impossible task as BBC Director-General of being both effective and popular (Dyke 2004: 1-33).

The crisis of 2004 has some almost eerie similarities with the disasters which overtook the BBC in 2012. Both centred on journalism – in 2004 it was Andrew Gilligan's allegation that the government had knowingly lied in making the case for war against Iraq; in 2012, *Newsnight's* untrue story about sex abuse in North

Wales and the furore over a spiked story, again by *Newsnight*, on Jimmy Savile. On both occasions, the BBC's mishandling of the crises undermined the director-general, who, as editor-in-chief, took final responsibility for the Corporation's journalism. Like Greg Dyke in January 2004, George Entwistle in November 2012 found that he had lost the support of the board and resigned (BBC Trust 2012a).

In the aftermath of both crises, hard questions were asked about the effectiveness of the BBC's governance arrangements, with an apparent political consensus that they were no longer fit for purpose and would need to be reformed at the next charter review. In 2004, the governors were described by a source close to Downing Street as 'the living dead' even though the charter still had another two years to run (Tait 2004); even before the investigations into Savile and the Public Accounts Committee inquiry into executive severance payments had been completed, the Trust had been dismissed as failing and facing the axe by a senior source at the Culture Department (Brooks and Hellen 2013). We now face the potentially hazardous prospect of the politicians imposing on the BBC what would be its third system of governance in the course of a decade.

Broadcasting is rightly a world that looks forward and focuses on the future. At present the challenges facing the BBC and other broadcasters as a result of the pace of technological change with digital convergence, the explosive growth of social media and the emergence of powerful new digital players (Royal Television Society 2013) mean that too much retrospection (or introspection) can seem as irrelevant to the future as the old debate about whether Betamax was a better format than VHS. But with that caveat, are there, perhaps, some lessons from a history of crises that does seem to have a tendency to repeat itself? I think there are number of possible conclusions to be drawn from the two rather sorry tales of 2004 and 2012 which may still have some relevance as the BBC contemplates a very different future in a converged world.

BBC journalism under fire
The first lesson from history is that although the BBC is often under fire for many faults, whether real or imagined, the truly toxic crises are always about journalism. Alasdair Milne, the first BBC Director-General to be fired, was at loggerheads with the Thatcher government over a series of news and current affairs programmes. He was sacked by the new BBC Chairman, Marmaduke Hussey, in January 1987 (Milne 1988: 201-202).

The 2004 crisis was over an item on *Today*. Andrew Gilligan, the programme's Defence Correspondent, had reported on 29 May 2003 that an intelligence source had told him that the Blair government's September 2002 dossier on *Iraq's Weapons of Mass Destruction* had been 'sexed up' by Downing Street to make the case for war more compelling. Had Gilligan stopped at that point, he would probably have won a Sony Award – for much of what his source had told him about the process was true (Jones 2010). But in one live interview that day, at

6.07 with John Humphrys, he went further, alleging that his source had told him that a key claim, that the Iraqis had chemical or biological weapons of mass destruction (WMD) deployable within 45 minutes, had been inserted into the dossier even though the government probably knew it to be wrong (Marsh 2013: 197-285).

A huge row with the government ensued. Gilligan's source was revealed to be a respected scientist, Dr. David Kelly, who committed suicide. The government set up an inquiry into his death under a judge, Lord Hutton, where Gilligan admitted that the 45 minute claim – the allegation of dishonesty rather than spin – was his own inference rather than a quote from his source. Lord Hutton's report cleared the government of any wrong doing but was highly critical of the BBC's management, led by Greg Dyke, and of the board of governors, who had stood 100 per cent behind what had turned out to be a flawed story (Hutton 2004). Within 36 hours, the chairman and director-general of the BBC had both resigned (Purvis and Hulbert 2013: 287-323).

The 2012 *Newsnight* story was about sex abuse in North Wales in the 1970s and 1980s. Angus Stickler, a freelance reporter working with the Bureau for Investigative Journalism, approached *Newsnight* with a source who claimed to have been abused by a senior Conservative politician. Although the report when broadcast did not name the politician as Lord McAlpine, a former Conservative Party Deputy Chairman, his identity leaked out and was widely reported on social media.

It rapidly became clear that Lord McAlpine had nothing to do with any alleged abuse and that he was the victim of a terrible case of mistaken identity – the BBC's source soon apologised to him for his mistake and the BBC also apologised unreservedly for the item (BBC Trust 2012b). The day after the BBC apology, on 10 November, George Entwistle, the BBC's newly-appointed Director-General, had a disastrous interview with John Humphrys on the *Today* programme where he admitted that he had known nothing of the *Newsnight* film until it was transmitted and had not been aware of press reports the following week that the BBC had made an appalling mistake. After an uncomfortable telephone discussion with the Trust later in the day (BBC Trust 2012a) he announced his resignation that evening after just 54 days in post (O'Carroll and Brown 2012).

Self-inflicted wounds, 2004 and 2012

Although there are plenty of differences between the two events, the similarities are in some cases quite striking. Both came from journalism from troubled programmes – when Kevin Marsh took over as Editor of *Today* in December 2002 he says his boss, Richard Sambrook, the BBC Director of News, told him baldly it was 'not what a BBC flagship should be. Wrong agenda and wrong attitudes' (Marsh 2013: 75). Ten years later, the problem child of BBC journalism was *Newsnight*. Sambrook's successor, Helen Boaden, told the Pollard review: '*Newsnight* is a bit like an old colonial power with a lot of old colonial power attitudes, refusing to accept a modern world with less resource, a digital challenge, and, at times, with a sort of contemptuous or sneering attitude to the rest of the News Group.' The editor, Peter Rippon, she added, was trying to deal with it (Boaden 2012: 182). *Newsnight's* presenter, Jeremy Paxman, argued that the problems were at least partly down to budget reductions which meant editors no longer had the space to make considered judgements (Paxman 2012: 6).

Both stories were attempts at investigative journalism on daily news programmes. While breaking news and revelatory journalism is a key part of any well run news programme, complex investigative journalism usually requires more time, more resource and more specialist expertise than is found in hard-pressed daily newsrooms. Marsh was worried that *Today* was straying into a 'tabloid agenda' with anonymous sources (Marsh 2013: 74-87); Boaden told the Pollard review that she did not think *Newsnight* had the skill to mount investigations and that the view of previous editors and heads of news was that the programme had tendency to rush them (Boaden 2012: 182).

Certainly, both stories were produced on a time scale that might seem leisurely for a daily news programme but dangerously fast for investigations making such serious allegations. Andrew Gilligan met David Kelly at the Charing Cross Hotel on 22 May 2003 – he was on the air with his account of what Dr. Kelly had said a week later. Angus Stickler approached *Newsnight* with his story on 28 October 2012; it was broadcast on 2 November. As the BBC's internal investigation pointed out, 'this was a highly complex story that went from commission to transmission within a week' (BBC Trust 2012b: 21).

History repeating itself?

Both stories depended on a single source – Gilligan's anonymous source was Dr. David Kelly, a government scientist and weapons inspector; Stickler's was Steve Messham, a victim of sexual abuse. Gilligan's further research found no one else to stand up the 6.07 allegation of dishonesty (Marsh 2013: 102-103); Stickler had in the past interviewed another abuse victim but he could not be found (BBC Trust 2012b: 14). After the Hutton Report, the BBC had tightened up its guidelines on the use of single sources. The Neil review, set up to learn the lessons of the affair (of which, to declare an interest, I was a member), recommended real caution in single source stories, and particularly when the source was anonymous (Neil 2004) – a view shared by other experienced editors (Rusbridger 2004).

In both cases, the BBC relied too heavily on the reporters' assurances that the story was fine. Andrew Gilligan maintained, until he gave evidence before Lord Hutton, that Dr. Kelly had, in fact, told him that the government had knowingly put false information into the dossier (Marsh 2013: 157-158); Angus Stickler had covered the North Wales sex abuse scandal in the past and the *Newsnight* team deferred to his expertise. The BBC's own internal investigation into *Newsnight* also found basic journalistic checks on the story were not made – the source was not even shown a photograph of Lord McAlpine before transmission – and insufficient attempts were made to validate the story beyond the reporter's assurances (BBC Trust 2012b: 10-20).

A second lesson from the past is that in both cases the management of the story was inadequate and those management mistakes made a poor situation far worse. The BBC ignored evidence that the 6.07 broadcast had gone beyond what Gilligan had agreed with his editors (Marsh 2013: 89-156) and that the allegation of government dishonesty was not supported by his notes of his meeting with Kelly (Purvis and Hulbert 2013: 306-323). In the case of the *Newsnight* story, the BBC never approached Lord McAlpine before transmission and ignored clear evidence from another journalist who had contacted him that he was vehemently denying any involvement and planning to sue for libel (Purvis 2012).

The Other Side of Jimmy Savile

At this point, 2004 and 2012 part company – because the untrue *Newsnight* sex abuse story was only part of a wider crisis around Savile which at times threatened to overwhelm the BBC. ITV's *Exposure* documentary, *The Other Side of Jimmy Savile*, in October 2012 on the scale of Jimmy Savile's criminal behaviour, much of it on BBC premises, would have been bad enough. What made it even worse for the BBC was the revelation that the BBC had passed on what was one of the stories of the year – a *Newsnight* team had had their own well-founded investigation into Savile spiked in December 2011 (Purvis 2012). They believed, wrongly, that the decision to drop their story was to protect two Savile tribute programmes in the 2011 BBC Christmas schedule (Pollard 2012: 22-42).

The BBC's initial reaction to both aspects of the Savile affair was inadequate – a cold press statement that the BBC had found 'an absence of evidence of any kind' of abuse on BBC premises and a blog from the editor of *Newsnight* about the spiked investigation which was challenged by the production team and had to be corrected. The BBC initially gave the impression that its own inquiries into its role in the affair would await the result of police investigations and then, under pressure, announced two separate investigations – one by Dame Janet Smith into Savile's abuse and the culture of the BBC and a second by Nick Pollard, the former Head of Sky News, into the reasons why the *Newsnight* item never saw the light of day (Marsh 2012: 19-28).

Dame Janet's report was due to be published in February 2014 but was then postponed till the summer to avoid prejudicing criminal proceedings. However, it was already clear from well-sourced leaks that it was going to be a devastating document – Savile had abused up to a thousand young people on BBC premises; although many of the cases were in the 1960s and 1970s the abuse had continued long afterwards – he had groped a young girl on his last *Top of the Pops* in 2006; BBC staff and executives were aware of his behaviour but took no action (Boffrey 2014). And when Pollard reported on 12 December 2012, his criticisms of current BBC management were severe. There had been no conspiracy to suppress the *Newsnight* story – the decision was flawed but made in good faith and not to protect the tribute programmes. But that was as good as it got for the BBC. Pollard was highly critical of what he saw as chaos and confusion in the BBC's attempts at crisis management (Pollard 2012: 22-23). The report also revealed tensions between the management and the Trust. The Trust, rather like the governors in 2003, had relied on the management's version of events – particularly the editor's blog – and had defended the BBC. It was embarrassed when the BBC changed its story (Purvis 2012).

The 'Mark Byford role'

And some of the witnesses who gave evidence to Pollard also looked back at the decision to make Mark Byford, the Deputy Director-General, redundant in 2011 and wondered if it had been the right decision to lose him and his role. Byford had been in charge of all the BBC's journalism and responsible for editorial standards across the organisation. He was an experienced troubleshooter. His role recognised the practical impossibility of the director-general having the time to be both chief executive of the BBC and at the same time, as editor-in-chief, be across the detail of difficult editorial issues.

Mark Thompson told Pollard that making Byford's post redundant had brought 'some potential level of risk' but there was a pressing need, encouraged by the Trust, to reduce executive board numbers (Thompson 2012: 7-14). Helen Boaden, the Director of News, said: 'We've made it much much harder for ourselves by getting rid of the Mark Byford role' (Boaden 2012: 141-142).

From my experience as a BBC governor and then Trustee from 2004 to 2010, where I worked closely with him, I thought Mark Byford played an invaluable supervisory role across all the BBC's journalism, was very good at crisis management and made the relationship with the Trust work well. The combination of Mark Thompson, Mark Byford and Helen Boaden at the top of the BBC editorial chain was a strong one. Throughout the period BBC news performed well and was very largely a crisis-free zone. The serious editorial problems which the BBC did encounter were in non-news areas – over Ross/Brand and phone-ins – and once they came to light they were effectively managed and resolved (Thompson 2012: 11-12). In May 2013, just a month after Tony Hall took over as Director-General, he announced the creation of new post – Editorial Director – without the seniority of deputy director-general, but with the same key responsibilities as the director-general's editorial troubleshooter (BBC News 2013).

Regime change at the BBC, September-November 2012

When the Savile crisis broke in October 2012 the BBC was in the middle of a radical regime change. Thompson had been appointed Chief Executive of *The New York Times* and had just left; Byford was long gone. In addition, Helen Boaden and her deputy were in the middle of the month 'recused' from involvement in anything to do with the Savile story. On top of that, the incoming Director-General, George Entwistle, who had been chosen after proposing radical changes to the BBC (Patten 2012: 33-34), was in the middle of restructuring his senior management with a much smaller management board. The Chief Operating Officer, Caroline Thomson, left; the Director of Audio, Tim Davie, was moving to run BBC Worldwide. Both had plenty of experience of crisis management and had themselves been interviewed for the DG's job – as had Helen Boaden (Entwistle 2012).

The BBC's history does show that regime change is almost always a tricky process, even when the director-general has not left unexpectedly. Even in calmer times, the appointment of a new director-general can be a fraught and potentially destabilising process as both John Birt and Greg Dyke found (Birt 2002: 314-322; Dyke 2004: 140-154). Mark Thompson's departure at some stage after the London Olympics had long been agreed and planned. But the BBC opted for a replacement timetable which meant it was a choosing its new chief executive and editor-in-chief right in the middle of the biggest summer of its history, with the coverage of London 2012 and the Diamond Jubilee bringing unique editorial, logistical and organisational challenges. Nor, after the appointment was made in July, was there much of a handover between Thompson and Entwistle, who took over on 17 September (Hough 2012). By a horrible irony, Mark Thompson's last day on the BBC payroll was 11 November 2012 – the day after his successor stood down.

The dire coverage of the Thames Pageant apart, where the BBC was lucky to have the weather to blame for what was in reality a truly terrible programme (Faulkner and Ledwith 2012), the coverage of the Olympics and the Jubilee showed the BBC at its very best. However, the pace of change at the top felt like rather too many control rods were being removed from the reactor at one time – and certainly it left Entwistle exposed when the Savile crisis broke. Like Dyke before him, he decided to take the lead in crisis management, despite the Neil review recommendation post-Hutton that the director-general should not get directly involved in complaints handling (Neil 2004). His performances at a select committee and on the *Today* programme sealed his fate (Marsh 2012: 19-28). Tim Davie stepped in as Acting Director-General while the BBC found a new chief executive.

Making a drama out of a crisis?

Was this, as the BBC's veteran world affairs editor John Simpson told *Panorama* 'the worst crisis I can remember in my 50 years at the BBC' (Sabbagh 2012)? Perhaps, but there is always a danger of the BBC itself or its staff making the worst of an admittedly bad job. One encouraging lesson from the history of 2004 and 2012 is that the BBC is a resilient organisation with, perhaps fortunately, both great powers of recovery and still very significant reserves of public support.

Within a few days of the publication of the Hutton Report in 2004, it was clear that the public was less convinced than the judge of the BBC's failings – by the end of the week opinion polls were showing that most of the public thought the report was a 'whitewash'. One poll for NOP showed that just 31 per cent of the public trusted the government to tell the truth while 67 per cent still trusted BBC news journalists (Jones, Leonard and Born 2004). Although at the height of the Savile scandal, a poll found half the public had less trust in the BBC than before (Deans 2012) the BBC's reputation has recovered since then and the BBC's news remains the most trusted journalism in the UK (BBC 2013a).

The BBC as an organisation recovered quickly from 2004. Although senior executive pay turned out to be his Achilles heel, Mark Thompson was a very effective leader of the BBC and overall deserves more credit than he is likely to get at present for his eight years in charge (Thompson 2012b). Tony Hall, after a very successful period as Chief Executive of the Royal Opera House, has already achieved a significant turnaround and built a strong management team to support him. Both have mapped the digital future of the BBC – with Thompson, the launch of the iPlayer; with Hall, the development of the concept of 'My BBC' – taking the iPlayer from catch-up TV into truly online TV (Hall 2013a).

The last governors 2004-2006
However, the Hutton Report was terminal for the BBC's old system of governance which, for all its evident flaws, had survived for nearly 80 years and had at least protected the BBC, unlike most public broadcasters in the world, from state control and excessive political interference. The board of governors had backed the management to the hilt in its battle with the government over Gilligan's story and was roundly criticised by the judge in his report. It was now accused of being unfit for purpose, being both a champion and a regulator (Cox 2003). It meant that the debate about the future governance of the BBC started with the question 'what should replace the governors?' rather than 'how can the BBC's governance be improved?' The BBC system of governance needed reform, certainly – but the 2004 crisis meant the argument for reform, rather than replacement, was probably lost before the debate began.

The government appointed an independent panel under Lord Burns to look at the options. In the end, what emerged from a season of seminars and committee reports, Green Papers and political wrangling was a compromise between the Burns panel's recommendations and the wishes of the BBC. Burns believed that the BBC should have a unitary board with a separate Public Service Broadcasting Commission (Independent Panel on Charter Review 2005); the BBC's proposal was to build on the reforms to the governors that Michael Grade had introduced when he took over as Chairman in April 2004. Grade's big idea was that by giving the governors the support of an independent Governance Unit to analyse proposals and help them deal with complaints they could avoid management capture (BBC 2005).

The BBC Trust 2006-?
From my own experience on the board at that time I think the new system deserved a chance to prove itself – it seemed to me that the Governance Unit, under the skilful management of its Director Nicholas Kroll, a former Chief

Operating Officer of the Culture Department, had solved many of the problems which had undermined the old governors (Independent Panel on Charter Review 2004). The government, however, rejected both the BBC proposal and the recommendations of its own advisers (Gibson and Conlan 2005). Instead, the government opted for its own idea – on 2 March 2005 Tessa Jowell, the Culture Secretary, announced the abolition of the governors and the establishment of the Trust (DCMS 2005).

The Trust was to have greater separation from the management – though, perhaps fortunately, the BBC was able to turn Kroll's Governance Unit into a Trust Unit, ensuring the new board of Trustees still had access to independent analysis and advice. But this compromise deal did not satisfy any of the BBC's critics and in record time the government that had forced the Trust on the BBC was disillusioned with it. Within three years Ben Bradshaw, the new Culture Secretary, was arguing that the Trust was 'not a sustainable model' (Robinson 2009).

Sustainable or not, the ten year term of the 2006 Charter rightly protected the Trust from being dismantled immediately. The potential fault lines in the system were always there – the relationship between the Trust and the non-executive directors over issues like executive pay: the regulatory overlap with Ofcom; trying to define how far the Trust's strategic role should influence how the executive ran the BBC. Despite that, the Trust developed some effective tools for holding the executive to account – particularly the service licences and five yearly reviews (Liddiment 2013). And the Trust got some big decisions right – rejecting the BBC executive's controversial proposals for local TV (BBC Trust 2009) and intervening quickly and effectively in both the premium phone calls scandal (BBC Trust 2008a) and the Ross/Brand case (BBC Trust 2008b). For a period under the chairmanships of Sir Michael Lyons and Lord Patten it had looked as though the issue of the BBC's governance was fading from prominence and would not dominate the next charter review.

'The Governance model is broken'

But the crises of the last two years have changed all that. Hard on the heels of Savile came executive pay and severance payments. The Public Accounts Committee's report in December 2013 was highly critical of the BBC's governance arrangements:

> Our examination of severance payments exposed a dysfunctional relationship between the BBC executive and the BBC Trust that casts doubt on the effectiveness of the BBC's governance model. The unedifying disagreements between witnesses and the conflicting accounts of what was disclosed about individual severance payments are symptomatic of a wider breakdown in the relationship between the BBC Trust and the executive. At present the governance model is broken. The Trust and the executive have a limited amount of time to demonstrate that the current governance model can be made to work (Public Accounts Committee 2013).

A few days before that report, the Trust and the executive, as in 2004, had come up with their own proposals to reform the existing system. Their own review was frank about the problems:

> … while the system itself is on the whole robust and effective, in some aspects of its operation the BBC's governance system has become too confused. There is currently too much overlap in practice between the roles of the BBC Trust and the executive board; the structures are too complicated; and people inside and outside the BBC do not always know who is responsible when things go wrong (BBC 2013b: 1).

The changes to be implemented from April 2014 included a greater separation between the Trust and the executive and a strengthening of the executive board – with Sir Howard Stringer, an industry heavyweight (former president of CBS and chairman of Sony), the first of a number of promised appointments (BBC 2013c).

The initial reaction to the BBC's proposals in Whitehall was not encouraging – they were, apparently, seen as 'mere window dressing' (Hewlett 2013). And the publication in December of the review into the failure of the £100 million Digital Media Initiative (DMI) again pointed to weaknesses in management oversight and governance (PWC 2013). The worry for the BBC is that the debate has moved on. On regulation, the political and industry consensus seems to have already coalesced around a different model – a unitary board and regulation by Ofcom – much to the alarm of the *Daily Mail* which suspended its normal criticism of the BBC to declare in an editorial it opposed Ofcom's involvement and stood shoulder to shoulder with the BBC on this issue (*Daily Mail* 2013).

When, however, BBC governance and regulation were debated at the Royal Television Society's Cambridge Convention in September 2013, the delegates voted overwhelmingly for the Ofcom solution (Brown 2013: 26). And as convergence brings the BBC more and more into the same online and on-demand space as commercial media, it faces increasingly forceful arguments from the commercial world that it should do less. Those arguments have recently been echoed by some respected BBC figures – Roger Mosey, the former Director of the BBC Olympics (Mosey 2013) and David Dimbleby, the BBC's general election presenter, have both argued for a smaller, more focused BBC (Linford 2013). In their evidence to the culture committee on the future of the BBC some of the BBC's main commercial competitors also re-opened the debate about 'top-slicing' the licence fee and sharing with other broadcasters and organisations. ITV thought the committee would want to debate the issue (ITV, 2013); Channel 4 talked about using the licence fee in partnerships (Channel 4, 2013); the Commercial Broadcasters Association thought there was a case to be considered for dividing the licence fee to fund other public service content (Commercial Broadcasters Association 2013).

Charter review and the BBC's independence

The debate about the BBC's future as we approach discussions on the next charter is likely to raise some fundamental issues – the BBC's monopoly of the licence fee, its overall market impact, the scale and role of its journalism. Tony Hall has set out a positive case for a strong, independent and well-resourced BBC for the future and has firmly moved the discussion on from the problems of the past – arguing that 'just because the BBC has got some things wrong doesn't mean it has got everything wrong. Far from it' (Hall 2013b).

But the current executive and Trust have a comparatively short time to make the case for their vision of the future and their preferred structure of governance and regulation in a sceptical, if not openly hostile, political and commercial environment (Hutton 2013). The self-inflicted wounds of the last two years will not make that task any easier. The BBC must hope that the politicians remember at least one lesson from history – that hasty changes to the charter in response to a short-term crisis are not the best way to ensure the BBC remains the strong and independent organisation it must be to serve its audiences as they expect and deserve.

References

Boaden, Helen (2012) *Evidence to Pollard Inquiry*, 21 November. Available online at http://downloads.bbc.co.uk/aboutthebbc/insidethebbc/howwework/reports/pdf/poll ard/helen_boaden.pdf, accessed on 3 December 2013

Boffrey, Daniel (2014) Revealed: How Savile abused up to 1,000 on BBC premises, *Observer*, 19 January 2014. Available online at http://www.theguardian.com/media/2014/jan/18/jimmy-savile-abused-1000-victims-bbc, accessed on 19 January 2014

BBC (2005) *Building Public Value*, London: BBC. Available online at http://downloads.bbc.co.uk/aboutthebbc/policies/pdf/bpv.pdf, accessed on 8 December 2013

BBC (2013a) *Public perceptions of the trustworthiness and impartiality of the BBC*, May. Available online at http://downloads.bbc.co.uk/aboutthebbc/insidethebbc/howwework/reports/pdf/bbc _report_trust_and_impartiality_report_may_2013.pdf, accessed on 10 December 2013

BBC (2013b) *Review of BBC Internal Governance*, 11 December. Available online at http://downloads.bbc.co.uk/bbctrust/assets/files/pdf/about/how we govern/governance_review_2013.pdf, accessed on 12 December 2013

BBC (2013c) BBC announces new plans to improve decision making and accountability, 11 December. Available online at http://www.bbc.co.uk/mediacentre/latestnews/2013/governance-review-exec.html, accessed on 12 December 2013

BBC News (2013) Roger Mosey named BBC Editorial Director, 8 May. Available online at http://www.bbc.co.uk/news/entertainment-arts-22447128, accessed on 16 December 2013

BBC Trust (2008a) *The BBC Trust's conclusions on the economic aspects of the use of Premium Rate Services by the BBC*, May. Available online at http://www.bbc.co.uk/bbctrust/assets/files/pdf/review_report_research/prs_pwc_rep ort.pdf, accessed on 17 December 2013

BBC Trust (2008b) *Editorial Standards Findings: Appeals and editorial issues considered by the Trust's Editorial Standards Committee: Russell Brand, Radio 2, 18 and 25 October 2008*, November. Available online at http://news.bbc.co.uk/nol/shared/bsp/hi/pdfs/21_11_08_brand_ross_moyles.pdf, accessed on 17 December 2013

BBC Trust (2012a) *Minutes of the BBC Trust meeting*, 10 November. Available online at http://downloads.bbc.co.uk/bbctrust/assets/files/pdf/about/minutes/2012/10_nov_1 430.pdf, accessed on 9 December 2013

BBC Trust (2012b) *Finding of the Editorial Standards Committee of the BBC Trust*: Newsnight *BBC2, 2 November 2012, Finding of 14 December 2012*. Available online at http://downloads.bbc.co.uk/bbctrust/assets/files/pdf/appeals/esc_bulletins/2012/ne wsnight_2nov.pdf, accessed on 3 December 2013

Brooks, Richard and Hellen, Nicholas (2013) Ministers to axe failing BBC Trust, *Sunday Times*, 8 September. Available online at http://www.thesundaytimes.co.uk/sto/news/uk_news/National/article1310987.ece, accessed on 3 December 2013

Brown, Maggie (2013) A Question of Trust, *Television*, October 2013 pp 24-26. Available online at

http://www.rts.org.uk/television-october-2013, accessed on 13 December 2013

Channel 4 (2013) *Written evidence submitted by Channel 4*, December 2013. Available online at http://data.parliament.uk/writtenevidence/WrittenEvidence.svc/EvidenceHtml/4166 (accessed 19 January 2014)

Commercial Broadcasters Association (2013) *Written evidence submitted by the Commercial Broadcasters Association*, December 2013. Available online at http://data.parliament.uk/writtenevidence/WrittenEvidence.svc/EvidenceHtml/4172 (accessed 19 January 2014)

Cox, Barry (2003) The BBC governors can't be champions and watchdogs, *Guardian*, 7 August. Available online at http://www.theguardian.com/politics/2003/aug/07/media.ofcom, accessed on 23 December 2013

Daily Mail (2013) Why the *Mail* stands shoulder to shoulder with the BBC, 16 September. Available online at http://www.dailymail.co.uk/debate/article-2422968/DAILY-MAIL-COMMENT-Why-Mail-stands-shoulder-shoulder-BBC-.html, accessed on 15 December 2013

DCMS (2005) *A Strong BBC, Independent of Government*, London: DCMS. Available online at http://news.bbc.co.uk/1/shared/bsp/hi/pdfs/02_03_05_bbcgreen.pdf, accessed on 8 December 2013

Deans, Jason (2012) Nearly half the public have less trust in the BBC since the Jimmy Savile scandal, *Guardian*, 18 December. Available online at http://www.theguardian.com/media/2012/dec/18/public-trust-bbc-jimmy-savile, accessed on 10 December 201

Dyke, Greg (2004) *Inside Story*, London: HarperCollins

Entwistle, George (2012) *Speech to BBC Staff*, 8 September. Available online at http://www.bbc.co.uk/mediacentre/speeches/2012/george-entwistle-to-staff.html, accessed on 5 December 2013

Faulkner, Katherine and Ledwith, Mario (2012) Man responsible for BBC coverage of Queen's Thames Pageant blames the rain as he is attacked on all sides for 'inane' and 'celebrity-driven drivel, *Daily Mail*, 5 June. Available online at http://www.dailymail.co.uk/news/article-2154424/Diamond-jubilee-BBC-attacked-inane-celebrity-driven-coverage-Queens-Thames-Pageant.html, accessed on 18 December 2013

Gibson, Owen and Conlan, Tara (2005) BBC governors to be scrapped, *Guardian*, 2 March. Available online at http://www.theguardian.com/media/2005/mar/02/bbc.broadcasting1, accessed on 14 December 2013

Hall, Tony (2013a) Director-General Tony Hall unveils his vision for the BBC, 8 October. Available online at http://www.bbc.co.uk/mediacentre/speeches/2013/tony-hall-vision.html, accessed on 8 December 2013

Hall, Tony (2013b) Speech, Voice of the Listener and Viewer Conference, 27 November. Available online at http://www.bbc.co.uk/mediacentre/speeches/2013/tony-hall-vlv.html, accessed on 14 December 2013

Hewlett, Steve (2013) A year of fireworks for the NSA and BBC, *Guardian*, 16 December. Available online at http://www.theguardian.com/media/media-blog/2013/dec/15/bbc-tony-hall-licence, accessed on 16 December 2013

Hough, Andrew (2012) Pressure on Lord Patten over BBC DG 'handover' rebuff, *Telegraph*, 18 November. Available online at (http://www.telegraph.co.uk/culture/tvandradio/bbc/9686151/Pressure-on-Lord-Patten-over-BBC-DG-handover-offer-rebuff.html, accessed on 13 December 2013

Hutton, Lord (2004) *Report of the Inquiry into the Circumstances Surrounding the Death of Dr. David Kelly C.M.G.* London: HMSO. Available online at http://webarchive.nationalarchives.gov.uk/20090128221546/http://www.the-hutton-inquiry.org.uk/content/report/index.htm, accessed on 4 December 2013

Hutton, Will (2013) The many challenges facing a beleaguered BBC, *Observer*, 3 November. Available online at http://www.theguardian.com/commentisfree/2013/nov/03/bbc-faces-many-challenges, accessed on 15 December 2013

Independent Panel on Charter Review (2004) *Governance and Regulation Seminar*, 3 December. Available online at http://webarchive.nationalarchives.gov.uk/+/http://www.bbccharterreview.org.uk/pdf_documents/gov_reg_seminar_transcript.pdf, accessed on 5 December 2013

Independent Panel on Charter Review (2005) *Final Advice to the Secretary of State*. Available online at http://webarchive.nationalarchives.gov.uk/+/http://www.bbccharterreview.org.uk/pdf_documents/050123a_Governance.pdf, accessed on 8 December 2013

ITV (2013) *Written evidence submitted by ITV plc*, December 2013. Available online at http://data.parliament.uk/writtenevidence/WrittenEvidence.svc/EvidenceHtml/4165 (accessed 19 January 2014)

Jones, Brian (2010) *Failing Intelligence: The True Story of How We Were Fooled into Going to War in Iraq*, London: Biteback

Jones, George, Leonard, Tom and Born, Matt (2004) Hutton was whitewash, say 56%, *Telegraph*, 30 January 2004. Available online at http://www.telegraph.co.uk/news/1453005/Hutton-a-whitewash-say-56pc.html, accessed on 6 December 2013

Liddiment, David (2014) TV diary, *Television*, January p. 8. Available online at http://www.rts.org.uk/television-%E2%80%93-january-2014, accessed on 23 December 2013

Linford, Paul (2013) Is BBC 'crushing' local press? Dimbleby reopens debate, Hold the Front Page, 20 November. Available online at http://www.holdthefrontpage.co.uk/2013/news/is-bbc-crushing-local-press-dimbleby-reopens-debate/, accessed on 20 December 2013

Marsh, Kevin (2012) Why the BBC's boss had to go, *British Journalism Review*, Vol. 23, No. 4 pp 19-28. Available online at http://www.bjr.org.uk/data/2012/no4_marsh, accessed on 8 December 2013

Marsh, Kevin (2013) *Stumbling Over Truth*, London: Biteback

Milne, Alasdair (1988) *DG: The Memoirs of a British Broadcaster*, London: Hodder & Stoughton

Mosey, Roger (2013) A smaller BBC would be good for audiences, *Times*, 8 November. Available online at (http://www.thetimes.co.uk/tto/opinion/columnists/article3916059.ece), accessed on 13 December 2013

Neil, Ron (2004) *The BBC's journalism after Hutton*, Available online at http://downloads.bbc.co.uk/aboutthebbc/insidethebbc/howwework/reports/pdf/neil_report.html, accessed on 7 December 2013

O'Carroll, Lisa and Brown, Maggie (2012) BBC in crisis as George Entwistle quits over *Newsnight* fiasco, *Observer*, 11 November. Available online at http://www.theguardian.com/media/2012/nov/10/bbc-crisis-george-entwistle-resigns, accessed on 8 December 2013

Patten, Lord (2012) *Evidence to The Pollard Inquiry*, 5 December. Available online at http://downloads.bbc.co.uk/aboutthebbc/insidethebbc/howwework/reports/pdf/pollard/lord_patten.pdf, accessed on 13 December 2013

Paxman, Jeremy (2012) *Evidence to The Pollard Inquiry*, 9 December. Available online at http://downloads.bbc.co.uk/aboutthebbc/insidethebbc/howwework/reports/pdf/pollard/jeremy_paxman.pdf, accessed on 15 December 2013

Pollard, Nick (2012) <i>The Pollard Review: Report.</i> Available online at http://downloads.bbc.co.uk/bbctrust/assets/files/pdf/our_work/pollard_review/pollard_review.pdf, accessed on 9 December 2013

Public Accounts Committee (2013) *Thirty-Third Report – BBC severance packages*, London: House of Commons. Available online at http://www.publications.parliament.uk/pa/cm201314/cmselect/cmpubacc/476/47602.htm, accessed on 16 December 2013

Purvis, Stewart (2012) The *Newsnight* crisis at the BBC: A new timeline from the death of Savile to the appointment of Hall, ProfPurvis. Available online at http://profpurvis.com/2012/11/22/the-newsnight-crisis-at-the-bbc-a-new-timeline-from-the-death-of-savile-to-the-appointment-of-hall/, accessed on 10 December 2013

Purvis, Stewart and Hulbert, Jeff (2013) *When Reporters Cross the Line*, London: Biteback

PWC (2013) *BBC Digital Media Initiative: Review of the BBC's management of DMI*, 17 December 2013. Available online at http://downloads.bbc.co.uk/bbctrust/assets/files/pdf/review_report_research/vfm/dmi/pwc_dmi.pdf, accessed on 18 December 2013

Robinson, James (2009) Ben Bradshaw attacks BBC Trust's cheerleader role, *Guardian*, 16 September. Available online at http://www.theguardian.com/media/2009/sep/16/ben-bradshaw-lays-into-bbc-trust, accessed on 8 December 2013

Royal Television Society (2013) Power shift: Who will control the future? RTS Cambridge Convention, *Television*, October. Available online at http://www.rts.org.uk/television-october-2013, accessed on 16 December 2013

Rusbridger, Alan (2004) The *Guardian*'s post-Hutton guidelines for journalists, *Media Guardian*, 30 January. Available online at http://www.theguardian.com/media/2004/jan/30/theguardian.pressandpublishing, accessed on 7 December 2013

Sabbagh, Dan (2012) Jimmy Savile row: *Newsnight* emails spark 'crisis' at BBC, *Guardian*, 22 October. Available online at http://www.theguardian.com/media/2012/oct/21/bbc-emails-jimmy-savile, accessed on 9 December 2013

Tait, Richard (2004) Britain's broadcast crisis, *Global Journalist*, 1 April. Available online at http://www.globaljournalist.org/stories/2004/04/01/britains-broadcast-crisis/, accessed on 4 December 2013

Thompson, Mark (2012a) *Evidence to Pollard Inquiry* 23 November. Available online at http://downloads.bbc.co.uk/aboutthebbc/insidethebbc/howwework/reports/pdf/pollard/mark_thompson.pdf, accessed on 5 December 2013

Thompson, Mark (2012b) *The BBC in 2012 and Beyond*, Speech at Royal Television Society 14 March. Available online at http://www.bbc.co.uk/mediacentre/speeches/2012/thompson-rts.html, accessed on 10 December 2013

Note on the contributor

Richard Tait is Professor of Journalism at the School of Journalism, Media and Cultural Studies, Cardiff. From 2003 to 2012 he was Director of the School's Centre for Journalism. He was Editor of *Newsnight* from 1985 to 1987, Editor of *Channel 4 News* from 1987 to 1995 and Editor-in-Chief of ITN from 1995 to 2002. He was a BBC Governor and chair of the Governors' Programme Complaints Committee from 2004 to 2006, and a BBC Trustee and chair of the Trust's Editorial Standards Committee from 2006 to 2010. He is a fellow of the Society of Editors and the Royal Television Society and Treasurer of the International News Safety Institute.

The BBC's cultural mission and how it interweaves with democracy and the economy

An outward-looking BBC sharing its cultural and economic capital with the nation: on this basis the BBC should win its next charter, argues Peter Bazalgette

BBC charter renewal is a sort of World Cup for the commentariat – it happens at regular intervals, is a festival of hot air for supporters and opposition alike and comes to a rather sudden finale. There will now be thirty months of chest beating and navel gazing before an eventual quick and dirty deal with the next elected government. Notwithstanding that, it's entirely healthy for public funding of all sorts to be subject to the scrutiny it now is. And as digital technology continues to disrupt our heritage media, it's right that the purposes of the BBC should be challenged, refreshed and, where necessary, redefined (just as the means of collecting the licence fee also need re-imagining).

The BBC represents a massive market and social intervention. Historically this has been justified by the delivery of three things: trusted and reliable news and information, substantial output of original programming and a sustained investment in creative talent. In this way the BBC has made a critical democratic, cultural and economic contribution to the life of our country. I do not think these principles have changed. But I will argue that the means of performing this role are changing and need to do so. In future, the Corporation should act less unilaterally and more as a partner. Here I will explore this theme chiefly in relation to the BBC's cultural mission, though it interweaves with the democratic and the economic.

Public investment in culture

So what is the BBC's cultural role? What is the purpose of the £3.6 billion public investment which the licence fee represents? This has best been summed up by the British Museum's Neil Macgregor: 'How we see ourselves and how the world sees us.' We make an investment in our national museums and Arts Council England for similar reasons (though, it must be said, a rather smaller one). At the Arts Council we have been doing some thinking about this, chiefly because we often meet folk in the public sphere who are generally in favour of Britain's public support for culture, but have actually forgotten why it's done. So we are developing what we call *the holistic case for public support of arts and culture*. It has four key elements:

• the intrinsic value of culture (first and foremost);

• the broader advantages to society;

• the symbiotic relationship with education;

• and the economic benefits.

This holistic case also offers a useful prism through which to focus on the BBC's cultural mission.

Intrinsic value of culture

It starts and must always start with culture's intrinsic value – as T. S. Eliot (1948: 27) put it 'that which makes life worth living'. There's our identity, national and individual. From *Who Do You Think You Are?* to the televising of the Olympic opening and closing ceremonies, the BBC performs an intimate service for each of us as we determine how we see ourselves. And there's our collective memory which is physically manifested by the BBC's archive. Is there anyone over the age of forty who hasn't indulged in the re-runs of *Top of the Pops* on BBC Four, with all the emotional baggage each era's tunes carry for us? A lively culture should also offer new ideas and fresh insights which inform us as empathetic citizens in a democracy – socially engaged, politically aware, understanding of others' lives and interests. Ofcom's 2013 survey of news consumption tells us that 53 per cent of our population still relies on the BBC as its primary source of news. Then, beyond that, the BBC claims that 96 per cent of the population use some element of its services every week. Music radio, the five funded orchestras and the Proms are an engine of this reach, providing an umbilical connection which appeals directly to our emotions. In our fragmented media world these are striking statistics.

The late W. G. Sebald argued that a healthy culture is one which is current. He regretted that German arts and culture was largely silent on the trauma of the Second World War for twenty-five years afterwards. Whether you watch *EastEnders, Question Time* or listen to the *Archers* or new bands on Radio One you will acknowledge how the BBC strives to hold up a contemporary mirror to us all. Finally, it's now recognised that the standing of post-war, post-empire Britain in the world is more determined by its culture than anything else. And, after Shakespeare and the English language itself, the BBC is by far the best known and most respected component of that. Witness Aung San Suu Kyi, under house arrest in Burma, listening to BBC music programmes and Mikhail Gorbachev, under house arrest in the Crimea, relying on the World Service to follow the progress of the 1991 coup against him. In summary, the BBC's contribution to national culture is, indeed, substantially to influence how we see ourselves and how the world sees us.

Culture and society

When writing about culture and society Jawaharlal Nehru (Narasimhachar 1961: 120) said it involved 'the widening of the mind and the spirit'. Yes, the widening, the enriching and the enlivening of the spirit. Older people, many isolated and living alone, rely on speech radio as their sole company. With local radio and Radios 4 and 5 the BBC is almost the sole supplier of this precious lifeline. And with landmark events such as the Diamond Jubilee, *Comic Relief* or *Children in Need*, the BBC provides the social glue that unifies us. Gareth Malone's harmonious marshalling of various community choirs in the past decade serves as a sort of wider metaphor for this quality. We are a digitally promiscuous generation. But at national moments of drama and high emotion we coalesce and still turn to the BBC.

Culture and education

When Lord Reith had to sum up the purpose of the BBC he famously adopted (and also adapted) the pithy phrase of the American radio pioneer, David Sarnoff, namely 'entertaining, informing, educating'. By the time it appeared in the BBC's charter it had been re-arranged: 'to inform, educate, entertain'. Note the order. The BBC has always had both a formal and informal education mission. If you want to see how they deliver on the former just Google BBC Learning and explore the Bitesize revision courses, the teacher packs, the co-operation with the Open University and the growing deployment of a digitised archive. Informal, lifelong learning is something the BBC offers us every night of every week in an extraordinarily rich output which we often take for granted, even as we rely on it. We may dislike this over-dramatic presenter, that director's clever-clever camera angles or the other's clumsy use of a music track, but the sheer force and variety of the politics, history, science and arts programming astonishes visitors to Britain who encounter it for the first time. 2014 will see a major campaign around the First World War, the focus will be Digital Creativity and Coding in 2015 and Shakespeare in 2016. The historian Thomas Carlyle (1827) had a philosophy even loftier than Reith's: 'The great law of culture is let each become all that he was created capable of being.' Lofty maybe, but impressively ambitious and an aspiration the BBC still seems to understand.

Culture and the economy

The fourth element of the holistic case is economic. Tessa Jowell, the long-serving Culture, Media and Sport Minister in the last government, once said that one of the purposes of the BBC was 'using the licence fee as venture capital for creativity'. What she had noted was that many of our successful independent producers started at the BBC; that many of our hit TV formats selling across the world were first tried out on BBC channels; that a sustained BBC presence in places such as Bristol and Salford can be an agent of regional regeneration; that investments in digital capacity such as BBC Online, Freeview and iPlayer were seeding fruitful new technologies. This is not just an economic argument. Empowered creatives exploiting these media are the people who articulate and re-interpret our culture for each generation. That's what the elected Mayor of Liverpool, Joe Anderson, had in mind when he said recently: 'Culture ... is the rocket fuel for our economy' (Bartlett 2013).

The holistic case – intrinsic culture, society, education, the economy – amounts to quite a list and one which gives us a rather broader definition of 'public service' than the narrow arguments about whether *Strictly Come Dancing* or the *Graham Norton Show* are suitable investments for the licence fee. It does us no harm to rehearse it, which is why charter renewal is a positive and valuable process. The BBC has no monopoly over our culture but it is probably the most significant player. In broadcasting others, such as Channel 4 and ITV, are real contributors too. But when we ponder how and whether to renew the BBC's charter we start from where we are. Over ninety years Britain has built up considerable cultural capital in this one institution and it would be rash to squander it. This doesn't mean, however, that it should not change. For me, the most important shift is that if the BBC is to remain the sole recipient of the licence fee it needs to share it much more widely. It must move from the unilateral to the bilateral, from the *dirigiste* to the collaborative, from Reithian aloofness to a spirit of partnership. This is already happening.

Partnerships or contested funding?

When I first worked for the Corporation in the 1970s, in BBC News and later in documentaries and factual entertainment, we were in truth pretty disdainful of our audience. We made programmes which interested us, we didn't treat complaints seriously or fairly and our grasp of proper budgeting (that is, deployment of the licence payers' money) was distinctly cavalier. The BBC today is a model of openness and transparency by comparison (in 2013 the Corporation received no fewer than 1,800 Freedom of Information requests). But the next big shift is that, in every sphere of its activities, it should be able to point to partnerships it has forged where, most often, the result is a whole that adds up to more than the sum of the parts. In other words, where the licence fee does dynamically more good than if it had simply been spent exclusively within the BBC. Perhaps the first example of this has been the enduring partnership with the Open University. And now that the OU is pioneering MOOCs (massive, open, online courses) via Futurelearn, imagine how exciting it will be if the BBC's remarkable archive is allied to these arts and science syllabi. Another extremely fruitful partnership has been the 25-year relationship with independent producers, now fuelled by the 'Window of Creative Competition'. This has had an undeniably beneficial effect on the BBC's programming, the economic health of the sector and the strength of Britain's programme and format exports.

The alternative to such partnerships is that the licence fee is shared out, via 'contested funding', to a much larger range of organisations which want to deliver on these public service objectives. I note that Roger Mosey, hitherto a BBC lifer who has run both news and sport in his time, has now settled into a Cambridge college and is arguing for just this. It is an important debate. Of course, during this current government small amounts of the licence fee were diverted to broadband roll out and the establishment of local television services (and valuably too, it must be said). This was not as novel as we might imagine. In 1930 some of the licence fee (in total, all of £1.47 million at the time) was, in effect, diverted to support the establishment of the Royal Opera House, with the Treasury using an equivalent amount of money to that which they taxed from the BBC (Squire 1930). The Prime Minister, Ramsey MacDonald, was also in favour of a similar conduit to enable a National Theatre but the Great Depression intervened and such ambitions were forgotten for 40 years. In fact, the way in which the BBC engages with the wider arts today provides the perfect model and exemplar for a future, more collaborative way of operating. If it pursues this wholeheartedly then there is no need for contested funding, the result of which could be a greatly diminished organisation. Mosey's biggest concern is too monolithic a voice in news output, in particular (Mosey 2013). But a greater commissioning of news and current affairs from outside companies could tackle this, as it has for Channel 4 News.

The artist as 'producer'

The BBC's coverage of the arts is a long and noble tradition. From *Monitor* and *Omnibus* through *Civilisation* and *Arena* to *Imagine* and the *Culture Show*. We think of the contributions of Huw Weldon, Humphrey Burton, Melvyn Bragg and Alan Yentob. But until recently it was all rather Reithian, as in, '*we* decide what to do and *your* job is to watch'. Spectrum was a scarce commodity, programme making a specialist skill and production equipment was expensive and 'professional'. Now spectrum is unlimited and every teenager is a programme maker using just a mobile phone to shoot and capture and the likes of YouTube to distribute. For artists and arts organisations this means they can create and share their own content. And it's already happening with the National Theatre, the Royal Opera House and the British Museum winning large audiences of their own in cinemas here and around the world. There are new aggregators such as HiBrow and new commissioners of content such as Tate Media. We are entering a different era and the BBC's role is to engage with these new producers and enable them. Tony Hall, now Director-General, is encouragingly making this a priority. He recently said that he wanted to appoint an Arts Executive 'who can help me build relationships with arts and artists ... we want more mainstream commissions ... with artists talking directly to audiences' (Mance and Pickford 2013).

This is exactly the idea behind the pop-up arts portal, the Space, established as a joint venture between the BBC and Arts Council England. It operated in 'beta' form during the Cultural Olympiad in 2012 and will be re-launched this spring as a fuller service. What it does is fund artists to create their own content, help to train them in production skills where necessary and provide a branded outlet for the programming. Already it has been the midwife to novel content partnerships with the Globe, Manchester Art Gallery, the Edinburgh International Festival and Birmingham Opera Company. And films by circus troupes, animators and musicians have gone on to win awards. This doesn't have to spell the end of traditional arts coverage on television but it does represent a radical departure. To their credit Sky Arts have also recognised this shift with their Ignition scheme for artists.

A charter for a partnership

Another example of a cultural partnership, a magnificent one, is the two radio series made by Radio 4 with Neil MacGregor and the British Museum: *A History of the World in 100 Objects* and *Shakespeare's Restless World*. Not just how we see ourselves, revealed through historical artefacts, but also how the world sees us, with the series heard throughout the world, boosting yet further the extraordinary visitor numbers to Bloomsbury. As it happens, 45 per cent of the views of the Space up to now have also been from abroad (MTM London 2013: 4). In the past that might have been questioned as an outcome for something publicly funded. But now there is a consensus that our cultural standing in the world is very much a public purpose. With a newly defined mode of operation, built on a rich tradition of public service, the case for a positive charter renewal becomes compelling. There are some in the Corporation who are still not clear how to spell the word *partnership*, but they need to learn. Those now leading the BBC certainly understand this. An outward-looking BBC sharing its cultural and economic capital with the nation – in essence, a joint venture – would have appalled that absolute monarch, Lord Reith. But its time has come. This is the basis on which the BBC should win its next charter.

So is the BBC in crisis? It has undoubtedly had its fair share of alarums and excursions of late, but no, it is not in crisis.

References

Bartlett, D. (2013) Culture will be the rocket fuel for Liverpool's economy, says Mayor Joe Anderson, *Liverpool Daily Post*, 4 April. Available online at http://www.liverpooldailypost.co.uk/news/liverpool-news/culture-rocket-fuel-liverpools-economy-5398728, accessed on 18 December 2013

BBC (2013) History of the BBC: 'entertaining, informing, educating'. Available online at www.bbc.co.uk/historyofthebbc/resources/indepth/reith, accessed on 18 December 2013

Carlyle, T. (1888) *Critical and Miscellaneous Essays*, London: Chapman & Hall

Department of Culture, Media and Sport (2006) Tessa Jowell in White Paper Introduction: *A public service for all: The BBC in the digital age*. Available online at http://www.official-documents.gov.uk/document/cm67/6763/6763.pdf, accessed on 18 December 2013

Eliot, T. S. (1948) *Notes Towards the Definition of Culture*, London: Faber

Mance, H. and Pickford, J. (2013) BBC will raise spending on arts coverage, *Financial Times*, 28 December

Mosey, Roger (2013) A smaller BBC would be good for audiences, Open Democracy, 14 November. Available online at http://www.opendemocracy.net/ourbeeb/roger-mosey/smaller-bbc-would-be-good-for-audiences, accessed on 13 December 2013

MTM London (2013) Evaluation of the Space, May. Available online at http://www.artscouncil.org.uk/media/uploads/MTM_Summary_Evaluation_of_The_Space_pilot.pdf, accessed on 18 December 2013

Narasimhachar, K. T. (1961) *The Quintessence of Nehru*, London: Allen & Unwin

Ofcom (2013) *News Consumption in the UK: Ofcom Research Document*, 25 September. Available online at http://stakeholders.ofcom.org.uk/binaries/research/tv-research/news/News_Report_2013.pdf, accessed on 18 December 2013

Squire, J. C. (1930) The opera subsidy, *Spectator*, 6 December. Available online at http://archive.spectator.co.uk/article/6th-december-1930/10/the-opera-subsidy, accessed on 18 December 2013

Note on the contributor

Sir Peter Bazalgette is Chair of Arts Council England. He is also a non-executive Director of ITV. Previously he chaired English National Opera, served on the Board of Channel 4 and was an independent television producer for twenty years.

• The opinions expressed in this chapter are his personal views.

Turning up the temperature:
The BBC and political pressure

Phil Harding argues that a BBC that was willing to lay down much stricter rules about its political accountability while at the same time opening a more open and direct relationship with the public who own it would become stronger – and much less prone to political bullying

Introduction

> The BBC shall be independent in all matters concerning the content of its output, the times and manner in which this is supplied, and in the management of its affairs.
>
> (BBC 2006)

Editorial independence is at the very heart of the BBC's existence. It is part of the reason for having a public broadcaster in the first place. At the same time, the BBC receives a very large amount of money from the public. It has to be accountable for that and it has to be open to public scrutiny for the way it discharges its responsibilities as a public broadcaster. There is a fine but important line between accountability and editorial independence.

In this chapter I want to suggest that in the midst of all the recent BBC's self-inflicted crises there has been a subtle but important shifting of that line away from editorial independence and towards political interference. The run-up to the next general election in 2015 will coincide with the negotiations for the next BBC charter and licence fee. It's a politically toxic period and one full of dangers for the BBC.

Editorial pressure/institutional pressure

There are two types of political pressure on the BBC. There is the pressure about editorial coverage and there is pressure on the BBC as a public institution. The latter includes how well it is managed, the scope and scale of the BBC and whether or not it should exist at all. I will explore each in turn.

Usually the two types of pressure are kept separate. While an editor might receive the most vigorous complaints about his or her programme they are never accompanied by a threat to cut the licence fee. That was what made the recent intervention by the current Conservative Party Chairman, Grant Shapps, in which he explicitly linked the future of the BBC licence fee to political coverage by the BBC's Home Editor, Mark Easton, so remarkable and why it provoked such a storm (Ross 2013). Shapps was, in fact, the fourth front-bencher to pick on Easton for his reporting. While some think that is because of the controversial nature of Easton's journalistic beat, others think the Conservatives are now calculatingly taking a page out of the Labour Party spinbook of dark arts, by singling out one individual journalist and then picking on them at every opportunity.

Pressure modern and ancient

Political pressure on the BBC is nothing new. Almost from its inception, relations with politicians have rarely been cosy, usually bracing and often abrasive. The BBC is usually under political pressure of one sort or another. After all, applying political pressure is what politicians do. It's their job. It's not the pressure that matters as much as what the BBC does in the face of such pressure. Part of the reason the BBC comes under so much political pressure is because it is so influential in public life. It has large audiences for its radio and television programmes. It has a high readership for its web and mobile services. It has a high reputation for providing quality coverage. It is the most trusted media source in Britain. Public and politicians have high expectations of it. It is also just about the only media outlet these days where politicians will receive extended coverage.

Neither is political pressure on the BBC necessarily a bad thing. If politicians complain about the coverage and seek to correct it, then it may just be that they have a point. Executives and editors should always listen. Political complaint and pressure can on occasion act as a necessary corrective to thoughtless or bad journalism.

A bit of history – the 'back channel'

In the 1970s and 1980s relations between the BBC and politicians were handled by two different routes. There was a front door and a back door. The day-to-day contacts and skirmishes over individual programmes were usually handled – as they are now – at a programme editor level. Sometimes a particularly fierce row would reach the head of department or the director of news but most were dealt with that day and forgotten by tomorrow. When I became the BBC's Chief Political Advisor in 1995 I became aware that there was a second parallel system in operation. It worked between the upper echelons of the BBC and the Chief Whips of the three main parties. This 'back channel' was where the big editorial disagreements between the BBC and the parties were discussed. It acted as an unofficial pressure valve for serious political discontent with the BBC. It wasn't a channel that was used often but when it was the BBC took it seriously.

One of the other main functions of this channel was to deal with the allocation of party election and party political broadcasts. This mattered because the allocation of air time for the election broadcasts formed the basis for deciding the rough allocation of time for the BBC's news coverage during a general election campaign. (For many years the ratio was 5-5-3/Conservative-Labour-Liberal Democrat.) As I discovered, the whole system of negotiation was liberally oiled by very large glasses of malt whisky in the office of the Government Chief Whip at No. 12 Downing Street.

The back-channel was a useful conduit – and helped avoid several potential clashes – though, of course, it didn't stop some of the big rows between the BBC and the Thatcher government over coverage of Northern Ireland, the Falklands war (of 1982) and the *Panorama* special, *Maggie's Militant Tendency* (broadcast on 30 January 1984). In the mid-1990s, this back-channel system had to be abandoned. Firstly, the allocation of party broadcasts was coming under increasing legal challenge – especially from the fringe parties. The keen advice of the BBC's lawyers was that the system would not withstand any serious legal challenge under Judicial Review. The second reason, which was to have even wider consequences, was the revamping of Labour's media operation – firstly under Peter Mandelson and then even more sweepingly under Alastair Campbell. The arrival of Campbell and his successful demand for full control and command of Labour's media relations meant that all issues about coverage were, in future, to be channeled through him – and only through him. As a result, any discussion with the Labour Chief Whip about media coverage was swiftly referred on.

The Campbell era

This change in Labour's media tactics – first in opposition then in government – meant that everything from the launch of campaigns to appearances on programmes to complaints about coverage minor and major all went through one route: Alastair Campbell. While this concentration of power doubtless had the effect of making Labour a much more disciplined campaigning force, it also meant that from the BBC's point of view it was no longer clear which complaints were being lodged because they were serious complaints and which were being lodged for party advantage. As the level of 'noise' increased so did the temptation for editors to ignore the complaints whether they were legitimate or not. This eventually culminated in the row about Andrew Gilligan's reporting of the Iraq dossier on 29 May 2003.

In this case, the removal of any 'back-channel' for taking some of the heat out of situation meant the row escalated without check. When a senior cabinet minister approached the BBC and offered to mediate in the dispute his approach was rejected. There was no longer a back-channel, trust had broken down. In the end, the Campbell approach of constant badgering and intimidation became counter-productive. Labour over-played its hand. Editors developed cloth ears.

Pressure today

These days a lot of the shouting and swearing has died down to be replaced by intensive texting. News editors at the BBC can expected to be bombarded two or three times a week by the new generations of spin doctors. Phrases such as 'totally inaccurate', 'lazy journalism', 'that story is far too prominent', 'totally unfair tone of that interview' will fly around. Conscious of the agenda-setting role of the *Today* programme, particular targets are the 6, 7 and 8 o'clock news bulletins. The BBC News website is increasingly important too. The government media operation complains more than Labour. Often the battle is over language: the 'bedroom tax' versus the 'spare bedroom subsidy' is a classic example.

In the run-up to the next general election the BBC can expect to start receiving even more texts and phone calls. Some editors say it had started before the end of 2012 already. At the same time we will have the negotiations for the next charter and licence fee. It's going to be a particularly febrile political time for a debate on the future of the BBC.

The licence fee and top-slicing

Even if the BBC were not such an influential political broadcaster, the fact that the level of the licence fee is set by the government of the day means that the negotiations over money and the BBC become intensely political. Often the final deal is only done with the Chancellor or the Culture Secretary on one side of the table and the BBC on the other. There has been a revival of talk in recent months about top-slicing the BBC's licence fee, perhaps even making all of the licence fee open to competition from all broadcasters (along similar lines to the Arts Council).

Already part of the licence fee has been quietly diverted. Starting in April 2015, the BBC will pay the Department of Culture, Media and Sport £12.5 million a month for two years (£300 million in all) to pay for the funding of the roll-out of broadband to rural areas across the UK. This pattern of using the licence fee for other public purposes was started with the 2006 licence fee settlement when part of the licence fee was allocated to the television digital switchover programme. From that point on the genie was out of the bottle.

The role of the National Audit Office

The BBC receives nearly £3.5 billion of the public's money via the licence fee. This means there must be proper external scrutiny of the BBC's expenditure. The self-proclaimed vision of the National Audit Office (NAO) 'is to help the nation spend wisely'. The NAO has taken an increasing role in the scrutiny by parliament of the spending of the BBC. It was first given access to the BBC's books in 2006 but with strict limitations. These restrictions have since been gradually removed until a new agreement in the autumn of 2015 has given the NAO the right to go where it chooses to go without seeking the prior permission of the BBC provided only that the NAO does not involve itself in editorial matters. It is a controversial role.

Recently, the NAO was described by the former BBC Chairman, Sir Christopher Bland, as being 'the most politicised auditor you can imagine', too focused in its reporting on 'whether they get a headline' (Plunkett 2013).

The argument about the BBC and the NAO crucially centres round the point that the BBC is not just another government department under the control of a minister. In order to keep its editorial independence it's important that it should not be treated as just another ministry. The line between legitimately assessing what is value for public money and allowing the NAO and MPs to decide on the BBC's editorial priorities is a thin one. For example, where would an examination of the BBC's spend on sporting rights fit? What is value for money if you are comparing the spending on say the Football World Cup versus the Ashes series? Though the current BBC Chairman, Chris Patten, professes himself to be relaxed about the new arrangements, others are less sure. This comment is from the BBC's former Director of News, Richard Sambrook:

> The worry is that a disgruntled MP might demand some immediate review of the BBC in retaliation for difficult questions being asked on *Newsnight* or *Today* – and the BBC would be powerless to resist. Or a competitor could raise questions for an MP to pursue in aid of its commercial advantage. A *Daily Mail* story on the number of staff sent to cover the World Cup, for example, might prompt calls for a hard look at value for money – surely commentators could do both radio and TV? If other broadcasters manage with one morning presenter, is that awkward one on the *Today* programme really necessary? Hard to imagine? No, not really (Sambrook 2013).

Each NAO report is, of course, laid before parliament which means there is then a grilling for the BBC by the Public Accounts Committee.

Select committees

Appearances before parliamentary select committees are seen as being an important part of the BBC's duty of public accountability. In 2013, the BBC has appeared before select committees at Westminster no fewer than 14 times. Of course, some of these appearances have been in response to the various self-inflicted crises: the Savile/*Newsnight* affair, the resignation of George Entwistle, the senior staff pay-offs and so on. By comparison five years ago there were three appearances, in 2002 there were two appearances. In addition, BBC executives and Trustees are now expected to appear before the relevant committees of the Scottish parliament and the Welsh and Northern Irish assemblies.

Even allowing for the fact that the past year has been an exceptionally bad one for the BBC, full of self-inflicted crises, there is clearly a longer-term trend here. Politicians are calling the BBC to give evidence more often and are taking a closer and closer interest in the internal workings of the BBC. The increasing numbers of appearances before select committees was recently described by one senior BBC executive as being 'totally out of control'. Many of the BBC's recent appearances before select committees have been marked by very aggressive and hostile questioning. The BBC, of course, has not been alone in this. In recent years, some of the committees seem to have come to see their job as holding the wider world to account by hostile grilling of people who hold no governmental role. This represents a significant extension of the select committees' powers which thus far has not been subject to much public debate. It certainly marks an increase in the powers that select committees think they have over the BBC.

There have also been some very singular lines of inquiry by MPs. A lot of the appearance by Lords Patten and Hall before the Culture, Media and Sport Committee in October 2013 was occupied by detailed questions about the differing accounts given to the Pollard Inquiry by Mark Thompson and Helen Boaden. Elsewhere, an appearance by three senior BBC editorial figures before the European Scrutiny Committee in February included questions about the make-up of a panel for one edition of *Question Time* and why their committee did not receive more coverage on BBC Parliament (European Scrutiny Committee 2013a).

It appears to have been increasing concern about the amount and scope of political scrutiny from select committees that led Chris Patten to write to the Chair of the European Scrutiny Committee, Bill Cash, turning down their invitation to appear before the committee in the following blunt terms:

> I have consulted my colleagues on the BBC Trust and this letter reflects our collective and unanimous view. It is incumbent upon the Trust under the terms of the royal charter to stand up for the independence of the BBC and, in particular, its editorial independence. We are bound to weigh this as of paramount importance when viewed against a request to appear before your committee which we believe to be inappropriate. Accordingly, I must decline your request. As part of our role I and my colleagues appear quite properly in front of the Culture, Media and Sport Select Committee and the Public Accounts Committee, and neither attempts to engage with us – as you are proposing to do – on the editorial decisions of the BBC. Since becoming BBC Trust Chairman in May 2011, I myself have appeared before these two committees a total of six times … We wonder if you have considered that the result of you asserting your right to call me before your committee on this issue is that BBC Trustees could in future be required to appear before any select committee to discuss the coverage of the BBC in its particular area of responsibility. It is not, therefore, beyond the bounds of possibility to conceive that in quite short order we could be expected to answer to say the Home Affairs Committee on the BBC's coverage of that area, or the Foreign Affairs Committee on international stories. We can't believe that is what was intended when the royal charter was drafted and we do not believe that it is consistent with the ideal of an independent Trust protecting the BBC from undue political interference (European Scrutiny Committee 2013b).

But this exchange looks unlikely to end there. The committee has repeated its invitation to Lord Patten and the Speaker of the Commons, John Bercow, has now intervened in support: '…..anybody who's invited to appear before a committee in this House should do so. No-one, no matter how senior, should imagine him or herself above such scrutiny' (Jeory 2013). This exchange could well turn into an important battle about the balance between the BBC's editorial independence and its proper accountability to politicians.

The BBC and the press

In recent years there has been a growing tension between sections of the press (the *Daily Telegraph*, *Daily Mail* and Murdoch's News UK groups, in particular) and the BBC. There are more and more critical stories often coupled with open contempt in the editorial columns. It's also perhaps no coincidence that two of the fiercest periods of attack by the press on the BBC have been at crucial times in the Leveson/royal charter press regulation debate. The crass incompetence of the Corporation in handling both its internal crises and the public's money has of course put it right in the firing line. But that's only part of the reason for the bad press. There have been two longer-running and deeper-seated causes.

First of all there is a growing commercial clash between the BBC and the various press groups. As media consumption and advertising spend moves more and more online and as newspapers have struggled to find a business model to fit, there have been increasing complaints that the BBC with its large online presence has been squeezing the living daylights out of the online operations of the commercial press. Secondly, there has been a growing line of political attack on the BBC. This comes from claims by the political right that, far from being the impartial editorial organisation it claims to be, the Corporation is, in fact, institutionally left-wing. This argument was expressed most fruitily by the Editor-in-Chief of the *Daily Mail*, Paul Dacre, in his 2007 Hugh Cudlipp lecture in an attack on what he saw as the subsidised liberal media:

> … the Subsidariat, dominated by the BBC monolith, is distorting Britain's media market, crushing journalistic pluralism and imposing a mono culture that is inimical to healthy democratic debate …. what is in front of one's nose is that the BBC, a behemoth that bestrides Britain is, as Cudlipp might have put it, TOO BLOODY BIG, TOO BLOODY PERVASIVE AND TOO BLOODY POWERFUL … What really disturbs me is that the BBC is, in every corpuscle of its corporate body, against the values of conservatism, with a small 'c', which, I would argue, just happen to be the values held by millions of Britons. Thus it exercises a kind of 'cultural Marxism' in which it tries to undermine that conservative society by turning all its values on their heads … Thus BBC journalism is presented through a left-wing prism that affects everything – the choice of stories, the way they are angled, the choice of interviewees and, most pertinently, the way those interviewees are treated (Dacre 2007).

The press and the politics

For some years the various press groups have been lobbying the government of the day over the size and scope of the BBC. The days of Rupert Murdoch being able to pop into Downing Street at will may have gone but the political pressures on the BBC from the press persist. Added to this is a new self-reinforcing alliance between some newspapers and some MPs who want to prune drastically the BBC (the latter described to me by one BBC executive as the 'tea-party faction'). This alliance sometimes takes the form of the newsdesk going to a particular MP for an attacking quote, sometimes the MP tabling a question which follows the particular agenda being pursued by that newspaper at the time.

Conclusion

The BBC will always be at the heart of political rows; it's almost part of its job. But as this chapter has argued, the political pressures on the BBC are mounting insidiously. It's been lots of small things: increasing pressure from MPs, the increasing numbers of appearances before select committees, the increasing acceptance that parts of the licence fee will be used for bits of national infrastructure, increasing scrutiny from the NAO, increasingly strident criticism from the press and the linking of editorial pressure with corporate pressure. It's been a bit like the story of the frog in the boiling water. The changes have been subtle and have taken place over a long period of time so that no one has really noticed how hot the water has become. So what is the way out of this dilemma? If the BBC is not to lose its editorial independence two things need to happen.

First, there need to be some new, clearer ground rules for appearances in front of select committees. The BBC has given ground on the activities of the NAO. In return it is time that MPs agreed that the BBC should normally only have to report to two select committees the Culture, Media and Sport Committee and the Public Accounts Committee, perhaps at fixed times of year and with a clearer understanding from the chair of the committee on the limitations of the questioning. At the moment, the balance is shifting dangerously close to editorial interference by MPs.

The second corrective is much broader and goes to the heart of the nature of the BBC as a public broadcaster. At present too much of the public's perception of the BBC is mediated by MPs and the press. The BBC needs to start building a much more direct relationship with the public whom it serves. It is a theme Tony Hall has started to develop:

> A central part of my vision for the BBC is that it is not just paid for by its viewers and listeners, it belongs to them, to you … Digital technology now means that we are able to hand to our listeners and viewers a huge amount of control that 30 years ago we kept to ourselves ... Services like the iPlayer bring you the programmes you want to watch and listen to whenever you want them. *Start The Week* in the middle of the week. *In Our Time*, in your time, the *Today* programme – tomorrow. The BBC you can have is catching

up with the BBC you want … There's a fundamental shift happening. I want a BBC that feels different, where our audiences are on the inside, helping us to be the best we can be (BBC 2013).

But this new vision needs to go beyond words and beyond what can be done with the iPlayer. The BBC needs to fully embrace the idea that the public *own* the BBC not just pay for it. That demands a big cultural shift. One of the ways that people have talked about involving the public in running the BBC is by instituting some sort of membership structure. Some in the Labour Party have talked about the 'mutualisation' of the BBC. There are some interesting ideas in Tessa Jowell's article for the Third Way booklet *Making it Mutual* (Jowell 2013). The idea here would be something along the lines of a National Trust with TV licences; every licence fee payer would become a member of the BBC. The BBC Trust would become accountable to the membership.

There is certainly something to be looked at here. But with the new technologies on offer the BBC could go much further. The BBC could become a truly open and porous organisation in which the boundaries between its professional operations and those of the public become increasingly blurred. There could be partnerships – real partnerships not token ones – with other bodies that provide public service value: local communities, councils, commercial media, production companies, cultural and educational bodies. The BBC may be a national treasure but at the moment the citizen has little engagement with how it is run. If every licence-fee payer felt they had a real personal stake and involvement in the BBC, then it could become a truly public broadcaster in every sense.

Some parts of BBC management, especially those who still think in terms of commanding fiefdoms, could find all this rather uncomfortable; so might some members of the BBC Trust. But a BBC that was willing to lay down much stricter rules about its political accountability while at the same time opening a more open and direct relationship with the public who own it would become a stronger, better BBC and one much less prone to political bullying.

References

BBC (2006) Charter. Available online at http://www.bbc.co.uk/bbctrust/assets/files/pdf/about/how_we_govern/charter.pdf, accessed on 21 December 2013

BBC (2013) Speech given by Tony Hall at Voice of the Listener and Viewer Conference, 27November. Available online at http://www.bbc.co.uk/mediacentre/speeches/2013/tony-hall-vlv.html, accessed on 21 December 2013

Dacre, Paul (2007) Cudlipp lecture, http://image.guardian.co.uk/sys-files/Media/documents/2007/01/23/CudlippDacre.pdf, accessed on 21 December 2013

European Scrutiny Committee (2013a) Minutes of evidence, HC 711, 6 February. Available online at http://www.publications.parliament.uk/pa/cm201213/cmselect/cmeuleg/c711-v/c71101.htm, accessed on 21 December 2013

European Scrutiny Committee (2013b) The visibility and scrutiny of the media. Available online at http://www.publications.parliament.uk/pa/cm201314/cmselect/cmeuleg/109/10911.htm, accessed on 21 December 2013

Jeory, Ted (2013) BBC Trust boss Lord Patten ordered to parliament to answer claims of biased coverage of EU, *Daily Express*, 5 December. Available online at http://www.express.co.uk/news/uk/446943/BBC-Trust-boss-Lord-Patten-ordered-to-Parliament-to-answer-claims-of-biased-coverage-of-EU, accessed on 21 December 2013

Jowell, Tessa (2013) Call to mutualise the BBC. Available online at http://thirdway.eu/2013/03/17/support-for-calls-to-mutualise-the-bbc, accessed on 21 December 2013

Plunkett, John (2013) BBC ex-chair says NAO more interested in headlines than value for money, *Guardian*, 12 September. Available online at http://www.theguardian.com/media/2013/sep/12/bbc-chairman-nao-headlines-watchdog, accessed on 21 December 2013

Ross, Tim (2013) BBC could lose right to licence fee over 'culture of waste and secrecy', minister warns, *Daily Telegraph*, 26 October. Available online at http://www.telegraph.co.uk/culture/tvandradio/bbc/10406971/BBC-could-lose-right-to-licence-fee-over-culture-of-waste-and-secrecy-minister-warns.html, accessed on 13 December 2013

Sambrook, Richard (2013) BBC faces being politicised, putting budgets and editorial content at risk, *Guardian*, 15 September. Available online at http://www.theguardian.com/media/media-blog/2013/sep/15/bbc-politicised-budgets-editorial-content, accessed on 21 December 2013

Note on the contributor

Phil Harding is a journalist and broadcaster. He is a former BBC executive and editor and held a number of jobs while at the BBC including Chief Political Adviser, Controller of Editorial Policy and Editor of the *Today* programme.

What Britons think of the BBC

Alice Enders draws on some of the recent surveys conducted by the BBC Trust and Ofcom to highlight the public's perceptions about the Beeb

The Culture, Media and Sport (CMS) Select Committee opened its 2013 inquiry on *The Future of the BBC* with the question 'What should the BBC be for and what should be the purpose of public service broadcasting?' to which the only obvious answer is that the BBC and public service broadcasting should be for the people of Britain. So that begs the question of what the people of Britain think of the BBC, answers to which are sketched out below.

There are many surveys in the public domain asking people what they think of the BBC. Below, I draw mainly upon the regular surveys conducted by the BBC Trust and Ofcom, because they have 'arms-length' relationships with the BBC executive, giving their surveys somewhat higher 'credentials' as is appropriate for a journalistic/academic publication such as this one. My focus is on (a) what the public at large thinks; and (b) what BBC TV audiences think, in the context of the UK's idiosyncratic system of PSB broadcasting. There is an important difference between the scope of these two populations:

- The public at large is 96 per cent of the UK's adult population of 52 million, interacting weekly with the BBC on at least one touchpoint (radio, TV, online), yielding an average of 18.5 hours per week of media engagement.

- On television, consumption totalled 26.7 hours per week in the nine months to September 2013, of which the BBC accounted for 8.5 hours weekly on average, 32 per cent of total television time amongst the four-plus UK population.

- However, there is a strong skew in BBC TV viewing share towards 55-plus adults, corresponding with their life stages, peaking amongst senior citizens that have lots of time on their hands to enjoy media in general and the

BBC in particular: those 55-plus spent 14.9 hours/week with BBC TV compared to 7.9 hours for the 35-54 demographic and just 4.7 hours by the 16-34 demographic.

Which matters more? The opinions regarding the BBC in the public at large or amongst BBC TV audiences? The public at large are the ultimate 'shareholders' of the UK government and its institutions, of which the BBC is, of course, unique in its role and function amongst cultural organisations serving the UK population. Most UK taxpayers live in UK TV households, paying the licence fee. So what the public at large thinks serves as a bellwether for notions of the position of the BBC in UK society at large.

Politicians too will tend to focus on opinions of the public at large, since voters are to be found in their midst. The House of Commons will tend to think more about voter opinions than audiences in its Annual Review of the BBC. So public opinion on matters of governance, Savile, etc… will perforce loom larger than what BBC audiences think.

The BBC Trust, as the overseeing authority for the BBC executive, thinks politically as it is answerable to parliament. But it will also think a great deal about audience opinions, assessed across all channels of delivery. Measurement is taken seriously at the BBC Trust because it drives recommendations to the BBC executive.

This serious approach to measurement is true as well of Ofcom. Its Annual PSB reports focus on PSB TV channel audience appreciation of channel fulfilment of public service remits.[1] Like other PSBs, the BBC is assessed through the 'performance gap' between audience expectations and fulfilment around phrases that interpret what PSB channels should be for to their audiences in terms of programming. These are the 'metrics' for PSB delivery that should inform policymakers when looking at the BBC, in terms of its role to 'inform, educate and entertain'.

What UK adults think of the BBC

The BBC Trust has produced adult population surveys annually since 2008, providing a valuable time series of results worth looking at in detail. The BBC executive too produces overlapping surveys, but those produced by the BBC Trust might be considered more trustworthy given its 'arms-length' relationship with the BBC. Some results from the last edition[2]:

- Testament to its importance, 80 per cent of UK adults would miss the BBC if it no longer existed, more than any other broadcaster.

- The majority of UK adults – 56 per cent – are 'high approvers' of the BBC, 32 per cent are mid-approvers and 10 per cent are low approvers. High approvers jumped 12 ppts from the 44 per cent recorded in the autumn 2011 edition, which has been consistent over time, suggesting a post-Olympics burst of enthusiasm for the BBC, on the back of the very successful coverage. Since the mids saw a 12 ppts decline, these results should be treated with caution.

- A majority of UK adults – 57 per cent – thought the licence fee was 'good value', overlapping with 'high approvers'. Except for 16 to 24-year-olds whose BBC approval rating was 57 per cent despite lower engagement with BBC TV programming, approval was correlated with age, rising to 61 per cent for those 55-64 and 65 per cent amongst those 65-plus. Amongst the nations, approval was higher in England (50 per cent) and Wales (60 per cent) than in Scotland (50 per cent or Northern Ireland (47 per cent), explaining the BBC's pledge to increase nations' programming.

- However, 43 per cent of respondents thought the licence fee was 'not good value', amongst which 66 per cent selected the factor 'cost and affordability' as an influence on value for money considerations. How well the BBC was run was a factor cited by 20 per cent of those in the good value for money camp and 31 per cent in the not good value camp.

Prospect magazine, in its 'How to rescue the BBC' cited a survey claiming that 48 per cent of UK adults in February 2013 found the licence good or very good value, compared to 23 per cent finding it neither good nor bad value, and 31 per cent finding it bad value. That still meant that less than a majority of UK adults considered the licence fee good value for money, which is disquieting.

The implications for the BBC and the licence fee of these important pieces of research need to be better understood. The licence fee is mandatorily paid by UK TV households, apart from exempted households (75-plus), which account for 16.5 per cent of 26,733 UK television licences. It's fair insofar as the applicable condition for the payment is the same for all households with television sets that are enjoying free-to-air programming, irrespective of the level of consumption, or of the main FTA supplier. The licence fee payer also makes a close link between the fee and the BBC's services.

At the same time, when viewed as a tax (which it is technically), the licence fee is regressive in claiming the highest share of household budgets of those least well-off in society. Although they may not seek to avoid paying the licence fee, these are households that are careful about any expenditure at all. £12.23/month may not seem like a lot in the grand scheme of things but for state pensioners below the 75-plus ceiling, it is still 3 per cent of the state pension. Unfortunately, there doesn't seem to be a ready alternative to the licence fee.

What UK adults think about the BBC's public service delivery
The BBC Trust oversees the delivery of the BBC's six public service remits grouped as follows: creativity; citizenship; nations: regions, communities; global; education; digital (Freeview, online, DAB radio). Since 2008, the BBC Trust has tested UK adult opinion on various statements for significance and delivery, testing 34 in its last edition of the *Purpose Remit Survey UK report*.

The single most important statement about the BBC is: 'The BBC makes high-quality programmes or online content' (important to 83 per cent of UK adults) with a deficit of 7 ppts in relation to the performance score (judged satisfactory by 76 per cent of US adults). The lowest scores (biggest deficits) are realised for the statements: 'The BBC has lots of fresh and new ideas' which the BBC Trust has highlighted as a failing of the BBC executive, and 'The BBC is good at representing my ethnic group.' The latter is perhaps understandable insofar as the BBC mainly produces programming for the majority of the UK population, which is not of ethnic origin, and this is amongst the genres designated for the PSB delivery of Channel 4.

In their regression analysis, NatCen Social Research for the BBC Trust tested the importance of statements for those 57 per cent stating the BBC was good value for money, and found the top 10 drivers are 'creativity', 'citizenship' and 'digital' statements.[3] Although the BBC has not picked up on this yet, a further focus on these three areas could drive higher approval on the licence fee.

What BBC TV audiences think of the BBC

On television programming, like other terrestrial broadcasters, the BBC is constrained to abide by the requirements of the PSB eco-system on the supply-side of programming, notably for news and current affairs programming, and other genres.[4] The highly regulated BBC contrasts with the less regulated commercial PSBs, which means that the BBC is the most important supplier of PSB programming.[5] PSBs with 95 per cent reach gain access to 'listed' events – the royal wedding, the Olympics and Paralympics, Wimbledon – which is also a driver of PSB audiences.

Despite fragmenting PSB channel audience behaviours due to the development of multichannel TV, PSB television consumption accounts for most of television time. The PSB eco-system is likely to remain of strong significance to UK audiences in the decade to 2027. So the measurement systems reported upon in this article will remain valid for the foreseeable future.

Television viewing has held up well in spite of the proliferation of other alternative content available via PC, mobile and tablets and through connected TV sets. In total, 3.8 hours/day were devoted to TV by the UK four-plus population in the nine months to September 2013, or 26.7 hours per week. Britons are well-known to be the outstanding couch potatoes of Europe.

However, there is a downward viewing trend across all television among under-55s, most markedly among children and teens. That said, as younger cohorts move into the next lifestage with families of their own, we believe that television will become more important, just as it has to previous generations, and their overall television consumption will increase.

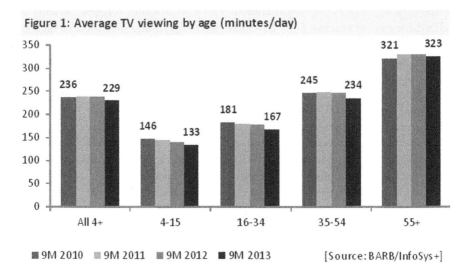

Figure 1: Average TV viewing by age (minutes/day)

■9M 2010　■9M 2011　■9M 2012　■9M 2013　　　　[Source: BARB/InfoSys+]

The BBC itself has held its audience share well over the past three years, with a 32 per cent share of television viewing in the nine months to September 2013. However, the BBC's share across 2013 is less than 25 per cent for under-35s (see Figure 2). Put together, these data imply that those 55-plus spent 14.9 hours/week with the BBC compared to 7.9 hours for the 35-54 demographic and just 4.7 hours by the 16-34 demographic. Total viewing share of the BBC is being hiked up by the viewing habits of the 55-plus UK adults, representing 18 million adults or 35 per cent of the UK's adult population of 52 million at 2012.

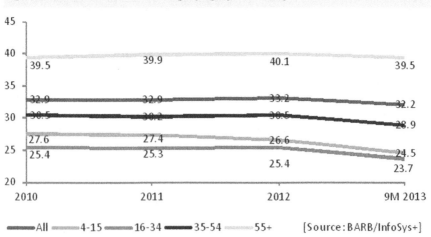

Figure 2: BBC share of TV viewing by age (% of total)

━━All　━━4-15　━━16-34　━━35-54　━━55+　　[Source: BARB/InfoSys+]

The BBC's biggest cross-platform audience is for news. BBC channels (including the parliament channel) accounted for a whopping 274 billion minutes of TV news minutes watched in the year to November 2013 (based on BARB/Infosys), just over 70 per cent of the total. On the terrestrial broadcast platform, the share of the BBC in news minutes was 76 per cent.

BBC One and BBC Two are also carried by non-terrestrial channels such as BSkyB and VMed. They benefit as PSB channels from preferential positions in the EPG, occupying numbers 1 and 2. While this may draw the attention of audiences to these channels, the appeal of BBC news is striking even in Sky households, which are served Sky News. Even here, BBC channels still manage to attract 65 per cent of the TV news minutes consumed by them in the year to November 2013 (BARB/Infosys).

Boasting 10.2 million unique users in the UK in the year to November 2013, the usage of BBC.com online extends and amplifies the presence of the BBC as the centre of news consumption in the UK. However, unlike the pre-eminence of the BBC on TV platforms, MailOnline.com gets more usage time: 8.5 million uniques devoted 8.5 billion minutes to site in the year to November 2013 (Nielsen), compared to 5.9 billion minutes to the BBC.

Ofcom reports on PSB channel audience fulfilment with respect to 12 common criteria. This method takes into account the demographic skew of BBC audiences towards 35+ adults, but not the greater amount of time they spend with BBC TV.

78 per cent of regular viewers of BBC One consider it delivers 'trustworthy' news programmes and also 'helps me to understand what's going on in the world'[6] which are the two PSB statements most important to UK PSB audiences (Figure 3). Audiences have a higher level of confidence in the BBC than other PSBs on most criteria.

Figure 3: Ofcom PSB channel summaries

Statements:	BBC One	BBC Two	ITV	Channel 4	Channel 5	PSBs combined
News programmes are trustworthy	78%	72%	67%	61%	46%	64%
Helps me understand what's going on in the world	78%	71%	58%	54%	34%	58%
Regional news is good quality	70%	-	65%	-	-	60%
Interesting programmes about history, science, arts	62%	79%	34%	45%	30%	47%

High quality soaps/dramas made in the UK	64%	48%	66%	45%	35%	47%
Portrays my region fairly to rest of UK	56%	42%	57%	36%	26%	40%
Shows different kinds of cultures within the UK	58%	58%	46%	55%	31%	43%
Shows well-made, high-quality programmes	81%	79%	68%	66%	48%	59%
Shows new programmes made in UK	65%	63%	55%	53%	33%	46%
Shows programmes with new ideas, approaches	56%	59%	47%	58%	35%	44%
Shows programmes that make me stop and think	62%	69%	40%	56%	31%	44%
Shows programmes I want to watch	69%	67%	63%	60%	48%	51%

[Source: Ofcom, *PSB Annual Report 2012*, Annex B]

Conclusions

It's crucial that policymakers engage closely with surveys asking Britons what they think of the BBC in the period of charter review that lies ahead, but also recognise the central role the BBC plays in supplying PSB programming to TV audiences. Conclusions include:

- A majority of UK adults back the BBC's licence fee, judging it good value for money, but there is a worrying 43 per cent that do not.
- Three of four Britons agree that 'The BBC makes high-quality programmes or online content'.
- Audiences have a higher level of confidence in the BBC than other PSBs on most criteria assessed by Ofcom, especially on the questions that concern the quality of news programming.
- The BBC's biggest cross-platform audience is for news, with BBC TV channels accounting for 274 billion minutes of TV news watched in the year to November 2013 (based on BARB/Infosys), just over 70 per cent of the total.
- TV remains the pre-eminent news channel despite the appeal of online news sites, which attracted 27 billion minutes of usage, just 10 per cent of the TV total.

Notes

[1] This rigorous and regular system of assessment does not apply to IP TV or satellite providers, just to the spectrum-using terrestrial TV broadcasters

[2] BBC Trust, *Purpose remit survey UK report*, June 2013

[3] Creativity statements: 'The BBC makes high quality programmes and online content'; 'The BBC makes programmes or online content that no other broadcaster would make'; 'The BBC helps me enjoy my interests, hobbies and passions'

Citizenship statements: 'The BBC helps me understand politics in Europe'; 'The BBC provides high quality independent journalism'; 'The BBC introduces me to new presenters, actors, writers and musical artists from the UK'

Digital statements: 'The BBC has a wide range of enjoyable and entertaining programmes and online content'; 'The BBC provides quality content that I find enjoyable or useful content on interactive TV'; 'The BBC provides quality content that I find enjoyable or useful on DAB digital radio'

[4] The PSB eco-system has evolved since the birth of BBC radio in 1927 to encompass BBC TV, Channel Four Television Corporation (C4C), a publicly-owned but commercially-funded broadcaster, Channel 3 licensees and Channel 5, the latter commercially-owned and commercially-funded and thus for-profit. UK audiences also enjoy channel broadcasts (due to must-carry) on pay-TV platforms BSkyB, Virgin Media and BT Vision, also all for-profit

[5] Ofcom enforces Tier 2 licence conditions on the broadcast of news programmes and current affairs programmes on the main channels of independent PSBs. In addition, PSBs Tier 2 obligations on commissioning original productions (as compared to 'bought-in' or in-house programming) set aside a quota for the independent production sector, including from companies located outside the M25 or in the Nations. The BBC's is the single largest amount

Ofcom's Annual PSB Reports indicate that compliance by PSBs, including the BBC, with quotas on news programming, current affairs programming, original, independent and regional programming is excellent and often exceeded

Tier 3 programming objectives are set out in Statements of Programme Policy (including by the BBC). Post-switchover, the fully commercial PSBs (ITV, Channel 5), have minimum Tier 3 obligations, thereby increasing the importance of the BBC and Channel 4 in the supply of Tier 3 PSB to UK audiences. Channel 4 of course has a much smaller audience than the BBC

[6] Ofcom, *PSB Annual Report 2012*, Annex B, pp 38-39

Note on the contributor

Alice Enders is Senior Media Analyst at Enders Analysis, a research and advisory firm based in London (www.endersanalysis.com). The company serves subscribers research on the media, entertainment, mobile and fixed telecoms industries, with a special focus on technology. Alice works on recorded music, the creative economy, content models and copyright licensing for the digital age. She was Senior Economist at the World Trade Organisation from 1988 to 2009 and holds a PhD in Economics from Queen's University (Canada).

The BBC as spectacle: Those who live by the camera, die by it

John Mair traces the recent history of the BBC and its appearances in front of parliamentary committees. The side show has become the main show – a modern day spectacle

The BBC has become the spectacle not the spectator at its own feast thanks to television and the rise of select committees in parliament. Far from simply reporting the story, the Corporation has too often become *the* story with month after month of BBC VVIPs appearing blinking in front of MPs and cameras. This month, the Culture Select Committee, the next the Public Accounts Committee, next the Foreign Affairs Committee. The merry-go-round simply never stops. It is a public spectacle or gladiatorial contest with no seeming end in sight. Watching the Beeb squirm is a spectacle sport of our times,

In 2013, BBC executives appeared before select committees a total of sixteen times (Patten 2013). Back in the Dark Ages – a decade ago in 2004 – there was just one annual trip from Portland Place to Westminster. The chairman of the BBC governors and the director-general would simply appear and amplify on the Corporation's annual report for the select committee on culture, media and sport. The then-Chairman, Gerald Kaufman MP, a former journalist and no slouch at self publicity, press released their conclusions in advance:

> After thorough discussion, the Committee has agreed a unanimous report. We do not believe that the status quo is an option for the BBC. Our recommendations are aimed at assisting the development of proposals that will take a strong and independent BBC, but also an accountable, open and efficient BBC, into what is an uncertain future for broadcasting. The current review of the BBC's royal charter is possibly the most significant in the Corporation's history (Culture, Media and Sport Committee 2004).

This all has a familiar ring to it in 2014. Back then, parliament itself would debate royal commission reports such as Annan in 1977 and Peacock in 1986 into the BBC, broadcasting and the licence fee plus their many early-day motions to let MPs praise or damn the Corporation for perceived triumphs or misdemeanours but, by and large, the two Estates remained separate.

No more. The road from W1 to SWI has become a well-travelled one and not always in peace. Director-General Mark Thompson did not cover himself in glory when threatening to shoot the Salford BBC baby at birth if no increase in the licence fee in front of a select committee in 2005. That was just the beginning of the nightmare. Think of poorly prepared then-D-G George Entwistle struggling to account for the Savile affair to the Culture, Media and Sport Select Committee (in the Thatcher Room of Portcullis House!) on 23 October 2012. It was a lamb and slaughter as the *Guardian* reported.

> Asked how many cases of sexual harassment the corporation knew about, he stumbled before answering there were 'between five and 10 serious allegations' relating to the Savile period. Later he changed that to 'between eight and 10'. This was not the sure-footed response needed to impress a committee that wrung a 'most humble day of life' apology out of Rupert Murdoch a year ago. It made it easy for Tory MP Philip Davies, no BBC loyalist, to land a blow. He accused Entwistle of a 'lamentable lack of knowledge' about the allegations of child abuse by now well-aired across every media outlet including the BBC. Davies quizzed him about what he knew about an alleged 'paedophile ring at the BBC' and wanted to know who was responsible for bussing vulnerable schoolgirls to Savile shows. 'I don't know,' Entwistle said, explaining the Corporation was trying to piece together documentation in relation to this. Asked who allowed underage children to go backstage with Savile, Entwistle responded: 'We are trying to answer the questions in the same way' (O'Carroll 2012).

Entwistle's time as D-G lasted just another three weeks after that.

Think of BBC Trust Chairman Lord Patten of Barnes losing his temper with Philip Davies MP calling his question about his daily routine 'impertinent' and asking: 'Do you want to know my toilet habits?' on 26 November 2012 and think of the worst spectacle of them all – the Six Not So Wise Men (and one woman) lined up, uncomfortably cheek by jowl and passing several bucks about executive pay-offs in front of the Public Accounts Committee on 9 September 2013. Live on the BBC's Parliamentary Channel, the BBC News Channel and many other non-BBC outlets. That single session did the Corporation much harm. One exchange between Margaret Hodge MP, the Chair, and Lucy Adams, the BBC Director of HR, illustrates the sheer bad temper and combative nature of the event:

> Chair: Just to be clear on that, because I am not having any more lies this afternoon, may I ask the NAO whether that document – the 7 October document, of which we were all given a copy – was also passed to the witnesses? Did they know what we were talking about?....

Lucy Adams: Yes, it was submitted by the Trust; it wasn't a document that I had seen. I apologise to the committee that I wasn't able to identify that document at the time. There was no attempt deliberately to mislead the committee. I immediately clarified upon parliament's return that I recognised the document as one to which I had contributed. In the committee meeting, I was clear that I couldn't with absolute certainty recall that document, but I was also clear that I was involved in advising Mark on the terms for Mark Byford. I have never sought to deny my involvement in that (Public Accounts Committee 2013).

The spectacle will be televised

Ironically, the BBC has created the transmission mechanism for its own appearance at the spectacle. Not just the massive News empire that is a relic of John Birt as Director-General with its big set piece built radio and television news programmes but the BBC News Channel, created in 1998 as BBC News 24, providing wall-to-wall news, twenty four hours a day seven days a week. That outlet is simply a sausage machine with a voracious appetite for content and stories. BBC bosses making a not very good fist of it in parliament live (and in later packages) is manna from heaven for them.

But worse there is the BBC Parliamentary Channel and Democracy Live both set up by the Corporation to try to bridge the democratic deficit between citizens and legislators. BBC Parliament – a channel run by the Corporation since 1998 – does what it says on the label. It features wall-to-wall UK Parliament, the Houses of Commons and Lords, the three devolved assemblies, the European Parliament, the London Assembly and all select committee sessions live and recorded. So too Democracy Live, the BBC News Online website launched at a cost of £3 million in 2009, streaming all parliamentary output live to the internet continually. There is now no hiding place in cyberspace for any politician or witness who appears in front of a parliamentary committee anywhere in the UK or Europe. It is a political anorak's dream.

So, parliaments of various sorts in the last decade have become the focus of the spectacle called accountability and transparency and the BBC has played its part in transmitting that spectacle and sometimes being the stars, albeit unwitting, of it all.

How did we get to where we are?

Select committees of parliament are newish boys on the Westminster block. They have existed only since 1980. Their purpose mainly is to shadow all government departments, interrogate their decisions and spending and report appropriately. They are, or should be, the legislature's check on the executive. Initially, they were anodyne and toothless but they soon found their range, especially when the Blair government took office in 1997 with its huge parliamentary majority. There was no real role in the chamber for backbench MPs so they might as well join a select committee and make a name for themselves/cause trouble on that. Committee rooms were a rare backbench platform. They could be a route to the ministerial red box (and car) for wannabe ministers but more often they were the refuge of the never-will-be-ministers, or those who once were but never will be again..

Select committees realised their power lay as much in 'naming and shaming' institutions and people as in carefully drafted and considered reports which would only gather dust on secretaries of state's shelves. The power of the press release and the spectacle of a live televised hearing were much more attractive than hours spent in line-by-line drafting of reports. Rather than long-term strategic questions they moved towards the simple headline-grabbing tactical ones.

In 2014, we have reached the position where some select committees are like the BBC's own *Newsnight* in redux but slower. An event or news story happens – in broadcasting, to the police, to the banks – and often within a week the representatives of that institution find themselves in front of the parliamentary watchdogs answering difficult questions. It has rapidly become part of the warp and weave of British public life. *Newsnight* does the story that night, select committees do it the week after

Along with the rise of the select committee as spectacle there has also been the rise of the select committee chairs (and some members) as stars. Give them a spotlight and they will find themselves under it. Keith Vaz MP is no shrinking violet. His Home Affairs Select Committee has become a publicity platform for this former minister in and out of parliament. Police misbehaving? They will be called to face his committee. Bulgarian migrants 'swamping' the UK? Vaz will be there at Luton airport to greet them-even if they are in single figures. No stone is left unturned by the Vaz PR machine.

Margaret Hodge MP is another ex-minister turned tormentor (of ministers and others). Her Public Accounts Committee has a wide remit on all government and public spending. She has used that to the full and most clinically in the last three years on the £3.65 billion of TV licence payers' money funnelled to the BBC. John Whittingdale MP was a Conservative Party spokesman on broadcasting in Opposition. Ministerial office was not to be his. Instead, he has turned his Culture, Media and Sport Select Committee into a running show on media matters; the *de facto Parliamentary Media Show*.

Newsnight in redux? The CMS select committee
The CMS select committee has become a televised Star Chamber. Most notably when it summoned Rupert Murdoch, the media *uber* mogul, to explain and justify phone hacking to them on 19 July 2011 after the closure of his *News of the World*. Murdoch's opening gambit then was a master stroke in dissembling. 'I would just like to say one sentence. This is the most humble day of my life.' This did not prevent him from being closely examined by the rottweiler of that committee, Tom Watson MP.

Mr Watson: Mr Murdoch senior, good afternoon, sir. You have repeatedly stated that News Corp has zero tolerance to wrongdoing by employees. Is that right?

Rupert Murdoch: Yes.

Mr Watson: In October 2010, did you still believe it to be true when you made your Thatcher speech and you said: 'Let me be clear: we will vigorously pursue the truth—and we will not tolerate wrongdoing'?

Rupert Murdoch: Yes.

Mr Watson: So if you were not lying then, somebody lied to you. Who was it?

Rupert Murdoch: I don't know. That is what the police are investigating, and we are helping them with.

Mr Watson: But you acknowledge that you were misled.

Rupert Murdoch: Clearly (Culture, Media and Sport Select Committee 2011).

On the other side of the committee and the House, Louise Mensch MP was much gentler than Bruiser Watson:

Louise Mensch: Mr Rupert Murdoch, you are the Chairman and Chief Executive of News Corp. You are the head of the global company. The buck stops with you. Given these allegations, indeed, when you opened the session, you said that this was the most humiliating day of your life

Chair: Humble.

Louise Mensch: Oh, I'm sorry – humble. I beg your pardon. That was a mistake. You said that it was the most humble day of your life. You feel humbled by these events. You are ultimately in charge of the company. Given your shock at these things being laid out before you and the fact that you didn't know anything about them, have you instructed your editors around the world to engage in a root-and-branch review of their own newsrooms to be sure that this isn't being replicated in other News Corps papers around the globe? If not, will you do so?

Rupert Murdoch: No, but I am more than prepared to do (Culture, Media and Sport Select Committee 2011).

Through the CMS Select Committee, Watson became the scourge of News International and, as a result, rose to Deputy Chair of the Labour Party. He later fell. Mensch decided parliament was too boring and small for her and retreated to the USA.

The CMS Select Committee has regularly turned its attention to the BBC in the last three years, as a search of Hansard reveals:

1. The BBC licence fee settlement, 15 December 2010: Mark Thompson, Director-General, and Sir Michael Lyons, then-Chairman of the BBC Trust, gave evidence.

2. The BBC Digital Media Initiative, 15 February 2011: Mark Thompson, Director-General, Erik Huggers, Director of Future Media and Technology, BBC, and Anthony Fry, Trustee, BBC Trust gave evidence.

3. The BBC Licence Fee Settlement and Annual Report and Accounts 2009-10, 19 May 2011: Committee report into this – as this had done for the previous decade.

4. One-off evidence session with outgoing BBC Director-General, 19 June 2012: Mark Thompson gave evidence of his achievements over the previous eight years and any setbacks, staff remuneration and the future of the BBC.

5. The BBC's response to the Jimmy Savile case, 23 October 2012: Director-General George Entwistle gave evidence about the two independent reviews; the safeguards and vetting procedures that would have been in place when Jimmy Savile was appointed by the BBC.

6. Priorities for the new Director-General of the BBC, 25 April 2013: On 2 April, Lord Hall started as the BBC's new Director-General. The committee held an early evidence session three weeks later with him to consider his priorities for the next few months.

7. The select committee questions BBC Director-General Tony Hall and BBC Trust Chair Lord Patten on the BBC annual report, 22 October 2013.

So, at least seven separate inquiries and reports into the BBC in less than three years. Whittingdale's committee is not done They are now holding a wide ranging inquiry into The Future of the BBC, ahead of its current royal charter ending in December 2016.

Accountable to the public?

Since 2011, the Public Accounts Committee and its investigative arm, the National Audit Office, have started to take a close interest in the BBC and BBC finances in at least three areas:

1. Evidence from the BBC on its efficiency savings programme, 21 November 2011.

2. BBC severance packages: Oral evidence, July and September 2013.

Two public hearings on executive severance packages resulting in a damning report on 16 December 2013 which made five tough recommendations

- The BBC should ensure that severance payments do not exceed what is absolutely necessary.

- The BBC should remind its staff that they are all individually responsible for protecting public money and challenging wasteful practices.
- To protect licence fee payers' interests and its own reputation, the BBC should establish internal procedures that provide clear central oversight and effective scrutiny of severance payments.
- The BBC executive and the BBC Trust need to overhaul the way they conduct their business, and record and communicate decisions properly.
- Given its overarching responsibility for the stewardship of public money, the BBC Trust should be more willing to challenge practices and decisions where there is a risk that the interests of licence fee payers could be compromised.
- The BBC Trust and the BBC executive need to ensure that decision-making is transparent and accountability taken seriously, based on a shared understanding of value for money, with tangible evidence of individuals taking public responsibility for their decisions.

3. Report on the BBC move to Salford, 16 October 2013.

My Lord … another committee

As if that's not enough, the House of Lords also has its own wide-ranging Communications Committee with a remit that includes the BBC. Their inquires have included:

1. BBC charter inquiry: BBC Chairman and the D-G gave evidence 18 July 2005.
2. BBC Trust: Mark Thompson gives evidence, 26 April 2011.
3. What will be on the box? Lords question BBC and Channel Four, 27 November 2012.

As part of their inquiry into media convergence, the Lords Communications Committee put questions to two public service broadcasters (PSBs), the BBC and Channel 4.

And even more…

The Foreign Affairs Select Committee looked at and reported on the Implications of the BBC World Service Cuts, in April 2011. And in the House of Commons chamber itself … on 21 October 2013, MPs took part in a general debate on the future of the BBC. Parliamentary scrutiny has clearly come upon the BBC with a vengeance in the last decade.

Spectacle of gladiators at the Coliseum?

So the spectacle of the BBC big-wigs up before the parliamentary beaks has become everyday. But is spectacle the best metaphor for the position in which the BBC finds itself? Could it be that a better parallel might be ancient Rome and the Coliseum in which gladiators fought off all-comers including wild animals like lions. The gladiators or swordsmen had to impress the audience with their ability to fight for their lives. Their job was not just survival but to achieve popular acclaim through the skills used in that. Through fight after fight the gladiators could buy their freedom. Is that what faces the Corporation over the next two years in the struggle for charter renewal and a decent licence fee settlement?

Just as in ancient Rome, what is happening in the Coliseum/parliament is there for the entertainment of an audience. In this case, licence fee payers informed and inflamed by a largely hostile anti-BBC national press. Leading the hate brigade, day after day, the *soi disant* voice of Middle England, the *Daily Mail*, a direct competitor to the Corporation in news and online provision (where MailOnline is trumping the BBC News Online into a cocked hat) and a vintage vehicle for BBC bashing. Two headlines on the PAC hearing and report on Executive pay offs in 2013 give a flavour: 'Thompson was firing away like a Spanish man o'war entering Gibraltar harbour' (*Daily Mail*, 10 September 2013). And 'Liars! MPs say BBC bosses lied to parliament about obscene pay-offs. There couldn't be a more serious charge, but don't expect any contrition' (*Daily Mail*, 17 December 2013).

Others in the 'balanced 'British press were equally shrill. For instance, 'BBC chiefs deny "losing the plot" over £1million pay-off' (*Daily Express*, 10 September 2013). And 'Accusations fly as BBC bosses argue over payoffs' (*The Times*, 10 September 2013). Newspapers feast on the spectacle of the 'BBC in the dock' for commercial and journalistic reasons like sharks or lions circling the wounded beast. In an ideal world they would like to see no BBC in 'their' market places to lessen their descent into oblivion. Only the sheer quality and popularity of their programmes, their range and the trust it engenders ensures the BBC's survival and that of the licence fee.

Egging on the crowds in this virtual Coliseum are rabble rousing politicians, usually Conservative. Home Secretary Theresa May – her intervention on local BBC Online News was noted earlier. Grant Shapps MP, the Conservative Party Chairman, called in October 2013 for the BBC licence fee to be 'top-sliced' next time round i.e. bid for and used by other public service broadcasters. His call did not fall on entirely fertile ground

The most persistent fly in the Corporation ointment is Rob Wilson, the Member of Parliament for Reading East. He has turned BBC bashing into his profession. No opportunity is missed to berate the national broadcaster. Unfortunately for them, he is the Parliamentary Private Secretary to Chancellor George Osborne who will probably be as crucial in setting the next licence fee as he was the last. D-G Mark Thompson and then-Culture Secretary Jeremy Hunt had to go to Osborne's office after their lightning 'negotiations' in 2010 to get his approval before going public,

What next for the spectacle?

Old BBC hands when confronted with the current panoply of woes shrug their shoulders and say: 'It will blow over, it always does.' Alas, this time the issues and problems may be more deep-seated. And more troubles may be on their way: Mark Thompson (again) in February 2014 will be at the Public Accounts Committee trying (*ex post facto*) to justify the Digital Media Initiative fiasco developed under his watch but written off later at the cost of £100 million – equivalent to all the licence fee payers of Glasgow. While in June 2014, the Dame Janet Smith report into the activities of Jimmy Savile (and others) within the BBC and the culture of the Corporation is due. That is literally a time bomb waiting to explode.

How many more times will the new BBC brahmins be called back to the Portcullis House gladiatorial arena? When and how will the spectacle end? Probably not until 31 December 2016 and then most likely in tears ...

References

Culture, Media and Sport Select Committee (2004) Press release, 10 December. Available online at http://www.parliament.uk/business/committees/committees-archive/culture-media-and-sport/cms-041210/, accessed on 23 January 2014

Culture, Media and Sport Select Committee (2011) Rupert Murdoch, James Murdoch and Rebekah Brooks questioned by MPs, 19 July. Available online at http://www.parliament.uk/business/committees/committees-a-z/commons-select/culture-media-and-sport-committee/news/news-international-executives-respond-to-summons/, accessed on 23 January 2014

O'Carroll, Lisa (2012) Jimmy Savile: Questions mount as George Entwistle squirms, *Guardian*, 23 October. Available online at http://www.theguardian.com/media/2012/oct/23/george-entwistle-bbc-jimmy-savile-scandal, accessed on 23 January 2014

Patten, Lord (2013) Comments to Culture, Media and Sport Select Committee. Available online at http://www.parliament.uk/business/committees/committees-a-z/commons-select/culture-media-and-sport-committee/news/131021-bbc-annual-report-2013/, accessed on 23 January 2014

Public Accounts Committee (2013) Minutes of evidence, 9 September. Available online at http://www.publications.parliament.uk/pa/cm201314/cmselect/cmpubacc/476/130909.htm, accessed on 23 January 2014

Note on the contributor

John Mair is a former BBC producer and director. *Inter alia*, he helped to invent *Question Time*. He has worked in the academe for the last eight years in Coventry, Kent, Northampton, Westminster and Brunel universities. He has also edited twelve 'hackademic' books with Professor Richard Lance Keeble.

Section 2:
Timewatch: From a historical perspective

Richard Tait

The sheer scale of the melodrama which has engulfed the BBC in the last couple of years has not, perhaps understandably, created much space for thoughtful, analytical journalism. The British press, after a number of years taking the incoming fire from the phone-hacking scandal and Leveson, could perhaps be forgiven for the relish with which it has piled into the troubles of an organisation which even its friends in the media can find hard to love and when digital convergence has brought print and broadcast into ever fiercer competition for audiences.

The BBC's inability (or failure) in 2012 and 2013 to bring closure to any of the major issues tormenting it in the way that it was able to draw a line under Hutton in 2004, and Ross/Brand and the dishonest programme-making around phone-in and competitions in 2008 and 2009, meant that the organisation appeared to be in permanent crisis. The postponement of Dame Janet Smith's report into Savile prolongs the agony over what is already admitted to be a truly shameful institutional failure; there are still questions around the Digital Media Initiative (DMI), running the real risk of another damaging bout of mutual recriminations from those involved; the new governance arrangements have to prove themselves; *Newsnight* needs a long, long period of great, accurate journalism and internal harmony.

The political context could not be worse, with individual MPs questioning the organisation whenever a loose end appears and parliamentary committees digging deeper and more often than ever before. The BBC is about to be reviewed to death in the run-up to charter renewal, and the politicians are looking forward to exercising their most important power over the BBC – the decision, through the licence fee settlement, on how much money the

Corporation will have for a number of years – in this case, probably, from 2017 to perhaps 2022. The BBC is always at its most vulnerable to bullying in the run-up to charter renewal and/or the setting of the licence fee – its terrible luck is that this time round both these processes will also coincide with a general election. The danger is that too much time and newsprint is being devoted to the short-term and the sensational and not enough to the less dramatic but really significant changes in the UK's media culture and structure which may have profound consequences for the BBC's future.

This section of the book is an attempt to put the breathless narrative of institutional car crashes in a more analytical context. Three of the best and most thoughtful media correspondents in the UK have looked back at the wreckage of the immediate past from a historical perspective.

Dangers ahead

Tara Conlan has written about the BBC for most of Fleet Street, was TV Editor of the *Daily Mail* and now contributes to the *Guardian*'s and the *Observer*'s media coverage. She has been talking to some of the key players in the BBC and elsewhere about the last few years and what emerges from a series of fascinating, on-the-record interviews, is what *Timewatch* would call 'the secret history' of the BBC – the really critical moments and the really serious underlying challenges to the future of the organisation. She believes that the flickering challenges on the horizon – financial, content, governance and politics – 'could combine to become a conflagration'.

For Ed Williams, the former BBC director of communications, the story that people are missing is money – the 2010 deal, freezing the licence at £145.50, is eroding the BBC, with perhaps much more pain to come with a further freeze in prospect. For Mark Thompson, the Director-General who did the deal, it was the best offer the BBC was going to get – 'a realistic deal in exceptional circumstances' was how he described it at the time – and even then it could have ended in disaster when the government tried to make the BBC pick up the tab for free licences for the over-75s. Thompson thought 'we were looking down the cliff' and had started on his resignation speech.

And longer term, an equally fundamental question is who's going to make the programmes? Ed Williams and the current Director of Television Danny Cohen discuss The Problem That Dare Not Speak Its Name – why should the best creative people want to work for the BBC? Why should anyone, for example, take a great idea or format to the BBC and see them exploit her or his intellectual property? Can in-house creative staff be incentivised to come up with a global hit? And with the pressure to make more and more air time available to independents, does in-house production outside of news have much of a future anyway?

The insider

The BBC's own journalism has come out of the last couple of years with mixed reviews. *Newsnight*'s lamentable performance over sex abuse in Wales, and the civil war on the programme over the spiked Savile investigation both make depressing reading. But when faced with an in-house story of epic proportions, the rest of the BBC news and current affairs operation did a very respectable job reporting the BBC's problems without fear or favour (and if you do not think that deserves any praise, just imagine the likelihood of a *Sun* investigation into phone hacking). *Panorama* on 'Jimmy Savile - What the BBC Knew' was a brave programme and cast serious doubts on the BBC's official position, though in the end, nothing could really compensate for the fact that ITV won the plaudits with an investigation into Savile that should have been on the BBC.

One of the calmest reporters in this madhouse was Torin Douglas, for 24 years the BBC media correspondent. In his chapter, 'Reporting the crisis from inside the beast', he gives a brilliant insider's account of what it was like covering your own organisation in meltdown and when one day's work (10 November 2012) is watching your editor-in-chief's career imploding as George Entwistle's disastrous *Today* interview with John Humphrys proved to be the last straw. Humphrys, too, deserves credit for not pulling his punches with the boss, although Douglas himself believes that some other BBC staff are both too gullible about what they read about the BBC in the newspapers and at worst, 'take a morbid glee in the reporting of the BBC's own failings'.

Douglas says that he rarely found his bosses trying to influence his reporting, which reflects well on them, as well. But it also underlines the value of experienced, specialist reporters with enough of a sense of history to report with perspective and balance. If Douglas were to present a *Timewatch* it would probably be 'The Case of the Disappearing Chairmen' – three times in recent years the BBC Chairman has suddenly left his role – Christopher Bland to become chair of BT, Gavyn Davies a few hours after the publication of the Hutton Report, Michael Grade to join ITV as Executive Chair. When you have had to report three such departures (one in the morning, one in the afternoon and one at night) in each case without any prior warning, I suspect very little about the BBC would surprise you.

Fixing the licence fee

Little surprises Raymond Snoddy, the doyen of media correspondents whose pioneering work at the *Financial Times* set the standard for modern media journalism. His focus is on the drama and low politics of licence fee negotiations, the detail of which is usually hidden from the public who actually pay for the BBC. Only twice in the modern history of the BBC have the real arguments between broadcasters and politicians leaked out into the public domain. In 1985, after a comparatively generous settlement, Margaret Thatcher's government set up the Peacock Committee which she hoped would recommend scrapping the licence fee and making the BBC take advertising. To her chagrin, it came up with, for her, the wrong answer – the licence fee was, in fact, the 'least bad' system.

Twenty five years later, the BBC faced another Conservative government toying with the idea of radical change. Snoddy reveals that George Osborne's Treasury wanted a fundamental review of the BBC's role and size which could have led to a much smaller BBC. The only alternative was to do a quick deal as part of the government's cuts in public spending. The controversial 2010 settlement was unprecedented – a frozen licence fee with the BBC taking over financial responsibility for the World Service and S4C. But the BBC avoided a process which could have been the end of the organisation's current size, role and scope.

Even so, the negotiations were fraught and dramatic – with a homeward bound Mark Thompson jumping off his evening train at Slough and heading straight back into London for overnight talks at the Culture Department and Deputy Prime Minister Nick Clegg intervening behind the scenes. The BBC is still struggling to cope with the budget reductions and additional responsibilities it agreed that night, but it was, as Thompson himself said, the best deal available.

The problem for the BBC, according to Snoddy, is that the next licence fee negotiations could be even worse – 'the most difficult and unpredictable there has ever been'. The scandals have weakened the BBC's reputation; as Snoddy puts it, 'the political vultures have already been circling'. The electoral timetable makes the outcome impossible to predict. Should talks start this year (ahead of the election) – or next? What sort of government will the BBC be dealing with in 2015?

Snoddy detects 'an emerging Conservative agenda for a smaller BBC, one that no longer has access to all the proceeds of the licence fee'. And regardless of the politics, he thinks technological change, with the growth of on-demand and the emergence of new players such as Netflix, means a fundamental examination of the purpose and funding of the BBC is inevitable.

But whatever the outcome of the reviews and analyses, the *Timewatch* perspective tells us that the single most important factor for the future development and scope of the BBC is its funding. The next licence fee negotiations are likely to be the most important for a generation. Follow the money.

View from a journalistic bystander

Tara Conlan argues there are a number of serious financial, content, governance and political challenges on the horizon for the BBC that are flickering and could combine to become a conflagration

When I asked people in the media if the BBC was in crisis, the most common response was 'Always.' So I asked 100 people outside media. Only 20 per cent of them said 'Yes' – the rest pointed to the high quality output on screen as an assurance that the BBC is not in crisis, echoing former director general Greg Dyke's assertion: 'It's the programmes, stupid.'

Yet some of their responses showed concerns. One said: 'I always associated the BBC with trustworthiness and integrity. Unfortunately, I do have to say that some of the recent scandals have made me change my views, and I do think they are in crisis.' Another said: 'I think crisis is too strong a word – it is still producing/broadcasting programmes I want to watch – but I think the management has lost its way and built itself an ivory tower, where it has forgotten about accountability.'

Between March 2012 and September 2013, according to published figures, the BBC spent a total of £20.3 million on consultants, the highly critical Pricewaterhouse Coopers report into the failed Digital Media Initiative (DMI) and on Jimmy Savile-related inquiries. To put that in context, BBC6 Music's annual budget is £11.5 million. The figures, combined with bad publicity over severance pay, the resignation of Director-General George Entwistle (the second to go within a decade) and the £100 million failure of DMI highlight a period of extreme turmoil.

Is it in crisis? I would argue it is certainly not in a crisis on the level of the one which followed the Dr David Kelly affair and the Hutton Report (2003-2004), when both the chairman and the director-general resigned and it seemed for a time that the BBC was locked in a battle for survival with the government. But there are serious financial, content, governance and political challenges on the horizon that are flickering and could combine to become a conflagration. And speaking to people within the BBC, former executives, suppliers, agents, rivals both UK and global, unions and broadcasting organisations, most of them agree.

That's life

Ed Williams, the former director of communications now Edelman UK CEO, steered the BBC through a number of high-pressure situations during his tenure, so he knows what a BBC crisis looks like. He says:

> Within the media bubble there's always a sense of crisis at the BBC because of the amount of scrutiny and interest that the BBC engenders. I felt that every day when I'd get the press cuttings and they would regularly be between 120 and 160 pages each day. If your diet was nothing more than the press cuttings of the BBC then you would absolutely get a sense that this was an organisation that was lurching from one difficult issue to another but actually you should look at the BBC over decades – not over days or weeks.

One of the issues facing the Corporation in the run-up to charter renewal and a new licence fee settlement (due to start in 2015-2016) is that in the digital era the newspapers that write about it consider it more of a rival as they bump into the BBC on the web. As Williams says: 'The narrative around the BBC in crisis is a very helpful one to certain parties though I think if you actually look at the BBC itself I'm not sure it is in crisis. However, that's not to say if you look at the BBC over decades that there isn't something potentially very alarming that's going on.' He cites money and programming.

> The BBC is slowly being eroded over time. It is a great granite cliff but the weather is getting to it. The licence fee settlement that we achieved when I was at the BBC as part of the Comprehensive Spending Review was deemed a success but it was a flat cash settlement. We had to find 20 per cent of savings, 16 per cent of real-terms cuts, 4 per cent to reinvest and that was a success! I think although there will be a lot of talk in the media about a new model, about mutualising the BBC, about a subscription model, I suspect what will happen ... as part of the next charter renewal process is that they turn the crank again and it's an extension of the licence fee ... and if it remains at £145.50 for another five years that will be mean even more painful cuts.

His former boss, Mark Thompson, says that the last settlement was one of two crises he faced during his eight years as director-general, although he says at the time it may not have felt like one to the outside world. When the government threatened to impose the £556 million of uncapped liability of free television licences for over-75s on the BBC, Thompson says: 'That was the one moment while I was there when I thought "I'm going to have to resign." I was just beginning to sketch out a resignation speech. I thought we were gone and the thing was decided the wrong way. That was the one moment when I thought we were looking down the cliff.' One thing is certain about the BBC – usually the worst crises cannot be predicted, as Thompson explains:

> Without question, the most emotionally difficult and trying crisis while I was D-G was the Alan Johnson abduction [the BBC reporter was kidnapped in Gaza by a Palestinian group for four months in 2007]. The stakes are just different when someone's life is in peril and you don't know how the story's going to end. For weeks and weeks it was gut-wrenching for everyone involved. Thank goodness it had a happy ending. It was my best day ever in the BBC [when Johnson was released] it was fantastic. For a D-G, that's lonely stuff, whereas rushing from studio to studio to be lambasted about Russell Brand – it's not much fun but you feel you're paid to do that.

Question time

For his successor Tony Hall unsettling political times are ahead. Chairman Lord Patten is due to step down in April 2015. A month later there is a general election, then the royal charter runs out at the end of 2016, plus a new licence fee settlement has to be agreed before March 2017. Home Secretary Theresa May and Conservative Party Chair Grant Shapps have fired some early shots across the BBC's bows. However, Williams says: 'The BBC has been here many times before and it is not a new tactic. The BBC has a very long institutional memory.'

And as his Edelman colleague and former *Financial Times* chief media correspondent Ben Fenton points out, 'it will go away the closer we get to a general election because there are no votes in bashing the BBC'. Arguably more worrying for public perception is what Williams says is a slow-burning 'programme crisis' that could be noticed on-screen in a few years.

> I think there's a series of very popular formats which over the next five to ten years will reach the end of their natural lives such as *Strictly Come Dancing, The Apprentice, Dragons' Den, Top Gear, The One Show*. These are all programmes currently very popular that reach large parts of the audience. But they will not be able to go on for ever and I think there's potentially an issue around revitalising and managing the portfolio ... that's not necessarily about money but about creative juices and insight and having the right people there. What I think is particularly challenging for the BBC is how can they make the case to get the best creative people at the BBC coming up with these ideas when actually if you've got a great idea why take it to the BBC, particularly if it's a format you could internationalise – why give away your own intellectual property?

BBC Director of Television Danny Cohen says that is 'a fair question and an ongoing question for the BBC'.

I think we need to keep looking at how we incentivise people, that's got to be a thing we do and how we use Worldwide to incentivise people – we need to look at that a bit. We have to make some of our own heroes: you get young people who come in who have good ideas and they are very proud to work at the BBC. A great idea can come from someone in their early 20s as well as 30s. We've got to take some bets on new people and we've got to work on incentivisation as well.

Cohen is honest about the situation: 'The truth is we haven't worked that through yet but I think the idea that if you come up with a global hit you should in some way benefit from that beyond your basic wage doesn't seem unreasonable. And I think if we want to bring in really smart people and generate IP – which will end up making money which will go back into the licence fee – people participating in that, in order to get the best people, then we have to look at and examine what's possible.' He continues:

I really believe in in-house. I believe it plays a critical role in the programme ecology of the BBC and beyond. I think it provides very important training – craft skills that aren't necessarily developed in the independent sector in quite the same way. So I believe in it. The area I'm working most around is development. I think most of the things you see made by BBC productions are extremely good if not excellent. I think where we've been less excellent is in the development of ideas and idea creation and we've got some wonderful examples of getting it right like *Strictly* and *Top Gear* and many programmes. But actually I'm not sure development has been as prized in the BBC or BBC productions as it has been in the independent sector. And you can't generate new IP and you can't keep your production base healthy unless you're coming up with lots of really good ideas. So I've spent a lot of time focusing recently on how we improve our development.

As one leading independent producer says:

Obviously there are some hideous things that have happened at the BBC in the last year but actually I think Danny [Cohen] as Director of Television is the best thing that the BBC could have at the moment. They just need to lick their wounds and carry on and they probably do need to sort out in-house. So obviously that's a threat to us but they do need to up their game. The truth is it's hard making programmes for the BBC because they give you less money than they used to. It's difficult and frustrating and I sometimes think they should just commission less and pay a bit more. Not keep trying to satisfy everyone. That puts us at risk because they would commission less programming but I still think that would be better. Obviously there are areas where the overhead is high but I think that it's quite a straightened place to work. I look at that compared to the other broadcasters – everyone is sort of battened down on expenses, it's already quite lean.

BBC Creative Director Alan Yentob agrees: 'People talk about a frozen licence fee but actually the BBC has had £700 million taken out of its budget by the Treasury. That is a very, very significant figure and obviously there are implications with that figure about how you make things work effectively. The BBC has never got much credit for saving money but it has been saving money. However, the next couple of years are tougher, much tougher.'

Flog it!

In 2008, the BBC had 17,677 public sector employees. By 2013 that had fallen by 1,143 (around 6 per cent) to 16,534. Independent production organisation Pact Chief Executive John McVay blames high staffing numbers on the policies adopted during Greg Dyke's time as Director-General of the BBC (from 2000 to 2004). And he thinks there is a 'compelling logic' for in-house to be cut as the Corporation would reduce 'overheads and you would not have all the property requirements so more money would be released – you would have the benefits of competition of the market'.

Independent producers face a dichotomy. They want a strong BBC as it buys their programmes and many of them are the broadcasting baby boomers who were trained by the Corporation before they went on to make their fortunes outside it. However, in the run-up to charter renewal they want changes to the BBC's 'window of creative competition', which guarantees 50 per cent for in-house producers, 25 per cent for independents and puts another 25 per cent up for grabs to both.

McVay points out that independents are able to deliver high quality shows such as the Paralympics or *Question Time*. 'I'll defend the licence fee but not bad management. It has to get with the 21st century in terms of their relationship with their supply base. The BBC has got to be more porous and flexible.' McVay argues that opening up more transmission hours to independents is an efficient way to 'maximise the licence fee' and adds: 'The BBC is not the sole trainer any more. Skillset can provide that. That doesn't stand up in the modern world.'

Producer and agent Peter Bennett-Jones says that while the BBC is 'not in crisis particularly' it 'probably needs remodelling. If you judge it by its output it's still pretty amazing'. He continues: 'We would miss the BBC if it was not part of our lives and culture, both indirectly and directly as a cultural institution. It's the biggest cultural institution for drama, comedy and radio output and in the end a very important part of what want think of what's great about Great Britain.' But he also thinks the structure of the Corporation could be changed: 'One of their problems is the relationship they have with the political set-up and the government, which is all linked to the news output. It doesn't matter who's in power they have a difficult relationship due to news and current affairs.'

World at One

Apart from money, content and structure, the BBC is also facing national and global challenges. If Scottish independence goes ahead will there be further fragmentation of the Corporation to the regions? Globally, Hall wants to increase news audiences from around 220 million to 500 million. However, one international producer says:

> I'm pretty sure 500 million watch BBC news anyway! The BBC is a great institution but it is not a proper global player. When you travel you realise they [BBC Worldwide] are feeding off crumbs. US studios combine their output with movie packages. You are buying certainty. US studios can sign up Michael Patrick King for five years and pay him a lot of money. Having to sell things on a series-by-series basis makes a huge difference to your ability to own your future.

He points out rivals such as al-Jazeera, National Geographic and Discovery have, unlike the BBC, 'unfettered commercialism', but says the BBC's reputation for quality, particularly in natural history programming, is an advantage. When such commercialism comes to BBC News, alarm bells ring. In 2012, BBC World Service journalists were asked in an email from Global News Director Peter Horrocks to come up with money-making ideas to help raise revenues for the Corporation's international services. Concerns were raised over editorial independence.

Food for thought

BECTU General Secretary Gerry Morrissey, who has been involved with the BBC in one way or another since 1977, says:

> There's always been some sort of crisis at the BBC but it depends how deep and grave it is. If you stay around long enough you see that everything is cyclical. The next licence fee is highly crucial. The issue is everybody wants everything but people don't want to pay for it. The difficult thing now is it negotiating from a very low base. The thing they've got on their side is popularity with the general public though they don't like taxes. They've got to come up with something which engages the government's programme for the country such as education. As a public service broadcaster how is it going to complement other parts of the public sector?

Yentob is concerned 'there's a sort complacency about the BBC ... people will miss it if it went, but by then it will be too late'.

Wasserman Media Group Global Media co-Managing Director David Kogan is in a unique position to ascertain if the BBC is in crisis having worked there and with it and once been in the middle of a political row between the BBC and the government while at Breakfast after Norman Tebbit intervened to get Cecil Parkinson pushed up the running order. Kogan says he does not think the

Corporation is in crisis but that it 'manages to inflict wounds on itself that are remarkable by almost any other public institution's standard'. 'It's trying to straddle these extraordinary divides – between being a huge public institution with public money, creating editorial content that will inevitably piss people off and cause short-term reactions and it's full of lots of ambitious people who are highly political who run into brick walls both of their own making or from external sources. This is compounded by a current corporate governance structure that is insane.'

He was brought in by Thompson to run the main negotiations between the BBC and Sky for iPlayer and the BBC channels going onto Sky which, he says, gave him an insight into the 'the extraordinary levels of myopia that take effect'. Talks had been taking place for five years but the main issue was neither side thought the other would agree on 'philosophical grounds'. Actually the real reason it could not be done was technical but that was relatively easy to solve and 'then it was down to politics'. 'And what one found in the Trust unit, the BBC strategy unit, the BBC policy unit, the BBC god-knows-what-else-they-all-do unit, was the vast numbers of people ... were so busy second-guessing each other in meetings of 20 people that none of them had a view of how to get anything done. That was my direct personal experience.' However, he adds:

> What saves the institution is that there are always a few very able men and women who can pull the irons out of the fire. In the case of this particular negotiation which took months to conclude there were two individuals within the BBC who turned it into reality. So in my view the BBC would save itself enormous amounts of time and trouble if it slimmed down the number of people internally who spend their time pretending to think and spent more time on a highly focused approach to the external market, including government. That would mean they could spend more resource on programme-making and a much more tailored approach to the way the world is changing.

A senior Tory politician told me around two years ago that if his party won the next general election he expected it to abolish the BBC Trust. And that was before the Jimmy Savile scandal and payoffs PR disaster. What might replace it though? Kogan points out Ofcom already has a wide remit and suggests an interesting alternative:

> I would introduce something like a PLC corporate board but one that's publicly appointed ...You can reflect regionalism, editorial and commercial and you can have a board that has various sub-committees in the way the Trust does except that it works like a big corporate board. Is that a board of governors? Maybe it is or maybe you call it something different? You call it the BBC Board – there's a radical view! Non-executive directors with fiduciary duties, charged with ultimate financial, editorial and other forms of safeguard for the public pound and for the editorial sanctity of the BBC

and the rest of it and with responsibility for very senior post holder hiring is a perfectly reasonable concept. It works all over the place in commercial businesses, why does the BBC need to be different?

Conclusions

On the one hand the BBC faces having to raise more revenue in the face of a licence fee freeze, while balancing its public service remit. When that balance goes it hits the headlines. That frustrates the staff at the coal face of the cuts, who as one staff member says 'go to work not to make loads of money, they go there to be focused on a specialist area ... and because it is something they want to do'. They say that 'within last two or three years' a real gap has opened up 'between graded staff and higher management'. The behaviour of highly-paid executives is 'seen as destroying the reputation of the BBC ... their actions have trashed the BBC's reputation' and that could have an effect 'on the licence fee'.

Having covered the Hutton crisis at the *Daily Mail* I have seen how, despite the sometimes fractious relationship between the *Mail* and the BBC, when the Corporation was under threat from the (albeit Labour) government, the *Mail* defended the BBC's independence. Those with vested interests need to ask themselves who else is going to try to improve religious literacy or put on *Songs of Praise* every week? Like *Farming Today* on Radio 4 you might not be able to remember the last time you tuned into it but it soothes the nation to know it is there.

There is obviously a case for the BBC around public service, value for all, competition, standards, impartiality, training and its ability to invest in genres that otherwise might not be made. But the Corporation can also reflect on the fact that despite the democracy of the digital age and the independence the internet has given creatives, television is still popular. According to Twitter sensor Bluurt, '40 per cent of evening tweets are about the programmes people are watching. This method of second screening (aka 'chatterboxing') is now a widespread phenomenon, with almost 50 per cent of people under the age of 35 and a quarter of all adults now 'chatterboxing as they watch'.

Note on the contributor

Tara Conlan is a freelance media writer mostly for the *Guardian* and *Observer*. She was formerly TV Editor of the *Daily Mail* and has written about media, business and the arts for *The Sunday Times, Evening Standard, Independent* and *Radio Times*.

Reporting the crisis from inside the beast

Torin Douglas provides a blow-by-blow account of the challenges he faced when reporting on the BBC's *annus horribilis* for the Corporation. And he stresses: 'In 24 years as the BBC's media correspondent, working under seven director-generals and six BBC chairmen, I rarely found my bosses trying to influence my reporting, other than in a legitimate editorial context'

Introduction

The events triggered by the death of Jimmy Savile at the end of 2011 prompted one of the most serious crises in the BBC's history. They damaged trust in the BBC's journalism, its management and its governance. The pay-offs to George Entwistle and other senior executives reignited the 'toxic' issue of high management pay which, alongside a £100 million write-off on the Digital Media Initiative project, led to an 'unedifying' breakdown of relations between the BBC Executive and the BBC Trust in front of the Public Accounts Committee. Yet BBC radio and television programmes remain highly popular and valued by the public – including readers of the newspapers most critical of the Corporation – and its website and the BBC iPlayer remain widely acclaimed.

In this chapter, I describe what it is like to cover such a crisis for the BBC's own outlets on the day George Entwistle resigned; compare it with previous crises such as the Gilligan/Kelly/Hutton affair, the early departures of three BBC chairmen, and the resignations of two channel controllers; and set out why – at the time of writing in January 2014 – I believe the BBC is not in crisis, but faces several very serious problems.

Covering the BBC from within

People have often asked me: 'Isn't it difficult covering stories about your own organisation?' One battle-hardened BBC correspondent told me: 'I wouldn't do your job for the world.' I tried to explain that it wasn't that hard, provided you treated the BBC like any other organisation, striving to be accurate and balanced

– and never referring to it as 'we'. 'But you have to report on your bosses!' he said.

That's not the biggest pressure, in my experience. In 24 years as the BBC's media correspondent, working under seven director-generals and six BBC chairmen, I rarely found my bosses trying to influence my reporting, other than in a legitimate editorial context, discussing the top line, interviewees and so on. I had no qualms about reporting criticism of the BBC and its executives, however virulent, provided I gave them the chance to respond. Sadly too often, in my view, they declined. I believe BBC News has a good record over the years in covering the Corporation's crises frankly and fairly. As a publicly funded, publicly accountable broadcaster, so it should, though it is probably unique among media organisations these days in the robust and balanced way it covers its own affairs (see Douglas 2009).

But BBC executives are less good at putting their heads above the parapet and answering their critics on the airwaves – even though the BBC demands that of every other organisation that finds itself in the news spotlight. And many BBC staff have – at best – a misguided view of how their own organisation works (being too willing to believe what they read in the newspapers) which goes beyond the natural journalists' scepticism about their own management. This has been exacerbated, understandably, by the BBC's high executive pay and pay-offs. At worst, staff can take a morbid glee in the reporting of the BBC's own failings.

For me, the biggest pressure was simply getting the story right and on the air fast, on as many BBC outlets as needed. As a specialist correspondent (and for the past ten years the only media correspondent), I reported round the clock for the national daily news bulletins and 'sequence' programmes on radio, television and online. Other BBC journalists have different pressures, covering stories for programmes such as *Panorama* and *The Media Show*, with a single weekly deadline and half-hour time slot. Getting it right and on the air fast has inevitably become much more demanding since the arrival of 24-hour news and the internet. There are more BBC outlets to serve, shorter deadlines and more competitors. Twitter has become a newsfeed in its own right, acting as a clearing house for media owners to trumpet their breaking stories amid the gossip, jokes, half-truths and occasional libels tweeted by others.

As media correspondent, you don't want major news about the Corporation to break on a rival media outlet. That is not easy to ensure when the BBC remains as leaky as it does and when, with the best of motives, it declines to confirm a story publicly until it has informed its own staff (which can mean, ironically, that they actually hear it from Twitter or a rival broadcaster or newspaper). And you don't want to get a BBC story wrong. That sometimes means waiting for confirmation, or more details, when the Corporation's competitors may be happy to fly kites or take a particular line. Programme editors find it very frustrating when the correspondent says they cannot confirm a story that is running on another media outlet and will try to push you on the air straight away. But 'never wrong for long' is not an acceptable philosophy for the BBC – especially about its own affairs.

The day George Entwistle resigned

The day George Entwistle resigned, 10 November 2012, provides a flavour of what it's like to cover such a story from within the BBC. That morning I was hoping – perhaps optimistically - for a bit of a lull, after a succession of 18-hour days, feeding the BBC's many news outlets, from 6am to midnight. It was a Saturday and the previous fortnight had been relentless, even by the standards of a story which by now had been running on front pages and news bulletins for more than 40 days. Since the end of September, when newspapers started previewing claims in an ITV documentary that Jimmy Savile had been a predatory sex offender, there had been questions over why *Newsnight* had not broadcast similar claims nine months before and how much the BBC had known about Savile's activities. The BBC had set up two independent inquiries, to be conducted by a former Appeal Court Judge, Dame Janet Smith, and the former head of Sky News, Nick Pollard.

There had been a *Panorama* programme in which two *Newsnight* journalists challenged their editor's version of events, leading the BBC to admit there had been errors in the editor's blog and the Prime Minister to say that the BBC had 'effectively changed its story'. MPs on the Culture, Media and Sport Select Committee had accused the new Director-General, George Entwistle, of an 'extraordinary lack of curiosity' over the Savile allegations and told him to 'get a grip'. The BBC Chairman, Lord Patten, had defended Entwistle's performance, saying he had been 'overwhelmed by a tsunami of filth'. At the end of October, Roy Greenslade wrote in his *Guardian* blog: 'In the history of "media feeding frenzies" the Savile story is already one of the most enduring, and it is obvious that there is plenty more to come.' Obvious, indeed – but none of us would have predicted just how much (Greenslade 2012).

The following Friday, as if to show it hadn't lost its bottle, *Newsnight* aired a report linking a 'senior Conservative politician of the Thatcher era' to the sexual abuse of children in care homes. It did not name him, but many on the internet did. A week later, on Friday 9 November, the BBC found itself in even greater disarray. On Radio 4's bulletins that day, I charted events as they unfolded (with some developments breaking minutes before major bulletins, demanding urgent rewrites). These are some extracts from across the day:

- After days of frenzied speculation, the former Conservative Party Treasurer, Lord McAlpine, has issued a categorical denial of allegations linking him to the sexual abuse of children from care homes in North Wales in the 1970s and 1980s ... The BBC's *Newsnight* programme had aired claims by a former resident of a care home in Wrexham, Steve Meesham, that he'd been abused by an unnamed senior Tory from the Thatcher era....

- This morning the *Guardian* named Lord McAlpine as being at the centre of the speculation but said it could have been a case of mistaken identity...

- Tonight, in a statement, Mr Meesham said he'd now seen a picture of Lord McAlpine and it was not the person he'd identified in the early 1990s from a photograph shown him by police. He offered his sincere and humble apologies to Lord McAlpine and his family…

- The BBC has apologised unreservedly … Lord McAlpine's solicitors said they'd be taking legal action against all media who had defamed his reputation…

The following morning's headlines summed up the story: 'BBC in turmoil as *Newsnight*'s Tory abuse story falls apart' proclaimed the *Guardian*. 'BBC faces inquiry after outcry over abuse claims' said *The Times*. Having read the early newspaper editions on Friday night and filed for Radio 4's midnight bulletin, I recorded the following piece for Saturday morning bulletins for Radio 4, making it also available for Radio 2, 5 Live, the BBC World Service and local stations:

> If the Jimmy Savile crisis were not enough, the BBC is now facing legal action from Lord McAlpine, whose solicitor has accused *Newsnight* of severely damaging his client's reputation, even though the programme never revealed his name. It's also facing questions about how the report came to be broadcast, without its allegations being put to Lord McAlpine, or his photograph being checked with his accuser. The BBC Director-General, George Entwistle, has asked the Director of BBC Scotland, Ken McQuarrie, to write an urgent report detailing what happened. He's also ordered a pause in all *Newsnight* investigations while their editorial robustness is assessed. The Conservative MP Rob Wilson said the *Newsnight* report had been 'shoddy journalism' but welcomed the Director-General's response. He has also written to the media regulator Ofcom asking whether it thought there were grounds for investigating the BBC broadcast.

That Saturday morning, I wasn't expecting a day off but I was hoping to handle my radio broadcasts from home, to recharge my batteries (metaphorically). I started with a two-way at 6.05am on Radio 5 Live, followed by *Today* an hour later. With luck, I might get no further demands till the Radio 4 lunchtime bulletin. Then I heard George Entwistle's *Today* interview with John Humphrys, in which he admitted he had not known of the *Newsnight* allegations till the following day and had not read the *Guardian* story which suggested Lord McAlpine had been wrongly accused. He insisted he was not going to resign. No lull for me then – on the contrary!

A Saturday morning in the BBC Newsroom is usually a very quiet time, with no senior executives taking charge (one did emerge later on). In their absence, at 9am I was summoned in to Television Centre in west London by an understandably keen newsdesk editor to cover the story for the day's TV bulletins, including hourly live analysis for the BBC News Channel. A colleague was deputed to handle most of the radio coverage. The TV reports turned out to be straightforward, since there were no developments for much of the day, apart from media and political commentators criticising Entwistle's performance on *Today*. For the teatime TV bulletin, I began my piece:

> Another day, another BBC crisis – and once again its flagship daily TV news programme is under the spotlight.

I included two clips from George Entwistle's *Today* interview, a highly critical clip from John Whittingdale, chairman of the Commons Culture, Media and Sport Select Committee, and my own 'piece to camera' observation: 'Weeks after the Jimmy Savile crisis began, the BBC is now facing more questions, not just about its journalism but about the way the organisation is run.' For Radio 4's 1800 bulletin, I recorded an analysis piece, with a more political take:

> Another day, another BBC crisis – but this one feels different. Over the years, the BBC has had bruising battles with governments of various persuasions – over the General Strike and Suez, over its coverage of Northern Ireland and the Falklands War under Margaret Thatcher, and over the Iraq War dossier under Tony Blair. That crisis cost the BBC its chairman and director-general. But though this one also involves a former political figure, it seems self-inflicted...

The Saturday evening TV bulletin was due to go out at 9pm and though my earlier piece merely needed tweaking, I decided to stick around until the bulletin went out, just in case. At 8.15, I got a call from the BBC Corporate Press Office saying a statement would be made at 9pm at New Broadcasting House, the BBC's glossy, glass-fronted headquarters in Central London. I jumped on a tube train and met the TV camera operator there, as a makeshift media scrum began to form in front of a microphone outside the main entrance. There was speculation, on rival media and Twitter – but no BBC confirmation – that George Entwistle was going to resign. The minutes ticked by. At 9.15pm, as the main BBC One news bulletin ended, Entwistle emerged with Lord Patten and spoke to the cameras, saying the 'unacceptable journalistic standards' of the *Newsnight* film had damaged the public's confidence in the BBC: 'As the Director-General of the BBC, I am ultimately responsible for all content as editor-in-chief, and I have therefore decided that the honourable thing for me to do is to step down.'

Minutes later, the camera was turned round so I could be interviewed on the BBC News Channel, together with the BBC's Home Editor Mark Easton in the studio in west London. Then, after I had spent the day reporting mainly for TV, the newsdesk asked me to switch horses and file for Radio 4's 10 o'clock news, while Easton took over the TV coverage from Television Centre. By now it was almost 9.30. 'Have as much time as you like' said the Radio 4 bulletin editor. 'It's a huge story'. Indeed, it was. I walked into New Broadcasting House, where I had a desk on the seventh floor, as part of the advance guard who had moved into the new building ahead of the newsroom teams. I bashed out two minutes of copy, reporting on the day's events, pressed the key to print it out – and nothing happened. I had been working in the west London newsroom all day, and the system had got confused.

It was now almost 9.50. I was keen to record my script, rather than read it live, because I had been broadcasting since 6 o'clock that morning after less than five hours' sleep, and that's when fluffs can happen. But either way I had nothing to read from! For a moment I felt a wave of panic. Because BBC News was still moving into the new building, the computer in the seventh-floor studio was not yet connected, so I could not read the script off the screen. The new lifts were temperamental, so to go down to the main newsroom on the lower ground floor might take several minutes. Switching on a computer in a studio there could take a few minutes more. So I decided to email my script to myself, and read it off my iPhone. That presents its own hazards. I would have to scroll down the screen very gently for fear of pressing too hard and losing the page altogether.

I was halfway through recording my two-minute script, with a few minutes in hand, when the studio manager said: 'I'm sorry, they've told me to transfer you to the bulletin studio – they say you've got to do it live.' So that's what I did, scrolling down the screen even more gently, for fear of losing my script live on air, on what was already a black enough day for the BBC.

How did this crisis compare with previous ones?

The sudden departure of BBC bosses is nothing new, and they are rarely timed conveniently for BBC news bulletins.

- In 2007, I covered the resignation of Peter Fincham as Controller of BBC One, when the BBC put out a trailer for a documentary wrongly suggesting the Queen had stormed out of a photoshoot. I was the first to interview him, while events were still unfolding, and after I switched off the recorder he said: 'I am in trouble, aren't I?' He had realised for the first time the full seriousness of his situation.

- The following year, Lesley Douglas resigned as Controller of Radio 2, after the station broadcast obscene phone calls by Jonathan Ross and Russell Brand to the actor Andrew Sachs. After a day of meetings and door-steppings, her resignation – and Ross's suspension – finally came through at five to six, desperately close to the 6 o'clock bulletins.

Three of the last four BBC chairmen left suddenly, before their time.

- Sir Christopher Bland resigned one morning to become Chairman of BT. Jeff Randall, then the BBC's Business Editor, broke the news on the *Today* programme shortly after the Stock Exchange opened. Unfortunately – some would say unforgiveably – he and his producer and the *Today* team had not told anyone else in BBC News, which left me scrabbling around at 7am trying to confirm it was true, so the BBC's many other breakfast outlets could carry the news too.

- Michael Grade left at 10pm one night to become Executive Chairman of ITV, one of the BBC's biggest rivals. Again, I was scrambled from home at short notice to confirm the news and give instant analysis.

- Gavyn Davies resigned following the Hutton Report in 2004, which was prompted by the BBC's mishandling of the *Today* broadcast about the Iraq War dossier and a ferocious battle with Alastair Campbell and the Labour government. Within hours of the report's publication, he revealed his intention to resign to Andrew Marr – then the BBC's political editor – who immediately reported it on News 24, leaving me to follow up on PM and other outlets. The revelation meant Davies had to resign straight away, before the crucial BBC governors' meeting which he had intended to chair, leaving little support for the Director-General Greg Dyke. The next day Dyke went too, leaving the BBC leaderless and me rushing from studio to studio to explain, as best I could, what was going on and the likely implications.

That remarkable episode puts the recent BBC troubles into some perspective. The Hutton story lasted many months, from Andrew Gilligan's early morning report on the *Today* programme, through the death of Dr David Kelly and weeks of evidence to Lord Hutton's Inquiry, to the publication of his report and its aftermath. One faint silver lining was that throughout that period BBC News was widely acknowledged to have handled the story fully and fairly, without trying to argue the BBC's case itself.

But in some ways, covering the Savile/*Newsnight* crisis was more difficult. When the Pollard Inquiry was set up, the key participants hired lawyers and the BBC's legal team became extra-sensitive, insisting that we should constantly state – even in a 30-second news summary – that one of those involved had not yet put their side of the story. At 2 o'clock one morning, I was still waiting to file my piece for the morning bulletins as a BBC lawyer debated its wording with the Radio 4 bulletin editor – four hours before I was due on air for my first live 'two-way' of the day. In addition, BBC News was on the back foot because *Newsnight* had spiked a hugely important story which ITV later exposed.

With Channel 4 and newspapers piling in with their own Savile revelations, some BBC editors understandably wanted to make up lost ground with their own exposés, both about Savile and the BBC's handling of the affair. *Panorama*, *The Media Show* and *Today* broke excellent new ground at various stages – most notably John Humphrys' fierce but fair interview with George Entwistle – demonstrating that at its best BBC News can genuinely and robustly hold its own organisation to account. But a few ran the risk of becoming 'part of the story', trying to fight their own corner, or that of BBC bosses they thought had been unfairly treated. And the *Newsnight* debacle over Lord McAlpine showed the danger of desperately searching for a scoop.

Is the BBC still in crisis?

For a month after George Entwistle resigned, the BBC was in a highly dangerous situation, as it waited to see whether anyone with the right qualifications could be persuaded to take on one of the toughest – and most high-profile – jobs in public life. Having made the wrong decision in the summer, there was huge pressure on Lord Patten and the BBC Trustees to make amends.

It should become a business school case study, demonstrating how, by appointing the wrong leader, a globally-renowned organisation can move 'from hero to zero' in a matter of weeks. On 17 September 2012, when Entwistle became Director-General, the BBC was basking in widespread praise for its extensive, ground-breaking coverage of the London Olympics and the Proms and dramas such as *Sherlock*, *The Hollow Crown* and *Parade's End*. Two months later, when the director-general had been paid off with twice his legal entitlement, the Corporation looked accident-prone, incompetent and careless with licence-payers' cash.

The BBC was fortunate that Tony Hall was prepared to take on the challenge. One former senior executive had texted him saying: 'This is your Lord Kitchener moment – the BBC needs you!' Had he not stepped forward, I'm not sure anyone else had the range of experience and, above all, the credibility to restore the BBC's reputation and prepare it for its next charter and licence fee settlement (Douglas 2012). Tim Davie did a good job as interim Director-General, steadying the ship and demonstrating the management skills that George Entwistle lacked. But Lord Hall's experience as a former Editor and Director of BBC News, and a successful Chief Executive of the Royal Opera House, put him head and shoulders above any competition that might have come forward.

Lord Hall is the right leader for the BBC, and he has made a good start, bringing together a fresh top team, including outsiders such as James Purnell, Anne Bulford and James Harding. He has announced plans to boost the BBC's arts and music output, enhance the iPlayer, improve access to the more intellectual radio programmes and treat licence-payers like 'owners', not just users, of the BBC (Hall 2013). But that doesn't make the job any easier and severe problems remain. None in itself amounts to a crisis but together they could still cause real damage to the Corporation.

The BBC's continuing problems

Jimmy Savile's legacy

At the time of writing, Dame Janet Smith's Review (of the culture and practices at the BBC while Jimmy Savile worked there) has yet to be published – but there can be little doubt that it will cause further damage to the BBC's reputation. The review has interviewed 140 witnesses and noted telephone calls with more than 340. Though it deals with the past, its findings could have legal ramifications which rumble on for years – and which also highlight continuing flaws in the BBC's current workplace practices.

The BBC's journalism

The director of BBC News, James Harding (who came from *The Times*) has hired people from other news organisations and so has the editor of *Newsnight*, Ian Katz (who came from the *Guardian*). Trust in the BBC has started to return (though some believe *Newsnight*'s flamboyant presentational techniques are distracting – and detracting – from its journalism). But the Savile/*Newsnight* crisis demonstrated real flaws in the editorial and management structure of the BBC news division, which grew like Topsy as it tried to integrate the Corporation's global and local journalism with its national news operations.

Does it need unpicking, as some have suggested? Or are there greater strengths in having a unified BBC news structure? Have management cuts – which closed the post of the deputy director-general in charge of journalism – left it (ironically) undermanaged, with too few 'wise heads' at times of major stories?

Executive pay and pay-offs

BBC executives were not always well-paid, which is one reason the Corporation offered a generous pension scheme. As a journalist, I took a pay cut to join the BBC in 1989, and my income fell further more than once, as its spending cuts started to bite. But for managers it has been a different story. Executive pay in the BBC has escalated dramatically, as it has in many other public organisations. Some have blamed the influx of London Weekend executives as BBC chairmen and director-generals, others the arrival of bankers and highly-paid directors as non-executive members of the BBC board and remuneration committee.

Others have blamed the much higher pay packets (and in some cases share options) at Sky, ITV, Channel 4 and the new digital and technology companies. Whatever the reason, high pay became, in the words of Lord Patten, 'a toxic issue', angering MPs and lowly-paid BBC staff alike. (Whenever I went into a studio to cover the BBC annual report, I would find studio managers beside themselves with fury at the salaries and bonuses awarded to the executive board.)

The over-generous pay-offs made matters worse, even though they speeded up the cuts in senior management (and the departure of George Entwistle) and so reduced the top pay bill more quickly. The Public Accounts Committee castigated the BBC for a 'culture of cronyism'. Tony Hall has now capped such pay-offs (at £150,000) and even quoted the old Morecambe and Wise joke about the BBC suit, as an aspiration to return to – 'small checks'. But it won't be easy. When, a few years ago, the BBC capped – and then abolished – management bonuses, and later cut a month's salary from the executive board's pay packets, no one took any notice. And Hall has already been criticised by John Whittingdale MP for the salaries he is paying his new senior appointments.

Budget cuts

As well as cutting its executive pay bill, the BBC has to manage its overall budget, on a licence fee reduced in real terms by 16 per cent. It budgeted for a further 4 per cent saving to invest in new projects and in October 2013 Tony Hall said his new plans would cost a further £100 million. From 2017, the BBC moves into a new licence-fee phase, with an income that, at best, is unlikely to increase.

'The eternal mystery of the BBC'

Yet despite all these problems, the BBC's programmes, both on radio and television and in the mobile and digital arena, remain enormously popular and much admired. So does its website. Indeed, the BBC is accused by its commercial rivals of being too popular and powerful, not too weak. It's as if the BBC's management failings occur in a parallel universe from its output. *The Times* put it well:

> The eternal mystery of the BBC is how an organisation that works so badly can work so well. As impressive a journalistic organisation as any, it is nonetheless a managerial basket case. When the spotlight shines on its internal workings, it diminishes in popular stature and deserves to (*The Times* editorial 16 December 2013).

Newspaper coverage of the BBC reflects that mystery, particularly in those most hostile to it as an organisation, which devote page after page to its programmes. On the day the *Daily Telegraph* reported the Public Accounts Committee's criticisms of the BBC executive pay-offs (on page 13), it carried a picture on its front page of Andy Murray, named BBC Sports Personality of the Year; devoted the whole of page 3 to the event, including eight photographs; carried four full-length photos of the *Strictly Come Dancing* finalists on page 9, as well as an article about the forthcoming return of *Sherlock* ('*Sherlock* explains even he cannot explain faked death'). On another page, *The Choir*'s Gareth Malone explained why he would not want Paul McCartney or Elvis Presley in his choir.

I don't believe the BBC is currently in crisis – and it has plenty of goodwill in the bank, as long as *Strictly Come Dancing, Sherlock, Doctor Who, Great British Bakeoff* and *Call the Midwife* (to name only its most popular drama and entertainment programmes) are winning audiences and acclaim; when Radio 4 is attracting its highest ever listening figures; and when the licence fee provides as much value as it does to millions of people for forty pence a day. But Tony Hall and his team have to tackle its problems, embrace real change and build a clear new strategy for the BBC, if it is to win the public's confidence for the next ten years of the licence fee.

References

Douglas, Torin (2009) Inside stories: On the media beat, *British Journalism Review*, Vol. 20, No. 2 pp 21-26

Douglas, Torin (2012) Tony Hall's challenges as direct general, BBC News, 31 March. Available online at http://www.bbc.co.uk/news/entertainment-arts-21977108, accessed on 7 January 2014

Greenslade, Roy (2012) Jimmy Savile and the BBC – the story that keeps on running, *Guardian*, 26 October. Available online at http://www.theguardian.com/media/greenslade+huttonreport, accessed on 7 January 2014

Hall, Tony (2013) Speech at the BBC Radio Theatre in London, 8 October. Available online at http://www.bbc.co.uk/mediacentre/speeches/2013/tony-hall-vision.html, accessed on 7 January 2014

Note on the contributor

Torin Douglas has reported on the media for 40 years, including 24 years as the media correspondent for BBC News and spells at *The Times*, the *Economist*, the *Independent* and LBC Radio. He is a Visiting Professor at the University of Bedfordshire and holds an honorary doctorate from the University of West London. He is the author of *The Complete Guide to Advertising* (Macmillan, 1985) and a Fellow of the Communications Advertising and Marketing (CAM) Foundation. He was awarded the MBE in 2013 for services to the community in Chiswick. He now speaks, writes and chairs events about the media and community issues.

BBC licence fee negotiations – past and future

Raymond Snoddy argues the Irish may well have landed on the 'least bad' system for funding public service broadcasting

There has been an unvarying pattern with BBC licence fee negotiations over the years. Once the vested interests and differing shades of political ideology have been stripped away it has usually come down to horse-trading over money. The BBC asks for more than it expects to get and implies that the end of civilisation is nigh if its 'entirely reasonable' demands are not met. The government of the day lops off a noticeable percentage so that it can appear to be tough and, above all else, not seem to be a patsy of the BBC, or to pay the Corporation back for previous sleights.

Labour governments tend to be a little more generous because of a warmer emotional attachment to concepts of public service broadcasting. This always has to be tempered by an appreciation of the impact of what is essentially a poll tax on the poorer voters. In general, a deal is done, the BBC makes some short-term cuts and then somehow, as if by magic, the Corporation finds enough money to continue expanding. The 'magic', of course, has included an increasing population, or more precisely, a growth in the creation of new households, each liable to pay the fee.

Two licence fee campaigns, however, stand out from the general run. The first was the award in 1985 of a £58 licence fee accompanied by a fundamental review of the financing of the BBC under the chairmanship of the free market economist Professor Alan Peacock. While the then-Home Secretary Leon Brittan emphasised that the purpose of the Peacock Committee was to come up with options rather than recommendations, it was widely seen as Margaret Thatcher's revenge on the Corporation. The BBC may have been given a relatively generous settlement for now, but that would certainly not be the end of the matter. Opening up the BBC to advertising and greater competition was the obvious longer-term solution.

Peacock, supported by another economist, Samuel Brittan, of the *Financial Times*, realised that advertising on the BBC would devastate the economics of commercial television. They, therefore, came to the 'wrong' political answer – that the licence fee was the 'least bad' system and that it should be indexed to inflation, though pensioners dependent on benefits should be exempt. It was a process that lasted 14 months and had the effect of putting to rest, at least for a generation, some of the more extreme theories about the financing of the BBC. They included everything from abolishing the licence fee to privatising the Corporation or even breaking it up.

2010 licence fee settlement 'by far the most exciting so far'

Peacock clearly made an impact and in retrospect can be seen as rather forward-looking. But in terms of sheer drama, the 2010 licence fee settlement was by far the most exciting so far, the most compressed in time there has ever been – a settlement where pragmatism and pressing financial realities largely swept aside ideology. Those close to the process say that George Osborne's Treasury would have welcomed a 'scale and scope' investigation into everything the BBC does and into whether it provides value for money or not. There was the implication that the Chancellor of the Exchequer wanted to explore options for a much smaller BBC, reduced to a more tightly defined range of overt public service responsibilities.

All such-longer term thinking was thrown out of the window by the fast-approaching Comprehensive Spending Review (CSR), the attempt to cut the budget deficit by reducing public spending drastically. During the negotiations the BBC, and the then-Culture Secretary Jeremy Hunt, thought a plan to force the BBC to pay the free licence fees of the over-75s had been rejected. Work and Pensions Secretary Iain Duncan Smith, desperate to get the £600 million cost (and rising) off his departmental budget, had apparently persuaded Osborne and Prime Minister David Cameron to his point of view.

There were implicit threats of resignations from the BBC Chairman Sir Michael Lyons and Director-General Mark Thompson in the face of what was seen as a crude threat to the BBC's independence. Apart from the initial £600 million a year bill, in an ageing population, the BBC would face an open-ended call on its finances. The Lib-Dem media spokesman Don Foster played an important role in alerting his leader, Nick Clegg, to the scale of the possible crisis. The entire BBC Trust was on the verge of resigning *en masse*.

It was a gloomy Thompson who headed for home in Oxford by train on the evening of Monday 18 October 2010 believing the game was up and that the battle of the over-75s licence fees had been lost. And then the call came that something was changing in the mood of Downing Street and could he get back to London as soon as possible? Thompson got off the train at Slough, crossed platforms and returned to London and straight to Hunt's office at the Department of Culture, Media and Sport for what turned out to be a night of negotiations. The pensioner's plan was dropped but Thompson had to decide whether to enter last-minute negotiations of the sort that would give horse-trading a bad name, or risk a prolonged 'traditional' round of licence fee negotiations that could have spread out across 2011 with unpredictable consequences.

Thompson and the BBC Trust choose the bird in the hand – a licence fee frozen until 2016 while at the same time taking over the BBC World Service, Monitoring services and most of the cost of the Welsh Fourth channel. In addition, the BBC would have to find £40 million for Hunt's pet project – local television. There had been nothing like it before, but despite cost cuts of 16 per cent or £700 million and 2,000 job losses, Mark Thompson insisted that the deal was 'the best of the available outcomes for the BBC and actually a pretty good outcome'.

How scandals have created 'a perfect storm for the BBC'

In the wake of current scandals facing the BBC, the up-coming licence fee negotiations, coinciding with the re-negotiation of a new ten-year royal charter, could be the most difficult and unpredictable there has ever been. The march of technology, the current political terrain and an unprecedented raft of scandals could all combine to create a perfect storm for the BBC. Certainly the BBC will never before have entered a licence fee round surrounded by the debris of such a number of internal embarrassments, many of them shrieking managerial incompetence.

The Pollard inquiry into the *Newsnight* affair found executives functioning in silos and communicating poorly with each other. The Public Accounts Committee (PAC) may have almost wilfully misunderstood the role of the BBC Trust – setting strategy rather than getting involved in the day-to-day operations of the organisation. But the PAC, under Margaret Hodge, did ruthlessly expose the fact that a number of departing senior executives left with more than their contractual entitlement, creating an impression of both waste and cronyism at the top of the organisation.

In terms of managerial competence the fiasco of the nearly £100 million wasted on the Digital Media Initiative is probably the most serious. Consultants Pricewaterhouse Coopers (PwC) found that the system designed to share digital and audio content across the Corporation had shown serious weaknesses in project management. The BBC had also taken too long 'to realise that the project was in serious trouble and was unlikely to deliver its objectives'.

There will almost certainly be further embarrassments to come for the BBC from the inquiry into the activities of Jimmy Savile. Each of the scandals is very different but they appear to share several things in common – complacency, arrogance and a lack of openness. Naturally the political vultures have already been circling with the Conservative Party Chairman, Grant Shapps, warning that the BBC could lose exclusive rights to the licence fee unless it tacked what he described as a culture of secrecy, waste and unbalanced reporting. Culture

Secretary Maria Miller suggested that without urgent action on governance, negotiations on a new royal charter could be brought forward.

It is difficult to predict what influence the electoral timetable will have on the future of the BBC. If talks are brought forward to this year (2014) then the Lib-Dems could have a restraining influence on gut Tory desires for a smaller BBC that would represent a lesser interference with the workings of the media market. Wait until after general election day on 7 May 2015 and the Conservatives could have free rein over the future of the BBC if they win an absolute majority. The need for a further round of Conservative-Lib-Dem Coalition cannot be ruled out entirely.

Calls for a smaller BBC

Meanwhile a couple of off-stage interventions have, deliberately or not, fed into the emerging Conservative agenda for a smaller BBC, or one that no longer has access to all the proceeds of the licence fee. In an interview on Radio 5 Live, the BBC's most senior presenter, David Dimbleby, who ran unsuccessfully for the director-general's job in 1987 and equally unsuccessfully for the chairmanship in 2004, outlined his vision for a very different Corporation. Dimbleby wondered whether the BBC had become too big and too powerful and asked if some licence fee money could not be used to help fund other commercial broadcasters so that a greater diversity of voices could be heard. BBC Four and BBC Two could be merged and then cut some of the gardening and cookery programmes. The corporation's online presence could also be reduced to prevent the BBC crushing local newspapers.

At around the same time, Roger Mosey, former Editorial Director and Head of News at the BBC was making similar points in an article in *The Times*. The scale of BBC News and its dominance in the market made BBC executives uncomfortable, argued the executive who had recently taken up the post of Master of Selwyn College, Cambridge. He added, in the Murdoch-owned newspaper which has campaigned for years for a smaller BBC, that two good TV channels might be better than four with resources spread too thinly. If implemented this would mean the closure of BBC Three and BBC Four. Mosey also advocated an element of 'top-slicing' the licence fee to give to other broadcasters.

Other ideas already circulating is one from Steve Morrison, the former Chief Executive of Granada, now Chairman of All3Media, the independent production company. Morrison believes the BBC should be allowed to hold on to all of its licence fee – but on one condition: that independent producers should have the right to compete for an extra 25 per cent of programme budgets. ITV later went further by arguing that all BBC output, apart from news, should be contestable in return for keeping all of its licence fee. The independent sector is already guaranteed 25 per cent of BBC output and can already compete for an additional 25 per cent. If the Morrison idea were adopted, the BBC would have absolute control of only 25 per cent of its non-news output.

Technological change, and the fact that more and more homes have a wide range of devices able to receive high quality online video from the internet and from OTT (over the top) suppliers such as Netflix, could raise questions over the wisdom, and even practicality, of continuing to try to impose a compulsory licence fee to watch television up to the year 2026. What if more and more people say they do not watch live television and only use computers and tablets to watch recorded material and, therefore, believe they should be exempt from paying the licence fee? There will almost certainly be a fundamental examination of the scope, purpose and funding of the BBC in the next few years whether it takes the shape of a formal inquiry or not.

The best hope for the BBC is that all the scandals will finally be out of the way before then, and that a nearly new management under Director-General Tony Hall will have put in place structures to try to ensure nothing of the like happens again. In the meantime a few concluding thoughts might help.

Conclusions

First, the idea that the BBC is too large and powerful seems misplaced. By definition the frozen licence fee and the 2,000 lost jobs means that the Corporation will become smaller in absolute terms. Even more important the BBC will inevitably continue to become smaller in relative terms given the growing competition in the market from satellite broadcaster BSkyB, the arrival of BT in the television market in a serious way and the impact of new players such as Netflix. It would also seem crazy to try to close down BBC Four and BBC Three. Four is the best thing the BBC does and Three provides a necessary link with younger audiences. People like cookery and gardening programmes and there seems no good reason to reduce their number if you want to justify a universal licence fee.

Top-slicing of the licence fee seems like a reasonable idea but actually isn't. It was thoroughly considered last time in the context of Channel 4 and rejected. The problem revolves around issues such as what new programmes should be funded by such methods, where are they going to be shown and who should benefit? Should money go to multi-millionaire independent producers or swell the profits of ITV or Richard Desmond's Channel 5?

It is obvious that as a society we can decide to have any shape or size of BBC we want. But remember that public service broadcasters across European are facing an increasing squeeze on their finances and if such institutions are irreparably damaged or lost they will never return. The signs are that the public, despite everything, is broadly satisfied by the current range of services provided by the BBC, and within reason, can be persuaded to fund them. All hell breaks loose when the BBC announces the planned closure of even an obscure, minority music station.

But if the decision is to continue with the licence fee system, and it still looks like the 'least bad' way of funding public service broadcasting, then the issue of who pays in the internet age should be clarified. The government could do worse than look at Ireland where the issue has been tackled and action taken. The Irish have gone for a 'public service broadcasting charge' which is 'device independent' and does not rely on the television set. It also will apply to 'occupiers' rather than owners which should help to eliminate the free-rider problem – the one-in-five Irish households who do not pay the licence fee at present. It could be part of a comprehensive licence fee and Royal Charter settlement that draws on the wisdom of Sir Alan Peacock – index the licence fee while taking pensioners on benefit out of the equation.

Note on the contributor

After studying at Queen's University, in Belfast, Raymond Snoddy worked on local and regional newspapers, before joining *The Times* in 1971. Five years later he moved to the *Financial Times* and reported on media issues before returning to *The Times* as media editor in 1995. At present, Snoddy is a freelance journalist writing for a range of publications. He presented *NewsWatch* since its inception in 2004 until 2012. The programme was launched in response to the Hutton Inquiry, as part of an initiative to make BBC News more accountable. His other television work has included presenting Channel 4's award-winning series *Hard News*. In addition, Snoddy is the author of a biography of the media tycoon Michael Green, *The Good, the Bad and the Ugly*, about ethics in the newspaper industry, and other books. Snoddy was awarded an OBE for his services to journalism in 2000.

Section 3:
Here is the news ... and it is not all good!

John Mair

The BBC – domestically and globally – is nothing without the news. It is the core of the Corporation, the backbone of the public trust in it worldwide. Damage that trust and you denigrate the rest of the output. The facts speak for themselves. As Alice Enders, of Enders Analysis, pointed out earlier in this volume the BBC's biggest cross-platform audience is for news, with BBC TV channels accounting for 274 billion minutes of TV news watched in the year to November 2013 (based on BARB/Infosys figures), just over 70 per cent of the total.

Most public rows – with governments, politicians, companies and individuals – start in and with the news. It used to be current affairs that were the engines of trouble but that abated when that genre was formatted to within an inch of its life and subsumed under news by Director-General John Birt a mini-generation ago. Post-Birt, BBC current affairs has never properly recovered its élan and healthy tendency to make mischief. *Panorama* is still the last bastion of good investigative journalism and. as a corollary, potential trouble in the BBC canon. The BBC it has always been said is 'one *Panorama* away from losing the licence fee' but the days of the massive public rows over *Yesterday's Men, Maggie's Militant Tendency* and too many Northern Ireland films to list now seem far away. Caution has been the BBC News watchword post-Birt and especially post-the 2004 Hutton Report on the Gilligan Affair when the Corporation came out leaderless, wounded and unsure of its own editorial judgement..

Using the term 'news' to include the nightly news analysis programme *Newsnight* the latest crises had their origins there and both to do with the (now confirmed) serial abuser, BBC presenter Jimmy Savile. *Newsnight*, as the media commentator Steve Hewlett well put it at the time (November 2012): 'Refused to transmit one film on Savile it should have done yet transmitted another it should not …' The first on Savile girls and an approved school in Staines was spiked by a not very courageous or convinced editor, the second commissioned and transmitted by a very inexperienced replacement. That led to a public apology, payment of libel damages to the late Lord McAlpine and a near death experience for *Newsnight*.

Vin Ray is (or was) a seasoned BBC News insider. The founding Director of the BBC College of Journalism set up in the wake of Hutton and before that a very experienced producer and editor. In an impressive piece of original reportage, 'Thirteen days in the life of *Newsnight*', he reconstructs the days leading up to and after the transmission of the *Newsnight*/McAlpine film on 2 November 2012. Ray has done what all good reporters do and gone and talked to the original sources – the journalism actors involved in that drama with the tragic end of the resignation of a director-general after just 54 days in office. It makes for racy reading.

> It had been a matter of weeks since the BBC had been plunged into crisis for *not* broadcasting something that turned out to be true. It could hardly get much worse. Except, of course, it just had. Because now they *had* broadcast something that turned out to be *not* true. In the early evening, a number of the BBC's most senior executives were scrambled onto a conference call with George Entwistle, the Director-General. Entwistle knew little of the detail but he knew it was serious. The discussion turned inevitably to the 'nuclear option': to take *Newsnight* off the air. To suspend the programme Entwistle had once edited himself: a programme that, firstly through the Savile story, and now through this McAlpine story, had brought him to the brink of losing his job. 'Is *Newsnight* toast?' asked Eddie Mair, live on that night's programme. Whether or not Entwistle would do it became immaterial. He didn't survive long enough.

Poor judgement at all levels of the BBC

Events had conspired against the new D-G, *Newsnight* and the BBC. Poor judgement at all levels, simple journalistic checks missed plus a hollowing out of news management to deal with the first Savile crisis (the film not transmitted) had created chaos, confusion and disaster.

> It had been a perfect storm. A director-general under siege had allowed a convoluted and confusing leadership structure in the News division. That caused blurred lines of accountability and put a huge strain on relationships. A severely weakened team at *Newsnight* was not shored up quickly enough. The story was wrong. Knowledge that existed internally was not shared. It was put to air too quickly. The legal advice was flawed. The deal with the BIJ (Bureau of Investigative Journalism) was broken. And so it went on, each domino knocking over the next.

Ray gets to the nub of the story first-hand and puts 'the worst crisis that I can remember in 50 years at BBC' as the veteran World Affairs Editor, John Simpson, put it at the time, into some context with huge style.

In 'A BBC anxious about making friends and ensuring survival has some very hard thinking to do', Peter Preston , who steered the good ship *Guardian* for twenty years but has since re-invented himself as a respected media commentator for the *Observer*, looks at the BBC local products. Preston's heart is still in newspapers and local ones like the *Loughbrough Monitor* where his distinguished career began with stints there during his university holidays. The 'locals' are in a bigger crisis than the BBC and they are falling like so many autumn leaves by the wayside. Their perfect storm of falling circulation and plummeting revenue seems to be never-ending. Those papers reach for the nearest soft target – the BBC's local output on TV, radio and online – as the source of their discontents. The Newspaper Society, their trade body, strangled the BBC hyper-local television experiment at birth in 2007 claiming 'unfair competition' and since have woefully underdeveloped video content on their websites. They now have the BBC local online sites in their cross hairs. They see that as unfair competition on the internet where they are very much the 'johnnie come lately' and often offering very poor products. This 'complaint' is taken up by politicians such as Home Secretary Teresa May with an eye on the main local and national chance. Preston expresses it well

> The plain fact – though it varies in force and impact from city to city and county to county – is that BBC local radio isn't seen as the friend of local journalism. It is, instead, a heavy boot kicking at the door. The websites the BBC run may not be very imposing; indeed, they may go out of their way to give surreptitious plugs to the paper newsrooms that, in fact, supply so much of the material that radio reprocesses. Nevertheless, they are viewed as an incursion and statement of ill intent. The BBC has a finger in this pie (as in all pies whilst the Birt theory of licence fee necessity lingers on). The sites themselves may not be packed or pulsating. Nevertheless, they exist – portending intervention when and if financial circumstances permit. As such, in inevitably small, local ways, they do nothing to alleviate a BBC sense of crisis. This is yet another battlefield on which print, broadcast and digital journalists are expected to make hostile forays. Worse, the politicians who hold this ring are instinctively on the side of print journalism, which has no obligation to imposed fairness and balance, as opposed to a BBC which can easily be seen to take sides and thus brings no great prospect of special assistance in train...

Post-2017, the BBC as universal provider of news locally, nationally and globally on and off the internet may be a feature of the past. Preston advises the BBC to 'make friends' to avoid salami slicing of services. The UK coalition government of the day has forced that friendship by *de facto* 'top-slicing' the last BBC licence fee settlement in 2010 to subsidise the setting up and day-to-day operation of the new, commercial, local TV experiment. Many feel this is good licence fee payers' money chasing a very bad cause.

BBC remains a trusted 'brand'

In a world of plentiful (and often free) sources of information thanks to the internet, the BBC still retains a name and is a trusted 'brand'. Commercial providers, especially of local radio and newspapers, will have to find another scapegoat to blame for their commercial misfortunes. Competition rules in all media markets – it just so happens that in some of those, the BBC can be nifty, crafty and find an audience. They can be good at business when they put their minds to it.

Professor Justin Lewis, Dean of Research in the Arts, Humanities and Social Sciences at Cardiff University, looks to the academic and para academic research on balance and impartiality in news – much of it commissioned by the BBC Trust in 'How the BBC leans to the right'. The BBC is 'owned' by all of us as licence fee payers yet politicians of all hues are not averse to using it as a political football to get their point of view, their ideology across:

> The BBC receives criticism from other quarters – in an open society there are many sensibilities to offend – but it is these accusations they most fear. The press can (and do) make a crisis out of the smallest drama, while there is justifiable anxiety about the way a Conservative government might behave whenever the licence fee is due for renewal. While this point is generally ignored, it is the BBC's cyclical dependence upon whoever happens to be in government during the licence renewal period that is the greatest threat to its impartiality. For those who value the BBC's independence, this a gaping flaw in the system – arguably a far more serious political infringement on journalistic freedom in the UK than anything proposed by Lord Justice Leveson.

Lewis looks at the research undertaken for the BBC Trust by John Bridcut in 2007, by him in 2008 and most recently in 2013 by his Cardiff colleagues under Professor Karin Wahl-Jorgenson. The last has been much under-reported by an often virulent, anti-BBC, right wing press. Is the BBC the 'Bolshevik Broadcasting' Corporation as Conservative 'loony right' MPs sometimes claim? Lewis demurs.

> Overall, the available evidence on the BBC centre of gravity does not suggest a leftist tilt. On the contrary, its dependence on certain dominant institutions – notably in the business world and the national print media – would appear to push it the other way. The evidence I have drawn on here is, of course, open to challenge and interpretation. But our response should be to pursue the question of impartiality with greater academic rigour. We almost certainly need more – and regular – independent research on media impartiality. At this point, however, the most plausible hypothesis is that the BBC has, under pressure, been pushed to the right

Professor Julian Petley, of Brunel University, London, concurs with Lewis. In a companion piece 'Facts, informed opinion and mere opinion', Professor Petley uses that Cardiff research and other contemporary research on impartiality by Stuart Prebble to argue that the BBC is trying to hold on to values of journalistic impartiality in a world in which partiality rules especially in the printed press in Britain.

> ...the problem for the BBC is that it exists in a culture in which these values have been wholly abandoned (if indeed they were ever embraced in the first place) by the vast bulk of the national press. To most of Britain's newspapers, in which the distinction between news and views has collapsed, readers are told what editors think they want to hear, 'flat earth news' predominates, and the ideological compass points to the extreme right wing of the Tory party (and now, in some cases, straight towards UKIP), the BBC's journalistic values must indeed seem anomalous. In truth, though, it is Britain's national press which is the anomaly when judged in 'normal' (that is, Western European and North American) journalistic terms – it would not be an exaggeration to call it an aberration. It would be an absolute catastrophe for democratic debate in this country if pressure from this quarter, hideously tainted as it is, were to tempt the BBC to follow such a deviant journalistic path.

David Edwards and David Cromwell, of Media Lens which monitors the media from a Chomskyite perspective, argue, in 'BBC in crisis: "The Westminster conspiracy"', that the BBC cannot be trusted to be impartial on any of the really important issues especially when it comes to reporting politics, business and the Middle East. They excoriate the work of the two titans of broadcast journalism, Jeremy Paxman, of *Newsnight*, and John Humphrys, of *Today*, for being anti-Iranian and pro Israeli as is, they argue, (too) much of the BBC output:

> ....media corporations, including the BBC, are closer to unaccountable, totalitarian tyrannies, with power flowing strictly top-down, than they are to democracies. Employees may contribute ideas, but power flows from the top. Journalists are expected to be 'team players', 'focused' and 'disciplined' – code words that refer to the need to remain focused on 'pragmatic', bottom-line goals. To attempt to take a moral stance in this environment is difficult; it risks raising issues that are deeply threatening to senior management.

So, as the Corporation faces up to the next charter and licence fee settlement in late 2016, it is not short of advice and advisors from the linked worlds of academia and journalism. The news on the news for the BBC, though, is not always positive.

Thirteen days in the life of *Newsnight*

Vin Ray revisits the *Newsnight*/McAlpine story and those extraordinary thirteen days that engulfed the BBC. It is a story that still raises more questions than answers, he argues, 'But there is a human aspect too.' Here he looks at the decisions, the mistakes and the life-changing consequences for the individuals involved

[In a tragedy] pity is aroused by unmerited misfortune, fear by the misfortune of a man like ourselves … a man whose misfortune is brought about not by vice or depravity, but by some error of judgement. Aristotle

Perfect storm [noun]: an especially bad situation caused by a combination of unfavourable circumstances. Oxford Dictionary

Melt-down

On the evening of Wednesday 24 October 2012, Adrian Van Klaveren, then-Controller of BBC Radio 5Live, was standing on the concourse at Euston rail station. He might well have been contemplating the holiday he was about to take in Wales. He was just about to board a train back to his base in Salford when his phone rang. The voice on the other end was that of the BBC's Director-General, George Entwistle.

It was a call that would change the course of Van Klaveren's career. Entwistle believed there was a melt-down in News; someone was needed to take the lead on matters related to the scandal surrounding the presenter Jimmy Savile. The leadership team needed help to get through a very difficult period. Van Klaveren did not board the train. He didn't take his holiday either: 'You have to start tomorrow,' he was told. It helped that he had once been Deputy Director of News and that he was now coming from outside the News Division. Help was, indeed, needed.

At the heart of the tensions was one programme: *Newsnight*. It was already the subject of a substantial investigation. The Pollard Inquiry was looking at why *Newsnight* had dropped an investigation into allegations of sexual abuse by Jimmy Savile. The programme's editor, Peter Rippon, had been asked to step aside for the duration of the review. Liz Gibbons, one of Rippon's deputies, had taken over as acting editor. The Director of News, Helen Boaden, and her deputy, Steve Mitchell had recused themselves from everything that was related to the Savile story. They had to, or they would have been in charge of reporting their own involvement in the Savile story – a clear conflict of interest. In theory it could work. The reality was chaotic. Fractious relationships that had simmered below the surface now spilled over.

To make matters worse, *Panorama*, the BBC's flagship current affairs programme, had also investigated what had happened at *Newsnight*. It was bad enough that one programme was investigating another programme in the same department. But one member of the BBC News board, Peter Horrocks, was overseeing a *Panorama* investigating the behaviour of other colleagues on the board. No news organisation in the world reports its own deficiencies as thoroughly as the BBC. But it is never without pain. Bitterness and betrayal filled the air.

One veteran of the News division said: 'I'd never seen it like that before. I'd never seen people so upset. And no one had any idea how to get out of it. Everyone was confused about who was in charge of what.' That confusion would come back to bite Van Klaveren. He had been asked to deal solely with 'Savile-related matters'. He would later wish that he had sought greater clarity about the remit of the role he was stepping into. Van Klaveren knew he had no choice but to 'step up'. But neither was he under any illusion that he was walking into a minefield. What he could not have known, was which particular mine would explode. For while he concentrated on the fallout and heavy demands from the Savile story and the Pollard Inquiry, another story was unfolding under the radar.

Old story, new context
On the very day that Van Klaveren had taken the call from Entwistle, Tom Watson, a Labour MP, had stood up at Prime Minister's Questions and made references to a potential cover-up of a paedophile ring linked to parliament. Watson's statement piqued the interest of a reporter at the Bureau of Investigative Journalism [BIJ], Angus Stickler. The BIJ is a not-for-profit organisation that works with media organisations on investigative stories. Stickler was a veteran investigative journalist who had won awards for his work across the years. Watson's allegations chimed with something Stickler had been working on since the early 1990s. In 2000, Stickler had made a radio documentary for BBC Radio 5Live about sexual abuse in care homes in North Wales. It is a powerful piece of broadcasting. The testimonies of the victims are hard to listen to. The documentary was broadcast in the wake of the Waterhouse

Tribunal, which had looked into the allegations of abuse. The tribunal heard from over 650 former residents who, as children, had been abused by the very people who were paid to look after them. The main thrust of the documentary was that previous police inquiries and the tribunal itself had not fully investigated allegations of a wider paedophile ring that included what it called 'a senior public figure'.

One of the victims interviewed for the documentary was Steven Messham. He claimed he was shown a photograph of that senior public figure, whom he identified as his abuser. He says he was then told by the police officer showing him that it was Lord McAlpine, a former Conservative Party Treasurer. This appeared to be corroborated by another victim who had appeared anonymously. This anonymous victim named Lord McAlpine more than once in his interview, though this was not used in the documentary. Nor, at any point, was McAlpine's name mentioned in the script. The fact that this 12-year-old programme had been through considerable legal and editorial checks would play a large part in the production team's thinking in the week ahead.

The Watson statement and, even more so, the Jimmy Savile scandal had created a new context for old story. Stickler saw an opportunity to look again at the issue.

First contact

On Sunday 28 October, Stickler left a voicemail on Liz Gibbons' phone, pointing her towards a piece in the *Mail on Sunday*. He suggested that in light of these new allegations of a cover-up *Newsnight*, in partnership with the BIJ, should revisit the perceived failure of previous police investigations and the Waterhouse Tribunal to fully investigate a wider paedophile ring. *Newsnight* had worked with the BIJ on four previous occasions, all with Stickler as the reporter. 'We trusted Angus and knew him of old,' one insider said: 'We'd dealt with him before and knew he had a long track record. The fact that he's done the broadly similar story for 5Live as well was also a factor. This was a story he was so familiar with. We trusted his journalism because of what he'd done previously.' Gibbons looked online to check the story. But the Waterhouse Tribunal report was not easy to decipher. She would not have known that Messham's name was replaced by 'witness B'; the name McAlpine by 'family x'. She was reliant on Stickler's expertise.

Stickler and Gibbons met the next day. The editor commissioned the piece. The reporter set to work. They were clear from the outset: they were not pursuing new evidence against Lord McAlpine, nor did they ever intend to name him. There was not enough evidence in 2000 and that was unlikely to change. The goal was to look at the failings of the police investigations. The story seemed simple: the inquiry had not done its job. The production process seemed simple too. It required little extra research.

Later that Monday, Van Klaveren met Peter Horrocks for a handover before Horrocks went off on holiday. Horrocks had been handling Savile matters up until this point. He called Gibbons during the meeting and asked her to pop up, say hello to Van Klaveren, whom she did not know, and give them a quick briefing about the programme. They talked mostly about the morale and staffing of the team. Before she left the meeting, Gibbons quickly ran through the stories they were working on. The list included Stickler's story. It was early days. The story had no shape. They were only just starting to look at it. It raised no alarm bells. What the meeting did do was to open a channel between Gibbons, who needed serious support, and Van Klaveren. This was important. Because whether Stickler's story was 'Savile-related' or not, it would be Van Klaveren she would turn to when she needed help later that week.

Into production

Stickler and his producer, Ming Tsang, talked to the lawyer, Roger Law, on the Tuesday and set about putting the piece together. Messham agreed to be interviewed again, as did his solicitor, Richard Scorer. Their stories were consistent with what they had said in the 2000 R5 documentary. But the anonymous victim who had also named Lord McAlpine could not be found. Stickler and Gibbons believed that, though 12 years old, this anonymous clip was still a legitimate second source: that if it was okay to use it in the original programme it was okay to use it now.

Gibbons was more concerned about the credibility of the abuse victims as witnesses: a notoriously difficult area. Many victims are damaged by the nature of the appalling abuse they have suffered. Gibbons says she had raised concerns about this but received assurances from the reporter. No one doubted Messham was a victim. But Gibbons was unaware of some crucial information that might have caused her to pause up. The Waterhouse Tribunal report, *Lost in Care*, had cast doubt on some of Messham's evidence. He was, the report said, 'severely damaged psychologically' and 'he presents himself as an unreliable witness by the standards that an ordinary member of a jury is likely to apply'. It also concluded that the second, anonymous, witness had probably been referring to a different abuser. Both had been incoherent under cross-examination. The name McAlpine had been raised at the tribunal so journalists had already had the opportunity to link Messham and McAlpine. Then, in 1994, a senior police officer had successfully fought a libel action against three publications after Messham had falsely claimed having been abused by him. Victims are still victims. It is crucial that their voices are heard. But it requires caution.

Stickler and his producer also sought interviews with the MP, Tom Watson, and former superintendent Peter Ackerley, the senior officer in charge of the North Wales police investigation. After some promising noises, neither materialised. So, in their minds, this was the context: the same reporter had used the same sources on pretty much the same story before and passed it through the normal legal and editorial processes; yes, it was a re-hash of an old story, but in a very different climate; and the alleged perpetrator was not being named. According to insiders, everyone – including the lawyers – was 'hugely comforted by the fact that they were not going to name him'. They were now working towards broadcast on the Friday night. There were concerns, of course, but on the Thursday things felt under control. What they could not know was that they were about to lose control in a way from which they would never recover.

A night in Oxford

On the evening of Thursday 1 November, a number of Oxford graduates, past and present, gathered in the black-tied, wood-panelled splendour of the university's Macmillan Room for a debate at the Oxford Union. Among them were the BIJ's managing editor, Iain Overton, and the Channel 4 News political correspondent, Michael Crick. As the pre-debate dinner reached coffee and mints, Overton began talking about how *Newsnight* and the BIJ were about to expose a senior Tory as a paedophile. According to Crick, others sitting nearby included Stephen Dorrell, a former Conservative cabinet minister, and Michelle Stanistreet, General Secretary of the NUJ. Crick pricked up his ears and began to push Overton for more details. Overton held his ground for a while but eventually volunteered that the man in question was Lord McAlpine. Crick was initially perplexed. He had assumed Overton had been talking about a current politician; he would never have guessed the name.

Whatever Crick learned or believed, he was fundamentally mistaken in one respect: at no point did it occur to him that *Newsnight* did not intend to name McAlpine: 'I'm sure that if you'd heard what Overton said you would also have assumed they were going to name their man.'

D-day

The following morning – the day of broadcast – Crick set about trying to find Lord McAlpine: he knew him vaguely of old. Crick worked his way through a range of numbers and eventually tracked McAlpine down to his converted convent in Puglia, southern Italy. After a few pleasantries Crick, embarrassed, began telling the peer that the BBC was about to allege that he had been engaged in sexually abusing young boys. McAlpine calmly explained that these rumours had been dismissed years ago and went in to a long and, according to Crick, plausible explanation about 'this place in Wrexham' and why it was a case of mistaken identity. McAlpine did not appear to be angry and even found time to joke about it. But he was clear what he would do: 'They'll get a writ with the breakfast toast,' he told Crick. They agreed to talk later in the day to see if the BBC had been in touch.

From the moment it had decided not to do the Savile story, the ship of *Newsnight* had been taking on water. But it was now about to hit an iceberg. While Crick was busy talking to McAlpine, Overton, the BIJ boss, took to Twitter. At nine minutes past ten on the Friday morning, the day of broadcast, Overton tweeted: 'If all goes well we've got a *Newsnight* out tonight about a very senior political figure who is a paedophile.' These twenty words put the programme in an impossible position, according to insiders. 'It was immediately a no win situation,' said one senior figure. 'If we went with it we risked rushing it and being accused of not using the name. If we didn't broadcast we would be accused of pulling a really difficult investigation – again. They would say we haven't got the bottle.'

Shortly after Overton's tweet, Gibbons, who was at home preparing her submission to the Pollard Inquiry, was called by the BBC press office. 'We're suddenly getting lots of calls,' they said. 'Are you outing a paedophile on tonight's programme?' The difficulty was not lost on Stickler. In an email marked 'URGENT', he told Overton: 'You've got to stop tweeting now. BBC press office getting calls – *Newsnight* spitting blood. If the tweet world starts suggesting that we are doing a certain person we will have to pull the piece.' Stickler eventually got through to Overton on the phone and lost his temper while repeating his plea to stop tweeting.

It was at lunchtime that Crick publicly entered the fray. His call to McAlpine had paid off. At six minutes past one Crick also took to Twitter: '"Senior political figure" due to be accused tonight by BBC of being paedophile denies allegations + tells me he'll issue libel writ agst BBC.' The twittersphere was now in overdrive. Alongside the speculation and names, there were suggestions that *Newsnight* would 'bottle it' again, by either not running the piece or not naming the perpetrator.

By around five o'clock Van Klaveren was becoming concerned about the reputational risk to the BBC, whether or not the piece was aired. In less febrile times he might have talked to any one of three experienced hands: Boaden, Mitchell or David Jordan, the Director of Editorial Policy and Standards. But all three had recused themselves of any stories that were Savile-related. So Van Klaveren referred up to the BBC's Board of Management. He had been told that the point of referral for that day was Peter Johnston, Controller of Northern Ireland. Johnston is not a journalist: he comes from a marketing background. He, in turn, told the Director of Communications. Neither told the Director-General. The situation had entered the system as a PR issue rather than an editorial one.

Around the time Van Klaveren was 'referring up', Crick called McAlpine again, as arranged. The result of that conversation was another tweet: 'The senior political figure due to be accused of paedophile activity by the BBC tells me that he still hasn't heard from them for response.'

At seven o'clock, Crick went live on Channel 4 News. The sensitivity of the situation was not lost on the Channel 4 team. There were several rehearsals. Certain phrases were agreed with the lawyers. 'I have never been so terrified doing a live,' Crick later admitted. Back at the BBC, Gibbons and Law watched as Crick tiptoed through the live interview, setting out how a victim of abuse in the North Wales scandal said he had been raped by 'a former senior Conservative official from the Thatcher era'. Note the wording: it had become far more specific than 'senior public figure' or 'senior political figure'.

At *Newsnight* there were now considerable worries about running the piece, because of the risk of identification. So it is no small irony that Gibbons and Stickler assumed Crick had a separate source and, in that sense, took heart: he too was on to the story. It never occurred to them that Overton might have told him. The BBC team found out that Channel 4 News were chasing Messham for an interview. It all added to the pressure to publish. 'After Savile,' one insider said, 'if we'd dropped a story about a paedophile and Channel 4 had run it we'd have looked like idiots.'

There was much to-ing and fro-ing with the lawyers about different aspects of the piece. They, too, decided they could go further in the way they labeled McAlpine. But the advice on which they based their decision to broadcast appears to have been that they were safe for two reasons: they were not naming anyone and there were now a sufficient number of names – around seven or eight – circulating around social media to prevent jigsaw identification. Gibbons interpreted the advice given to her to mean that there was a bigger risk in asking for a right of reply than not. There was, by now, a clear disjuncture between expectations. Those on the inside had thought they were doing a story about failed police investigations. Those on the outside perceived a story about one man: Lord McAlpine.

The final draft of the script was signed off by the lawyer, Roger Law, and Van Klaveren just before quarter past nine in the evening – 75 minutes before the programme was due to go on air. The final green light had been given. It was just five days since Stickler had pitched the story. The stage was set. And so it was that, at 10.30pm, the *Newsnight* titles rolled. 'Good evening,' said Gavin Esler, the presenter. 'A *Newsnight* investigation into the abuse of boys at children's homes in Wales can reveal that two victims say they suffered sexual abuse at the hands of a leading Conservative politician from the Thatcher years.'

Aftermath

At the Monday morning editorial meeting, an argument broke out about the *Newsnight* piece. Ceri Thomas, then Editor of the *Today* programme, was particularly vocal. He argued that this was an old story: the Waterhouse Inquiry and previous investigations had been through all this. But his bigger concern was about the way the story was handled: 'You've turned us into the internet.' Van Klaveren argued that *Newsnight* was trying to give a voice to a victim. That airing it in this new climate was the right thing to do. At least two senior editors supported Van Klaveren. One person at the meeting said: 'I think those who knew a lot about the North Wales inquiries were much more sceptical. Those who knew much less about it felt that it seemed the right thing to do.'

But the story had taken on a momentum of its own. The Prime Minister, David Cameron, announced two inquiries, one to look into the conduct of the original inquiry and the second into the police handling of complaints at the time. Prominent tweeters were openly inferring that McAlpine was the culprit (an act they would live to regret). Later that week, Cameron was handed a list of suspected abusers live on ITV's *This Morning* programme. The presenter, Phillip Schofield, said he had found the names after spending 'about three minutes' trawling the internet.

Despite these developments, by Wednesday a general sense of unease at the BBC began to crystalise into a realisation that something might be seriously wrong. Ever since the broadcast, BBC Wales – who had covered the original inquiries comprehensively – had been expressing concerns about Messham and his testimony. Then, late on the Thursday, the *Guardian* published the results of its own investigation: 'New evidence obtained by the *Guardian* suggests that the senior Conservative figure at the centre of sex abuse allegations broadcast last week by BBC2's *Newsnight* has been a victim of mistaken identity.'

Much has been made of the fact that *Newsnight* omitted to test the veracity of Messham's claims by showing him a photograph of McAlpine. '... A terrible error on my part for which I am profoundly sorry,' Stickler said afterwards. But as Crick argues: 'The most amazing thing – and this is an indictment of us all – is that none of us, not just *Newsnight*, showed Messham a photo.'

'That's certainly not the man...'

Friday 9 November – one week after the broadcast – began calmly. On the 0915 conference call at the BBC there were differing views about the seriousness of the problem. One senior executive said it was 'low level': part of the warp and weft of a normal week – the media were always after *Newsnight*. But others saw it for what it was: much more serious. Any doubt was quickly removed: McAlpine finally went public. In a long statement, he said that Messham was mistaken and that he had only ever been to Wrexham once in his life. The allegations were, 'wholly false and seriously defamatory'. In the end, the *coup de grace* was delivered by the story's star witness: Steve Messham. Sometime after five in the evening, he called Stickler. He had just seen a photograph of Lord McAlpine: this was not the person who had abused him. Stickler immediately called the BBC and asked Messham to write a short statement.

Newsnight that night was presented by Eddie Mair in what one newspaper called 'a masterclass in humility'. There was no 'Good evening'. His opening words: 'A new crisis for *Newsnight*. Tonight, this programme apologises.' Shortly afterwards, the headline sequence cut to Steve Messham: 'Humble apologies to Lord McAlpine. That certainly is not the man that abused me. That's certainly not the man I identified as abused me to north Wales police in the 90's.' Later in the programme, the media commentator, Steve Hewlett, was excoriating: 'It's all very well to talk about trial by Twitter. In actual fact, this was trial by *Newsnight* ... What people out there are asking is who is running this show?' He didn't just mean *Newsnight*.

It had been a matter of weeks since the BBC had been plunged into crisis for *not* broadcasting something that turned out to be true. It could hardly get much worse. Except, of course, it just had. Because now they *had* broadcast something that turned out to be *not* true. In the early evening, a number of the BBC's most senior executives were scrambled onto a conference call with George Entwistle, the Director-General. Entwistle knew little of the detail but he knew it was serious. The discussion turned inevitably to the 'nuclear option': to take *Newsnight* off the air. To suspend the programme Entwistle had once edited himself: a programme that, firstly through the Savile story, and now through this McAlpine story, had brought him to the brink of losing his job. 'Is *Newsnight* toast?' asked Eddie Mair, live on that night's programme. Whether or not Entwistle would do it became immaterial. He didn't survive long enough.

It had been a perfect storm. A director-general under siege had allowed a convoluted and confusing leadership structure in the News division. That caused blurred lines of accountability and put a huge strain on relationships. A severely weakened team at *Newsnight* was not shored up quickly enough. The story was wrong. Knowledge that existed internally was not shared. It was put to air too quickly. The legal advice was flawed. The deal with the BIJ was broken. And so it went on, each domino knocking over the next.

Cloud-spotting

Part of the art of being a great editorial leader is having the judgement, intuition and antennae to spot which of the many clouds on the horizon is likely to rain on you. How easy it is to write that. In reality, life gets in the way. When the Irish broadcaster, RTE, went into its own melt-down over allegations about a Catholic priest, the then-Director of News, the highly-respected Ed Mulhall, was heavily involved with President Obama's visit to Ireland – one of the most important live events they had ever staged. Mulhall was one of a number of executives who lost their jobs. Throughout the short gestation of the McAlpine story, Van Klaveren was submerged in dealing with lawyers about what material should be handed over to the Pollard Inquiry. Liz Gibbons, too, was preparing for Pollard as well as planning for her trip – leaving that weekend – to the US for the elections. If editorial leadership has an Evil Spirit then its favourite trick is what magicians call misdirection: it is easy to worry about the wrong thing.

Even if you are worrying about the right thing you can still ask the wrong questions. Investigations begin – consciously or not – with a hypothesis. It is part of an editorial leader's job to make sure that the production team is testing that hypothesis as rigorously as they can; to ensure that the team is not blind to evidence that does not support their hypothesis; to ensure that they believe what they see and not just see what they believe. An editor's enthusiasm and encouragement must be tempered with robust questioning: what the BBC Trust, in its report into the affair, called 'authoritative editorial challenge'.

Less experienced leaders often believe that they need immediately to have all the right answers; more confident leaders realise that it is more important to have all the right questions. Chief among those is: 'How do you know that?' 'How can we test that?' 'How can we be sure?' Basic questions, for sure. But there's no point worrying about the risk of defamation if the story is not true in the first place. In any story of this nature there will be a danger of over-reliance on one journalist's beliefs and expertise. Of course, at some point, it must come down to trust. As the Ben Bradlee character in the film *All the President's Men*, says: 'I can't do the reporting for my reporters, which means I have to trust them. And I hate trusting anybody.'

Trust has wider implications too. It's not clear how widely known the story was during its production. It is not uncommon for investigations to be kept under wraps to prevent leakage. Some insiders believe that this was more tightly controlled than usual and that this might have meant there was less chance for alarm bells to sound. But it was not a secret by the time of the 3.15pm meeting on the day of broadcast, where it was openly mentioned in the presence of editors from across the BBC. Either way, the BBC was not joined up about it. The story had already been offered to at least one other programme. On the Sunday he first called *Newsnight*, Stickler had already pitched the story to Ceri Thomas at the *Today* programme. Thomas, who had worked on the north Wales story for the past 20 years, turned it down: he did not think there was anything new to say. BBC Wales, who knew more about the story – and Messham – than anyone, were not consulted.

New world

Social media did not exist when almost exactly the same story was first run, 12 years previously. Despite a reluctance to criticise, there is no disguising some frustration with the legal advice. One senior insider said that the advice, 'didn't understand how Twitter conversations unfold and where it was likely to go next. It was a very narrow view … ignoring the speed and implications of social media.' But it's unlikely that anyone involved in this story understood the speed, ferocity and implications of the way speculation can break across the internet. The risks of publishing were increasing exponentially throughout the day of broadcast. Of course, as the lawyers might point out, it would have been handy if the story had been true.

Wise heads

A resilient organisation needs experienced people at the top to avoid (and handle) crises. BBC News is a huge operation. It broadcasts a vast amount of output every day. The capacity for mistakes is there every hour. It needs experienced hands. So it is perhaps worth reflecting on the number of senior news executives who had left in the run-up to this crisis. Richard Sambrook, former Director of Global News, was no longer there. Mark Damazer, former Controller of Radio 4, had left. Pat Loughrey, former Director of Nations and Regions, had gone. All of them had lived through crises. To compound that loss, Mark Byford, the Deputy D-G, who had been described as the 'glue' holding together the various parts of BBC's journalism, had also left. Roger Mosey was still there but was now in charge of BBC Vision. When the Savile crisis erupted, this drain of wise heads came home to roost. The most experienced executives remaining – Boaden, Mitchell and Jordan – had all recused themselves of dealing with any matters to do with the very crisis that was pulling them under. What would, until recently, have been a raft of old hands on which to call, had gone. The cupboard marked 'experience' was almost bare.

In the end, Van Klaveren and Gibbons faced disciplinaries and were moved to different jobs. The BBC paid Lord McAlpine £185,000 in damages. The *Guardian* continued to make the running in unraveling and debunking the *Newsnight* story. Its coverage was overseen by the newspaper's Deputy Editor, Ian Katz. He will have used the experience for a job interview: six months later Katz was appointed as the new editor at *Newsnight*.

Of course, missing from all this are the most important people of all. For while the media concentrates, quite predictably, on the deficiencies of the BBC, it is easy to ignore the victims of abuse. We must remember that we still have a duty to air their voices. There are still many unanswered questions about the tribunal and the police investigations. Whatever the merits of this unfortunate episode, the victims' stories remain matters of the highest public interest.

Someone like you

So this is a story that still raises more questions than answers. There are myriad lessons to be learned. But there is a human aspect too. It is a defining characteristic of the best leaders that they do not melt away when the going gets tough. They step up. Van Klaveren, a veteran of the News division with a long and unblemished record, did just that. The circumstances were acute and he probably had no choice. But had he said 'no' and taken his holiday, there is every chance he would now be Director of News, the job for which many people thought he was the favourite.

Liz Gibbons had also stepped up. She was under the most intense pressure. She was handling so much more than this story. That she felt physically sick she attributed to the pressure. Not an implausible reason, until she discovered the reality during the week: she was pregnant. She was prescient too. At lunchtime on the day of broadcast she texted her partner: 'I think I may be about to lose my job.' Overton resigned almost immediately from the Bureau of Investigative Journalism. Colleagues say that at one point he was so distraught they feared for his health. A BIJ statement announcing his departure left no room for conjecture: 'Any role by the bureau or its officers in this story was strictly contrary to the fundamental principles and standards of the bureau.' That meant Stickler too, who resigned some weeks later. At the point of departure, Stickler asked the BIJ board if he could say a few words to the team before he left. Stickler had withstood extraordinary pressure running tough investigations across the years. But seeing his colleagues gathered round was too much. Too emotional to speak, he left the room – and his colleagues – to start the search for another job.

Early on the morning of Saturday 10 November, George Entwistle walked voluntarily to the gallows of the *Today* programme studio. He looked exhausted and ill, according to one member of the production team. The presenters' rota exemplified his bad luck: John Humphrys would be his interrogator. What followed was hard to listen to. Entwistle was spent. These were his final words: 'I am accountable to the BBC Trust … If they do not feel I am doing the right things then obviously I will, I will, be bound, bound by their judgement.'

And so it was that some 12 hours later, Entwistle and Lord Patten, the BBC Chairman, emerged from New Broadcasting House and stood on almost the exact same spot where, 54 days earlier, they had triumphantly announced Entwistle as the new D-G. Entwistle spoke for one minute and 29 seconds: '… the wholly exceptional events of the past few weeks have led me to conclude that the BBC should appoint a new leader,' he said. He quickly disappeared back into the building, collected his coat and left. It was his son's 18th birthday.

Note on the contributor
Vin Ray is a writer, media consultant, teacher and Visiting Professor of Journalism at Bournemouth University Media School. He left the BBC in 2010 after a 23-year spell in which he had been Foreign Editor, Executive Editor and the founding Director of the BBC College of Journalism. He is the author of two books: *The Reporter's Friend* and *The Television News Handbook*.

'A BBC anxious about making friends and ensuring survival has some very hard thinking to do'

Peter Preston suggests the BBC's strategy to date has been to spread resources more thinly across the piste, but not to withdraw from any major commitment. 'The answer for the next ten years looks to be somewhat different'

Modern newspaper life seems to offer only a toxic blend of perplexity and paranoia. Print is on the way out. Digital, with its bewilderingly obscure permutation of revenue streams, is taking over – brushing aside the safe old world of conventional journalism. National papers have to find fresh ways of charging for the news they present. But how do you do that when the BBC, replete with licence fee cash, offers much the same online service at no added cost? Even newspapers that traditionally champion the heirs of Reith have difficulty here. See the *Guardian*'s CEO grow pensive. And if Fleet Street feels threatened, the chill winds of fear blow stronger still at local level.

In many ways, too, this resentment feels more bitter, more acrid, on the streets where we live. Local newspapers may not be dying in droves as yet, but staffing has been slashed year after year. The big companies that control so much of the market have stripped away production resource from newspaper offices down your way and sited them many miles distant in purpose-built sub-editing factories (rather like battery chicken sheds). HQ managers, whether in London or Edinburgh, appear more worried by share price slumps than the survival of individual papers. There's a feeling of helplessness that corrodes hope. No wonder embattled editors thrash round looking for someone or something to blame. No wonder, too, that the BBC is public service Enemy Number One. And because local MPs are inevitably enmeshed in the passions of local world, resentment travels up the chain to Westminster just as speedily – and perhaps more authentically – as the lobbying once press barons come to call at Number Ten.

So when the Home Secretary of the day has to address an editors' conference, she chooses a theme that guarantees instant applause. Theresa May champions the *Maidenhead Advertiser* and puts the boot into BBC Berkshire. It's not fair to undercut the *Advertiser*'s website, she says. The BBC encroaches too much, a giant whale gulping plankton. Back off – or the government will start pushing back itself!

Thus Paranoia Gulch suddenly becomes a much bigger canyon running down Langham Place. The BBC is under pressure, too. The next royal charter – and vital licence fee settlement – has to be won. Fear cuts both ways. But how far is any of this reality? Are local radio stations and the websites they produce true threats, or just rather desperate excuses? The quick answer for anyone scanning such sites seems initially reassuring. BBC Berkshire, produced and designed to a national formula, is unthreatening in its scope and range. Just a three or four anodyne stories from around the county, a dollop of sport, perfunctory cross-references to better tales in the *Advertiser* and other Berks journals. It looks thin and under-resourced, which isn't remotely surprising, because that's exactly what it is. A few random clicks, however, doesn't tell the whole of this story or reveal the basic dilemma of local journalism. That needs a little history added, and more than a little human context: which means starting with BBC local broadcasting itself, trying to discern why it's there and what keeps it going, essentially unchanged, through an era of profound digital upheaval. You don't find good answers by tackling newspaper neuroses in isolation.

Delving back to the BBC's fifties and sixties

The significant thing, delving back to the BBC of the fifties and sixties, is how little anything local mattered – indeed, by today's standards, how little news itself mattered. We tend to take the BBC we know now on its own self-evaluation: as the nation's greatest newsroom, bringing us vital facts without the taint of prejudice. That's the Corporation's touted reason for existence as a trusted counsellor. That, incessantly repeated, is what justifies the licence fee. But long ago, in a world without FM, news was a far sparser commodity. Then the pitch to governments (for funds) and the pitch by governments (for due deference) were predicated on wavelength scarcity. Remember the 'Home Service' and 'Light Programme'. Look in vain for the full range of news worlds from *One* to *PM* to *Tonight* and *Weekend*. Think back to the beginnings of *Today*, with Jack Di Manio presiding over a cuddly collation of human interest tales. No Radio Five Live until 1994, no TV News Channel until 1997, not even *Newsnight* until 1980. And see, time and again, how reactive many of these expansions seemed.

It was Sky which set the 24-hour news ball rolling. It was the mushroom growth of commercial local radio – and Independent Radio News, launched in 1973 as a pioneer LBC began broadcasting to London – that made Five inevitable (if much delayed). As a matter of fact, too, it wasn't news at all that sparked the foundation of so many BBC outposts around England, but the need to counter the arrival of pirate radio pop stations and their mainland commercial brothers – and thus to start Radios One and Two. With so much local musical activity – 250 or so stations coming and in many cases going – could the BBC sit on its hands and cede the local air space? Of course not. That was the driving force of the 39 English local radio stations we have today. Their rationale, specifically targeting audiences over-50, was music, chat and some local news for the grey panthers of their various catchment areas. It is signal, and very important, to note how marginally that has altered over the years. Indeed, given a few casualties and amalgamations through repeated spending cuts, the era that Radio Leicester began in 1967 has not changed in its fundamentals.

BBC local websites 'barely more than cursory add-ons'

The succession of websites that so alarm newspaper editors are barely more than cursory add-ons. The budget for English local radio – just under £115 million on the latest reckoning – has to stretch across 39 stations and, on average, pay for the activities of 12 to 14 editorial people required to cover and present the news of traffic hold-ups, weather forecasts and actual stories over a 75-hour broadcasting week. It's not surprising that the news on the sites, like the news on the air, can sometimes seem pretty vestigial. More, there's an obvious lack of what we can properly call coherence. The news beyond that 75-hour mark will come straight from Radio Five. The chat, away from prime commuting time, is increasingly shared out between several station areas. Nothing of immediate relevance at all. The appeal of the truly local comes – and then goes. James Harding, from *The Times*, takes over as Head of News and boldly proclaimed that local resources will be more integrated, more vital, more revered. But that's a million miles from present practice. What we see, increasingly, is a kind of third-tier national service of shared programming with regular local moments.

This isn't surprising when you look wider. Commercial radio has, for the most part, been merged into a series of big chains – in the same way that local newspapers have become part of Trinity Mirror, Newsquest and the rest once the families that founded them grew old and sold out. The BBC, an engine of centralisation in any case, its Trust prescribing reporting balances from and approved approaches from Cairo to Corby, is not ideally fitted to be broadcasting's voice in local world. The 39 stations may be used as 39 steps to charter renewal, as an argument that shows the Corporation's proclaimed purpose in serving all its subscribers, but they are mostly bits of background scenery in any serious crisis, one reason for renewal amongst many. It is, of course, significant that Scotland, Wales and Northern Ireland are left to go their own way, without any meaningful replication of England's pattern. Put that down to profound national differences, if you like: but also, perhaps, to the way the 'local' fashion faded as it moved further away from London. And when it's necessary to cut, there's natural opportunity for 'efficiency' trimmings that affect only small, separate spots around the country rather than obliterate an entire national channel.

Note, especially in England, what fuzzy concepts the words 'local' and 'regional' anyway convey. Counties – say the 'Radio Three Counties' of Beds, Herts and Bucks that were reckoned to share a single local station – are nebulous entities. Broadcasting regions are no better: we may have Radio Derby, Radio Leicester and Radio Nottingham on air, but lump them together as the 'East Midlands' for regional television purposes and the result is that two-thirds of the news conveyed is almost completely irrelevant. The three cities live different lives. Radio Merseyside has the reality of a single, large community to it. Radio Manchester, ringed by substantial towns in the Bolton and Blackburn category, doesn't. Radio London – local radio for a 'locality' with the population of Austria – is a misnomer wrapped in an enigma. By contrast, local newspapers, founded bottom up in existing communities, are more natural growths with deeper ties. Broadcasting, state superintended, carves up the map for bureaucratic convenience and feels bound to sketch in national deadlines to any main bulletin, because that's what the audience expects. Newspaper journalism, by contrast, knows its time and its place in the survival of the locally fittest.

Tensions and suspicions

That's one tension. Add in a rulebook – extrapolated from largely irrelevant US experience – that rations ownership overlaps between local papers and local commercial broadcasting (with the BBC playing irritant on the side) and you can sense further friction. Load on a seeming BBC wish to move into 'hyperlocal TV' as the millennium turned (an ambition swiftly abandoned in leaner times). Suspicion festers. Even on a personal, very local level, relationships don't run smooth. Local print journalists are notoriously badly paid. Local BBC journalists have their place on a national scale. They are much better paid. When John Myers, the noted commercial radio guru, looked at local radio as part of a broader review, he questioned the need to have £100,0000-a-year station managers running each of the residual 39. Couldn't they look after three or four stations each? Apparently not, the BBC decided – but didn't pause to inquire how many local newspaper editors can aspire to six figure salaries for themselves. Talk the green eyes of envy if you like: but also think red rags to bulls.

The plain fact – though it varies in force and impact from city to city and county to county – is that BBC local radio isn't seen as the friend of local journalism. It is, instead, a heavy boot kicking at the door. The websites the BBC run may not be very imposing; indeed, they may go out of their way to give surreptitious plugs to the paper newsrooms that, in fact, supply so much of the material that radio reprocesses. Nevertheless, they are viewed as an incursion and statement of ill intent. The BBC has a finger in this pie (as in all pies whilst the Birt theory of licence fee necessity lingers on). The sites themselves may not be packed or pulsating. Nevertheless, they exist – portending intervention when and if financial circumstances permit. As such, in inevitably small, local ways, they do nothing to alleviate a BBC sense of crisis. This is yet another battlefield on which print, broadcast and digital journalists are expected to make hostile forays. Worse, the politicians who hold this ring are instinctively on the side of print journalism, which has no obligation to imposed fairness and balance, as opposed to a BBC which can easily be seen to take sides and thus brings no great prospect of special assistance in train.

Look a few years down Paranoia Gulch as local editors and reporters do. Perhaps print copy numbers and print advertising clout will go on diminishing. Perhaps the *Maidenhead Advertisers* of this world will turn into local news blogs (of the kind already starting to make a big city living). Perhaps very local advertising and hyperlocal readership will offer local journalists a future of the autonomous, self-starting kind sketched out by David Montgomery, CEO of the new Local World chain. But, in every way and in every case, the BBC presence isn't automatically seen as propitious. It chips away possibilities, not enhances them. If unique visitors to a live-saving website matter, then here are some visitors going elsewhere. If local TV and local newspapers can form an economic bond before print vanishes, then here's an extra complication that does nothing to speed solutions (especially up in London where Ofcoms and Monopolies Commissions meet).

Thus – in a way that frankly doesn't add up the cash and risks at stake too accurately – the gloom is generalised, the hostility vague but prevalent. And here's where a BBC anxious about making friends and ensuring survival surely has some very hard thinking to do. How far can the public's tolerance stretch as the licence fees goes ever onwards and upwards? Where is the connection between an aspirational half a billion BBC viewers and listeners worldwide and the seven million or so who still tune in to BBC local? How far can 'broadcasting' as a concept be stretched? Beyond television and radio to smartphones, mobiles and the rest? Is the mission to expand driven from within or due, henceforth, to be conditioned by evolving technology? If local, in the purest community sense of the word – your street, your family, your friends – is best served by bloggers who ask for nothing and expect no reward bar recognition, then where does the heavy, expensive technology of BBC existence chip in?

Reassurance and entertainment to (ageing) millions

It's easy, you fear, to see any retreat, any retrenchment, as selling the pass. What the BBC has, in the name of Birt, it must inevitably strive to hold: and there are very good practical reasons for embracing that position. BBC local offers reassurance and entertainment to (ageing) millions. It is a friend calling in. Some of what it provides is basic information: the weather, travel and news very close to home. Some of it offers a stage to disk jockeys and entertainers on the way up - or down. Most of it performs to a consistently high professional standard. (Not today, thank you, Alan Partridge!)

By these lights, there's no call to pull back, to retreat from a fight. To the contrary, duty calls. But the crucial questions here aren't really asked by the press, I fear. The questions that matter are posed from within. For the BBC, no matter how united it tries to appear, is wracked by internal debates. Very simply: if the licence fee can't go growing in these hard times for hard working families, how do we survive on progressively less? The answer thus far has been to spread resources more thinly across the piste, but not to withdraw from any major commitment. The answer for the next ten years looks to be somewhat different.

You can make extra money abroad – BBC worldwide, in fact – by selling more programmes and formats. You can cast a long shadow across the internet of globalisation. You can find new opportunities by leaving Britain (poor little Britain) behind: not fit for all-conquering website purpose. But the part of current operations that doesn't quite fit then stands out more starkly. There is no money in local public service. There is no real national power or impact along that path. There is just an old, dying audience that, in essence, only exists in England anyway, pursuing the dreams of forty years ago in a context that has changed mightily. Is there a better way of serving that audience: by subscription, by blogs or joint websites, by drawing on newspaper resources direct? Perhaps there will have to be. Don't take Theresa May's homily to the *Maidenhead Advertiser* too seriously. Politicians come and go. But don't fall into the reverse of that ominous trap: believing that somehow things can just potter on unaddressed.

Note on the contributor
Peter Preston edited the *Guardian* from 1975 to 1995. He is currently a director of the Guardian Foundation, a media commentator for the *Observer* – and a founding partner of the new European Press Prize.

How the BBC leans to the right

Justin Lewis examines claims about breaches in BBC impartiality, taking particular note of some the impartiality reviews commissioned by the BBC Trust. He concludes: 'The most plausible hypothesis is that the BBC has, under pressure, been pushed to the right'

Look right, look left, look right again: The BBC under attack

Social scientists like myself like to see claims and assertions enlightened by a solid body of evidence. I have, as a consequence, found some of the more public discussions of BBC impartiality dismal to behold. Accusations of BBC bias are now part of a political game in which forms of self-interest are played out against a backdrop of anecdotal evidence and half-truths.

Leading the charge are conservative media owners and their press outlets. Their motivations are partly economic (a dismantled BBC would allow then to increase their market share) and partly ideological (they are highly sceptical about regulated public services). Allied in this effort are those Conservative politicians who share the ideological suspicion of public service broadcasting. Their interests are also strategic, since political pressure – they hope – obliges the BBC to bend over backwards to avoid accusations of a leftist tilt.

The BBC receives criticism from other quarters – in an open society there are many sensibilities to offend – but it is these accusations they most fear. The press can (and do) make a crisis out of the smallest drama, while there is justifiable anxiety about the way a Conservative government might behave whenever the license fee is due for renewal. While this point is generally ignored, it is the BBC's cyclical dependence upon whoever happens to be in government during the licence renewal period that is the greatest threat to its impartiality. For those who value the BBC's independence, this a gaping flaw in the system – arguably a far more serious political infringement on journalistic freedom in the UK than anything proposed by Lord Justice Leveson.

Despite the highly partial origin of claims about the BBC's propensity to lean leftward, any serious accusations of this kind deserves proper examination. I have often heard it said that if the BBC is being criticised from both political flanks, it is probably getting it about right. This is, with all due respect, a lazy supposition (so, for example, a centrist bias is still a breach of impartiality), and if this chapter is a plea for anything, it is that impartiality is sufficiently important to be subject to systematic, independent scrutiny. We also need to consider the possibility that attacks from the right are having the desired effect. While the BBC can, at times, be robust in defending its independence, it can also be risk averse. There is a real possibility that this understandable caution has led the BBC to seek shelter in more conservative enclaves.

Recent evidence from the most recent BBC Trust commissioned impartiality review appears to support this view. The research, by my colleagues at Cardiff, compared BBC news when Labour were in power (in 2007) with coverage under a Conservative-led coalition (in 2012). The study found, by a series of measures, that 'Conservative dominance in 2012' of BBC news was 'by a notably larger margin than Labour dominance in 2007' (Wahl-Jorgenson et al 2013: 5).

Beyond the main parties, the study suggested that the BBC is more likely than either ITV or Channel 4 to use sources from the right, such US Republicans or UKIP, and less likely to use sources from the left, such as US Democrats and the Green Party. But it is the imbalance between Conservative and Labour – by margins of three to one for party leaders and four to one for ministers/shadow ministers – that was most striking, especially since the research indicated that this rightward shift was a strictly BBC phenomenon. The study found no similar patterns on either ITV or Channel 4 (ibid: 83). These were not findings the BBC Trust was especially keen to draw attention to, and – oddly for a review about impartiality – they were played down in the subsequent report. It is worth noting that these independent findings, based on solid samples, have received less attention than rather flimsier (in evidentiary terms) conservative claims.

Measuring impartiality

Impartiality goes beyond matters of party political representation: it encompasses the issues a news outlet chooses to cover and the way those issues are framed and reported. Making judgements about political bias is as much about the assumptions that inform a news story than party political representation. So, for example, conservative newspapers tend to give far more coverage to issues that interest the political right (such as immigration or abuses of welfare) than those that concern the left (such as poverty or inequality)

The first problem facing any analysis of BBC imp, neutral centre of gravity, no golden objective mean departure. Locating the centre is a matter of context, choices. The BBC's approach to the coverage of politi uses Westminster as its touchstone, with its centre of the Speaker's Chair. This point was made clearly by th the BBC Trust's commissioned study of political coverage in a post-devolution era (Lewis et al 2009; Cushion et al 2009). The research found that despite the significant devolution of political power to Scotland, Wales and Northern Ireland, political coverage remained heavily focused on Westminster. At best, this meant ignoring the different policies pursued outside England, at worst it meant that England (whose governance remains at Westminster) became a stand-in for the UK as a whole.

The BBC, to its great credit, took action to remedy some of the weaknesses identified by the King Report. Follow up research suggested that this intervention improved coverage in a number of areas, with greater representation of policy regimes across the four nations (Cushion et al 2010). Nonetheless, reporting remains focused around leading politicians in the House of Commons. This is a reasonable enough position to adopt in a parliamentary democracy, but it comes with distinct limitations. Most notably, it relies upon the main political parties to give voice to a range of well informed perspectives. As a consequence there are many parts of the political terrain – such as the EU, (immigration) or economic growth – where debate takes place within a very narrow frame of reference.

So, for example, debates about Europe are invariably framed by a main party debate which sees 'Europe as a problem for the UK, particularly in terms of national sovereignty' (Wahl-Jorgensen et al: 51). The recent BBC Trust commissioned review found 'very little room for sources presenting a broader range of views, and for substantive information about what the EU actually does and how much it actually costs' (ibid: 52). What we end up with is less a discussion about the merits of the EU than who can best represent UK interests. Important, no doubt, but limited in scope.

Similarly, there is now a growing body of evidence suggesting a model of permanent economic growth is of dwindling benefit to wealthy countries such as the UK. Research now shows that GDP growth is no longer linked to improvements in health or happiness (Bok 2010; Layard 2011), is environmentally unsustainable (Jackson 2010) and stretches commodity choice far beyond the time we have available to us as consumers (Offer 2006; Lewis 2013). In short, there is a serious debate about whether wealthy consumer economies still rely on growth to generate prosperity. But it is not one to be heard in the House of Commons – or, as a consequence, on the BBC, where GDP growth is invariably assumed to be an objective good (Lewis 2013). The BBC thereby reflects a series of assumptions that inform the political mainstream. It is both pro-democracy and pro-monarchy. It upholds liberal Western values and a series of economic assumption based on a global market economy (in which, for example, economic growth is seen as more important than the climate change it helps create).

The BBC, in this very Reithian sense, reflects the assumptions of some of our ⟨domi⟩nant institutions. This is an easy position to defend, although it sometimes ⟨shows a⟩ certain myopia, constraining wider and more critical discussion. The failure of the BBC's economic experts to anticipate the credit crash, for example, was a function of its reluctance to go outside a narrow range of mainstream economic debate and incorporate those more critical economists who *did* see it coming (Berry 2013). Similarly, the BBC's reliance on military top brass for discussions about military spending levels means that such discussions are decidedly lop-sided. Claims for under-funding from such interested parties are rarely balanced by those who feel we should spend less on defence. The UK is one of the world's largest military spenders (a point rarely made) while discussions of the merits of such spending, research suggests, is becoming increasingly one-sided (Lewis and Hunt 2011).

The BBC Trust's first impartiality review, which suggested moving from a 'see saw' (generally left vs right) to a 'wagon wheel' approach, did not really explore these ideological assumptions. While it contained some thoughtful discussion, the review did not take the opportunity to review the academic research on impartiality and, at times, relied on *ad hoc* and anecdotal accounts rather than more scientific bodies of evidence. Its conclusions were based on the sense that traditional left/right divisions were breaking down, making the old 'see saw' balancing act a less appropriate guiding metaphor. Its advocacy of the 'wagon wheel' was an attempt to move beyond such limitations:

> The wheel is not exactly circular, it has a shifting centre, the 'spokes' are not necessarily evenly spaced, nor do they all reach the edge of the wheel, nor does one 'spoke' necessarily point in a directly opposite direction to another. So opinion is not confined to 'left' and 'right' but ranges through 360 degrees. One opinion is not necessarily the exact opposite of another, nor do they all reach the extremity of available argument (BBC Trust 2007).

The flaw in the metaphor is, perhaps, revealing. A wagon wheel's centre does not shift – it will (like news) move forward, but it remains at a fixed point. The assumptions behind locating the centre remain an issue. What it does make possible, in a way the see-saw does not, is space for perspectives that question those assumptions. Moving from a see-saw to a wagon wheel is, however, easier said than done. It requires a radical appraisal of the range and type of sources typically used to inform news, and a commitment to looking beyond the usual suspects for a well-informed diversity of perspectives. The latest BBC Trust impartiality review, designed to test how far the BBC had made this metaphorical move, found the see-saw still firmly in place (Wahl-Jorgenson et al 2013), with a small number of dominant institutions – notably parliament – continuing to dominate debate.

Impartiality and the range of BBC sources

The BBC's model of impartiality – the location of its centre, if you like – is inevitably limited by its tendency to favour some institutions over others. A 2007 study, for example, found that around half of those sources used on BBC news were from just four professions: the worlds of politics, business, law and order and the news media. By contrast, the main knowledge-based professions and civic voices (from the academy, medicine, science and technology, thinks tanks, government/public agencies and NGOs) made up, between them, only 10 per cent of all sources (Lewis and Cushion 2009).

This concentration was confirmed by the recent BBC Trust review of television news, which suggested that the dominance of these four groups as news sources has increased over the last five years – with a particular rise in the use of business and media sources (Wahl-Jorgensen et al 2013: 80, which found similar trends on the Radio 4 *Today* programme). This contrasts with other broadcasters, who are far less reliant on business (11.1 per cent of sources on BBC news, but only 3.8 per cent on ITV and 2.2 per cent on Channel 4) or media (8.2 per cent of sources on BBC news, 1.6 per cent on ITV and 5.9 per cent on Channel 4). Both ITV and Channel 4 make significantly more use of sources from the academy, medicine, science and technology, thinks tanks, government/public agencies and NGOs: these groups make up 16.4 per cent of sources on ITV and 22.7 per cent on Channel 4, but only 9.7 per cent on the BBC.

This not only narrows the range of expertise available on BBC news, it has implications for impartiality. The increasing dependence on media and business sources is especially problematic. Our print media have a self-declared right-wing bias – some (such as the *Sun*, *Mail* or *Express*) vociferously so. While the BBC undoubtedly tries to negotiate this bias (sometimes balancing, for example, the *Guardian* against the *Telegraph*), it is often guilty of using the press as a substitute for public opinion. This, in turn, provides a loudspeaker for those instances when polling majorities lean to the right – on issues such as immigration, on which sections of the press campaign – than when they lean to the left – on issues such as the privatisation of Royal Mail, on which they do not (see Jordan 2013).

The assumption that, for example, the views of *Daily Mail* readers are represented by the newspaper's editorial line is not borne out by a detailed examination of public opinion data. In short 'Middle England' is far more politically diverse than *Mail* editorials would suggest (Lewis et al 2005). Majorities may be anti-immigration, but they are also opposed to further privatisation of public services and sympathetic to nationalisation of others (such as the railways). A reliance on the range of opinions expressed by the press will invariably push debate to the right of the broader public.

In a similar way, the growth of business news (Svennevig 2007) and the widespread use of business sources raises important questions about impartiality. A business perspective will *tend* to lean to the right: representatives of business (for reasons of economic self interest) will, for example, favour corporate tax cuts over public spending, and opt for less rather than more regulation on employment rights or environmental protection. In the past, these perspectives were balanced against voices from the trade union movement. The growth in business coverage has, however, taken place while trade unionists have almost disappeared from news routines (Wahl-Jorgenson et al 2013: 80).

A review of UK Business Reporting for the BBC Trust (BBC Trust 2007) sidestepped the broader question of whether a focus on business creates a slant toward a particular view of the world. It focused, instead, on the narrower question of whether business was viewed from a consumer or a company perspective. The report's desire for a more consensual approach – avoiding such antagonisms – glossed over the different interests of producers and consumers (consumers want the best product at the cheapest possible price, while businesses want to spend as little on the product as they can and sell it for as much they can). More importantly a broader and more critical view of the role of business in society has no place in this framework. Although the BBC Trust review did not explore this point, they did acknowledge it, observing that:

> Around 29 million people work for a living in the UK and spend a large proportion of their waking hours in the workplace. However, little of this important part of UK life is reflected in the BBC's business coverage … the audiences are served in their identity as consumers. But they are not that well served in their role as workers (ibid: 9).

As workers, we have distinct interests – we want well-paid, secure jobs with profits shared amongst the workforce, rather than passed to owners, shareholders or consumers. For both businesses and consumers cheap labour is a good thing, for workers it is not.

Overall, the available evidence on the BBC centre of gravity does not suggest a leftist tilt. On the contrary, its dependence on certain dominant institutions – notably in the business world and the national print media – would appear to push it the other way. The evidence I have drawn on here is, of course, open to challenge and interpretation. But our response should be to pursue the question of impartiality with greater academic rigour. We almost certainly need more – and regular – independent research on media impartiality. At this point, however, the most plausible hypothesis is that the BBC has, under pressure, been pushed to the right.

References

BBC Trust (2007) *Report of the independent panel for the BBC trust on impartiality of BBC business coverage*, London: BBC Trust

Berry, M. (2013) The *Today* programme and the banking crisis, *Journalism*, Vol. 14, No. 2 pp 253-270

Bok, D. (2010) *The Politics of Happiness: What Government Can Learn from the New Research on Well-Being*, Princeton: Princeton University Press

Bridcut, J. (2007) From Seesaw to Wagon Wheel: Safeguarding impartiality in the 21st Century. Available online at http://www.bbc.co.uk/bbctrust/assets/files/pdf/review_report_research/impartiality_21century/report.pdf, accessed on 13 December 2013

Cushion, S., Lewis, J., and Groves, C. (2009) Reflecting the four nations? An analysis of reporting devolution on UK network news media, *Journalism Studies*, Vol. 10, No. 5 pp 655-671

Cushion, S., Lewis, J., and Ramsay, G. (2011) The impact of interventionist regulation in reshaping news agendas: A comparative analysis of public and commercially funded television journalism', *Journalism*, Vol. 13, No. 7 pp 831-849

Jackson, T. (2010) *Prosperity Without Growth? The transition to a sustainable economy*, London: Sustainable Development Commission

Jorden, W. (2013) Two-thirds of public oppose Royal Mail sell-off, YouGov. Available online at http://yougov.co.uk/news/2013/07/11/two-thirds-public-oppose-royal-mail-sell/, accessed on 13 December 2013

Layard, R. (2011) *Happiness Lessons from a New Science*, London: Penguin Books

Lewis, J. (2013) *Beyond Consumer Capitalism: Media and the Limits to Imagination*, London: Polity

Lewis, J. and Cushion, S. (2009) The thirst to be first: An analysis of breaking news stories and their impact on the quality of 24-hour news coverage in the UK, *Journalism Practice*, Vol. 3, No. 3 pp 304-318

Lewis, J., Cushion, S., Groves, C., Bennett, L., Reardon, S., Wilkins, E. and Williams, R. (2008) *Four Nations Impartiality Review: An analysis of reporting devolution*, London: BBC Trust. Available online at http://downloads.bbc.co.uk/bbctrust/assets/files/pdf/review_report_research/impartiality/appendix_a_cardiff_u_analysis.pdf, accessed on 13 December 2013

Lewis, J., Inthorn, S. and Wahl-Jorgensen, K. (2005) *Citizens or Consumers: The Media and the Decline of Political Participation*, Maidenhead: Open University Press

Lewis, J. and Hunt, J. (2011) Press coverage of the UK military budget: 1987 to 2009, *Media, War and Conflict*, Vol. 4. No. 2 pp 162-184

Offer, A. (2006) *The Challenge of Affluence: Self-Control and Well-Being in the United States and Britain since 1950*, Oxford: Oxford University Press

Wahl-Jorgensen, K. et al (2013) BBC Breadth of Opinion Review: Content Analysis. Available online at http://downloads.bbc.co.uk/bbctrust/assets/files/pdf/our_work/breadth_opinion/content_analysis.pdf, accessed on 13 December 2013

Note on the contributor
Professor Justin Lewis is Dean of Research in the Arts, Humanities and Social Sciences at Cardiff University. He has written many books about media, society and the creative industries, his most recent being *Beyond Consumer Capitalism: Media and the Limits to Imagination*, published by Polity.

Facts, informed opinion and mere opinion

Julian Petley highlights a 'worrying picture' which, he claims, emerges from the BBC Trust's response to commissioned content analysis by researchers at Cardiff University: 'a pre-emptive defensiveness about the liberal values which the BBC's numerous and vociferous enemies on the right never lose any opportunity to excoriate'

From Seesaw to Wagon Wheel

In July 2013, the BBC Trust published a review of breadth of opinion in BBC output (BBC Trust 2013). One of its main purposes was to examine the extent to which the BBC had adopted the recommendations of John Bridcut's 2007 report *From Seesaw to Wagon Wheel*. This argued that impartiality was a matter of reflecting a wide spectrum of opinion and not simply achieving a balance of left-wing and right-wing views. According to Bridcut: 'Impartiality must continue to be applied to matters of party political or industrial controversy. But in today's more diverse political, social and cultural landscape, it requires a wider and deeper application' (BBC Trust 2007: 33). The report notes that the political and cultural landscape has changed dramatically in recent years: the main Westminster parties are less sharply differentiated, party membership has dropped, voter turnout declined, and parliament is widely held in low esteem and now competes for attention with alternative forms of political discourse in the new media. Consequently, Bridcut argues:

> There are many issues where to hear 'both sides of the case' is not enough: there are many more shades of opinion to consider ... parliament can no longer expect to define the parameters of national debate: it can sometimes instigate it, but more often it has to respond to currents of opinion already flowing freely on the internet and in the media. The world no longer waits on parliamentary utterance, and parliamentary consensus should never stifle the debate of topical issues on the BBC – because it does not always correspond with the different strands of public opinion (ibid: 34).

For those who have long argued that the terms of political debate on the BBC are too narrow and dominated to a democratically unhealthy degree by political discourse from inside the 'Westminster bubble', this was a welcome development, although it is also one which is fraught with difficulties, as we shall see.

The Cardiff University content analysis

To help it assess the extent to which Bridcut's recommendations had been adopted, the Trust commissioned a content analysis from Cardiff University which, among other things, examined breadth of opinion in BBC coverage of immigration, religion, and the UK's relationship with the EU in one month in each of 2007 and 2012. In its discussion of the content analysis the Trust noted that:

> Cardiff found no clear statistical evidence of a change of approach between 2007 and 2012 but there was a slight increase in the breadth of opinion across the years in the samples regarding the three topics. A significant finding of the content analysis was the dominance of political voices. Political voices have become more, not less, dominant in coverage of the EU and immigration between 2007 and 2012 (BBC Trust 2013: 5).

As far as it goes, this is an accurate summary of part of the Cardiff analysis, and, judged in Bridcut's terms, is surely disappointing. But when one digs down into this part of the analysis, another, equally worrying, picture emerges. This concerns partiality in a straightforward political sense, and this aspect of the research is entirely ignored by the Trust in its report.

Political partiality

Thus in the relevant period in 2007, when Labour was in government, Labour accounted for 45 per cent of all sources for which a political affiliation could be determined, and the Tories for 41 per cent. But in the relevant period in 2012, when the Coalition was in government, the Conservatives accounted for 48.4 per cent of all politically affiliated sources, and Labour 26.3 per cent. As for the Liberal Democrats, the figure for 2007 was 9.0 per cent and for 2012 it was 6.0 per cent, although it needs to be noted that in the latter year the figure for Coalition sources was 5.0 per cent. Similarly, although in 2007 and 2012 the Prime Minister was the most newsworthy single source, Gordon Brown was used 46 times in 2007 and David Cameron 53 times in 2012. Meanwhile, Cameron was used 27 times as leader of the opposition in 2007 and Ed Miliband 15 times in 2012. In 2007, there was an almost equal number of references to 'Conservatives' (28) and 'government' (26). By contrast, in 2012, 'government' was referred to 35 times and 'Labour' only 22 times. Similarly, sources representing the Shadow Cabinet and Ministers went down from 3.9 per cent of all sources under Cameron's opposition leadership in 2007 to 1.5 per cent under Miliband in 2012 (Wahl-Jorgensen et al 2013: 15-16). These figures clearly point to a distinct bias towards the Conservatives. Of course, this is a bias only in quantitative terms, but it is surely consistent enough to merit further investigation in qualitative ones.

The EU as a problem

However, the Cardiff analysis also uncovers something which goes beyond the Conservatives receiving more airtime than other parties for their views. In broadcast stories concerning the EU, in the relevant month in 2007, Labour spokespeople were actually sourced more frequently (32 times) than the Conservatives (21), but the only thoroughly Europhile party, the Liberal Democrats, was sourced only twice. Given that the two largest parties contain considerable numbers of Europhobes, privileging those parties as sources would almost inevitably have the effect of amplifying anti-EU sentiment on the BBC. The Trust does, in fact, acknowledge that 'the content analysis indicated that the EU was more often treated as a problem in BBC content than otherwise' (op cit: 9) in both years, but this does not adequately convey the extent to which the BBC's broadcast news coverage can justifiably be considered as presenting the EU in a negative light, as a consequence of the main sources on which the BBC drew in its coverage of the issue. Thus, for example, in 2007, as the Cardiff analysis explains:

> The reporting of the Lisbon Treaty was largely dominated by the perspectives of the two main parties (Conservative and Labour) and the debate was focused around the procedural issues of 'red lines', 'opt-outs' and referendums. There was very little extra-parliamentary opinion from areas of civil society or substantive debate about what the Lisbon Treaty actually involved. There were also limited attempts to actually make the case for Europe making a positive contribution to Britain. Instead, most of the debate focused on the Conservatives stressing that the EU was further encroaching on British sovereignty and Labour insisting that this was not the case. So despite the limited presence of UKIP there was a greater proportion of opinion which framed Europe as a threat than an opportunity. On the whole, it appears that the way in which the story of the Lisbon Treaty was told in BBC programming tended to reflect a narrow range of opinion, strongly focused on issues of national sovereignty, and tensions between the two main Westminster political parties (op cit: 46).

The Cardiff researchers conclude that in both years:

> The positive case for Europe tends to be framed solely in terms of economic benefits and political influence. There is very little room for sources presenting a broader range of views, and for substantive information about what the EU actually does and how much it actually costs ... The reliance on Westminster sources means that the relationship of the UK with the EU is usually covered within a framework where the EU is seen as a threat (ibid: 52).

Adding still further to the anti-EU discourse was the fact that, although in 2007 UKIP was sourced only twice, 'the party's political views were amply represented by other sources' (ibid: 43). It is also notable that in 2007, of the ten references to newspaper coverage of the Lisbon Treaty on the *Today* programme (presumably in its round-up of the day's main newspaper stories), no less than seven were from anti-EU papers, and at least three of these were straight editorialising: 'This act of betrayal will haunt Mr Brown till the end of his political days' (*Sun*, 19 October); 'The *Sun* says that Gordon Brown has rolled over in abject surrender' (*Sun*, 23 October); 'The new treaty is 96% identical to the defeated constitution. Don't let Britain down by signing up' (*Mail*, 18 October).

Why the BBC feels the need to amplify, on a daily basis, propaganda (and not simply on the subject of the EU) posing as news stories in hyper-partisan newspapers, the vast bulk of which lean heavily to the right, is a question which it needs urgently to ask itself – not least given these newspapers' incessant onslaughts on the Corporation itself. And yet, in spite of the dominance of sources which were either frankly hostile to the EU or simply viewed it in a negative or sceptical light, the BBC Trust seemed to take the view that the Cardiff findings suggested that not enough of such voices had been heard, noting that in 2012:

> The low coverage given to UKIP on the sample of programmes that were the subject of the content analysis looks at odds with the levels of support the party was receiving in public opinion polls at this period, though the sample period was shortly before the 2013 local elections and the rise in UKIP coverage associated with those elections (op cit: 11).

(For an account of the Cardiff analysis by one of those actually responsible for carrying it out, one which paints a very different picture from that presented by the Trust, see Berry 2013.)

For and against immigration

A similar line was taken by the Trust with regard to the Cardiff analysis of coverage of immigration. This showed that 'while political sources were less prevalent in the immigration sample than in coverage of the UK's relationship with the EU, they still accounted for more than half of all sources in 2007, declining to two out of five in 2012' (op cit: 54). As a consequence:

> Stories on immigration frequently focused on political infighting over the management of immigration, as well as reactions to official government reports and statistics. However, our analysis demonstrates that though political sources once again strongly framed the debate, stories about immigration also occasionally gave voice to a broader and more diverse range of sources, including immigrants and asylum seekers, as well as members of the public (ibid: 53).

In the Cardiff researchers' view, sources for stories on this topic were carefully balanced, but in such a way as to present immigration 'primarily as a topic on which there were arguments for and against, rather than a broader range of views' (ibid: 59). Such stories tended to focus on specific cases rather than on how 'the larger story of how immigration may affect British society for better or worse. Just as in the case of the EU debate, the broader context, in terms of both information and opinions, has limited presence in the BBC programming we examined' (ibid: 63). However, the lesson which the Trust chose to draw from this part of the research was that:

> Whilst the choice of stories can never be expected to be chosen in proportion to public interest the Trust was interested to note that Cardiff University's research suggested that the number of stories on immigration did not appear to reflect the level of public concern on the issue, which has consistently appeared in the top five when people are asked by Ipsos MORI to name the most important issue facing the country. The BBC executive will wish to reflect on the nature and amount of its coverage on this subject (op cit: 10).

'A range of people and organisations'

The main questions raised, albeit in different ways, by the Bridcut report and the Cardiff research are: if a wider spectrum of views is to be represented across BBC output, how wide should that spectrum be, and to what extent should political views which fall outside the Westminster consensus be included? Although this is nowhere stated explicitly, these questions inform the independent assessment undertaken by Stuart Prebble for the Trust and included in its breadth of opinion review. Prebble explains that in order to compile his report he identified

> … a range of people and organisations operating within the subject areas which provide our focus – the EU, immigration, and religion and belief; people with a point of view who might not feel that their own or similar voices had been sufficiently represented on the airwaves. I would contact as wide a range of opinions as I reasonably could, and invite them to tell us whether they felt their views were represented appropriately, or under-represented, on the BBC. Then I would do what I could to investigate individual concerns (BBC Trust 2013: 25).

On the topic of immigration he argues that although mainstream politicians have been reluctant to raise the issue (a judgement with which many would strongly disagree), it is a subject of widespread concern within the community, so much so that 'only the economy is seen by the public to be a more significant issue'. However, he argues, 'despite the demonstrably high levels of popular concern, advocates of the need for a public debate on the subject have felt that the BBC has been hesitant in the past in raising it' (ibid: 27).

So, what range of people and organisations outside the BBC did Prebble contact to discuss immigration? Those quoted either directly or indirectly in his report are Sir Andrew Green and Alp Mehmet (both of Migration Watch), Robin Aiken (author of the book *Can We Trust the BBC?*), Rod Liddle, University of Lincoln academic and former BBC correspondent Barnie Choudhury (in the context of a controversial *Today* piece, commissioned by Liddle, on no-go areas for whites in Oldham), and Frank Field and Nicholas Soames (in their role as co-chairs of the Cross Party Group on Balanced Migration). Sir Andrew, according to Prebble, who mentions him no less than thirteen times, 'has struggled over many years … to get an appropriate hearing on the BBC' (ibid: 28). Yet we discover that in February 2005 Helen Boaden (Director, Radio, and until recently Director, BBC News) invited him to speak to BBC editors, and that he was invited again a year later by Boaden's then-Deputy, Stephen Mitchell, to address editors in BBC Radio (ibid: 29). Field and Soames, who are mentioned four times each, 'claim that their appearances, or indeed of anyone representing their point of view, are few in relation to the importance of the topic they are raising. When they or colleagues with the same views do appear, they claim, they are sometimes treated by the interviewer in a more combative fashion than are their opponents' (ibid: 29).

Muted voices

In other words, not a single figure from among the BBC's many critics who claim that BBC news programmes are far too prone to follow the anti-immigration agenda set daily by much of the press, and that the BBC should spend more time probing the *bona fides* of Migration Watch as a self-proclaimed independent and non-political body and less in giving it a platform for its far-from-disinterested views. Thus it is hardly surprising that Prebble ends up asking: 'Is it fair to say, as some of the BBC's critics do, that its coverage assumes a disposition sympathetic to immigration, and that it excludes from the airwaves a range of the voices which might oppose aspects of it?' (ibid: 32), when one could equally well ask if its coverage assumes a disposition unsympathetic to immigration, and if it excludes voices which are in favour of it. Such critics most certainly exist, but, particularly given the nature of the British press, their voices are considerably more muted than critics of the kind with which Prebble has concerned himself. Indeed, at one point Prebble himself lists a number of *Panorama* programmes which might well back up these critics' views: 'My Big Fat Fake Wedding' (sham weddings involving immigrants); 'Breaking into Britain' (routes followed by those trying to get into Britain); 'Britain's Child Beggars' (the exploitation of children by criminal gangs from Romania); 'Britain's Secret Health Tourists' (foreigners coming to Britain to use the NHS); 'Britain's Crimes of Honour' (so-called 'honour crimes').

Given the above list, even Prebble is forced to conclude that, 'taken in conjunction with other coverage of the subject on TV and radio, it seems difficult to sustain the charge that the BBC is suppressing voices critical of aspects of immigration into the UK' (ibid: 34). Nonetheless, he seems to be constantly at pains to suggest that such a charge is, indeed, sustainable.

'The full context'

Take, for example, his analysis of a *Today* piece by BBC Home Editor Mark Easton, which suggested that the phenomenon known as 'white flight' is not necessarily the result, as is habitually suggested by most newspapers, of white people moving out of neighbourhoods as non-white populations move in, but may also be explained in terms of working class aspiration and economic success. One of the participants in the item, Professor Danny Dorling, is described, entirely unnecessarily, as having been dubbed by Simon Jenkins as 'Geographer Royal by Appointment to the Left', and the presence of the former Labour MP Oona King as the other participant in the item calls forth the judgement that this was 'perhaps not a perfect example of balance between differing points of view, or of a range of opinions' (ibid: 37). But for Prebble, the main problem appears to be that, judging from comments on the BBC website, a section of the audience strongly disagreed with Easton's analysis. Another dissenter was the ubiquitous Sir Andrew Green, whose letter to Helen Boaden is quoted as 'expressing disappointment at the handling of this topic today which seemed to be blind to the real concerns of the public' (ibid). Prebble concludes that this episode 'underlines the need for BBC reporters to take even greater care than usual to anticipate potential responses and provide the full context when reporting on these sensitive areas' (ibid: 38).

However, it's by no means clear what is meant by the 'full context'. But perhaps a clue can be gleaned from a comment about other *Today* items on immigration, of which he remarks that 'if there is a criticism to be made, it is perhaps that the coverage is largely dry and clinical, and more about statistics and the performance of the official agencies, than it is about the impact of all this on the wider community' (ibid: 34). He continues:

> What may be missing from the *Today* coverage is much sense of what the impact of immigration is on the ground. In the period reviewed, the people mainly expressing concern about immigration levels are Sir Andrew Green from Migration Watch, Jon Cruddas (Labour MP for Dagenham and Rainham) and Peter Lilley (Conservative MP for Hitchin and Harpenden). Given its importance as an issue to the country at large, perhaps *Today*'s reporters might have been used more extensively not just to illustrate and enliven but to examine and underpin the stories. Longer pieces about pressure on services, on land, on cultural stresses and changes would also create their own, off-diary, stories, allowing the programme to rely less on following the newspaper or newsgathering diary agenda (ibid: 35).

Prebble does not actually use that patronising phrase 'ordinary people', but the gist of his argument does appear to be that the BBC should air more of their views on why immigration is such a bad thing. However, anyone looking at the comments under immigration stories on the BBC website will see that these views are present in such abundance, and with such vehemence, that it might be mistaken for the BNP website. Indeed, it could be argued that, rather than seeking out more anti-immigration views (not exactly a difficult job) to put on air, the BBC would be better employed moderating the comments on its website – not as an exercise in censorship but in the kind responsible editorial judgement to be expected of a public service broadcaster.

Knowledge and belief

The real problem here for the BBC is that every single reliable piece of research which has been carried out in the UK into public perceptions of issues related to immigration shows a lamentable degree of ignorance about the subject. For example, in its end of year review for 2013, Ipsos MORI found that respondents calculated that black and Asian people made up 30 per cent of the population, whilst the actual figure is 11 per cent, whilst the proportion of the population who are Muslims was thought to be 24 per cent as opposed to 5 per cent (see http://www.slideshare.net/IpsosMORI/ipsos-mori-great-britain-the-way-we-live-now). Given the prevalence of such beliefs, it is hardly surprising that many people do indeed blame stresses on local services and shortages of housing on what they call 'immigrants' (many of whom were actually born here). However, even though such an 'explanation' is reinforced on a daily basis by most of the national press, that doesn't make it any the more valid, nor does it detract from the fact that far more plausible culprits are savage cuts in local authority spending and regressive housing and land policies (all of which are vociferously supported by most of the national press). So, the question for the BBC is: should the fact that a particular point of view, however ill-informed, is widely held, guarantee it a place on the spectrum of views regularly represented across BBC output?

'An impressively wide range of programming'

Prebble follows a similar line on Britain and the EU, noting that the dominance of mainstream political sources 'meant that there were fewer opportunities for non-party political opinions to be expressed' (op cit: 41). As a consequence:

> Those in favour of a vigorous debate on the subject of British withdrawal from the EU believe that the BBC, in the past at least, has not given it the coverage it merits. Such debate as there has been, they claim, has been weighted to discussion between those who generally agree that the UK should remain in the EU, albeit with renegotiated terms. The 'withdrawalist' tendency has, it is claimed, had more popular support within the country than has been reflected either by politicians, or in the news (ibid).

However, when Prebble himself goes on to produce a list of BBC programmes in order to point to the 'impressively wide range of programming in which it has examined the EU from different angles' (ibid: 45), those he cites all fit into the problem/threat category identified by the Cardiff research, whilst several have a distinctly Eurosceptic tinge. The list includes television programmes in which Robert Peston 'examined the costs of the dream of monetary union'; 'self-confessed "confirmed Eurosceptic"' Michael Portillo went to Greece and interviewed 'a very broad range of local opinion and which questioned the survival of the EU'; John Humphrys interviewed 'a wide variety of Greek voices'; Andrew Neil questioned Britain's application of European human rights laws; and *Panorama* looked at whether the EU's vast farm subsidy system was working, broadly concluding that it was not doing so, at least as far as Britain was concerned – the programme's introduction asking: 'Why are we paying out millions of pounds in public money and asking for virtually nothing in return?' Meanwhile Radio 4 programmes included a *File on 4* which examined the cost of the EU; *The EU Debate*, in which former UK Permanent Representative to the EU Sir Stephen Wall 'faced the arguments of four persuasive Eurosceptics'; an edition of *Analysis* entitled 'Eurogeddon'; a programme which asked how widespread Euroscepticism was in the Labour Party; and *This Eurosceptic Isle*, which examined the reasons for the rise in British Euroscepticism (ibid: 45).

Specifically with regard to UKIP, he notes that in 2012, *Today* sent Evan Davis to the UKIP conference in Birmingham and carried 'an unusually long package', in which he interviewed a 'healthy mix of conference attendees' (ibid). UKIP representatives appeared on *Question Time* five times in the six months from October 2012 and twice on *Any Questions?* EU budget negotiations, increasingly strident calls for an in/out referendum in the UK, and the Eurozone crisis, put the EU high up the news agenda in the final months of 2012, and Nigel Farage was back on *Question Time* in January 2013. After that, as Prebble correctly observes, 'coverage of the Eastleigh by-election in February and of May's local elections led to a noticeable increase in UKIP appearances' (ibid: 46).

It's thus extremely hard not to read Prebble on the subject of the BBC and the EU without coming to the conclusion that anti-EU voices actually receive an extremely fair (some might say distinctly over-generous) hearing on the BBC. These are not simply 'Eurosceptic' voices from the two largest Westminster parties, but, as noted above, 'withdrawalist' voices from UKIP, which currently has no MPs at all. Now, if one agrees with Bridcut and Prebble that political voices on the BBC should not be confined to those of the main Westminster parties, then this is not in itself problematic. But it does immediately raise the question of why, among the minority parties, UKIP should be singled out for special treatment.

Party political imbalance

For example, why should not the Green Party be treated equally generously? This has one member in the Commons, one in the Lords, and two in the European Parliament. At the 2010 General Election it polled 265,187 votes (0.96

per cent of the total), and at the European Parliament Elections in 2009 it secured 1,223,303 votes (8.7 per cent of the total). Meanwhile UKIP has no members in the Commons, three in the Lords, and nine in the European Parliament. At the 2010 General Election it polled 919,471 votes (3.1 per cent of the total) and at the European Parliament Elections in 2009 it secured 2,498,226 votes (16.5 per cent of the total). In terms of local authorities, UKIP holds 135 seats on County Councils and the Green Party 19; the figures for Unitary Authorities are UKIP 23 and the Green Party 35; for the London Borough Councils UKIP 11 and the Green Party two; for the Metropolitan Borough Councils UKIP four and the Green Party 21; for the District Councils UKIP 44 and the Green Party 62; for the Scottish Unitary Authorities UKIP none and the Green Party 14; and the Welsh Unitary Authorities UKIP two and the Green Party none. Overall, at local level, UKIP have 219 seats and the Green Party 153 (see http://www.gwydir.demon.co.uk/uklocalgov/makeup.htm).

By this token, the Green Party should be sourced almost as frequently as UKIP by the BBC, but this manifestly is not the case. In its defence, the BBC might argue that UKIP's policies are of greater popular concern than those of the Green Party, but this could be at least partly because the BBC has given a great deal more space to UKIP than to the Green Party.

The knowledge gap

Furthermore, if the BBC really is determined to give yet more space to the 'withdrawalist' perspective, it will need, as in the case of the anti-immigration views discussed above, to come up with a very convincing answer to the question raised by what, for the sake of politeness, we will call the knowledge gap regarding the EU. According to *Eurobarometer 75* (Spring 2011), of all the members of the EU, the British are the most ignorant about it. In 15 of the 27 EU Member States a majority claim to understand its nature and workings. In the UK, 58 per cent of respondents claim not to understand how it works, representing, along with Malta, the highest level of ignorance in the EU. Two-thirds of Europeans know that the EU consists of 27 members. With the sole exception of the UK, at 48 per cent, an absolute majority in each of the EU countries calculated the number of member states correctly. 62 per cent of Europeans think of themselves as citizens of the EU. This is a minority opinion in only four states, the UK, Greece, Bulgaria and Latvia, with the UK scoring lowest at 41 per cent. Hand in hand with ignorance of the EU goes hostility to it. In 22 of the EU's 27 members, a majority believe that EU membership is beneficial. In the UK this is a minority view, since only 35 per cent of those questioned thought it was beneficial, whilst 54 per cent took the opposite view. 40 per cent of Europeans state that they have a positive image of the EU. The percentage of positive opinions is equal to or above the EU average in 13 member states, and below the average in fourteen states, especially the UK at 22 per cent. In the EU as a whole, 41 per cent state that they tend to trust the EU whilst 47 per cent express distrust. In the UK the corresponding figures are 24 per cent and 63 per cent (see http://ec.europa.eu/public_opinion/archives/eb/eb75/eb75_publ_en.pdf).

Now, rather than inviting yet more Europhobes on to the airways, the BBC should seriously ponder its own contribution to this knowledge vacuum. As a start, it should ban locutions such as the following, which are absolutely habitual across its services: 'Talking on *The Andrew Marr Show*, Mr Cable agreed with Liberal Democrat leader and Deputy Prime Minister Nick Clegg that a proposed cap of 75,000 people coming to the UK from the EU would not work' (see http://www.bbc.co.uk/news/uk-politics-25484056). This should of course read 'coming to the UK from *elsewhere* in the EU', but this infuriating semantic tic in BBC stories about the EU serves only to reinforce the profoundly mistaken belief (see above) that the EU is some kind of alien imposition upon the UK rather than an organisation of which the UK is a member. No doubt there are those British (or rather English) people who believe that they are not European in any sense at all, but since such a belief flies firmly in the face of at least two millennia of history and culture, there is no more reason to give it airtime (other than to interrogate it) than regularly to air the views of those who believe that the earth is flat and that the sun revolves around it.

A matter of opinion

The real question for the BBC here is whether it should be giving space to a wide range of informed views, or to ill-informed views which happen to be held by a significant number of people and are amplified daily by ideologically-driven newspapers. In this respect it should be noted that, in response to Professor Steve Jones' assessment of the accuracy and impartiality of BBC science coverage, the BBC Trust agreed that 'programme makers must make a distinction between well-established fact and opinion in science coverage and ensure the distinction is clear to the audience' (BBC Trust 2011: 3) and that 'there should be no attempt to give equal weight to opinion and to evidence' (ibid: 7). Or as Jones himself put it:

> Equality of voice calls for a match of scientists not with politicians or activists, but with those qualified to take a knowledgeable, albeit perhaps divergent, view of research. Attempts to give a place to anyone, however unqualified, who claims interest can make for false balance: to free publicity to marginal opinions and not to impartiality, but its opposite (ibid: 16).

There is surely every reason to apply such an approach to any other topic in which the actual facts of the case contradict mere opinion. After all, if one wants to hear the latter one simply has to go to the pub, pick up a newspaper or get on a bus – not pay a licence fee,

Searching the liberal soul

It's very hard to read Prebble's report and the Trust's remarks about both it and the Cardiff analysis without sensing a pre-emptive defensiveness about the liberal values which the BBC's numerous and vociferous enemies on the right never lose any opportunity to excoriate. These values aren't mentioned specifically but are certainly implied in Prebble's remark that '"people like us" work from an assumed consensus, which can have the effect of narrowing debate, and prevent us from gaining a real understanding of points of view we do not share' (op cit: 62), and by the Trust's conclusion that 'we should guard against "group think" by asking ourselves whether we are including the widest possible range of voices and views, and by challenging our own assumptions about the shared consensus within which these debates should be conducted' (op cit: 66).

But buried deep within all this searching of the liberal soul is actually a very simple and sensible proposition stated *en passant* by Prebble, namely that 'perhaps it is not too paternalistic or patronising to conclude that it is the BBC's job to inform the public of what they need to know in a democracy, whether they like it or not' (op cit: 41). Indeed, and it's what any rational person should expect from the BBC, as do those members of migrant communities interviewed for the audience research part of the Trust's project who stated that they wanted…

> … the public debate in 'flagship media' such as the BBC to move on from perception and possibly prejudiced emotional 'opinion' towards a real debate based on statistics and facts. These groups, particularly Muslim Asians, said that they regarded factual-based debate as their best defence in the dispelling of myths. They saw the role of the BBC as being to help everyone move towards a much fuller understanding of this controversial issue (op cit: 32).

Exactly the same should be true of any other issue with which the BBC deals.

Conclusions: Journalism and the Enlightenment project

If journalism is a modern-day expression of the Enlightenment project, and if the core purpose of that project is rational enquiry in order to explain the society and, indeed, the world in which we live, then the values which journalism must surely embrace are those of objectivity, impartiality, accuracy, truthfulness, and scepticism – particularly towards received opinion and 'common-sense' explanations of social reality. These are liberal values, but they are more a matter of methodology than of ideology, which is why it's perfectly possible to be a Conservative or a socialist journalist and to embrace these values wholeheartedly.

But the problem for the BBC is that it exists in a culture in which these values have been wholly abandoned (if indeed they were ever embraced in the first place) by the vast bulk of the national press. To most of Britain's newspapers, in which the distinction between news and views has collapsed, readers are told what editors think they want to hear, 'flat earth news' predominates, and the ideological compass points to the extreme right wing of the Tory party (and now, in some cases, straight towards UKIP), the BBC's journalistic values must indeed seem anomalous. In truth, though, it is Britain's national press which is the anomaly when judged in 'normal' (that is, Western European and North American) journalistic terms – indeed, it would not be an exaggeration to call it an aberration. It would be an absolute catastrophe for democratic debate in this country if pressure from this quarter, hideously tainted as it is, were to tempt the BBC to follow such a deviant journalistic path.

References

BBC Trust (2007) *From Seesaw to Wagon Wheel: Safeguarding Impartiality in the 21st Century*, London: BBC. Available online at http://www.bbc.co.uk/bbctrust/our_work/editorial_standards/impartiality/safeguardin g_impartiality.html, accessed on 27 December 2013

BBC Trust (2011) *BBC Trust Review of Impartiality and Accuracy of the BBC's Coverage of Science*, London: BBC. Available online at http://www.bbc.co.uk/bbctrust/our_work/editorial_standards/impartiality/science_im partiality.html, accessed on 27 December 2013

BBC Trust (2013) *A BBC Trust Review of the Breadth of Opinion Reflected in the BBC's Output*, London: BBC. Available online at http://www.bbc.co.uk/bbctrust/our_work/editorial_standards/impartiality/breadth_o pinion.html, accessed on 27 December 2013

Berry, Mike (2013), Hard evidence: How biased is the BBC? The Conversation, 23 August. Available online at http://theconversation.com/hard-evidence-how-biased-is-the-bbc-17028, accessed on 27 December 2013

Wahl-Jorgensen, Karin et al (2013) *BBC Breadth of Opinion Review: Content Analysis*, University of Cardiff: Cardiff School of Journalism, Media and Cultural Studies. Available online at http://www.bbc.co.uk/bbctrust/our_work/editorial_standards/impartiality/breadth_o pinion.html, accessed on 27 December 2013

Note on the contributor

Julian Petley is Professor of Screen Media in the School of Arts at Brunel University, Chair of the Campaign for Press and Broadcasting Freedom and a member of the advisory board of *Index on Censorship* and of the editorial board of the *British Journalism Review*. His most recent book is the edited collection *The Media and Public Shaming* (I. B. Tauris, 2013).

BBC in crisis: 'The Westminster conspiracy'

David Edwards and David Cromwell argue that the BBC cannot be trusted to be impartial on anything that matters

The BBC is part of a high-level 'conspiracy' obstructing radical changes needed to reform a UK democracy that is manifestly failing. More to the point, it is part of 'the Westminster conspiracy', with senior BBC managers, trustees and government cabinet ministers working together to keep fundamental change off the BBC's agenda. They 'don't want anything to change' for a simple reason: 'It's not in their interests.'

We do not ordinarily resort to conspiracy theories to explain media performance and, originating from us, the above comments would be dismissed as 'loony left' myth-making. But, in fact, these are the opinions of none other than former BBC Director-General Greg Dyke as published on the BBC's own website in 2009 (Wheeler 2009). Dyke commented:

> I tried and failed to get the problem properly discussed when I was at the BBC and I was stopped, interestingly, by a combination of the politicos on the board of governors, one of whom was married to the man who claimed for cleaning his moat, the cabinet interestingly – the Labour cabinet – who decided to have a meeting, only about what we were trying to discuss, and the political journalists at the BBC.

He added:

> A lot of the governors were what I call semi-politicians and they liked the present system and ... maybe they were right – it's not the job of the BBC to change the political system and to start questioning the political system. I happen to not agree with that but, you know, we didn't get anywhere (ibid).

If we care about genuine freedom of speech, then Dyke's claims certainly do point to a grave crisis at the BBC – one simultaneously threatening both UK

134

democracy and press freedom. It is particularly disturbing that Dyke highlighted the role of 'the political journalists at the BBC' in obstructing his attempts to challenge the *status quo*. In fact, these journalists are watchdogs for the *establishment*, not the people, as Dyke explained:

> In the end political journalists live in the same narrow world as politicians do and they don't see a need to change because they think it's the world. They just don't understand that out there it's very different (ibid).

Since the 2004 Hutton Report (into the events surrounding the death of weapons inspector Dr David Kelly) and Dyke's departure soon afterwards along with BBC chairman Gavyn Davies, further disasters have engulfed the Corporation. In November 2012, having earlier dropped a report on claims of sexual abuse against the late BBC DJ and television presenter Jimmy Savile, the BBC's flagship *Newsnight* programme wrongly implicated Tory peer Lord McAlpine in child abuse. As a result, Director-General George Entwistle 'stepped down' after just 54 days in the job. The BBC's head of news, Helen Boaden, was also 'asked' to 'step aside'. Peter Rippon, the *Newsnight* editor responsible for the Savile decision, had already 'stepped aside'.

Newsnight's journalistic 'failures' on child abuse were, indeed, appalling. But there was no comparable pressure for senior staff to resign over the BBC's far more catastrophic refusal to challenge the US-UK governments' propaganda campaign before the 2003 Iraq war. BBC performance helped facilitate an attack on Iraq at a cost of perhaps one million lives (Patrick 2013). This pro-establishment bias was, and is, absolutely standard. As BBC founder Lord Reith noted in his diary of the government, and as Dyke surely understands: 'They know they can trust us not to be really impartial' (Robinson 2012: 556).

In their highly respected study of the British media, *Power Without Responsibility*, James Curran and Jean Seaton wrote of 'the continuous and insidious dependence of the Corporation [the BBC] on the government' (Curran and Seaton 1991: 144). The inevitable, and entirely taboo, reality is that the BBC can be trusted 'not to be really impartial' on everything that matters.

The claim can be tested easily enough against the performances of even the BBC's most highly-rated journalists. Consider, for example, much-vaunted *Newsnight* anchor Jeremy Paxman's confession on Iraq in 2009:

> As far as I personally was concerned, there came a point with the presentation of the so-called evidence, with the moment when Colin Powell sat down at the UN General Assembly and unveiled what he said was cast-iron evidence of things like mobile, biological weapon facilities and the like ...When I saw all of that, I thought, well, 'We know that Colin Powell is an intelligent, thoughtful man, and a sceptical man. If he believes all this to be the case, then, you know, he's seen the evidence; I haven't.' Now that evidence turned out to be absolutely meaningless, but we only

discover that after the event. So, you know, I'm perfectly open to the accusation that we were hoodwinked. Yes, clearly we were (Paxman 2009).

Government submission of evidence *ought* to mark the point where serious journalism begins rather than ends. Paxman would have us believe that this is also his view. He commented of the BBC's purpose:

My own view is that it's to do to the best of its ability the ordinary business of journalism – which is finding things out and telling it as straight as you can tell it … I'd plea for an unwillingness to believe what you're told. It seems to me you want to have an instinctive distrust of powerful vested interests (ibid).

The difference between what Paxman *does* and what he *claims* to do is emblematic of the gulf separating the public relations image from reality at the BBC. It is not true that Powell's evidence on Iraq was revealed to be 'absolutely meaningless' only 'after the event'. In fact, it was *immediately* evident. Scott Ritter – who had been exposing US-UK claims on Iraq for several years – immediately responded to Powell's claims: 'He just hits you, hits you, hits you with circumstantial evidence, and he confuses people – and he lied, he lied to people, he misled people' (Ritter 2003).

Sadly, Paxman's touchingly naive response is the norm at the BBC. His high-profile colleague on *Newsnight*, Mark Urban, referred to 'President Bush's grand design of toppling a dictator and forcing a democracy into the heart of the Middle East' (Urban 2005). On the 21 February 2005 edition of *Newsnight*, Matt Frei described 'a war [in Iraq] fought primarily not to defend America, but to create democracy in a distant land' (Frei 2005). BBC reporter Paul Wood commented on the BBC's *News at Ten*: 'The coalition came to Iraq in the first place to bring democracy and human rights' (Wood 2005).

The same propaganda version of reality prevails at Radio Five Live, where a phone-in asked: 'Are 100 British soldiers' lives too high a price to pay for democracy in Iraq?' (Radio Five Live 2006). Rarely, if ever, did BBC journalists give the impression that anything illegal was happening in Iraq. Certainly, there was no sense that a truly historic war crime was underway. As US tanks blasted their way into Baghdad on 9 April 2003, the BBC's *Breakfast News* presenter, Natasha Kaplinsky, beamed as she described how Tony Blair 'has become, again, Teflon Tony' (Kaplinsky 2003). The BBC's royal and diplomatic correspondent, Nicholas Witchell, agreed: 'It is absolutely, without a doubt, a vindication of the strategy' (Witchell 2003).

On the same day, political editor, Andrew Marr, addressed a national audience on prime-time TV from Downing Street: 'Frankly, the main mood [here] is of unbridled relief. I've been watching ministers wander around with smiles like split watermelons' (Marr 2003). Marr added:

Mr Blair is well aware that all his critics out there in the party and beyond aren't going to thank him – because they're only human – for being right when they've been wrong. And he knows that there might be trouble ahead, as I said. But I think this is very, very important for him. It gives him a new freedom and a new self-confidence … He said that they would be able to take Baghdad without a bloodbath, and that in the end the Iraqis would be celebrating. And on both of those points he has been proved conclusively right. And it would be entirely ungracious, even for his critics, not to acknowledge that tonight he stands as a larger man and a stronger prime minister as a result (ibid).

On his Sunday morning television show of 25 September 2005, Marr observed: '25,000 civilians have died in Iraq over the last two years.' He continued: 'About a third of those people were killed, *no doubt in absolutely legitimate operations*, by British and American soldiers' (Marr 2005, our emphasis). Like Paxman, Marr talks a good fight when it comes to selling himself as a fiercely independent journalist: 'When I joined the BBC, my Organs of Opinion were formally removed' (Marr 2000).

A 2003 Cardiff University report found that the BBC 'displayed the most "pro-war" agenda of any broadcaster' on the Iraq invasion. Over the three weeks of the initial conflict, 11 per cent of the sources quoted by the BBC were of coalition government or military origin, the highest proportion of all the main television broadcasters. The BBC was less likely than Sky, ITV or Channel 4 News to use independent sources, which tended to be the most sceptical. David Miller, of Strathclyde University and co-founder of Spinwatch, concluded: 'BBC managers have fallen over themselves to grovel to the government in the aftermath of the Hutton whitewash ... When will their bosses apologise for conspiring to keep the anti war movement off the screens?' (Miller 2004).

John Humphrys' 'moral glow'

If, like Paxman, we are tempted to treat the coverage of Iraq as an unfortunate one-off, as a 'failure', we can pick almost literally any other topic to discover essentially the same performance. In 2011, a report by the BBC's deputy political editor, James Landale, on Nato's Libya 'intervention' resonated with uncanny echoes of Marr's memorable performance eight years earlier:

> But all that caution has been matched by some satisfaction and optimism. Satisfaction that all David Cameron's critics, who said that this couldn't be done – that aerial bombardment would not work – have been proved *wrong*. And also a sense of optimism that, *if* the diplomacy works, if the TNC [the 'rebel' Transitional National Council] do as they have promised, it's just possible this *could* end the right way. And if it *does*, that would be an achievement this administration [thumb jabbing over shoulder at the door of Number 10] would claim some credit for (Landale 2011).

In October 2011, the BBC's Political Editor Nick Robinson waxed lyrical: 'Libya was David Cameron's first war. Colonel Gaddafi his first foe. Today, his first real taste of military victory' (Robinson 2011). In an interview with the UK

Defence Secretary Philip Hammond, John Humphrys asked of Libya: 'What apart from a sort of moral glow – and there's nothing wrong with that – have we got out of it?' (Humphrys 2011). The BBC's Chief Political Correspondent, Norman Smith, commented: 'I imagine, privately, David Cameron must surely feel vindicated because the Libyan enterprise was a big political risk' (Smith 2011).

These celebrations of Cameron's war crime in Libya – the brazen abuse of UN resolution 1973 in pursuit of the entirely illegal goal of regime change – was offered as Libya rapidly sank into militia-run chaos. A UN report in October 2013 found: 'Torture and brutality are rife in Libyan prisons two years after the overthrow of leader Muammar Gaddafi.' Around 8,000 prisoners were being held without trial in government jails on suspicion of having fought for Gaddafi (Evans 2013). In the aftermath of Nato's 'humanitarian intervention', torture, bombings and assassinations are now par for the course in Libya (see: Interventions Watch 2013).

In similar vein, following yet more unsubstantiated claims of possible Syrian government use of chemical weapons, a front-page BBC report read: 'World "must act" over Syria weapons' (BBC website 2013a). And yet a BBC article indicated the lack of certainty: 'There is no doubt Syria's government has used sarin during the country's crisis, says France's foreign minister ... But he did not specify where or when the agent had been deployed; the White House has said more proof was needed' (BBC website 2013b). A UK government statement observed merely: 'There is a growing body of limited but persuasive information showing that the regime used – and continues to use – chemical weapons.' Readers will recall that intelligence indicating the existence of Iraqi WMD was also said to have been 'limited but persuasive'.

BBC performance on Syria may have exceeded even its coverage of Iraq in 2002-2003 in selling the US-UK case for war, with endlessly hyped atrocity stories inevitably blaming the Syrian government, supplied by the tinpot Syrian Observatory for Human Rights based in Coventry: 'an unlikely home to prominent Syria activist', as Reuters (2011) observed. The warmongering BBC bias on Syria has been so extreme that even 'mainstream' commentators have noticed. Peter Hitchens wrote in the *Daily Mail* that UK government policy was being 'disgracefully egged on by a BBC that has lost all sense of impartiality' (Hitchens 2013).

In September 2013, John Humphrys told listeners on the BBC's *Today* programme that 'there will be high-level meetings to find ways of Iran giving up its nuclear weapons programme in exchange for sanctions being dropped'. Peter Oborne (2013) responded in the *Daily Telegraph*: 'Unfortunately for Humphrys, Iran does not have a nuclear weapons programme, and US intelligence knows this even if he doesn't. It regularly briefs Congress that Iran has no Iranian nuclear weapons programme. It is incredible that a senior BBC broadcaster should make this mistake ...' Oborne continued: 'I have rarely heard such ignorant or biased broadcasting.'

Head of BBC News balance – 'I am pro-Israel'

The role of BBC News as handmaiden to power is exemplified by its reporting on Israel's assaults on Gaza. On the first day of Israel's Operation Pillar of Cloud (14 November 2012), thirteen Palestinians, including three children, were reportedly killed, and about 100 wounded. Israeli forces succeeded in their objective of 'assassinating' Hamas military chief Ahmed al-Jabari in a clear act of extrajudicial state murder. By 16 November, Israel was reported to have bombed 150 sites in Gaza the previous night, with 450 attacks in total. And yet the main BBC headline that morning read: 'Egypt PM arrives for Gaza mission.' We can perhaps imagine a rather different headline, if 450 targets had just been hit by high-tech bombs, missiles and artillery in Tel Aviv. The BBC reported the Israeli attacks as 'retaliation' for Palestinian 'militant rocket attacks' on southern Israel. In a study of news performance in 2001, the Glasgow Media Group (2001) noted that Israelis 'were six times as likely to be presented as "retaliating" or in some way responding than were the Palestinians' in media reports. A BBC correspondent in Gaza said 'there are now fears now (sic) of a major escalation of violence'. But the Israeli execution of Ahmed al-Jabari was itself a *major* escalation of violence.

Another safe pair of hands was found to replace Helen Boaden as head of BBC News. James Harding (2011), formerly Editor of the Rupert Murdoch-owned *Times*, had earlier stated: 'I am pro-Israel.' He added: 'I haven't found it too hard' reporting on the Middle East under Murdoch because '*The Times* has been pro-Israel for a long time.' Amena Saleem (2013), of Palestine Solidarity Campaign, noted that another new senior BBC appointee, former Labour MP James Purnell, who became Director of Strategy and Digital, is also avowedly pro-Israel and served as Chair of the pro-Israeli parliamentary lobby group Labour Friends of Israel from 2002-2004.

Saleem argued that the BBC 'gave up all claims to impartiality when it spectacularly pulled from its schedule a documentary questioning the scale of the Jewish exodus from Jerusalem nearly 2,000 years ago – the exodus on which Zionists base the Jewish "right to return" and to colonise what was once Palestine'. The documentary, scheduled to appear as part of a BBC Four series on archaeology, was dropped at the eleventh hour. When questioned about this late and dramatic development, a BBC email explained: 'We have decided that it doesn't fit editorially and are no longer planning to show it as part of the season.' But, added Saleem: 'Ilan Ziv, the Israeli-born documentary maker who made the hour-long film, has said that the official reason given by the BBC for pulling the documentary contradicts the reasons given to him in private.' Ziv (2013) summed up: 'This is ultimately a sad saga of what I believe is a mixture of incompetence, political naiveté [and] conscious or subconscious political pressure.' Tim Llewellyn, the BBC's former Middle East Correspondent, told Saleem:

The BBC is now culturally and socially stuck in the Zionist frame. Whether this is fear of the Zionist lobby and its many friends in the three British political parties, sheer inbuilt prejudice, ignorance of the facts, history and nuances that every reporter, producer and editor should by now know, I am not sure. I suspect a combination of all three (ibid).

Professor Greg Philo, of the Glasgow University Media Group, related a discussion he had with senior producers on television news, including the BBC, one of whom said to him candidly (Pilger 2010): 'We wait in fear for the telephone call from the Israelis.'

Climate change

Inevitably, the BBC's establishment bias is also reflected in its extremely poor coverage of climate change. According to former BBC correspondent and editor Mark Brayne, who was privy to internal editorial discussions in 2010, the BBC has 'explicitly parked climate change in the category "Done That Already, Nothing New to Say"' (Romm 2010). Brayne added:

On climate change, that BBC journalistic urgency to be *seen* to be fair now means, after a period between Al Gore's Inconvenient Truth and the disaster of [the 2009 UN Climate Summit in] Copenhagen when global warming was everywhere in the output, that the Corporation has been bending over backwards to reflect the opposite, sceptical view.

Consider the analogy of two men at a bar, says Brayne. One man claims that two plus two equals four, and the other that two plus two equals six. The BBC solution to this disagreement? 'Put them both on the *Today* programme, and the answer clearly lies somewhere in the middle.' *Today*, BBC Radio 4's 'agenda-setting' morning programme, is a serial offender when it comes to irresponsible climate coverage. On 13 July 2013, John Humphrys interviewed Ralph Cicerone, president of the US National Academy of Sciences. Humphrys commented:

But to say nearly every spot on the globe has warmed significantly over the past 30 years and indeed the entire planet is warming is different from saying it's going to continue to warm to such an extent that we have to spend vast and unimaginable amounts of money to protect ourselves against a catastrophe that many people, some distinguished scientists say, isn't actually proven.

Cicerone replied: 'Well, of course, the way you've worded it, it was quite strong; "vast and unimaginable sums of money", I don't think I've heard anybody make such a proposal.' Moments later, Humphrys said: 'You can't absolutely prove that CO_2 in the atmosphere is responsible for global warming.' As climate writers Christian Hunt and Ros Donald put it politely (Hunt and Donald 2012): 'If the *Today* programme brought this level of research and preparation to interviewing politicians, it probably wouldn't be taken particularly seriously.'

Meanwhile, BBC News has supplied a long stream of articles and broadcasts about Britain's 'dreadful weather' and how it has, for example, 'cost rural Britain £1bn' (Heap 2012) in lost income. But readers and viewers will be hard pressed to find any links drawn between these extreme events and human-induced global warming. In an article entitled, 'Whatever happened to climate change?' Paul Vallely (2013) wrote in the *Independent on Sunday*:

> BBC news outlets – normally a voice of sanity on science – are paralysed by their adversarial paradigm of giving 'equal space' to both sides. Faced with the prospect of having to give climate change deniers the same airtime as the 97 per cent scientific consensus the BBC has largely descended into silence on the issue. The BBC has a bigger responsibility than balance here.

The BBC's culture of fear

It is important to remember that media corporations, including the BBC, are closer to unaccountable, totalitarian tyrannies, with power flowing strictly top-down, than they are to democracies. Employees may contribute ideas, but power flows from the top. Journalists are expected to be 'team players', 'focused' and 'disciplined' – code words that refer to the need to remain focused on 'pragmatic', bottom line goals. To attempt to take a moral stance in this environment is difficult; it risks raising issues that are deeply threatening to senior management. An article in *Press Gazette* (Ponsford 2013) notes a 'strong undercurrent of fear' amongst BBC employees. A survey of BBC staff, commissioned in the wake of the Jimmy Savile sex abuse scandal, had raised 'alarm bells about bullying and a culture of fear about speaking out'. The authors of the survey report said:

> Throughout our conversations we heard a strong undercurrent of fear; fear of speaking out, fear of reprisal, fear of losing your job, being made redundant, fear of becoming a victim, fear of getting a reputation as a troublemaker and not getting promoted if an employee, or further work if a freelancer, supplier or contractor.

Jenni Russell (2012), a former BBC editor, commented:

> Nothing makes the BBC as nervous as the prospect of its own journalists inquiring into its behaviour. It is the one moment the BBC's otherwise admirable system of editorial independence often breaks down. No one in the organisation is ever unaware of the possible damage to the BBC's brand when news starts asking critical questions of the BBC itself. The corporate centre's instinctive response is to block and discourage criticism, and any ambitious editors and executives in news are constantly aware of that.

And she continued:

In theory the BBC believes in the freedom of its journalists to inquire into itself; in practice, as I found in eight years of being an editor in current affairs there, the organisation is astoundingly defensive whenever it is challenged. Trying to get a reaction out of senior executives either in news or the corporate centre always sent it into hedgehog mode, making it bristling, fearful and unresponsive.

Is it any wonder that the term 'Orwellian' appears ever more appropriate to describe the UK's 'best' news organisation?

References

BBC (2013a) World 'must act' over Syria weapons, 5 June. Available online at http://www.medialens.org/images/stories/alerts_images/bbc-propaganda-world-must-act-over-syria.png, accessed on 26 November 2013

BBC (2013b) France's Fabius 'confirms sarin use' by Syria regime, 5 June. Available online at http://www.bbc.co.uk/news/world-middle-east-22773268, accessed on 26 November, 2013

Curran, James and Seaton, Jean (1991) *Power Without Responsibility: The Press and Broadcasting in Britain*, London: Routledge, fourth edition

Evans, Robert (2013) Torture rife in Libya's jails two years after Gaddafi: UN, Reuters, 1 October. Available online at http://www.reuters.com/article/2013/10/01/us-libya-torture-idUSBRE99012J20131001, accessed on 26 November, 2013

Frei, Matt (2005) BBC *Newsnight*, 21 February

Glasgow Media Group (2001) Bad News from Israel. Available online at http://www.glasgowmediagroup.org/content/view/4, accessed on 26 November 2013

Harding, James (2011) Cited in *The Times*, Editor urges BBC to 'learn to apologise', Westminster News Online, 5 April. Available online at http://www.wnol.info/the-times-editor-urges-the-bbc-to-%E2%80%9Clearn-to-apologise%E2%80%9D/, accessed on 26 November 2013

Heap, Tom (2012) Weather 'cost rural Britain £1bn', BBC News online, 9 September. Available online at http://www.bbc.co.uk/news/science-environment-19521845, accessed on 26 November 2013

Hitchens, Peter (2013) We set Syria ablaze: Now we're hurling in explosives, *Daily Mail*, 2 June. Available online at http://www.dailymail.co.uk/debate/article-2334411/PETER-HITCHENS-We-set-Syria-ablaze--Now-hurling-explosives.html, accessed on 1 December 2013

Humphrys, John (2011) BBC Radio 4 *Today*, 21 October

Humphrys, John (2013) email to Ian Sinclair, 27 September

Hunt, Christian and Donald, Ros (2012) 'You can't absolutely prove, can you, that CO_2 is responsible for global warming?' The *Today* programme out of its depth on climate science, The Carbon Brief blog, 13 July. Available online at http://www.carbonbrief.org/blog/2012/07/the-today-programmes-ill-researched-climate-change-interview, accessed on 26 November 2013

Interventions Watch (2013) Some headlines from the *Libya Herald*, 24 July. Available online at http://interventionswatch.wordpress.com/2013/07/24/some-headlines-from-the-libya-herald/, accessed on 26 November, 2013

Kaplinsky, Natasha (2003) BBC *Breakfast News*, 9 April

Landale, James (2011) BBC 1 *News at Six*, 22 August

Marr, Andrew (2000) Andrew Marr, the BBC's political editor, *Independent*, 13 January

Marr, Andrew (2003), BBC 1, *News At Ten*, 9 April. Available online at https://www.youtube.com/watch?v=5_JC371jxPI, accessed on 26 November, 2013

Marr, Andrew (2005) *Breakfast*, BBC1, 25 September

Miller, David (2004) Media apologies?, ZNet, 15 June. Available online at http://www.zcommunications.org/media-apologies-by-david-miller.html, accessed on 1 December 2013

Oborne, Peter (2013) John Humphrys' ignorance about Iran is par for the course in all Western media, *Daily Telegraph* blogs, 26 September. Available online at http://blogs.telegraph.co.uk/news/peteroborne/100238184/john-humphrys-ignorance-about-iran-is-par-for-the-course-in-all-western-media/, accessed on 26 November 2013

Patrick, Melanie (2013) *Gross Miscalculation*, Pluto Press, 30 October. Available online at http://plutopress.wordpress.com/tag/gross-miscalculation-infographic/, accessed on 26 November 2013

Paxman, Jeremy (2009) Is World Journalism in Crisis?, Coventry University online interview, October 29. Available online at http://coventryuniversity.podbean.com/2009/10/29/is-there-a-crisis-in-world-journalism-jeremy-paxman/, accessed on 26 November 2011

Pilger, John (2010) Greg Philo quoted in The War You Don't See, first broadcast on ITV, 14 December. Available online at http://dartmouthfilms.com/war-you-dont-see, accessed on 26 November 2013

Ponsford, Dominic (2013) Review prompted by Savile scandal reveals 'strong undercurrent of fear' at BBC, *Press Gazette*, 2 May. Available online at http://www.pressgazette.co.uk/post-jimmy-savile-respect-work-review-reveals-strong-undercurrent-fear-bbc, accessed on 26 November 2013

Radio Five Live (2006) BBC, 1 February

Reuters (2011), Mohammed Abbas, Coventry: an unlikely home to prominent Syria activist, 8 December. Available online at http://uk.reuters.com/article/2011/12/08/uk-britain-syria-idUKTRE7B71XG20111208, accessed on 26 November 2013

Ritter, Scott (2003) Ritter dismisses Powell report, Kyodo News, 7 February. Available online at http://www.insideassyria.com/archive/5/messages/11703.html, accessed on 1 December 2013

Robinson, Nick (2011) BBC 1 *News at Six*, 20 October

Robinson, Nick (2012) *Live From Downing Street – The Inside Story of Politics, Power and the Media*, London: Bantam Press

Romm, Joe (2010) Mark Brayne quoted in 'Exclusive: Former correspondent and editor explains the drop in quality of BBC's climate coverage', Climate Progress blog, 22 September. Available online at http://thinkprogress.org/climate/2010/09/22/206766/bbc-climate-change-coverage-mark-brayne/, accessed on 26 November, 2013

Russell, Jenni (2013) Could *Newsnight*'s editor really have acted alone on the Jimmy Savile story?, *Guardian*, 23 October. Available online at http://www.guardian.co.uk/commentisfree/2012/oct/23/newsnight-editor-jimmy-savile-story, accessed on 26 November 2013

Saleem, Amena (2013) BBC airs Israeli 'Independence Day' propaganda presented as documentary, Electronic Intifada, 5 May. Available online at http://electronicintifada.net/blogs/amena-saleem/bbc-airs-israeli-independence-day-propaganda-presented-documentary, accessed on 26 November 2013

Smith, Norman (2011) BBC News online, 16:34, 21 October

Urban, Mark (2005) BBC *Newsnight*, 12 April

Vallely, Paul (2013) Whatever happened to climate change?, *Independent on Sunday*, 22 September 2013. Available online at http://www.independent.co.uk/voices/comment/whatever-happened-to-climate-change-8831686.html, accessed on 26 November 2013

Wheeler, Brian (2009) Dyke in BBC 'conspiracy' claim, BBC, 20 September. Available online at http://news.bbc.co.uk/2/hi/uk_news/politics/8265628.stm, accessed on November 26, 2013

Witchell, Nicholas (2003) BBC *Six O'Clock News*, 9 April

Wood, Paul (2005) BBC1, *News at Ten*, 22 December

Ziv, Ilan (2013) The Exiling of my Film, 'Exile A Myth Unearthed', Outsider on the Inside blog, 28 April. Available online at http://ilanziv.com/2013/04/28/the-exiling-of-my-film-exile-a-myth-unearthed-in-the-bbc-2/, accessed on 26 November, 2013

Note on the contributors
David Edwards and David Cromwell are the editors of Media Lens (www.medialens.org), a UK-based media analysis website which they co-founded in 2001. They are the co-authors of *Guardians of Power* (Pluto Books, 2006) and *Newspeak in the 21st Century* (Pluto Books, 2009). Edwards is also the author of *Free To Be Human* (Green Books, 1995) and *The Compassionate Revolution* (Green Books, 1998). Cromwell is the author of *Private Planet* (Jon Carpenter, 2001) and *Why Are We The Good Guys?* (Zero Books, 2012) and co-editor, with Mark Levene, of *Surviving Climate Change* (Pluto Books, 2007).

Section 4:
Casualty: Crises – past and present

Richard Lance Keeble

We all remember the interview George Entwistle, the embattled Director-General of the BBC, gave with John Humphrys on the *Today* programme of 11 November 2012. The D-G was effectively mauled by one of his own employees as he stumbled (and quite often fell silent) through what should have been a routine Q and A (see *Guardian* 2012 for a full transcript). What did the D-G know about the *Newsnight* investigation which had wrongly accused a senior Conservative figure of child abuse? Very little, it appeared, until after it was broadcast. Oh dear.

Former Culture Secretary David Mellor stuck the knife in even further: 'I feel so disillusioned that such a man can rise without trace to be Director-General. He came across as so out of touch, it made me think Winnie the Pooh would have been more effective.' Soon afterwards the inevitable happened. After just 54 days in the hot seat, Entwistle was forced to resign. Humphrys, for his part, went on to win a top Sony Award for the interview. 'It's sad,' he said, 'to be praised for something you'd rather not have had to do. Once you start an interview like that the years of doing it take over and you don't think: "That is my boss." You just do your job; then, when it's over, you think: "Oh my god"' (WalesOnline 2013).

Richard Peel knows a lot about PR. A former Head of PR for BBC News, he has been a senior communications professional for more than 25 years and is currently the Managing Director of Richard Peel Public Relations. He begins this section by arguing (perhaps not surprisingly) that good PR could have saved the

BBC much heart ache. And Entwistle, he says, didn't need to give that disastrous interview with Humphrys:

> What is apparent is that any plan to put the BBC back on the front foot was totally scuppered as a result of the *Today* programme interview. And Entwistle did not need to do it. At all times, the BBC's PR machine should treat the BBC the same as any other media organisation and not give favours. A well-rehearsed statement outside Broadcasting House and return back into the building to 'get on with the job' would have been a better way forward.

Peel also suggests, controversially again, that the Corporation needs to have a stronger grip on its communication across the organisation, including feedback from a network of PRs, and greater control over its journalists and presenters. 'They must act in the best interests of the organisation and not be critical or offer advice on how best to tackle its problems at public events or interviews. The BBC is their paymaster. They should be loyal and respectful and, if they have advice, offer it discreetly and internally.'

Threats from outside the BBC

Jean Seaton is more concerned about the threats from outside the BBC. As Professor of Media History at the University of Westminster and author of the official history of the BBC, *'Traitors and Pinkoes': The BBC and the Nation 1974-87* (to be published by Profile Books in September 2014), she is well acquainted with the series of crises which have gripped the Corporation over recent decades.

> It was battered far more than its commercial rivals during the long (and still festering) conflict in Northern Ireland. Mrs Whitehouse was a formidable opponent and brought down one of the greatest Director-Generals, Sir Hugh Carleton Greene. The remaking of the nation during the 1970s and 1980s repeatedly brought the Corporation to an economic and political brink with the Labour government and a political and economic one with Margaret Thatcher's Conservatives. On the way it lost one Director-General, Alasdair Milne, bloodily, and another, the decent, reforming, efficient Michael Checkland, through eviction … Would the Hutton Inquiry into a programme which, however 'right', had casually accused a prime minister of lying in an unscripted two-way early in the morning, mean the end? The roll call of BBC conflagrations went on and on.

But this time round, Seaton argues, there is no BBC crisis: 'The BBC has made mistakes. But it is the array of powers arraigned against it that should worry us and the fragility of the institutions that we might expect to save it.' The civil service, she says, used to defend the BBC, recognising it as an institution that shared its values of impartiality and independence. But now the civil service is less able to protect any autonomous notion of the public interest, more concerned with management than it was in the past. 'In particular, it is policy making capacity in the civil service which has been privatised and politicised. The Department of Culture, Media and Sport has been especially hard hit by cuts. The BBC is consequently more vulnerable.'

Tim Crook, Visiting Professor of Broadcast Journalism at Birmingham City University, also draws on the historical record to conclude, somewhat ominously: 'Mistakes are not permitted, rarely forgiven, and the future is less certain and secure for the BBC than it has ever been in its 92-year history.' Crook examines in some detail three major radio controversies. Firstly, those surrounding the broadcasting of the (now long forgotten) plays of Reginald Berkeley, the Tom Stoppard of his day, between 1925 and 1927. Next he looks at the row which exploded with the government following Andrew Gilligan's early morning two-way on the *Today* programme on 29 May 2003 (see BBC 2003):

> That the New Labour government had published a dossier in September 2002 which had been rewritten to make a better case for war in Iraq than the intelligence justified seems unassailable. His source Dr David Kelly, who effectively died for the story, has been posthumously vindicated. But the controversial nature of the politics involved, a context of aggressive news management by government communications, and on-air mistakes by the reporter in his use of language plunged the BBC into a ritual of political and legalistic trial and examination that would exploit its most vulnerable weaknesses. On matters of legal judgement it has no control, and in matters of funding and regulation it is subject to the will of executive and legislature who will exercise it when they believe public and judicial opinion is on their side.

Gilligangate/David Kelly Affair ultimately led to the damning Hutton Report and the resignations of both BBC Chairman and Director-General in 2004. Finally, Crook examines the *Mail*-induced moral panic after BBC Radio 2 comedy artists Russell Brand and Jonathan Ross made prank calls to the actor and writer Andrew Sachs about his granddaughter, Georgina Baillie, who performed in the burlesque dance group, Satanic Sluts Extreme (*Daily Mail* 2008). Again prominent heads rolled – and this time Ofcom landed the BBC with £150,000 fine and damned the voicemail messages as 'gratuitously offensive, humiliating and demeaning' (Holmwood 2009). Crook concludes: 'This is a narrative without an ending and with all of the prospects of an unhappy one ... The BBC can only hope that when next cornered, its hunters are not inclined to decide on termination.'

'The real crisis is yet to happen'

Steven Barnett, in the next chapter titled 'Crisis? What crisis? The real BBC catastrophe is yet to happen', argues, along with the conclusions of a major study published by the Reuters Institute in February 2013, that the real danger for the BBC is a progressive decline in funding to the point where it is incapable of fulfilling its task as a comprehensive public service broadcaster.

The authors note the gradual diminution of the licence fee as a proportion of total industry spending on television, projected to fall from its current 22 per cent of the total to 18.5 per cent by 2016. This 'salami-slicing' – which accelerated with the 16 per cent cuts imposed by the newly-elected Coalition government in October 2010 – is progressively eroding the BBC's ability to maintain its status as a major cultural force in Britain. According to the authors, 'it is not scaremongering to project that, if the current policy continues (i.e. even if the more radical proposals for scaling back the BBC are rejected), within a generation it will have been reduced to a barely relevant sideshow, the UK equivalent of PBS in America.

Barnett, Professor of Communications at the University of Westminster, predicts a concerted attack on the BBC's size, funding, governance, impartiality, competence and standing in British society as anti-BBC MPs (mostly from the Conservative benches) join forces with ferociously anti-BBC national newspapers which are determined, for self-serving commercial as well as political reasons, to undermine the Corporation's legitimacy and funding base. To avoid a genuine crisis, he suggests, supporters of the BBC both inside and outside of parliament will have to struggle to have their voices heard.

Finally in this section, Professor Brian Winston, of the University of Lincoln, takes issue with Steve Hewlett, ex-editor of *Panorama*, current presenter of Radio 4's *Media Show* and a leading *Guardian* media commentator, who wrote:

> The BBC's independence is widely recognised as its greatest asset. And it's a fragile flower – depending on an array of understandings and conventions (this being Britain there is no 'constitution' to protect it) that, in turn, rely on all parties understanding and respecting them (Hewlett 2013).

Winston draws on his deep knowledge of constitutional history and law to challenge Hewlett. In particular, he refers to Dicey's seminal *Lectures Introductory to the Study of the Law of the Constitution*, of 1885, where it is suggested that a part of the UK constitution are rules (emphatically not laws) that:

> … consist of conventions, understandings, habits, or practices that – though they may regulate the conduct of the several members of the sovereign power, the Ministry, or other officials – are not really laws, since they are not enforced by the courts. This portion of constitutional law may, for the sake of distinction, be termed the 'conventions of the constitution', or constitutional morality.

So, Winston argues, Hewlett is quite right to note that the 'fragility' of the BBC's 'independence' is because of its reliance on 'understandings and conventions'. But his 'conventions' comfort blanket 'pulls wool over his eyes'. Many believe, like Hewlett, that the BBC's 'independence' is protected by conventions when, in fact, they don't really exist. All that protects the BBC,

Winston concludes, 'is politics; "political morality", forsooth!' A rousing note, then, on which to end this section.

References

BBC (2003) The *Today* audio timeline, 29 May, 6.07 am. Available online at http://www.bbc.co.uk/radio4/today/reports/politics/hutton_audio_timeline_2004012 8.shtml, accessed on 1 February 2014

Daily Mail (2008) Grandpa came to watch me be a Satanic Slut – and he liked it, says Georgina Baillie, *Daily Mail*, 5 November. Available online at http://www.dailymail.co.uk/tvshowbiz/article-1083254/Grandpa-came-watch-Satanic-Slut---liked-says-Georgina-Baillie.html, accessed on 2 February 2014

Guardian (2012) John Humphrys interviews George Entwistle – transcript. Available online at http://www.theguardian.com/media/2012/nov/10/john-humphrys-george-entwistle, accessed on 2 February 2014

Hewlett, Steve (2013) Grant Shapps may have crossed the line on the BBC – but so did Tony Hall, *Guardian* Media Blog, 1 December. Available online at http://www.theguardian.com/media/media-blog/2013/dec/01/bbc-grant-shaps-tony-hall, accessed on 1 December 2013

Holmwood, Leigh (2009) BBC fined £150,000 over Russell Brand and Jonathan Ross phone prank scandal, *Guardian*, 3 April. Available online at http://www.theguardian.com/media/2009/apr/03/russell-brand-jonathan-ross-bbc-fine, accessed on 1 February 2014

WalesOnline (2013) John Humphrys wins Sony Award for interview with former BBC director-general George Entwistle, 13 May. Available online at http://www.walesonline.co.uk/lifestyle/showbiz/john-humphrys-wins-sony-award-3708651, accessed on 1 February 2014

BBC and the PR challenge

Richard Peel argues that the BBC must justify its existence to the public with a convincing, forward-thinking argument explaining why we can't live without it

The BBC is one of most scrutinised, praised and criticised public bodies in the world and is routinely presented with enormous PR challenges as any accountable organisation should be. It is still regarded across the globe as the creator of extraordinary programmes and a reliable and accurate source of news and information, although, in terms of quality, BBC World, has dented that reputation somewhat – particularly through the eyes of UK critics. But the original dramas, the prolific and stunning output of the BBC's Natural History Unit in Bristol, rich and diverse radio output, international 'hits' such as *Doctor Who* and a website with around 40 million unique users a week, means its reputation plays well in an environment where brands are fighting it out on a daily basis for recognition and respect.

According to the YouGov brand index, the BBC iPlayer still ranked as the top brand in the UK at the end of 2012 (YouGov 2012) despite the departure of the Director-General, George Entwhistle. But can that brand value diminish and is the BBC – partly because of the way it presents itself to the outside world – in the throes of a deep crisis, so entrenched it can't be rescued?

The BBC has never been particularly good at looking outwards. It is a giant 'family', is all-consuming and so disparate and exciting in what it does, that it would be possible as an employee to almost ignore what goes on elsewhere – except for the fact that its journalists are supposed to reflect the world where we live, back to the licence fee payers. Melvyn Bragg put that sense of insularity aptly during an interview when he talked about internal BBC promotion 'The Club [the BBC] becomes the most important thing in their lives. When you talk about politics to BBC people, they immediately assume you mean BBC politics, not relations between the parties or superpowers but who's going to be the next D-G' (cited in Paxman 1990).

This self-centeredness is borne of privilege. The licence fee does provide a cushion. There is no bottom line to be concerned about and the BBC's shareholders – the licence fee payers – are not in a position to heist the chief executive if its reputation takes a battering. So, unlike a conventional organisation, where brand value is the lifeblood and where sales and profit can be badly damaged by a careless comment or a product disaster, the BBC is largely immune. Of course, there are repercussions if government is offended or the defence of the organisation is not robustly managed – the Gilligan affair, the Ross/Brand debacle and the hesitancy and flat-footedness over the Savile stories, are good examples – but, as we have seen, the BBC can get away with much more than a commercial organisation and still plough on, because it is unique and well established as a valued institution – for the moment.

Threats of privatisation
But will the public, now faced with a plethora of choice, and the government, of whatever hue, want to retain the licence fee when it seems like an anachronism to the BBC's critics? Not that it hasn't been close to privatisation before – although, in the end, even Mrs Thatcher did not have the stomach to go down that route. One of the biggest crises occurred in 1985 when the BBC PR Department was caught in the ludicrous position of trying simultaneously to answer for the actions of the Board of Management and the Board of Governors, who were at loggerheads over the screening of *Real Lives* – a documentary on Northern Ireland. 'Which side are you on?' was the awkward question fired by delighted journalists at a BBC Press Office, under siege.

This was a period when the BBC was, arguably, at a lower ebb than now. At the Edinburgh Festival in 1984, Max Hastings boomed: 'Never has the leadership of the BBC seemed more pitifully inadequate, bankrupt of ideas, lost for course…' As Michael Leapman recorded in his book *The Last Days of the Beeb* (1986), *The Times* ran a series of articles in the eighties advocating the fragmentation and privatisation of the BBC and Leapman predicted that in the final decade of the century in a world of satellite and cable the BBC would have a greatly diminished role 'far removed from its heyday as a dominant force in British culture' (ibid).

Mercifully, Leapman's predictions did not come true. But the odds against the survival of the licence fee are stacking up, bolstered by the digital revolution and multiple choices across a range of television channels and new digital platforms, and encouraged by the self-mutilation of BBC executives. In 2013, the Corporation was rocked by scandal after scandal and in many instances looked complacent, sometimes arrogant and always disorganised. None of these traits will find favour with those set on dismantling the BBC and it can ill afford to lose its few friends with self- interested media opponents circling, a new charter approaching and a general election on the horizon.

Long-term strategy

As with all large organisations, the starting point for a good public image and strong public relations is a solid, credible long-term strategy that is fully understood by internal and external stakeholders, is exciting to relate and brings positive benefits to all. At the root of this, for the BBC, are quality, attractive, original programming and rock solid, revelatory journalism. Coupled with that, the BBC needs a strong narrative that draws on its incomparable history, its range and depth of programming, its creative and journalistic skills, its cultural significance, value for money, and its relationship with viewers and listeners. Its rebuttals need to be confident, swift and evidence-based and the apologies forthcoming when mistakes are made. Bob Dulson, ex-BBC Head of Corporate Media Relations, has these words of advice:

> With charter review around the corner and the Tories at the helm, the pressure's on: the BBC has to find its feet and fast. It should rediscover and demonstrate its core values. One word above all other defines the corporation's USP – trust. It is respected around the world because of its honesty, independence and integrity. Those qualities are essential ingredients, not just in its products but in its whole ethos. The BBC is the UK's finest 'export'. It says more for Britain than any other company or commodity.

Until the arrival of Lord Hall, there was little sense of a long-term strategy – even now the vision is not comprehensive – and the BBC's record of reacting quickly to breaking news stories was hardly exemplary. Director-General Greg Dyke was not across Gilligan's *Today* programme report until well after the event. Director-General George Entwistle – incredibly – was unaware of the *Newsnight* scandal and Chairman, Chris Patten, claimed not to have been told about executive pay-offs. This is hardly a sign of joined-up management or governance and suggests that PR advisers were either being ignored, were not persistent, did not have enough authority, or were simply inept.

One of the roles of PRs in any organisation is to sniff out the positive stories but also to anticipate and intuitively predict what Ron Neil, former BBC Director of News, called at the time, the 'flying omelettes'. These are stories that will embarrass and even humiliate the organisation. For a Corporation the size of the BBC the risk register should be massive and each of those risks can impact on the organisation's reputation. In most cases large corporations hold their director of communications or corporate affairs responsible for managing the fall-out from crises. This person is responsible for ensuring that the right messaging is in place to use when the crises occurs; that there can be a rapid response to calls from the media and that inquiries can be managed efficiently, effectively and fast.

Communications on the board

To understand the nature of potential risks the individual responsible for the organisation's brand needs to be at the heart of the decision-making process and fully across the strategy, emerging policies and the tittle tattle. It follows that this individual should have a position on the board but the BBC abandoned this policy more than a decade ago and at one point did not even have communications or corporate affairs representation in the management tier below the board. This is ill-judged and dangerous. Says Dulson:

> In my view the move to a marketing-led strategy was the root of the problem. In its haste to be slick, smart and competitive (even on pay!), the Beeb took its eye off the ball. It demands a system that is PR, rather than marketing-led – a communications team with information management skills and disciplines, a boss at board level, and the core values at its heart.

Not only does the director of corporate affairs need to be on the board, he or she also needs to have a 'special' relationship with the director-general. One where there are no secrets and where there is mutual honesty and respect. The director of corporate affairs is not there necessarily to air views on policy – although there is no reason why they shouldn't – but what they are there to do is to make plain the consequences of actions and ideas, speeches and initiatives so the public relations outcomes can be managed sensitively and positively.

Coached and grilled

The same goes for select committee appearances, or interviews on radio or television or with the press. The D-G, and others in the management team, need to be briefed, coached and put through a rigorous Q & A grilling to make sure they are equipped to respond to difficult questions and in a position to get the right messages across. There was not much evidence of this during George Entwistle's tenure, either in front of politicians at the select committee, or the media. Although to be fair to those involved in PR at the time, there was a suggestion that he was reluctant to take advice. What is apparent is that any plan to put the BBC back on the front foot was totally scuppered as a result of the *Today* programme interview. And Entwistle did not need to do it. At all times, the BBC's PR machine should treat the BBC the same as any other media organisation and not give favours. A well-rehearsed statement outside Broadcasting House and return back into the building to 'get on with the job' would have been a better way forward.

These were the kind of issues and tactics always discussed at a daily morning meeting, dropped for a long spell, where senior representatives of BBC management, including the D-G, director of corporate affairs and director of policy and others, used to convene to discuss coverage in the day's newspapers, online and on air. They would make decisions on messaging and positioning in relation to running stories about the Corporation. As with the National Health Service – barely a day goes by without one.

Apart from having a strong grip on its communication across the organisation, including feedback from a network of PRs, it also needs to have greater control over its journalists and presenters. They must act in the best interests of the organisation and not be critical or offer advice on how best to tackle its problems at public events or interviews. The BBC is their paymaster. They should be loyal and respectful and, if they have advice, offer it discreetly and internally.

PR peers put the boot in

So, what were the consequences of a seemingly broken PR machine trying to support a dysfunctional management which seemed barely capable of communicating with itself? It is not often that PR professionals turn on their peers so savagely, but the *Newsnight* debacle led to the PR fraternity piling on the criticism on top of the media attacks from the national newspapers, broadcasters and the negative spice added from bloggers and a steady stream of tweets.

For example, the PRCA (2013) conducted a survey amongst senior PRs on their perception of the BBC's PR performance following Entwistle's departure. The outcome was predictable. Francis Ingham, PRCA Director-General, commenting on the results, said: 'The BBC's reputation has been thoroughly trashed by its handling of the two *Newsnight* fiascos. That's the clear verdict of PR leaders. It's also clear that Entwistle's resignation hasn't drawn a line under the affair, but has actually damaged rather than helped the BBC's position. As an organisation, it clearly remains in an existential crisis.' The BBC communication team's reaction to a critical piece about its operation was, perhaps symptomatic of an organisation with a severe dose of the jitters. Challenged by *PR Week* (Turvill 2013) about the numbers of people employed in communications – a total of 147 – following a Freedom of Information request, the BBC's limp, uninspiring response was bereft of statistics and substance. It said:

> Every week the BBC Communications division handles several thousand enquiries relating to its television, radio and online output at a regional, national, and international level. The team promotes a wide range of programmes such as *Panorama* and *Strictly Come Dancing* in newspapers, magazines and broadcast media. In addition, there is a corporate team that responds to a huge array of queries about the Corporation itself. There is also an internal communications team for staff matters and the public affairs team that liaises with politicians nationwide. The division is vital for keeping licence fee payers informed about the BBC's content and how the organisation is being run.

During the same period, Mark Borkowski, one of Britain's leading PRs, said the BBC were 'the architects of their own crisis'. He claimed: 'The BBC ... is now culturally inept at dealing with a situation of this size.' Colin Browne, who has been at the sharp end of PR at the BBC as Director of Corporate Affairs and is now Chairman of the Voice of the Viewer and Listener, has a more measured and, perhaps, realistic view:

> Everyone feels they own the BBC. This is a consequence of the privilege of the licence fee. So the BBC has to communicate with an incredibly wide range of stakeholders, often with widely diverging interests. This is a much more complex communications scenario than faced by a plc, never mind a privately owned company.

He adds: 'The fact that the BBC is, broadly, constrained from taking a view on contentious issues can leave it very vulnerable to attack from those who are committed to one view or another. Its hands are tied.' And the organisation has certainly been on the rack. Even the *Economist*, not renowned for its Beeb-bashing, weighed in (*Economist* 2012) and the story began its inevitable transition into an examination of its future.

Referring to the Savile story, an *Economist* writer opined: 'Out of this mishandled mess, the BBC has lost a newly appointed director-general and much credibility. Its own "key values" commitments include "quality" and "trust" and it has squandered both in this sorry saga.' They continued: 'There is also a broader cultural problem which attaches to a broadcaster funded through a levy on viewers which they are compelled to pay if they own a TV set. When funding is (more or less) assured, it is easier for group-think to set in, in the higher echelons, whose inhabitants believe that the BBC is inherently superior and can never be at fault. Too much of this has accompanied the story so far.'

A story about sloppy journalism had quickly, as it always has in the past, escalated into a major PR crisis with the Tories calling for BBC blood and the Corporation, initially, relying on others to present their case. Tristram Hunt, in the *New Statesman*, (2012) made the following observations about the disproportionate political onslaught:

> The ongoing implosion of BBC News has given the Conservative right another opportunity to urge the elimination of the licence fee … with 425,320 hours of TV and radio output last year (a figure the BBC Press Office should have used in its statement) the BBC's encroachment on the market is an important debate, as is its eternally bloated management structure. But with those managerially responsible having departed or, in Reithian terms 'stood aside', that debate bears only passing relevance to a scandal that is ultimately about shoddy standards of journalism at one current affairs programme.

In the end, of course, it should be the public and not the media or politicians who decide the fate of the BBC. As Mark Damazer, former Controller of Radio 4, put it in an *Observer* column (2013): 'The BBC is almost always in crisis or on the verge of a crisis … and yet the public has not decided that the game is up. And the public is right.' This sentiment was echoed by Will Hutton, also in the *Observer* (2013). Highlighting conservative ideology and the BBC, he wrote: 'This is the toughest battle yet in it (the BBC's) history with the most vicious of enemies. It is time for the BBC to show some nerve, enlist its audience and stand up against the bullies.'

So, the BBC is far from out of the woods and its PR machine will continue to be at full stretch. The *Sunday Telegraph*'s ICM poll (Ross 2013) that showed 70 per cent of voters believe the BBC licence fee should be abolished or cut was an early example in the run-up to licence fee renewal of how the Tory supporting media will use public sentiment to beat the BBC. The article concluded. 'The findings follow warnings from cabinet ministers over the future of the licence fee and demonstrate the extent of public hostility to the current system.'

To add to the PR burden, MPs announced an inquiry into the role and purpose of the BBC, and whether the licence fee should continue in its current form after 2016, when the current charter expires. John Whittingdale, Chairman of the Commons Media Select Committee, said the poll demonstrated that there was 'considerable public dissatisfaction' with the current funding arrangements. 'In my view, the licence fee is becoming very difficult to sustain,' he said. 'It is a flat rate poll tax, which is highly regressive without any kind of means testing, it is very expensive to collect and there is a very high level of evasion.'

Providing further ammunition for the media, the Public Accounts Committee then accused the BBC of cronyism and *The Times*, in one of their damning editorials, described the Corporation as a managerial 'basket case' while the *Daily Mail* said the BBC's governance was 'broken'. And so it goes on. What can the BBC do to win back favour? According to Professor Patrick Barwise, commenting in a Channel 4 News online story (Channel 4 2013): 'The only way to earn trust is by keeping your promise. The Beeb's promise is that they apply the highest standards of objectivity and credibility. They've just got to tighten up and get a grip on their journalism.'

Conclusion

Unquestionably, the BBC is entering another crucial phase in its history. To survive, from a PR perspective, it needs to be transparent, confident but not arrogant, clear on its goals and its mission; it must listen more assiduously to licence fee payers and act on what it hears and it must ensure that the right framework is in place to guarantee editorial accuracy, independence, originality and authority.

It cannot afford any more major crises in the run-up to the next licence fee settlement. It must justify its existence to the public with a convincing, forward thinking argument explaining why we can't live without it, underpinned by its output of unique programmes, news and current affairs you can trust and its ability to record the big occasion with a sense of history and authority. Unless it can re-capture the public's imagination and rebuild its image, at the very least, it will be wounded and weakened.

References

Channel 4 (2012) How can the BBC recover from crisis?, 12 November. Available online at http://www.channel4.com/news/bbc-crisis-trust-entwistle-davie-patten, accessed on November 23 2013

Damazer, Mark (2013) The many challenges facing a beleaguered BBC, *Observer*, 3 November. Available online at http://www.theguardian.com/commentisfree/2013/nov/03/bbc-faces-many-challenges, accessed on December 8 2013

Economist (2013) What's gone wrong on planet Beeb?, *Economist*, 12 November. Available online at http://www.economist.com/blogs/blighty/2012/11/bbc-crisis, accessed on 22 November 2013

Hunt, Tristram (2012) Why the Tories' knives are out for Chris Patten, *New Statesman*, 15 November. Available online at http://www.newstatesman.com/politics/politics/2012/11/settling-old-scores, accessed on 28 November 2013

Hutton, Will (2013) How does the beleaguered BBC confront the future, *Observer*, 3 November http://www.theguardian.com/commentisfree/2013/nov/03/bbc-faces-many-challenges, accessed on December 8 2013

Leapman, Michael (1986) *The Last Days of the Beeb*, London: Allen and Unwin

Paxman, Jeremy (1990) *Friends in High Places*, London and New York: Penguin

PRCA (2013) Leader's panel. What should the BBC do next? *PRCA*, 15 November. Available online AT http://www.prca.org.uk/%5CPRLeadersPanelWhatnextfortheBBC, Accessed on 18 November 2013

Ross, Tim (2013) BBC licence fee should be cut or scrapped poll finds, *Telegraph*, 2 November. Available online at http://www.telegraph.co.uk/culture/tvandradio/bbc/10423117/BBC-licence-fee-should-be-cut-or-scrapped-poll-finds.html, accessed on November 5 2013

Turvill, William (2013) Astonishment over BBC's 147 PR staff, *PR Week*, 14 January. Available online at http://www.pressgazette.co.uk/bbc-employs-147-pr-staff-outsourced-work-during-savile-scandal, accessed on 14 November 2013

YouGov (2012) Brand Index Rankings. Available online at http://www.brandindex.com/rankings/2012-annual, accessed on 14 November 2013

Note on the contributor

Richard Peel has been a senior communications professional for more than 25 years and is the Managing Director of RPPR (Richard Peel Public Relations). He has held corporate affairs directorships and other key communication roles in the Media, Health, Broadcast, Sport, Local Government, and Gaming sectors. He spent 10 years with BBC News, heading its communications and marketing from the late 1980s when all of the BBC's radio and television news and current affairs programmes were brought together in a single directorate. Website: www.rppr.biz.

The coming crisis

Jean Seaton argues that the array of powers arraigned against the BBC – and the fragility of the institutions we might expect to save it – should worry us all

The BBC's crisis is not as it seems; not the interlocked series of self-inflicted disasters that have broken over in the last year. They are, however shocking, grindingly uncomfortable or infuriating, being dealt with. Leadership, management structures, new people in new jobs, and the vision for the BBC are all being shaken up. The relationship between the BBC and the Trust, and the functioning of the board of management are evolving. The relationship with the public (over Savile) has to be dealt with un-flinching propriety. Yet neither the idea of the BBC nor its governance structures need ripping up.

The real problem is that as a consequence of the ruthless pursuit of an agenda that says the BBC and its constitution are 'broken', the BBC will be fatally weakened. It is what is being made of serious but not irreparable errors that is so threatening. If the BBC were to be demolished, that would happen despite the public's keen appreciation of public service content, and with no regard to the public or national interest. The danger is another constitutional revolution, further 'top slicing' of the licence fee, and a slashing of the Corporation's revenues. If every time there is a row the BBC's constitution is altered, then its precious independence will be demolished, and its creativity stifled – as its enemies want. The pumping up of the case against the BBC and the ruthless repression of its defence might well mean that the Corporation were so reduced in size, diminished in revenue and hamstrung in purpose that it would stop being itself.

For the first time every newspaper has a direct commercial interest in the BBC being smaller and less good. Moreover, whatever the long term consequences of the Leveson dispute over the regulation of the press – one thing is clear and perturbing. The press have learnt how to coordinate a response to anything they don't like. They suppress any challenging evidence and deny opponents a voice. Even *Private Eye* seems to have adopted a 'position' on press regulation and gives no space for any information that is seen as opposed to that interest. The power of the press to set the agenda has increased rather than diminished as circulations waver. In a febrile pre-election period they have an exaggerated effect on the political classes, setting the tone and agenda.

The message, that the BBC is 'broken' and 'in crisis', rammed home by a large part of the press with their own interests, fanned by those who talk regretfully of the need for reform but really seek the destruction or emasculation of the BBC, is made by long-term commercial and ideological political opponents, in the name of 'freedom' and 'choice'. On its side the Corporation has no organised collective defence mechanisms. There are few organisations (let alone lobby groups) who defend it, or permit the expression of the wider public interest.

And unlike the past when both politicians and the civil service moved behind the scenes to protect the Corporation, the worry now is that the role, purpose, and sheer capacity of the civil service have been radically reduced by the present government, with numbers slashed so that the ability to recognise and argue against insistent lobbying is weaker. The civil service used to defend the BBC, recognising it as an institution that shared its values of impartiality and independence. But now the civil service is less able to protect any autonomous notion of the public interest, more concerned with management, than it was in the past. In particular, it is policy making capacity in the civil service which has been privatised and politicised. The Department of Culture, Media and Sport has been especially hard hit by cuts. The BBC is consequently more vulnerable.

Then there are politicians. Time and again Liberal Democrat ministers have intervened to assist the BBC in the last three years. During the licence fee negotiations of 2010, forced through in order to find No. 10 more money for the Ministry of Defence, Danny Alexander, Chief Secretary to the Treasury, played a vital role in defending the BBC. And in the days of panic that culminated in George Entwistle leaving, Lib Dem ministers were steady. But as the election approaches their impact within the coalition is weakening.

In the past, big ministers who used to be in charge of the BBC were powerful cabinet members. Many had a genuine love of the arts and creativity, or a respect for the world role of the BBC, or recognised that the BBC helped create a national discussion and brought the nation together. Home Secretaries from Roy Jenkins to Douglas Hurd and Leon Brittan, or Culture Ministers from Virginia Bottomley to David Mellor, to Tessa Jowell understood that their Department, of Culture, Media and Sport (DCMS) had guardianship of great bits of British culture, the beacons of Britishness in the world and significant industries. They have often been critical of the BBC, but have all been concerned to craft policy with respect for the Corporation not out of knee-jerk hostility to it. Nor have they treated it casually; they listened and sometimes at least rejected partisan lobbying against it. Conservatives defended it from the far right, and Labour, in the seventies and eighties, needed to defend it from the far left.

A peculiarly dangerous moment for the BBC

However, the fate of the BBC is currently in the hands of a minister appointed not because of interest in the subject, but because the prime minister needed to appoint someone from the tribal right of the cabinet. Of course, this political position may be to the advantage of the Corporation, she may well be able to bring some of the more extreme critics of the BBC (often with objections to the BBC in principle) with her. However, if the example of press regulation is considered the record is worrying. It shows she had 29 formal, face-to-face meetings with newspaper editors on press regulation between January and September 2013. There were presumably many other non-formal meetings, telephone calls, or lobbying with her staff. In that time she had two meetings with what might be called the 'other' Leveson side. Can she summon the clout, understanding and independence to protect the BBC against a concerted lobbying campaign?

Last summer a group of senior Indian and Pakistani journalists, brought delicately together for the first time on a pioneering Foreign Office course, visited the BBC's Northern Ireland office on Ormeau Avenue, in Belfast. A marvellous building, although hardly a pretty one, it has a presence. It is plain, and stern, at a crossroads in the non-partisan centre of town. It has been bombed and battered repeatedly: one of its achievements was to construct an innovatory new kind of bomb-proof studio. At the heart of its labyrinthine corridors, the newsroom remain much as it was during the troubles – dark and hugger mugger. The visiting editors and reporters were told by one journalist there, with 25 years' experience of telling difficult stories into the divided community she also lived within, that 'everyone's personal politics had always been left at the door with their coats as they come in'.

The visitors were visibly shocked. When the BBC staff took their visitors on a trip around Belfast's 'peace walls', one of the Indian journalists said it was the only thing he had seen that made Kashmir look peaceful. BBC journalists briefed them on the central economic and political problems, took them to a community centre, explained the arguments around one acutely political story, and put them at the back of an audience for a live session with a loud, engaged and opinionated local audience. The Indians and Pakistanis who also share so much across a fissile border were enthralled and inspired. 'It was the political realism combined with principle, and such carefulness,' said one Delhi editor. This being Northern Ireland there were also very good jokes, a natural courtesy, and a lot of biscuits.

It was the BBC at its local, important, intelligent, thinking, concerned best. But as we walked through the corridors I noticed a certain furtive scurrying. It was the day Rolf Harris had been indicted for allegedly abusing yet another raft of young, vulnerable women. His (absolutely ghastly) self-portrait was being hurriedly removed from the BBC's corridors. But did that invalidate everything else the intrepid Indians and Pakistanis had found so exciting and useful? I think not.

The Savile abuses were shocking. But the BBC's handling of how they were reported was dreadful. It did, however, in the end, lead to the loss of a director-general. The trail of minor broadcasting celebrities being prosecuted for allegedly violating young women now seems endless. Meanwhile the pay-offs to senior executives sticky with 'sweeteners' seemed wrong and absurd. Some were simply part of a negotiation to get people out of the door. Some were leaving jobs that were not disappearing. However, the payoffs not only infuriated the public but demoralised and dismayed hard working, stretched BBC staff facing cuts.

Ritual humiliation of some serious BBC players

It has all been compounded by the ritual humiliation of some serious BBC players scourged by Margaret Hodge with the full finery of righteous public indignation in the Public Accounts Committee. The casual demolition of public servants several of whom – Chairs of the Trust, Sir Michael Lyons, Lord Patton and the principled Head of the Trust, Nicholas Kroll – had been attempting to reshape the BBC much as the public wanted, made for compelling gladiatorial fun. But it added another layer of damage. Then the digital initiative collapsed costing a good deal more money, although it had been a quite proper attempt to solve the problems of sharing a digital archive with the public – as opposed to commodifying and narrowing access which the other large players are trying to do. How it was handled however did demonstrate a kind of 'silo' battle within the BBC.

Combined with the imminence of a vital charter renewal, many say that it looks like a perfect storm. It has been a nasty mess; it is potentially dangerous. The environment in which the BBC operates is politically more hostile than at any time since the 80s. Proposals to rip up the Trust, export the oversight of the BBC, slice up the licence fee even further are to be found everywhere.

Nevertheless, the recent troubles also need putting in some perspective. The BBC has had more perilous crises and near-death experiences than the public perhaps understands or, indeed, than its own mandarins comprehend. Institutional memories are short. The BBC has survived repeated attempts by governments to take it over. It has sustained slippery and sly, as well as bruising and overt, attempts to usurp its editorial independence. There have been secret plans to control its money; plans to drive it into debt; plans to make it part of general taxation or responsible for providing services that ought to be paid for separately. These have all been considerable threats to the BBC's necessary financial autonomy, since if it had to compete head on with welfare or health it would lose its independence.

Then, nearly all prime ministers have railed about it and spent morose afternoons contemplating how badly it has treated them and plotting revenge. Since Baldwin, prime ministers have often seen it at times as biased (against them) and have considered how to curtail its impact. After all, the BBC was created in the heat of a nation being torn apart by the General Strike: emerging as a public service not a state broadcaster required delicate and shrewd judgements. But it also needed luck. As Asa Briggs, the official historian, pointed out, it was only because the press barons of the time, Beaverbrook and Northcliffe, did not understand what the BBC might become that they did not mobilise their power to strangle it at birth. Its ingenious engineers saved it from being commandeered and shut down in 1938 before the Second World War; the Opposition saved it after the Suez debacle in 1956; and the SDP defended it from being condemned as a traitor during the Falklands conflict of 1982.

It was battered far more than its commercial rivals during the long (and still festering) conflict in Northern Ireland. Mrs Whitehouse was a formidable opponent and brought down one of the greatest Director-Generals, Sir Hugh Carleton Greene. The remaking of the nation during the 1970s and 1980s repeatedly brought the Corporation to an economic and political brink with the Labour government and a political and economic one with Margaret Thatcher's Conservatives. On the way it lost one Director-General, Alasdair Milne, bloodily, and another, the decent, reforming, efficient Michael Checkland, through eviction.

Would John Birt's 'Producer Choice', an early, partly justified, partly misguided, version of outsourcing, nearly wreck the BBC? Would the Hutton Inquiry into a programme which, however 'right', had casually accused a prime minister of lying in an unscripted two-way early in the morning, mean the end? The roll call of BBC conflagrations went on and on.

The different kinds of BBC crises
There are different kinds of BBC crises. There is the BBC versus government car crash. This can take place with governments of every political complexion. The Corporation's accumulated authority means that it does have to exercise responsibility about politics. It lasts longer than governments. Politicians in tight corners – that being what politics requires – resent and lash out at it when it does not support them. The public is quite frequently (but not always) on the Corporation's side in these arguments: over Northern Ireland the nation was divided and rows over programmes divided the public; over Hutton and the Iraq war the public was on the BBC's side.

The second kind of crisis involves a real or perceived editorial error. Inevitably the BBC makes mistakes but sometimes the problem is distance between the mores of different audiences; the Corporation has made unthinking assumptions that are indefensible; sometimes judgements over individual programmes have been wrong. But as long as the BBC worries and corrects these errors the public has understood in the longer run. That has been because, beside the periodic crises, there have been the everyday pleasures and decencies, the satisfaction of interesting programmes that mean far more than episodes of error. Although the public is occasionally outraged it also usually quite enjoys the debacle: tutting has its own pleasures.

The third kind of crisis is to do with money (and most BBC crises are ultimately about money). The BBC is a peculiar organisation in that it spends the public's money in a commercially competitive world. Quite a lot of BBC money goes on entertainers and fripperies and that's just what the audiences want.

The Savile crisis was different: it was between the BBC and its audiences, not the BBC and government. It continues to be deeply painful for the Corporation because it involved what turned out to be a sustained betrayal of public confidence and trust over decades. It is bitterly dreadful that Savile abused vulnerable young women and used his power as a popular celebrity to exploit and silence them. That he operated within a form that was peculiarly of the BBC – a combination of charitable work and vulgar fun – makes it very uncomfortable.

However, generations of BBC viewers were involved in what they now with revulsion feel to have been complicity with a man they undoubtedly believed to be odd, but whose good-hearted intentions a whole series of authoritative institutions appeared to guarantee. That sense of personal investment, the children who loved *Jim'll Fix It*, the teenagers who liked *Top of the Pops*, the grans who thought he did so much for charity, meant that much of the British public feels as if their pleasure in his performance and, indeed, their enthusiasm for him, was used in a vile way. However, of all of the creators of Savile – and the NHS, his charities, and the police who failed to pursue allegations against him are all implicated – the BBC is the only one whose inquiry is large, public, transparent. The Smith review is chilling. But the BBC commissioned it.

None of this demonstrates that the BBC governance structure is 'broken'. Good governance structures evolve, they are not invented. If every time there is a crisis the BBC were to have a new 'structure' imposed, then how long would independence last? Since the Public Accounts Committee hearings, the Trust has clarified its independence, the BBC executive has new members, Tony Hall feels like a man invigorated not beaten down by the challenge. Indeed, although it is not fashionable to say it, 'structures' are also a matter of personality and the times. The appointment of a new director-general changes the BBC more profoundly than many other organisations: because it is above all creative, the ideas that animate it have to be allowed to flourish from the top and bubble up from the bottom.

Even more unfashionably, it is worth saying that the structure in place was in many ways performing as it should. Another of the crises – the scandal over pay-offs – was a direct consequence of the BBC Trust bearing down on executive pay and numbers with a determined focus, long before the banks and the NHS had begun to do so. Indeed, the BBC Trust had been pursuing a strategy to reduce salaries and numbers since Sir Michael Lyons became Chair. Lord Patten had pursued this policy with great determination. Bringing pressure to bear on the Director-General to reduce numbers of executives took ruthless and persistent action. But the Trust does not, and ought not to, 'manage' the BBC. Nearly all those who attack the BBC's governance use this as a disguise for their political and economic hostility to the very idea of the BBC; pulling on the thread of the constitution is a way of unravelling the whole thing. There was a Trust strategy and it was working. Indeed, it was doing what the public wanted. But the Trust also thought that the BBC was less collegiate and more dominated by a powerful DG than was healthy. George Entwistle was appointed as a solution but proved unable to deal with the Savile crisis.

The real question is why did BBC salaries get so large? Every BBC pound is also a political currency. The top of the BBC seemed to lose sight of this. Then another issue were the non-executive directors appointed from outside on to the board of management. The philosophy behind their appointment was that people from 'outside' brought 'commercial' realism to the BBC. But they did not seem to understand the rather different business of public service, and they brought with them the nineties and noughties belief in and casual acceptance of gross salaries. Getting rid of people and structures can bring its own problems – Mark Thompson reduced the number of bureaucratic roles – but every increase in responsibility led to an increase in salaries. And the changes had consequences: Mark Byford presided over a journalism committee, set up in the wake of Hutton to scout out and deal with potential crises before they broke. It survived but he, together with Caroline Thompson who also went, were calm, decent, sorters of big problems. The mishandling of the Savile crisis happened three months later. It is not that the BBC can exist without bureaucrats: it just needs the right ones in the right places.

A BBC peculiarity: The 'beheading' of the top executive

One of the brilliant peculiarities of the BBC is the beheading of the top executive: very few director-generals have left when they intended to. But it is also a very good way of refreshing the BBC. Tony Hall was a good choice: it is his last big job, so he is fearless. He has dissolved management committees. He has overturned the nostrums of management theory, and quite rightly put individual responsibility in the place of meetings. But he is determined to make the culture more collegiate, choosing some brilliant new top managers. James Harding, fresh from *The Times*, is putting sharp, disciplined, news-focused energy back into News. James Purnell, a wily strategist with a love for the BBC, started out in Policy and Planning under the redoubtable Patricia Hodgson in the Birt era. Danny Cohen has the flamboyance that BBC entertainment needs.

The World Service has been written into the Trust's responsibilities although the revolution there – prompted by cuts – is disturbing. It needs watching in the national interest. Nevertheless the Trust has clarified what it has responsibility for and what the management has responsibility for. Dame Janet Smith has opened all of the ghastly cupboards in the place. Hall feels in charge. And yet there is a crisis. It is not, however, a BBC crisis. The BBC has made mistakes. But it is the array of powers arraigned against it that should worry us and the fragility of the institutions that we might expect to save it. We need a bold, imaginative BBC giving a voice to the less powerful and using its creativity to express an optimistic cultural high-mindedness taking the best of everything to everyone. We may have to rally round it right now to protect it.

Note on the contributor

Jean Seaton is Professor of Media History at the University of Westminster and Director of the Orwell Prize for political writing and journalism. She has written widely on broadcasting history, conflicts, security, politics and the media. Her most recent book was *Carnage and the Media: the Making and Breaking of News about Violence* (Penguin). Her volume of the official history of the BBC *'Traitors and Pinkoes': The BBC and the Nation 1974-87* will be published by Profile Books in September 2014.

BBC Radio censorship rows: Lessons from history

Tim Crook examines three major crises to have shaken the Corporation and concludes: 'Mistakes are not permitted, rarely forgiven, and the future is less certain and secure for the BBC than it has ever been in its 92-year history'

BBC Radio – powerful and vulnerable

The BBC continues to be the most powerful radio and sound publisher in British society. At the time of writing its listening figures and online presence vastly exceeds that of its independent and commercial competitors. The paradox is that in 1922 it began by being powerful, controversial and vulnerable at the same time, and it continues to be. The dilemma and problem is existential. It is positioned within a framework of accountability to politicians, state governance and legalistic policing and, indeed, from time to time trial and inquiry by judiciary. This means it will always have to deal with peaks of social, political and cultural crises arising out of the inevitability that its publications are going to be controversial.

Managing agitation and containment

BBC streaks of controversy are by their very nature agitational. When the internal containment fails and the external political and legal containment is over-charged the BBC risks losing power. I would argue that it was the *Today* programme radio crisis of 2003-2004 over Andrew Gilligan's live two-way about the government's intelligence dossier arguing for war that catalysed an ongoing disempowerment. Condemnation by judicial public inquiry, the immolation of its executive management, the destruction of its system of governance and the failure to negotiate an inflation index-linked licence fee means that there will be continuing decline. The fact that there is a growing consensus that BBC regulation should be transferred to Ofcom is another clear indication of future diminishing independence.

This continuum of crisis is cyclical as this chapter will demonstrate by focusing on three radio censorship rows. The BBC's conflict with the writer and politician Reginald Berkeley between 1925 and 1927 has been somewhat lost to history. The controversy was concerned more about what the BBC decided not to broadcast in the genre of sound drama. It was the beginning of the BBC's engagement with the political controversy of its role as a state approved and later 'public' broadcaster and how this would always have legal and political consequences when it made mistakes.

The BBC Radio 4 *Today* broadcast by Andrew Gilligan about the 'sexing up' of the first Iraq war dossier followed by the death of his source for that story, Dr. David Kelly, and the subsequent Hutton Inquiry of 2003, was about what it decided to broadcast in the frame of news and current affairs. The Russell Brand and Jonathan Ross BBC Radio 2 crisis of 2008 was about what the BBC was accused of wrongly broadcasting in the realm of radio comedy. It was investigated and condemned for failing to censor its content in terms of taste and decency or what had been reconstrued as harm and offence, and the new legal doctrine of privacy (Crook 2013: 110).

Social justice and commercial competition

Other qualifiers are at work. The BBC is dependent on the life-blood of licence fee payment by anyone watching live television online or by analogue and satellite reception. In the result television income by taxation subsidises BBC radio. Hundreds of thousands of people every year are criminally prosecuted (BBC News 2013) for watching television and not paying the licence fee. Hundreds used to be jailed for failing to pay the fine. When BBC 'talent' and senior executives receive controversially high fees, salaries and severance, and the BBC, as a public and indirectly state financed media institution, 'wastes' millions of pounds through incompetence, issues of social justice and fairness are raised.

The BBC's privilege and vulnerability in being given publication power by legislature and executive means that its entrepreneurial activities will always be controversial. This was true when it decided in 1923 and 1929 to publish the *Radio Times* and the *Listener*. Questions about the BBC abusing the privilege of its publicly funded power by seeking unfair gains in the commercial marketplace continue in the late 20th and early 21st century. Its popular music radio channels are repeatedly accused of draining potential income from its independent competitors by conjuring quasi-commercial arrangements in promotional events (Spence 2013). The courageous establishment in 2000 of the independent Oneword digital radio channel, pioneering a unique format of spoken word, drama and comedy, was undermined by the BBC's then commercial arm buying up the station's main shareholder Chivers, and the launch of BBC Seven (now BBC R4 Extra) with an almost identical format. BBC Seven had the advantage of the BBC's drama, comedy and, indeed, Chivers spoken-book back catalogues.

Oneword ceased transmission on 11 January 2008 and was replaced with the sound of looping birdsong (CRCA 2004: 23-24).

Reginald Berkeley and his plays – 1925-1927

Reginald Berkeley was the Tom Stoppard, or Sir David Hare of the 1920s. He was also a lawyer and a politician having been Liberal MP for Nottingham Central between 1922 and 1924. His enthusiasm for the new genre of radio drama greatly assisted the BBC's development of the microphone play; so much so that in 1925 he wrote the first original one-hour play, *The White Chateau*, for the new medium. The play had an anti-war theme but did not explicitly demonise the Germans in the Great War propagandist style of 'evil huns'. Transmission time was moved to avoid any potential ill-will with Weimar Republic Germany poised to sign the Treaties of Locarno and gain admittance to the League of Nations. Berkeley had to resist a BBC management decision to cut his play in half because of fears that listeners could not follow drama in such great length (Berkeley 1925).

The publisher of the play's script, Williams and Norgate, had to sue the BBC, in the first ever defamation action for 'slander by microphone'. The BBC and Berkeley had been working with the publisher to promote the first ever book publication of a radio play. They were jointly running a competition for listeners who after transmission on Armistice night could send in essays about their impressions of the drama. But on 4 November 1925 the BBC had incorrectly announced that the printed version of the play was not available because of a printer's strike. Despite broadcast corrections in the days that followed, the publisher still sued and won what Mr Justice McCardie described as 'so novel an action' (*Times* 1926). In the decades that followed the BBC would not find itself such a stranger to actions for defamation.

In 1926 Berkeley had a bitter public row with the BBC when without his permission it 'amputated' the final scene of his play *The Quest of Elizabeth*. Management had decided that listeners could not cope with his exploration of the consciousness of a dying child in a hospital emergency. The young girl had been knocked over by a car while searching for her mother and father, unaware they had previously died in the same accident. The BBC's decision to excise the scene where the girl dies herself on the operating table provoked Berkeley into effusions of outrage in the press (*Nottingham Evening Post* 1926). He instructed his agent to withdraw the BBC's rights to an outside broadcast of one of his stage plays (ibid) and publicly rebuked the BBC's managing director John Reith when the script was published in May 1926 (Berkeley 1926).

Worse was to follow when the BBC decided not to produce the next play commissioned from Berkeley: *Machines*. The BBC believed the dramatic characterisation of politicians from named parties, along with an apparent denunciation of capitalism and depiction of adultery between the middle and working classes was 'politically controversial': something the BBC believed it was banned from broadcasting in its then agreement with the government.

Berkeley had no law to sue the BBC with, but he published the banal and embarrassing correspondence with its executives in a stinging *J'accuse* against censorship along with the play itself and had it produced in the West End with the approval of the then process of theatre censorship by Lord Chamberlain (Berkeley 1927).

The BBC survived this scandal. It was negotiating its transformation into public corporation and its exit from any perceived obligations to avoid making politically controversial programmes. Berkeley went to Hollywood and never wrote for them again. The casualty was dramatic truth in broadcast form. The gain was a maturing of broadcast content, unleashed from the shackles of a *cordon sanitaire* around anything politically controversial, and a development of relative autonomy from government control.

Today, Dr David Kelly, and the Hutton Inquiry – 2003-2004

So much has been written and debated about this affair; not least Lord Hutton's inquiry report which ran to 750 pages in 13 chapters and 18 appendices (Hutton 2004). But in the context of the BBC's broadcasting history, it is being argued that this was a politically controversial radio news story that the BBC got largely right as the findings of the subsequent Butler Inquiry into the government's use of intelligence for its case for war (Butler 2004) and evidence given to the recent though not yet reported Chilcot Inquiry would seem to indicate. The report's text containing the inquiry's conclusions runs to more than one million words and is being delayed by difficulties in getting government documents declassified (Chilcot 2013).

The gist of most of Andrew Gilligan's radio reporting for the *Today* programme – that the New Labour government had published a dossier in September 2002 which had been rewritten to make a better case for war in Iraq than the intelligence justified – seems unassailable. His source Dr David Kelly, who effectively died for the story, has been posthumously vindicated. But the controversial nature of the politics involved, a context of aggressive news management by government communications, and on air mistakes by the reporter in his use of language plunged the BBC into a ritual of political and legalistic trial and examination that would exploit its most vulnerable weaknesses. On matters of legal judgement it has no control, and in matters of funding and regulation it is subject to the will of executive and legislature who will exercise it when they believe public and judicial opinion is on their side.

The Editor of *Today* at the time, Kevin Marsh, in his book *Stumbling Over Truth* argues that Lord Hutton did not know 'how the *Today* or any news programme or newspaper works. And because he decided he didn't need to hear how I'd considered the allegations of Gilligan's source, he assumed I hadn't thought about them at all' (Marsh 2012: 101-102). There is no structured process of appeal against the findings of public inquiries, though Marsh was advised by his lawyers that he had a case for judicial review because of the unfounded attack on his reputation.

Marsh analyses the way in which Hutton misunderstood how Gilligan came to erroneously report his source saying that the government included the claim that Iraq could launch weapons of mass destruction in 45 minutes and probably knew that it was wrong. Gilligan conceded that Dr Kelly had not told him 'actually the government probably, erm, knew that that 45-minute figure was wrong, even before it decided to put it in.' Gilligan added: '…in hindsight I should have scripted that item' (ibid: 213). As Marsh says, the item was scripted: 'Gilligan knew exactly how every BBC editor planning to run his story, including me and the overnight editor at *Today*, expected him to word those allegations' (ibid).

Marsh's book demonstrates the depth and wretchedness of the BBC's political, legal and constitutional defeat over the Kelly, Gilligan, Hutton affair. The BBC's journalism was informed by much more than Gilligan's bumbling representation of his meeting with Dr. Kelly at the Charing Cross Hotel. Marsh and his presenter John Humphrys had had lunch with the Chief of MI6, Sir Richard Dearlove, who had told them: 'On any Cartesian analysis, Iraq was not the main threat' (ibid: 117). He argues that time and again the BBC was accused of things it had not done or said and conceded and apologised for things it had got right over and over again: 'The BBC whom I'd trusted had let me down. Hutton had trashed my reputation unjustly and unfairly and without allowing me a hearing' (ibid: 299).

Brand, Ross and Radio 2 comedy – 2008

This scandal gained traction when prank calls by BBC Radio 2 comedy artists Russell Brand and Jonathan Ross to the actor and writer Andrew Sachs about his granddaughter who performed in a pop group were given focus by the *Mail on Sunday* (Goslett and Roberts 2008). 'Harm and offence' in cutting edge comedy may well be a matter of subjectivity but when questioned and attacked the BBC learnt that this was an area of subjectivity it could not afford. The hyperbole surrounding Jonathan Ross's multi-million contract added petrol to the fire. This affair demonstrated that the BBC faces a multiplicity of problems when mistakes are made: resignations of executives, including the much respected network controller; the departure of the offending talent eventually, and investigation as a breach of privacy and harm and offence by both the BBC and Ofcom who had dual regulatory jurisdiction.

The Ofcom Sanctions Committee fined the BBC a total of £150,000 and observed that the material aired had 'a cumulative effect which resulted in it overall being exceptionally offensive, humiliating and demeaning' (Ofcom 2008). The BBC Trust's apology for the programming and condemnation of the behaviour of the artists, and editorial decision-making that approved the broadcasts was not sufficient (BBC Trust 2008).

How past radio crises inform present corporate debacles

The crisis of *Newsnight* and the exposure of Jimmy Savile's sexual abuse of children in 2012-2013 were primarily about a decision not to broadcast journalism on television. This was followed by a decision to broadcast another *Newsnight* story about the sexual abuse of children which was conceded by legal settlement to be libellous (BBC News 2013). In the political maelstrom the BBC became the responsible party, even though the burden of proof in libel law being on media defendants had protected Savile when he was alive and was a factor needing consideration on the threshold of proof required for post-mortem attack on his reputation. Multi-million pound charities for good causes depended on his good name whether dead or alive.

The BBC became the responsible party for the second problematic *Newsnight* story that was broadcast. It originated from the City University London-based Centre for Investigative Journalism that apparently 'champions critical, in-depth reporting and the defence of the public interest' (CIJ 2013). Lord McAlpine so wrongly libelled by inference had not been explicitly named by the BBC. The nuances of justice in media law became an irrelevant sideshow.

The Savile scandal blew up because of division in the ranks at *Newsnight* and internecine tensions and a paucity of collective communication and cooperation at executive corporate level. Internal governance and the contingency of editorial mistake became yet again matters of political and state investigation. Publication decisions had to be examined by the legalistic ritual of 'external' and 'independent' inquiry, editorial executives had to be represented by counsel, and then judged by the forensic theatre of 'transparent' and 'accountable' evaluation. This was editorial trial by hindsight in the political spotlight again, and the self-infliction of more media institutional lesions costing millions.

As with the Hutton Inquiry findings, those of the Pollard Inquiry would be flawed by the omission of significant evidence. Hutton never heard from Andrew Gilligan's editor at *Today*, Kevin Marsh, who had insisted on the preparation of a legally and journalistically correct script for his reporter's notorious 6.07 am two-way and was powerless when his reporter, Andrew Gilligan, went *off piste*. The BBC's pre-publication editorial system of supervision was the very opposite of what Hutton condemned them for (Marsh 2013). Pollard did not include in his report key evidence given to him by the BBC's Director of Journalism, Helen Boaden, that she had briefed the BBC's Director-General Mark Thompson about *Newsnight*'s investigation into Jimmy Savile's sexual molestation of children (Pollard and Oborne 2013).

The BBC's 2013 *annus horribilis* has been compounded by the wretched vista of alleged greed in executive remuneration, and catastrophic waste of expenditure by alleged executive incompetence. The House of Commons Select Public Accounts Committee, chaired ferociously by Margaret Hodge, is legislative inquisition by democratically elected politicians. Combining this with the scrutiny of the National Audit Office leaves the BBC uncomfortably wedged in a constitutional vice of barbed condemnation (Hodge 2013). There is also the context of the BBC's hostile competitors in the multimedia-sphere whose critical noise impacts on public opinion and arcs its lightning between newsprint and online. The radio dimensions to this crisis are ever-present. The digitisation of the BBC's radio archive should be a straightforward process of analogue to digital transfer, rights clearance, storage and access management on network computer servers, but appears to have been subsumed into an abandoned £100 million 'Digital Media Initiative'.

The starting salary of a BBC broadcast journalist in local radio appears to be on a ratio of 1:20 to the highest paid radio executive. The rhetoric of social justice will not go away when the prospects for debt-ridden and post-graduate educated entrants to broadcast journalism are diminished by waning BBC income and performance. Large sections of the BBC's radio audience are living in a society where distribution of wealth is in reverse.

Conclusions to be drawn for an ongoing narrative

This is a narrative without an ending and with all of the prospects of an unhappy one. Political accountability involves legislative inquisition by parliamentary committee, the hysterical chatter of multi-media hostility from competitors, the flagellating expiation of corporate executive resignations, legalistic trial in court, public or corporate inquiry, punishment by diminishing income whether through direct grant or licence fee agreement, and a merry-go-round of diminishing independence through reforms in governance and regulation. The BBC has lost all of its separate World Service funding from the Foreign and Commonwealth Office. The licence fee has been frozen for a period of six years from 2010.

The analysis of the three radio crisis case histories, Reginald Berkeley (1925-1927), Hutton (2003-2004) and what became known as Sachsgate (2008) demonstrates that the BBC has lost its ability to withstand political firestorms without experiencing severe collateral damage. The BBC's first managing director and Director-General, John Reith (1922-1938), was adept at survival and development despite being authoritarian, brutally ruthless, an admirer of Hitler and Mussolini, and corruptly hypocritical in persecuting homosexuality and infidelity amongst his staff when he concealed his own life-long gay affair advanced by nepotism (Dyke 2007).

The performance of current and former BBC and BBC Trust executives before the Commons Parliamentary Public Accounts Committee investigating severance payments on 9 September 2013 reached a nadir that must have been unimaginable to Reith and his successors from the last century. BBC News correspondent Nick Higham tweeted: 'There was an audible cheer in the BBC newsroom when Margaret Hodge accused BBC HR director Lucy Adams of lying to the PAC' (ITV News 2013). Hodge had, in fact, said in different exchanges: 'I'm not having any more lies this afternoon ... You're developing a habit of changing your evidence' (Hodge 2013: 31 and 52). In my opinion the written transcript of the feeble arguments and lamentable explanations from the

BBC's representatives failed to convey a sense that the row had run out of words with politicians, broadcasters and regulators seeming almost speechless.

Hodge spoke of 'incompetence, a lack of central control, and a failure to communicate for an organisation whose business is communication. At worst, we may have seen people covering their backs by being less than open' (Hodge 2013: 53). It was like imperial prize-hunters cornering the King of the Jungle only to find him bloated and semi-conscious with indulgence and the last of his species. The choice was either annihilation or mercy. Hodge chose the latter course: 'All of us round the table, and I am sure you do down that end as well, really believe and value and recognise the absolute central importance of the BBC as an institution. It is one that we want to protect and promote' (ibid). If there is any conclusion to be drawn it is that mistakes are not permitted, rarely forgiven, and the future is less certain and secure than it has ever been in its 92-year history. The BBC can only hope that when next cornered, its hunters are not inclined to decide on termination.

References

Books

Berkeley, Reginald (1925) *The White Chateau*, London: Williams and Norgate Ltd

Berkeley, Reginald (1926) *The World's End and Other Plays*, London: Williams and Norgate Ltd

Berkeley, Reginald (1929) *Machines: A Symphony of Modern Life*, London: Robert Holden & Co.

Butler, Lord Frederick E. R. of Brockwell et al (2004) *Review of Intelligence on Weapons of Mass Destruction: Report of a Committee of Privy Counsellors*, London: Stationery Office

Crook, Tim (2013) *The UK Media Law Pocketbook*, Routledge: Abingdon, Oxon

CRCA (2004) Memorandum submitted by Commercial Radio Companies Association (CRCA) in evidence to Culture, Media and Sport Committee, ev 43-44, *A public BBC First Report of Session 2004–05, Volume II, Oral and written evidence*, London: Stationery Office

Hodge, Margaret et al (2003) *BBC severance packages: Thirty-third Report of Session 2013–14*, House of Commons Committee of Public Accounts, London: Stationery Office

Hutton, Lord Brian (2004) *Report of the Inquiry into the Circumstances Surrounding the Death of Dr David Kelly C.M.G.*, London: Stationery Office

Marsh, Kevin (2012) *Stumbling Over Truth: The Inside Story of the 'Sexed Up' Dossier, Hutton and the BBC*, London: Biteback

Pollard, Nick (2013) *The Pollard Review: Report*, London: Reed Smith LLP and BBC Trust

Newspaper archive

Nottingham Evening Post (1926) Captain Berkeley's Indignation, 8 February p. 1; No Broadcast of Captain Berkeley's Play: The Right of Censorship p. 2

The Times (1926) High Court of Justice, King's Bench Division: Alleged Slander by Microphone, 24 April, *Times* p. 5

Online

BBC News (2013) TV licence prosecutions hit new peak, 22 August. Available online at http://www.bbc.co.uk/news/entertainment-arts-23792388, accessed on 12 December 2013

BBC News (n.d.) Savile Inquiry. Available online at http://www.bbc.co.uk/news/uk-20286888, accessed on 12 December 2013

BBC Trust (2008) *Editorial Standards Findings: Appeals and editorial issues considered by the Trust's Editorial Standards Committee in Russell Brand et al and Radio 2 and Radio 1*, October. Available online at http://news.bbc.co.uk/nol/shared/bsp/hi/pdfs/21_11_08_brand_ross_moyles.pdf, accessed on 12 December 2013

Centre for Investigative Journalism, (CIJ) (n.d.) Available online at http://www.tcij.org/about-cij, accessed on 20 December 2013

Chicot, Sir John (2013) Chair of the Iraq Inquiry. Available online at http://www.iraqinquiry.org.uk/, accessed on 23 December 2013

Dyke, Greg (2007) Greg Dyke on Lord Reith, BBC 4, 23 and 24 May 2007. Available online at http://www.bbc.co.uk/programmes/b0074tml, accessed on 12 December 2013

Goslett, Miles (2008) Russell Brand and Jonathan Ross could face prosecution after obscene on air phone calls to Fawlty Towers actor, 78, 26 October , *Mail on Sunday*, Available online at http://www.dailymail.co.uk/news/article-1080621/Russell-Brand-Jonathan-Ross-face-prosecution-obscene-air-phone-calls-Fawlty-Towers-actor-78.html, accessed on 12 December 2013

ITV News (2013) Audible cheer at BBC when HR boss accused of lying, 9 September. Available online at http://www.itv.com/news/update/2013-09-09/audible-cheer-at-bbc-when-hr-boss-accused-of-lying/, accessed on 24 December 2013

Oborne, Peter (2013) Lord Patten must find out the truth about Jimmy Savile, Mark Thompson and the Pollard Review, *Daily Telegraph*, 21 November. Available online at http://blogs.telegraph.co.uk/news/peteroborne/100246954/lord-patten-must-find-out-the-truth-about-jimmy-savile-mark-thompson-and-the-pollard-review/, accessed on 12 December 2013

Ofcom (2008) *The British Broadcasting Corporation, the BBC, in respect of Radio Two*, Content Sanctions Committee: October. Available online at http://stakeholders.ofcom.org.uk/binaries/enforcement/content-sanctions-adjudications/BBCRadio2TheRussellBrandShow.pdf, accessed on 12 December 2013

Roberts, Laura (2009) Just vile: Brand and Ross 'joke' about breaking into Andrew Sachs' home to sexually abuse him as he slept, *Daily Mail*, 29 October. Available online at http://www.dailymail.co.uk/news/article-1081528/Just-vile-Brand-Ross-joke-breaking-Andrew-Sachs-home-sexually-abuse-slept.html, accessed on 12 December 2013

Spence, Alex (2013) Middle-brow Radio 1 is squeezing us out, say commercial rivals, *Times*, 21 December. Available online at http://www.thetimes.co.uk/tto/news/medianews/article3961517.ece, accessed on 21 December 2013

Note on the contributor

Tim Crook's publications include *Comparative Media Law and Ethics* (Routledge 2009) and the *UK Media Law Pocketbook* (Routledge 2013). He has been an award-winning journalist, author and broadcaster for 38 years. He is Visiting Professor of Broadcast Journalism at Birmingham City University and Reader in Media and Communication at Goldsmiths, University of London where he has originated undergraduate and postgraduate courses in radio, scriptwriting, and comparative media ethics and law.

Crisis? What crisis? The real BBC catastrophe is yet to happen

Steven Barnett predicts a concerted attack over the next 18 months on the BBC's size, funding, governance, impartiality, competence and standing in British society – as anti-Corporation MPs join forces with ferociously anti-BBC national newspapers

There is no crisis at the BBC.

Let me put that another way. There is a permanent crisis at the BBC. In fact, narratives about the BBC in crisis have been all the rage ever since Michael Leapman's apocalyptically titled book *Last Days of the Beeb*, published in the midst of clashes with the Thatcher government in 1986. Anyone under 50 will barely remember a time when the BBC wasn't in crisis.

In the wake of the Hutton Report and subsequent resignation of both BBC Chairman and Director-General in 2004, it was hard to escape stories about meltdowns, irrevocable damage and terminal crisis. The BBC recovered. In the ten years since, we have had the 'crisis' of BBC chairman Michael Grade defecting to ITV, the 'crisis' of Queengate and a trailer which appeared to show the Queen storming out of a photoshoot instead of walking in, the 'crisis' of fake phone calls to phone-in programmes and fake competition prize winners, the Ross-Brand 'crisis' when Jonathan and Russell left abusive messages on actor Andrew Sachs's answer phone, the 'crisis' when the BBC refused to broadcast a charity appeal in aid of Gaza refugees, and the 'crisis' when footage from a *Panorama* investigation into Primark (obtained from a third party) appeared to have been doctored.

And so we arrived at 2012-2013. A daft editorial decision by *Newsnight* to drop a story exposing Jimmy Savile as a paedophile (which ended up on ITV) was followed by an even dafter *Newsnight* film which mistakenly named former Conservative Party Treasurer Lord McAlpine as involved in child abuse in North Wales. Following another D-G resignation from George Entwistle after just 54 days in the chair, the newly-installed Lord Hall was faced with evidence of inflated senior management salaries and – even worse – pay-offs to departing executives far in excess of their entitlement.

Each of these episodes has at different times exposed failures in some part of the BBC's operation: managerial incompetence, poor editorial judgement, crass mishandling, bureaucratic bungling, flawed understanding of the public service ethos. Each has been characterised as signalling fundamental malaise if not terminal decline. For many years now, this narrative has been deliberately and mischievously fanned by powerful press groups deeply antagonistic to the size and scope of the BBC on both ideological and commercial grounds. To some extent, twas ever thus. But the noise of these self-interested attacks is louder, the excuses are flimsier, and the commercial imperatives are much stronger as the long-standing business model of print journalism goes pear-shaped. So while we should expect and demand that the BBC rectify its corporate mistakes and misjudgements – and ensure that any repetition is minimised if not eliminated – we should also be clear about the blatant exaggerations of crises that simply do not exist. And – much more importantly – we should also be clear about what constitutes the genuine, life-threatening crisis that could eventually engulf the BBC completely.

Non-crisis of governance

Without doubt, the most unedifying BBC spectacle of 2013 was the sight of executives trying to explain to the Public Accounts Committee of the House of Commons why tens of millions of licence fee payers' money had been handed out in generous – and unearned – severance payments to departing senior executives. This palpable failure to exercise proper stewardship over public money – which was, in fact, a failure of BBC management and its non-executive directors – inevitably raised questions about the BBC's governance structures given that the BBC Trust was established to act as 'the eyes and ears of the licence-payer'.

It is not unusual – nor even necessarily wrong – to question governance structures after such public displays of incompetence, and the Culture Secretary Maria Miller lost little time in calling on the BBC to address what she called 'ongoing confusion' between the respective roles of Trust and Management. In a gross but predictable overreaction, many MPs – not to mention the usual suspect columnists and BBC critics – queued up to condemn the governance system as 'broken'. The BBC responded with a joint Trust/Executive review, published in December 2013, which committed to a series of actions designed to bring greater clarity and greater separation 'with the Trust clearly responsible for setting the overall strategic framework for the BBC and the Executive responsible for delivering within this' (BBC 2013).

It is easy to forget that this is precisely the basis on which the Trust was established in 2006 to replace the system of governors which had long been seen as too intimately bound to BBC management. In a world where public funding demanded independent scrutiny, the Trust was designed to make both a geographical and conceptual break in how BBC governance would operate. For the first time, not only did the BBC have six newly articulated public purposes enshrined in their 2006 royal charter, but each of their individual services – every TV channel and radio station as well as its online offering – was required to have a detailed 'service licence' established by the Trust and reviewable every five years to enable it to 'monitor and ensure the performance of the Executive in delivering individual services'. Moreover, every BBC programme must fulfil one of five 'public service characteristics'; and any new service or any 'significant change' to an existing change must be subjected by the Trust to a 'Public Value Test' (PVT).

This 'triple lock', as the then-Culture Secretary Tessa Jowell called it, provided a clear basis on which the Trust could scrutinise the BBC's activities and ensure that it continued to operate in accordance with its public purposes. That crucial element of the new governance structure has worked well, despite attempts to condemn the whole operation as effectively bust. Just as under the old system of governors, there has been criticism of the 'dual role' played by the Trust, as BBC 'cheerleaders' protecting it from government interference while at the same acting as scrutineers of management. In fact, that tension is implicit in the very existence of a publicly funded broadcaster which is not an arm of the state. There is no counsel of perfection for BBC governance, and any arrangement will involve some kind of compromise.

While the current system might be improved by appointment of a BBC non-executive chairman to take on an explicit cheerleading role – and allow more distance for the chairman of the Trust – the oft-quoted idea of the BBC coming under Ofcom is both unworkable and undesirable. To have the same regulator which is responsible for a thriving commercial sector also responsible for looking after a public sector with a wholly different culture, rationale and history would create huge difficulties for the future of a healthy and dynamic BBC.

Non-crisis of influence

Another favourite assertion of BBC critics is that the BBC's size and scale is 'crowding out' its commercial rivals, either preventing the growth of existing media enterprises or stifling new commercial initiatives. Moreover, they insist that this unhealthy influence extends to the reach of BBC news, because of its popularity with viewers and online users. Less than a year after a procession of democratically elected prime ministers publicly conceded to the Leveson Inquiry that they had surrendered too much power to big media corporations – and, in particular, to Rupert Murdoch's News Corporation – a government review of media plurality suggested that the BBC might be incorporated into a new plurality framework. Without irony – and encouraged by some carefully targeted ministerial briefings – newspaper coverage gleefully interpreted this as evidence that, in the *Daily Mail*'s words, 'the BBC could be curbed under government plans to rein in dominance of media giants'.

In revenue terms, of course, the BBC's £3.5 billion revenue pales into insignificance next to the massive global giants of Google, Facebook, and Amazon, let alone the £7 billion annual revenues of BSkyB. Even within the newspaper world, despite declining circulations and an increasingly defective advertising-based business model, Ofcom's figures show that 40 per cent of the population still 'use daily newspapers for news', of which a quarter read the *Sun* and one in five read the *Daily Mail*. Alongside a further 9 per cent who read *The Times*, a combined figure of one third of newspaper readers still read papers owned by Rupert Murdoch's News UK – the same proprietor who continues to own a controlling 39 per cent in BSkyB (Ofcom 2013).

Nevertheless, that same Ofcom report is being brandished by those desperate to see a weakened, diminished BBC because of its attempt to develop a quantified assessment of cross-media consumption. This 'bespoke cross-media metric', called Share of References, is based on the frequency with which consumers use different news sources and is heavily weighted towards television consumption simply because television viewing is far more woven into people's lives than online or newspaper consumption. Using this metric, Ofcom calculates that the BBC commands 44 per cent of 'Share of References' with ITN on 14 per cent, Sky on 13 per cent and all the newspaper groups straggling along at less than 5 per cent – figures gleefully seized on by the BBC's enemies.

However, these bald statistics give an entirely misleading impression of BBC power. They take no account of the ability to influence opinion which is implicit in the freedom to promote impassioned, one-sided arguments that is – quite properly – an integral part of any free press. Nor do they take account of the power of Britain's national press to set news agendas. While there is little rigorous research, anecdotal evidence points to a major role for our national press in driving news agendas. Broadcast newsrooms are famously immersed in mountains of newsprint, and informal conversations with BBC journalists reveal a high level of editorial anxiety when bulletins are not covering a story featured prominently in the press.

On a different level, Ofcom's approach takes no account of the power to influence elite groups and policy makers – government ministers, MPs and peers, senior civil servants, regulators, policy advisers and members of think tanks. In their evidence to the Leveson Inquiry, former and serving government ministers told of how powerful newspaper proprietors sought to exert influence over government policy, and former *Guardian* journalist Malcolm Dean has described a series of social policy case studies where governments have clearly been influenced by press policy agendas (Dean 2013). That kind of power and influence is not measured by Ofcom, and is certainly not wielded by the BBC whose invitations to Downing Street are neither cast nor interpreted as opportunities to impart advice.

Non-crisis of bias

Almost as predictable as calls for greater regulatory scrutiny of the BBC are allegations of outrageous left-wing bias and a 'crisis' of editorial incompetence. Mostly, these are prompted by a particular programme or individual, suggesting anecdotally that the BBC is gripped by a collective left-wing culture. Occasionally, these anecdotes are turned into 'hard evidence' by an organisation or publisher determined to 'prove' that a left-wing bias exists through some kind of attempted quantification.

That is precisely what happened when the *Daily Telegraph*, along with *Press Gazette* and several other papers, announced a study in August 2013 which claimed to have 'statistical evidence' of the BBC's left-wing bias. The pre-announced report from the Centre for Policy Studies, an avowedly right-wing think tank, claimed that the number of BBC website mentions given to political think-tanks correlated much more closely with the *Guardian* than with the *Daily Telegraph*. This shocking demonstration of left-wing manipulation was compounded by a finding that right-of-centre think-tanks were far more likely to receive health warnings than their left-of-centre counterparts.

Although it was never officially published, the 16-page report is still available on the CPS website and a swift reading demonstrates its lack of robustness (Latham 2013). Amongst the many basic methodological errors are:

- an assumption that the *Guardian* and *Telegraph* represent polar opposites (they each have more sophisticated news values);
- that BBC online represents all BBC output (subsequent television news bulletins have quoted Policy Exchange, MigrationWatch and the Taxpayers Alliance with no health warnings);
- that online is representative of BBC news consumption (the vast majority of BBC exposure is to TV news);
- that each think tank output is equally newsworthy (many are propaganda rather than research-based, and editors make editorial decisions accordingly);
- that the BBC is out of line with other broadcasters (there was no attempt at comparative analysis with Sky or ITN);
- and that the list of think-tanks was appropriately drawn up (it is, for example, amusing to see the right-of-centre Institute of Economic Affairs positioned to the left of the spectrum while the left-of-centre Institute for Public Policy Research is to the right).

As has long been the case, both left and right view the bias debate through their own partisan lenses, and this will not be the last time that a politically partisan think-tank produces a blatantly politicised report. Genuinely independent and rigorous studies are difficult to find, but one of the most recent comprehensive studies was conducted by the highly respected Cardiff University research group. It examined evidence for bias in the BBC's coverage of Europe and the City and concluded that 'the BBC tends to reproduce a Conservative, Eurosceptic, pro-business version of the world, not a left-wing, anti-business agenda' (Berry 2013). Strangely, Cardiff's 112-page report attracted virtually no publicity. Meanwhile, the British public continue to place their faith in the BBC: asked of all the news sources, which *one* source they were most likely to turn to for impartial news coverage, 49 per cent spontaneously answer the BBC. Its closest rivals are ITV on 14 per cent and Sky News on 6 per cent.[1]

The real crisis is funding

As a major study published by the Reuters Institute in February concluded, the real danger for the BBC is a progressive decline in funding to the point where it is simply incapable of fulfilling its task as a comprehensive public service broadcaster. The authors note the gradual diminution of the licence fee as a proportion of total industry spending on television, projected to fall from its current 22 per cent of the total to 18.5 per cent by 2016. This 'salami-slicing' – which accelerated with the 16 per cent cuts imposed by the newly elected Coalition government in October 2010 – is progressively eroding the BBC's ability to maintain its status as a major cultural force in Britain. According to the authors, 'it is not scaremongering to project that, if the current policy continues (i.e. even if the more radical proposals for scaling back the BBC are rejected), within a generation it will have been reduced to a barely relevant sideshow, the UK equivalent of PBS in America' (Barwise and Picard 2014). As well as public and consumer detriment this continuing decline will impact on the UK's independent production sector since the commercial sector cannot make up the shortfall.

That is the real crisis for the future of the BBC. If Britain wants to sustain a cultural institution which is still trusted and enjoyed by the vast majority of its own citizens while being consistently praised and admired throughout the world, we must have the political will to make the resources available. We urgently need manifesto commitments from all three major parties to guarantee that they will, after 2016, reinstate a licence fee index-linked to inflation.

That agenda will not be pursued by our national or regional press. Over the next 18 months, we can expect a concerted attack on the BBC's size, funding, governance, impartiality, competence and standing in British society as anti-BBC MPs (mostly from the Conservative benches) join forces with ferociously anti-BBC national newspapers which are determined, for self-serving commercial as well as political reasons, to undermine the Corporation's legitimacy and funding base. Let's not forget that in the White Paper review which preceded the last BBC charter renewal in 2006, there was an unprecedented joint submission by three major UK newspaper conglomerates – Associated Newspapers, News International and the Telegraph Group – which combined forces to call for a below-inflation increase in the licence fee to 'curtail the width of the BBC's remit in the digital arena'. The submission was also signed by the Commercial

Radio Companies Association and the Newspaper Society, representing the local and regional press.

That same alliance – whether explicitly or not – will be operating this time around, and will be very keen to extend the 'BBC crisis' narrative which has been so vigorously promoted over the last 10 years. It will not be the first time that BBC supporters both inside and outside parliament – who represent the great majority of the British public – will struggle to have their voices heard. But if the BBC is to avoid a genuine crisis, it might be the most important.

Notes

[1] Ipsos MORI for the BBC, UK adults 16-plus who follow the news (1,873) interviewed face-to-face, February 2013. Reported in BBC Response to DCMS Consultation on Media Ownership and Pluralism: Annex 2

References

Barwise, Patrick and Picard, Robert G. (2014) *What If There Were No BBC Television? The Net Impact on UK Viewers*, Reuters Institute for the Study of Journalism, February

BBC (2013) *Review of BBC Internal Governance*, BBC, December. Available online at http://downloads.bbc.co.uk/bbctrust/assets/files/pdf/about/how_we_govern/govern ance_review_2013.pdf, accessed on 22 December 2013

Berry, Mike (2013) Hard Evidence: How biased is the BBC?, *The Conversation*, 23 August. (The full report, by Karin Wahl-Jorgensen et al, is available online at http://downloads.bbc.co.uk/bbctrust/assets/files/pdf/our_work/breadth_opinion/co ntent_analysis.pdf, accessed on 23 December 2013)

Dean, Malcolm (2013) *Democracy Under Attack: How the Media Distort Policy and Politics*, London: Policy Press

Latham, Oliver (2013) Bias at the Beeb: A quantitative study of slant in BBC online reporting, Centre for Policy Studies, August. Available online at http://www.cps.org.uk/publications/reports/bias-at-the-beeb/, accessed on 23 December 2013

Ofcom (2013) *News Consumption in the UK – 2013*, 25 September. Available online at http://stakeholders.ofcom.org.uk/binaries/research/tv-research/news/News_Report_2013.pdf, accessed on 23 December 2013

Note on the contributor

Steven Barnett is Professor of Communications at Westminster University and an established writer, author and commentator, who specialises in media policy, broadcasting, regulation, and journalism ethics. He has acted several times as specialist adviser to the House of Lords Select Committee on Communications, most recently for their inquiry into Investigative Journalism, and was twice called to give oral evidence to the Leveson inquiry. Over the last 30 years, he has directed numerous research projects on the structure, funding, and regulation of communications, and in April 2013 he began an 18-month AHRC fellowship study on developing new policy approaches to media plurality. He sits on both the Management and Editorial Boards of the *British Journalism Review* and writes frequently for the national and specialist press. He is the author or co-author of a number of books, of which the most recent, *The Rise and Fall of Television Journalism*, was published by Bloomsbury Academic in November 2011.

The conventions of the BBC

The BBC's independence, it is commonly believed, is protected by 'conventions', there being no written constitution. Wrong on both counts, argues Brian Winston. It does have a constitution, its charter and agreement, but there are no meaningful 'conventions' to protect it – only politics

'Political morality'

Steve Hewlett, ex-editor of *Panorama*, current presenter of Radio 4's *Media Show* and a leading *Guardian* media commentator, expresses a received opinion when he writes:

> The BBC's independence is widely recognised as its greatest asset. And it's a fragile flower – depending on an array of understandings and conventions (this being Britain there is no 'constitution' to protect it) that, in turn, rely on all parties understanding and respecting them (Hewlett 2013a).

Hewlett knows more than most about the BBC, but, like most, it would appear he knows less than he might about Albert Venn Dicey, Vinerian Professor of English Law at Oxford, 1882-1909, the man who introduced the concept of 'constitutional conventions' in his *Lectures Introductory to the Study of the Law of the Constitution*, published in 1885 (Dicey 2013 [1885]). Part of the UK constitution, in Dicey's formulation, are rules (emphatically not laws) that:

> … consist of conventions, understandings, habits, or practices that – though they may regulate the conduct of the several members of the sovereign power, the Ministry, or other officials – are not really laws, since they are not enforced by the courts. This portion of constitutional law may, for the sake of distinction, be termed the 'conventions of the constitution', or constitutional morality (Dicey 2013 [1885]: 186 [420].

'Constitutional morality', to make its oxymoronic quality clearer, is elsewhere glossed as a species of 'political morality' (ibid: 203 [453]). 'Conventions', then, exist for the exercise of 'discretionary authority' not *prima facie* as a means for constraining it except as, say, between the will of parliament and the will of the crown. Moreover, as Dicey pointed out, these conventions are in fact 'fictions' – comforting shibboleths – nothing more than, in his words, the 'most fanciful dreams of *Alice in Wonderland*' (cited in Ward 2004: 33).

So, Hewlett is quite right to note that the 'fragility' of the BBC's 'independence' is because of its reliance on 'understandings and conventions', but his 'conventions' comfort blanket pulls wool over his eyes (and, it must be said, over the eyes of many others too). It is widely believed that the BBC's 'independence' is protected by conventions when:

a) these would do no such thing if they actually existed in any Dicerean sense; and

b) anyway, they don't.

All that protects the BBC is politics; 'political morality', forsooth! It might be thought the capstone right of free expression, which is after all what is fundamentally here at stake, needs more than that.

Ever since the 17th century Civil War and the failed attempts of the Crown in the 1690s to re-impose autocratic censorship structures on organs of expression, you can rely on one establishment voice or another (let's call them Whigs) being raised in defence of free expression whenever other voices attack (Tories?). Thanks to Mr Hitler and the BBC's brilliant response to his war, this mechanism still works to the BBC's advantage. That is why, when a Grant Shapps (the Conservative Party Chairman) threatens the BBC's continued existence, he is reminded – even by some of his own government – that he shouldn't (BBC News 2013). But to think that a 'convention', much less legally protected 'independence', is in play here is to be grievously mistaken. The outcomes of such interventions, the reality of the menace they represent, are far more matters of raw politics than of the niceties of supposed 'conventions'.

The general miasma about the BBC's constitutional position extends to the question of its supposedly unwritten constitution in general: 'this being Britain, there is no written "constitution"', writes Hewlett (op cit). The scare quotes echo Walter Bagehot's high Victorian opinion that Britain was far better off without such revolutionary texts as those adopted by the French and the Americans. Ironically, though, the BBC is an exception to the usual British preference for dealing with constitutional complexities – such as the situation of a state broadcaster which must not appear to be an organ of the state – by remaining silent. However, in fact, the BBC does have – in plain sight – a written constitution: its charter and agreement (Secretary of State for Culture etc 2006a, 2006b).

The *Oxford English Dictionary* has 'constitution' defined as 'decree, ordinance, regulation': the dictionary notes that this meaning of constitution is especially apposite for 'an enactment made by an Emperor'. True, the lexicographers were thinking of ancient Rome, but the specific gloss applies in 20th century Britain, too. The BBC's charter – that is, its royal charter – is one half of its written constitution. The first iteration of the charter in 1926 stated: 'We [i.e. the Throne] deem it desirable that the Service [i.e. radio] should be developed and exploited to the best advantage [by] ... a corporation [i.e. the BBC] charged with these duties' (cited in Briggs 1995: 327). A charter is defined as a 'document ... granting privileges and rights' – in this case, the right and privilege to broadcast. The device of a charter indicates, as it was designed to do, an implicit measure of independence. That it does not do this in fact is because of the second written element, initially the licence.

What is all too often conveniently overlooked is that the charter did not – does not – stand alone. There was also this licence which detailed how the right and privilege bestowed by the first document was to be operationalised. The BBC's constitution, therefore, was a charter and licence. This second element is also covered by a further OED definition of 'constitution': 'The system or body of fundamental principles according to which a national, state or body politic is constituted and governed.' It was no accident that the implicit 'privilege' of a charter was hedged about by the actual restrictions of a licence.

Because today the BBC's use of the spectrum is licensed by another state organ, Ofcom, the operationalising element is now termed the agreement and the state supervision of the BBC is exercised by it as well as the Secretary of State for Culture (Secretary of State for Culture 2006b). The use of the term agreement is, like charter, confusing. In reality, the agreement does not mean agreement in its dictionary sense of a bargain freely forged through 'mutual understanding'. It is still an imposed document. By it the Secretary of State for Culture still has oversight. For one thing she chooses and pays the BBC's Trustees (as the governors have become). In fact, she is mentioned 78 times in the 61 pages of the current iteration of the agreement.

So, in short, the BBC does have a written, two-part detailed constitution; but this is not to say the BBC is entirely supine. It has, as it were, Whiggery on its side. Certainly from the outset in 1926, each decadal (more or less) renewal of its constitution has occasioned serious manoeuvrings between the Corporation and the government of the day but always with the politicians holding the trumps. The discussions are far more conditioned by *realpolitik* than by constitutional protections and it is, needless to say, erroneous to believe the BBC's charter 'by convention cannot be changed without the BBC's full agreement' (Hewlett 2013b: 32). This is simply not so. The BBC can lose the argument and have no legally sanctioned redress.

'Controversy'
In the 1920s, radio threw up many tricky issues for the authorities. As a communications system, initially limited to military use, wireless telegraphy, in British official thinking, fell clearly with the purview of the Postmaster General.

He already had control of telegraphy and telephony and he was charged, by domestic law and international treaty obligations, with the allocation and licensing of the radio spectrum. In 1922, having been pestered for some years by radio manufacturers for transmitting licences to encourage the sale of domestic receivers, the Postmaster General , with rather bad grace, agreed to issue these, if the companies agreed (in the dictionary sense) to cooperate. Much was made of the chaos of American broadcasting at the time to justify the creation of a monopoly. The deal which then established the British Broadcasting Company was essentially concessive as it was to be managed with 'the maximum freedom which Parliament is prepared to concede' (Briggs 1979: 50). The following year, the legitimacy of this Broadcasting Company was (belatedly) confirmed by a Committee of Inquiry headed by Sir Frederick Sykes, MP.

A state-created licensed commercial monopoly was a rare but no unique thing. At exactly this time, for example, the government passed considerable state subsidies to the similarly nascent commercial airline companies to merge into what became Imperial Airways, another (eventually) *de facto* state-licensed monopoly. The difference was that the BBC was an organ of opinion and, as such in a democracy, should not enjoy so close a relationship with the state. It was assumed that a better, potentially less conflictive, way would need to be found and in 1925 another committee of inquiry under Lord Crawford was established to determine final arrangements for the nation's radio service. (Briggs 1991: 299-328). The question of political influence and independence, however, was no more fully discussed by Crawford than it had been when the Company was established in 1922 or at the Sykes inquiry in 1923. The range of lobbyists who came before Crawford – from the Church and the 'hams' to the newspaper barons and the entertainment industries – all were eager to exploit or stunt radio's growth. None were concerned about independence or the shadow the PMG cast over the whole business.

Crawford's proposed use of the medieval instrument of the royal charter mechanism (not to make a town a city or a college a university as was its usual purpose but to create a public broadcasting corporation) was a fig leaf to cover what Whig opinion might consider the improperly close relationship of broadcasters and politicians. Praying in the charter was a PR masterstroke. England is, after all, the country of *Areopagitica* (of 1644), subtitled: *A speech of Mr. John Milton for the Liberty of Unlicenc'd Printing, to the Parlament of England.* Milton's key demand of, and the key to, a right of free expression is succinctly contained in the word 'unlicenc'd'. Licensing modes of expression is unacceptable to the British political psyche. It smacks too much of autocracy. Distracting public debate from the *Licence* and the question of independence by way of the *de facto* red herring of a royal charter was the name of the game. In the same wise, this charter called for 'governors', despite the connotation of prisons and colonies, rather than the Cromwellian 'commissioners' which was the alternative being suggested at the time (Briggs 1979: 49). It is even not really part of the record who the genius who thought of this ploy was. Asa Briggs' official BBC history fails to name names, as if the idea was too obvious, too natural, to warrant a credit. And it certainly worked. There was again no discussion of any constitutional guarantees of independence.

This was all the stranger because the question of independence was clearly being refracted as the issue of 'controversy' – and this at least was being, if only marginally, considered. John Reith, the Broadcasting Company's CEO, had been properly concerned with the PMG endlessly seeking to prevent the Broadcasting Company airing 'controversy'. Forbidding this was one of the terms of the Company's licence which Reith thought ought not to be repeated in the charter. By 1925, 'controversial' content had been deemed to include, for example, a politician of the Postmaster General's own party mentioning on air the 1919 Treaty of Versailles without prior Foreign Office clearance and the banning of his own chancellor from broadcasting a report on the budget (Briggs 1995: 243-245). Aside from Reith and his colleagues, though, the impropriety of such censorship had hardly been noticed and never seriously debated, much less acted on. But events allowed Reith to find a way of dealing with these interventions to achieve a *modus vivendi* with government.

Two months after Crawford reported, in March 1926, recommending a monopolistic royal corporation, the General Strike occurred, causing the establishment to believe it was witnessing an early replay of the recent Soviet revolution in England's green and pleasant land. Churchill, then Chancellor of the Exchequer, wanted to take the Broadcasting Company over directly. Reith brilliantly resisted, by pusillanimously doing everything a Churchill could have desired and thereby established a basis for removing the Postmaster General's dead-hand. In the memo he sent his managers after the nine days that did not shake the world and the strike collapsed, can be seen the contours of this accommodation:

> There could be no question about our supporting the Government in general, particularly since the General Strike had been declared illegal in the High Court. This being so, we were unable to permit anything which was contrary to the spirit of that judgement, and which might have prolonged or sought to justify the strike. ... The only definite complaint may be that we had no speaker from the Labour side. We asked to be allowed to do so, but the decision eventually was that since the Strike had been declared illegal this could not be allowed.

Briggs' opinion of the significance of this cannot be denied: 'The Company existed on 8th May [the first day of the strike] by sufferance' and it only maintained 'a precarious measure of independence throughout [it]' (Briggs 1995: 330, 347). But Reith was able then to argue successfully that, on the basis of the BBC's coverage of the strike and its subsequent editorial record over equally vexed issues, broadcasters could be trusted to handle 'controversy'. In 1928, he wrote to the Postmaster General promising that:

… it appears from universal experience that the broadcaster himself is the most important censor of the form and extent of controversial matter, and that even where government control is so remote and loose as to be negligible, the self interest or sense of responsibility of the broadcaster requires that controversy should be prudently or tactfully introduced (Scannell and Cardiff 1991: 42).

The government agreed. The Postmaster General's censoring powers were curtailed and the BBC's independence was allowed to flourish. A convention might be said to have been established; but given these circumstances, the 'independence' which was allowed to bloom was, and – as Hewlett points out – is, fragile.

'Controversy' might now be countenanced but there are still 40 references to 'content' in the 2006 agreement, starting on page ii: 'The content of the BBC's UK Public Services must be high quality, challenging, original, innovative and engaging, with every programme or item of content exhibiting at least one of those characteristics.' None of these terms, mind, is defined – a particular danger in this Dicerian 'wonderland', where, it will be remembered words mean what Humpty Dumpty says they mean. It is no stretch to see this charter and agreement as more a constitution for regulators than for broadcasters. As such, it can be further noted, the content demands are echoed by the *de facto* censoring Ofcom content codes which also now apply to the Corporation.

The overwhelming technical need, reinforced by law and treaty, was for the state to allot bandwidth. This necessity allowed the politicians and, subsequently, the statutory regulatory creatures they created to control broadcasting, to cross the line unimpeded between such legitimate infrastructural allocative functions and improper content controls. To this day: Ofcom now perfectly illustrates how we have confused allocation with censorship. It properly controls the infrastructure and improperly constrains content. It does this last with a further display of the English genius for governance. 'Censorship' is defined as 'laying no *previous* restraints on publications' (Blackstone 1979 [1769]: 151, emphasis in the original); so, as Ofcom does not vet content, and cannot do so by law, it can claim that it does not offend the 'no prior constraint' doctrine. It does not, by its own logic, censor. Instead it 'regulates' by producing detailed content rules and, in the event of a transgression against them, acts only after transmission. In this way, with chilling effect, its codes force the broadcasters to do its prior constraining for it. Broadcasting is a world of 'compliance officers' within its institutions and, therefore, between 'regulation' and 'censorship' lies only a distinction without a difference. To pretend there is no censorship is another aspect of the shibboleth of broadcasting freedom – commercial as well as the BBC.

Of course, day-to-day this matters little. Working at the BBC does not entail constantly looking over one's shoulder at the government and, to most intents and purposes, content is no more constrained than it is at other broadcasting institutions. Moreover, incidents have occurred which indicate that Whiggish protection is possible if any serious prior threat to editorial integrity is presented. In 1956, for instance, the Leader of the Opposition, Hugh Gaitskell was allowed (eventually) to broadcast Labour's hostility to the Suez adventure in the teeth of Tory Prime Minster Eden's objections (Chignell 2013). A more overt piece of 'convention' making occurred in 1972, at the outset of the Ulster Troubles. The Home Secretary, Reginald Maudling, threatened to use his powers under the charter and licence to control coverage of the province but the Chair of the Governors, Lord Hill, resisted – and, moreover, let it be known that he would let it be known if the BBC were censored. Whiggish sensitivities prevailed. But, note, this last is no longer – if it ever was – a 'convention' as it is now part of the written agreement (Secretary of State for Culture 2006b: 81). The BBC has a right to reveal if it has been subjected to prior constraint – nakedly 'censored'.

Do these incidents 'prove' the BBC's independence, or are they exceptions to a general rule of (albeit occasional but not necessarily rare) control? They suggest that actual protections soon find their way into writing. They, therefore, cannot be presumed to exist in any meaningful fashion if unwritten. Basically, beyond the anyway chilling effects of the content codes, we cannot know how often pressure improper in a supposedly open democracy is actually exerted and to what effect. The belief that the limitations imposed by the charter, agreement and Ofcom are constrained by 'conventions' is a species of flat-earthism, mere cognitive dissonance.

Licence fee

In 1926, though, for Reith, the problem was not only to escape the Scylla of his bosses, the wireless-set manufacturers who owned the Company, while avoiding a much as possible Charybdis, i. e. the Postmaster General, who licensed its operation. More pressing was the fact that the PMG controlled the Company's and, after 1 January 1927, the Corporation's future through the licence fee. The subterfuge of the royal charter has worked brilliantly to preserve the BBC for nearly a century but the method of its financing, ultimately, gave (and gives) it no protection. How could this be otherwise given the irresistible attractions of power to the political class? And what greater power is there than control of finances? Against this, the BBC can deploy only Whig assumptions as to the desirability of free expression. Thus lightly armed it has to renegotiate its existence and its finances with parliament once a decade and sometimes more often than that, e.g. as in 2011 (Secretary of State for Culture 2011). The plain fact is that the BBC was handed a poisoned chalice by the Broadcasting Company – and the poison was the licence fee.

An antidote, of course, is commercial advertising. As happened with the newspapers in the 19th century, government money, in the form of bribes, was (finally and totally) replaced by advertising revenue. These put the recipients into thrall but advertisers, certainly individually, were no match in power to the state. Reith, apparently sensing the dangers of reliance on state funding, quietly objected to a prohibition against advertising being a clause in the charter (Briggs 1995 [1961]: 329), but to no effect. The US example had convinced the Post Office not only that a single corporation was needed but, equally significantly, the crassness of American radio advertising ruled out commercial sponsorship. The possibility was buried almost without trace and, anyway, already to hand, was the licence fee sharing arrangements of the GPO and the Broadcasting Company. Continuing this for the BBC was the obvious answer. Distributing revenue raised from domestic receiver licence-holders between the Post Office and the Corporation to fund programming was deemed as reasonable in 1926 as it had been in 1922. The Corporation was going to be forced into dealing directly with government as the sole source of its funding in perpetuity or until its (likelier sooner) demise. Reith's immediate concern, therefore, was to argue for the greatest percentage of the fee, set at the highest level possible, as he could get. Everyone of his successors has fought the same battle. The implicit threat to independence is the inexorable consequence of this dependence. If a Shapps gathers enough around him, no convention will protect the BBC's funding.

And, once again, this starts to matter very much. As Hewlett notes, the BBC's independence – whatever its reality – 'is most at risk whenever the BBC's corporate interests – financing, governance, charter review and so on – are in play' (Hewlett 2013a). And they are certainly in play now. Facing licence fee negotiations followed by the renewal of the charter – this time to allow the Corporation to enter its second century – the BBC finds itself in a somewhat parlous state. Hollowed out by Birt's manageralism and Thompson's over-enthusiastic embrace of the 'ethos' of late capital, challenged by new media and old scandals, the Corporation enters this phase in far less good order than it has on previous occasions. But there is an opportunity here.

For a start, for too long and far too well has *public institution, private world* (Burns 1979) described the BBC. The old Reithian habits of elitism and haughtiness in the BBC's conduct of its affairs must be transformed. This is not, of course, to say anything about its programming. Rather, it is to suggest that the best defence of its independence, as Alexander Hamilton put it in another connection, 'must altogether depend on public opinion, and on the general spirit of the people and of the Government' (Hamilton *et al* 1864 [1788]: 632). If the government's will is uncertain it is then only society's Whig instincts which stand in its defence.

Conclusion: Need for a proper, grown-up debate

And if those instincts are to have real political impact, the upcoming debates cannot be conducted in Thatcherite secrecy. We must return to the tradition of public inquiries which Thatcher abandoned the better to aid Murdochian broadcasting ambitions. We need to have a proper grown-up debate about the 90-year-old fudge which so fractures the foundation of the BBC's independence.

In the 1920s the problem was the creation of a state broadcaster which must not appear to be an organ of the state. The solution of charter and licence/agreement was brilliant but it is looking threadbare. We need less talk of 'conventions' but more of how, truly, in a democracy, we can have an organ of opinion funded, but not compromised, by the receipt of public money.

The BBC's second century is soon upon us: it is, as the Americans say, time to fish or cut bait.

References

BBC News (2013) TV licence 'faces cuts unless BBC rebuilds trust' – Shapps, 27 October. Available online at http://www.bbc.co.uk/news/uk-24690002, accessed on 22 December 2013

Blackstone, William (1979 [1769]) *Commentaries on the Laws of England: A Facsimile of the First Edition of 1765-1769, Vol. 4*, Chicago: University of Chicago Press

Briggs, Asa (1995 [1961]) *The History of Broadcasting in the United Kingdom: The Birth of Broadcasting 1896-1927*, Oxford: Oxford University Press

Briggs, Asa (1979) *Governing the BBC*, London: BBC

Burns, Tom (1977) *The BBC: Public Institution, Private World*, London: Macmillan

Chignell, Hugh (2013) BBC Radio News and Current Affairs and the Suez Crisis, *Media History*, Vol. 19, No. 1 pp 93-106

Dicey, A. V. (2012 [1885]) *Lectures Introductory to the Study of the Law of the Constitution* (ed. Allison, J. W. F.), Oxford: Oxford University Press

Hamilton, Alexander (1981 [1788]) Certain General and Miscellaneous Objections to the Constitution Considered & Answered, *The Federalist Papers: A collection of essays written in support of the Constitution of the United States*, Baltimore: Johns Hopkins University Press

Hewlett, Steve (2013a) Grant Shapps may have crossed the line on the BBC – but so did Tony Hall, *Guardian* Media Blog, 1 December. Available online at http://www.theguardian.com/media/media-blog/2013/dec/01/bbc-grant-shaps-tony-hall, accessed on 1 December 2013

Hewlett, Steve (2013b) Opinion is divided press regulation – or is it?, *Guardian* 21 October. Available online at http://www.theguardian.com/media/media-blog/2013/dec/01/bbc-grant-shapps-tony-hall, accessed on 4 January 2014

Scannell, Paddy and Cardiff, David (1991) *A Social History of Broadcasting Vol. 1 1922-1939: Serving the Nation*, Oxford: Basil Blackwell

Secretary of State for Culture etc (2006a) *BROADCASTING: Copy of Royal Charter for the continuance of the British Broadcasting Corporation: Presented to Parliament by the Secretary of State for Culture, Media and Sport by Command of Her Majesty October 2006*, CMD 6925, London: Stationery Office

Secretary of State for Culture etc (2006b) *BROADCASTING: An Agreement Between Her Majesty's Secretary of State for Culture, Media and Sport and the British Broadcasting Corporation Presented to Parliament by the Secretary of State for Culture, Media and Sport by Command of Her Majesty. July 2006*, CMD 6872, London: Stationery Office

Secretary of State for Culture etc (2011) *BROADCASTING: An Agreement Between Her Majesty's Secretary of State for Culture, Olympics, Media and Sport and the British Broadcasting*

Corporation Presented to Parliament by the Secretary of State for Culture, Olympics, Media and Sport by Command of Her Majesty February 2011, CMD 8002, London: Stationery Office

Ward, Ian (2004) *The English Constitution: Myths and Realities*, Oxford and Portland Oregon: Hart

Note on the contributor

Brian Winston holds the Lincoln Professorship at the University of Lincoln. He is the author of *A Right to Offend* (Bloomsbury 2012), *The Rushdie Fatwa and After* (Palgrave 2014) and edits the 'ourBeeb' blog for openDemocracy (http://www.opendemocracy.net/ourbeeb).

Section 5:
The Money Programme: The BBC 'Officer Class' fill their boots

John Mair

Just one mistake can determine a leader's legacy. In the case of Prime Minister Tony Blair it was the war in Iraq. For Mark Thompson, one of longest-serving and best BBC Director-Generals of the modern era, it was the executive pay-off scandal of 2010-2013. Nothing to date has dented public trust in the Corporation as much and brought so much opprobrium to it. It had even the BBC's most loyal friends running for cover.

Put very simply, the Director-General was told by the BBC Trust to reduce the size of the 'officer class' – senior managers – to save money following a not very generous licence fee settlement in 2010. Thompson did reduce the numbers by shrinking the employment of senior managers from 624 in March 2010 to 445 in March 2013, saving £35 million in total (and ongoing savings every year after that in the future). According to the National Audit Office (NAO) report presented to parliament by the Secretary of State for Culture, Media and Sport in July 2013, the BBC spent a total of £25 million in that period (2010-2012) on all severance payments to departing senior managers. Out of the 150 cases in total, £1.4 million was spent which the BBC was not contractually obliged to pay.

It meant Thompson 'letting go' some of his most senior lieutenants and closest friends. He did but with a twist – many of them received hugely enhanced pay-offs to sweeten the joys of parting. This brought an acerbic response from the Chair, Margaret Hodge MP, when the 'Magnificent Seven' (BBC Very Senior Executives) appeared before her Public Accounts Committee in September 2013:

> ... in my view there was also a culture where the people at the top of the BBC had known each other for years and years and years, probably come

in as graduate trainees together, and it seemed right that they should look after each other by when they lost their job giving out lots of public money in unacceptably high pay-offs.

The list and rewards for those allowed to go does not make for pretty reading for the licence payers of Britain. The first and best known case to come to light was that of then Deputy Director-General (and BBC lifer) Mark Byford. He became a near millionaire in severance pay alone – £949,000 – when declared redundant in 2011. The former DD-G received 12 months' salary of £474,500, with a further £474,500 pay in lieu of notice (in fact, he continued to work until well into 2012 as the BBC's London 2012 Olympics supremo). When he was presented with his formal notice in June 2011, the BBC would have been legally obliged to pay him a shortfall of four months' pay in lieu of notice instead of the entire twelve months. The extra £300,000, according to then-Director-General Mark Thompson, was to keep Mr Byford 'fully focused'. Byford is not known to have taken any paid employment post-BBC.

The Director of Nations and Regions, Pat Loughrey, also found himself in the redundo money. When he took redundancy in December 2009, he accepted a pay-off cheque of £866,288 – 12 months' salary at £300,000, 12 months in lieu of notice and £266,000 in pension enhancements. He went on to be Warden of Goldsmiths College, University of London, at an annual salary of £206,000.

Roly Keating left the BBC's employ in May 2012 to become Chief Executive Officer of the British Library. Keating had been a well-regarded Controller of BBC Two and Four, BBC One briefly, a former Head of Music and Arts and was latterly Director of Archive Content. He was given a 'golden goodbye' of £376,000 (one year and a half's pay plus legal fees) even though his post was not being made redundant. It was felt he needed the 'sweetener' to accept the BL offer at a salary lower, it is thought, by £100,000 per year. When this payment came to light, Keating repaid it in full in July 2013 telling the new Director-General, Lord Hall, it was 'a matter of principle. I would never wish to benefit from a payment that could not be demonstrated to have been fully and appropriately authorised'.

Another seeming special case...

Sharon Baylay was another seeming special case. Her role as Director Marketing, Communications and Audiences was closed in February 2010 leaving a problem. She had only seventeen months' continuous service to the BBC and thus ineligible for any severance. Problem solved simply by Baylay going on maternity leave taking her into the qualifying period and a severance package of £394,638. She now works as an executive coach and for Dot Net Solutions and Havas EHS.

George Entwistle turned out to be the shortest-ever serving BBC Director-General. He was effectively invited to fall on his sword after just 54 days in office on 10 November 2012. His contract stated that he was entitled to six month's notice if he resigned; twelve months if dismissed. Although Entwistle resigned, and the Trust never actually told him he should go, the Trust agreed on legal advice to treat him as if he had been dismissed – giving him . a year's pay in lieu of notice – a £470,000 severance payment including legal costs, private medical insurance and communications support, making his total remuneration for 2012-2013 £802,000. He is not known to have taken paid employment since leaving the BBC. Currently, he is an unpaid trustee at the Public Catalogue Foundation and is reported to have enrolled for a part-time Master's degree in Design at the University of Oxford.

The person he pipped at the post to get the D-G's job, Chief Operating Officer Caroline Thomson, saw her role made redundant. She, too, left the Corporation. As Entwistle entered the D-G's office, Thomson left by another door. She did not leave empty-handed – but with a total severance package of £680,400. Although she offered to work her notice, the BBC said no. She has worked since as the Executive Director of the English National Ballet, Chair of Digital UK and she is also chair of Tomorrow's People Trust's Ambassadors Group.

Perhaps the most perplexing pay off case to come to light (eventually) is that of Jana Bennett. She was the BBC's Director of Vision (and had been for nigh on a decade) who was moved from the Public Service (licence payer funded) arm to BBC Worldwide (the commercial arm) as President of Worldwide Networks and Global iPlayer in February 2011.She left that job in June 2012 and accepted a severance package of £687,333 (£404,000 for loss of office and £283,333 pay in lieu of notice – two months more than she was entitled to).

That money was reclaimed by BBC Worldwide from BBC Public Service in March 2013 but when that emerged into the public domain via the PAC, the transaction was reversed in September 2013. The shareholders (including the BBC) paid rather than the licence payers. Ms Bennett was appointed at President of the Biography Channel and Lifetime Movie Network at A+E Networks in New York, in June 2012. The salary for that is not known.

But the saga does not end there. John Smith left office as CEO of BBC Worldwide, the commercial, non-licence fee payer funded arm of the BBC, in December 2012. Smith, who was not being made redundant, received a total payment in 2012/13 of £1,396,000 including 12 months' salary, another 12 months in lieu of notice, a bonus of £222,000, another £386,000 of deferred bonus payments and additional profit share plan payment and taxable benefits. His BBC pension pot after 24 years' service to the BBC was around £5 million in March 2013. Mr Smith has since paid back six of the 12 months' salary in lieu of notice (£205,000). He took up the post of CEO of Burberry in March 2013 earning £575,000 annually.

Many of these payments only emerged once the National Audit Office and the Public Accounts Committee started to investigate. The new BBC Director-General, Lord (Tony) Hall, announced as one of his first decisions in April 2013 that severance payments would in future be capped at £150,000.

Origins of the 'sense of entitlement'

In this section of the book, two former BBC staff have their say on 'the officer class filling their boots'. Nicholas Jones was for thirty years a BBC News Industrial and Political Correspondent. In 'How BBC executives lost the public service ethos', Jones chronicles how the self indulgence of a cohort of departing BBC executives in agreeing between themselves the size of their pay-offs and pension pots came as no surprise to many of the journalists and producers who had worked alongside them. He traces the origins of a sense of entitlement that took root in the upper echelons of the Corporation and which uncoupled an 'officer class' (as Tony Hall has labelled them) from their obligations to the licence payer. It all goes back to the John Birt era and the introduction of commercial managerialism in the 1990s. Jones was able to observe from the poop deck of the newsroom the rise and rise of 'the 'officer class' and the sheer increase in the size of that cadre

> My distaste of the well-funded self aggrandisement of the BBC's 'officer class' is laced with memories of some bruising encounters from my years as an industrial and political correspondent. Line managers came and went, some rising inexorably to positions within a managerial layer that maintained a packed diary of engagements but which seemed remote from the demands being placed on editorial and programme staff. When I reflect on the passage of many of the BBC's executives of my era, I may perhaps be permitted to misquote the unforgettable line from the Falklands War reporting of my former colleague Brian Hanrahan: 'I counted them in and I counted them out.' As they journeyed through the BBC, I experienced at first hand the results of their efforts to make the BBC more cost-effective and competitive; I also saw how with the introduction of a bonus culture bequeathed by Birt they were able to reward themselves handsomely in the process.

There grew up a false sense of the commercial worth of BBC public servants, a drive to commercialism that grew pretty silly (I recall as a producer in the 1990s not being able to access the BBC in-house facilities at Southampton as they were all rented out to commercial corporate clients…). And a feeling that different parts of the BBC were competing 'businesses' which was to say the least difficult in an environment with guaranteed revenue and, in Mark Thompson's words, wallowing in 'a jacuzzi of cash' after a generous licence fee settlement. Thompson was CEO of Channel Four at the time.

Suzanne Franks was a BBC brahmin in waiting. She was selected after Oxford and Harvard Universities to be a 'RAT' (research assistant trainee) – the pathway to glory in a 1979 cohort which included the future Director-General, Mark Thompson. She rose to become a producer on *Newsnight* and *Panorama* before first joining the real world of independent production– her company started the televising of parliament – and then to academia where she is currently Professor of Journalism at City University London. She is coruscating in her critique of her former BBC colleagues and their 'snouts in the trough' culture. In 'Sweet partings ...', she too counts them all in and counts them all out:

> Similar principles were being used to defend the high payments for key staff members who were easily able to demonstrate that they could command more outside the corporation – in particular roles as such as finance director or heads of commercial operations. Yet at this point there was an elision which started to include all kinds of other roles in the same bracket. Lifetime BBC managers whose roles were not translatable far outside the Corporation were being paid eye-watering salaries on the basis that this was what the market required to retain their talents. But it was never really explained where exactly the temptations might come from to lure away their services.

Faux commercialisation

Franks, like Jones, sees the faux commercialisation and artificial creation of markets in the BBC as being the source of many of the recent discontents:

> ...in addition to ever increasing salaries compatible with private sector habits, they were also seamlessly retaining all the benefits, security and comforts of a reliable public service berth – such as the gold-plated pension scheme. So it is this conflation of two cultures which was at the heart of the discontent about pay-offs; for if these were roles that lived and died by the market with all the brutal insecurity that entailed, then individuals could argue they were entitled to high salaries as they would be in any private enterprise. Yet different rules should apply if these were in effect public servants who deserved to be looked after if they were eased out after long-term tenure on the basis that they could not easily expect to find another job and had given a lifetime to the Corporation on a comparatively modest salary. In the way in which the pay-offs were being applied it looked as if it were a case of 'heads the BBC manager wins and tails the licence payer loses' or for the executives 'have your cake and eat it'.

No words are minced by Franks. She concludes:

> Even the Corporation's staunchest supporters and friends cannot find words to defend such practices. Indeed, they shake their heads in disbelief.

Hear, hear!

The executive pay-off scandal has not proved to be the BBC's finest moment. It has become the Achilles Heel of the Thompson D-Gship. It could yet become the hole below the waterline of the Good Ship Auntie as she goes begging for a licence fee to the next government.

- The author would like to thank Catherine Chapman and Raya Raycheva, postgraduate journalism students at Brunel University, London. Their original research forms the basis of this introduction.

How BBC executives lost the public service ethos

The self indulgence of a cohort of departing BBC executives in agreeing between themselves the size of their pay-offs and pension pots came as no surprise to many of the journalists and producers who had worked alongside them. Nicholas Jones, a BBC correspondent for thirty years, traces the origins of a sense of entitlement that took root in the upper echelons of the Corporation and which uncoupled an 'officer class' from their obligations to the licence payer

While some employees found the collective strengths and ideals of 'auntie' BBC outdated and restrictive, many of my contemporaries ended fulfilling careers acknowledging they had been well-rewarded. Most are comforted in retirement by their good fortune in being the beneficiaries of what for them has been a generous final-salary pension scheme. But those of us who stayed the course cannot help but reflect on the gulf that grew ever wider between editorial and production staff and the multiplying layers of upper management. In seeking to explore the factors that led executives to detach themselves from the ethos of a public service financed by a compulsory licence fee, I realise that my own behaviour over the years, and the fact I too am currently the fortunate recipient of a BBC pension, might render my observations as nothing more than a misplaced, self-serving exercise in bashing the BBC.

Indeed, the BBC's director of television Danny Cohen has railed against 'on-screen talent and some former members of staff' who have chosen to 'join the daily chorus of BBC bashing'. He called on 'critical friends' to explain why the BBC 'really matters and sits proudly at the heart of public service broadcasting' (Cohen 2013). Cohen's plea echoed that of the Director-General Tony Hall who has argued in a series of speeches that the BBC should be 'more aggressive' in making the case for the licence fee; the audience should be treated not merely as licence-fee payers but owners; and 'every time we spend money', the BBC had to remember that being funded by a licence fee was a tremendous privilege. 'The people of this country make a bold and generous commitment in paying for the

198

BBC. Every day we are going to show that we are worthy of that commitment' (Hall 2013a).

Hall and Cohen probably have little comprehension of how reassuring their approach has been to former employees who watched with despair as high-flying editors and directors appeared to have little difficulty manipulating pay offs and pensions to their financial advantage; more often than not their 'early retirement' was a sham as many moved on seamlessly to highly-paid posts in other publicly-funded organisations. What had always marked them out for me was not only their lack of hesitation in playing fast and loose with licence-fee income but also the way they seemed to distance themselves from what sustained the BBC's independence; they rarely if ever mentioned, let alone defended, the principle of a universal charge on every household with a television set. But even they, I suspect, lacked the effrontery, let alone credibility, to have delivered the kind of undertaking which the director-general has now offered licence-fee payers.

Birt's legacy: A corporate structure that sidelined the licence fee

The challenge for Hall and Cohen is to ensure their worthy declarations do bring about a change in a deeply-entrenched management mindset. In his eight years as the BBC's Director-General John Birt launched an era of unprecedented innovation and expansion. He also bequeathed a corporate approach that spawned a bonus culture which, according to the National Audit Office, resulted in the BBC paying out £1.4 million to 22 former executives that went beyond their contractual entitlements (National Audit Office 2013).

During the early 1990s, Birt built up elite departments handling corporate and strategic relations. Rather than proclaim openly and publicly what the BBC required from licence-fee negotiations, Birt and his acolytes preferred to deal directly but privately with the government of the day, adviser to adviser, strategist to strategist, a process that accelerated once Tony Blair was elected Prime Minister and their appointees became part of a revolving and self-perpetuating web of advisers, lobbyists and the like. Increasingly I sensed that the historic importance of the licence fee was being sidelined in much of the BBC's public discourse, as though it was a founding principle that dared not speak its name. That omission was all too evident in the approach of Mark Thompson, Hall's predecessor as Director-General. Whenever I heard or read of his representations regarding the BBC's finances in what after all had become the era of top slicing the licence fee, he seemed content to talk loosely about the government of the day having to 'provide more money for public service broadcasting'.

I had become so incensed by the management's reluctance to speak with conviction about the incalculable value of the BBC's relationship with licence payers, and the sense of self-discipline that this responsibility should impose, that this disconnect became the theme of my contribution at a conference on new threats to media freedom organised by the National Union of Journalists in early 2008. Top slicing was the key issue of the moment: the loss of £14 million to fund the digital switchover, and then more to finance the start-up of new rival services, was seen as a first step towards direct government control over the BBC's income. My fury was aimed at the executives who in previous years I had worked alongside but who had retreated into the corporate jargon of what had come to be known as 'Birtspeak'. Where, I asked, were BBC heavyweights punching for the BBC's independence, singing the praises of the licence fee? 'I am not ashamed of a compulsory charge on every household. Being upfront like that, having the guts to defend a universal licence fee, has to be the foundation of any future campaigning. It is the activists who are going to have to dig in to defend BBC values and independence' (Jones 2008).

Until now I have held my counsel and refrained from joining in the recent chorus of criticism but the sheer greed of managers awarding themselves pay-offs higher than stipulated in their contracts is a scandal that gets to the heart of the struggle to find a future road map for publicly-funded organisations such as the BBC, especially when so many similar institutions have been privatised and when market forces are considered the final arbiter. For the BBC its very survival, independent of government and still funded by the licence, will be no mean achievement. As the BBC Trust was struggling to explain its failure to police goings-on at the top of the Corporation, the Royal Mail was being floated off in the City of London, a reminder if one was needed that governments are quite capable of thinking and enacting the unthinkable.

A Thatcherite free-for all in broadcasting eroded BBC values

Having joined the BBC in 1972, and having managed very briefly against the odds to celebrate my 60th birthday while still an employee, I hope I have the credentials to look back with a degree of informed insight into the circumstances that gave rise to the shameful episodes of recent years. How did the BBC end up being controlled by quite so many selfish executives? For me the starting point has to be the challenge which the Corporation faced in adjusting to the rapid expansion of radio and television services during Margaret Thatcher's premiership. Opening up the airwaves to competition and loosening the stranglehold of the BBC-ITV duopoly were steps which helped to create and then sustain the vitality of the vibrant broadcasting industry we have today. But the well-ordered structures of 'auntie' BBC could not always cope with the repercussions of a Thatcherite free-for-all; new services came and went as ratings and market forces eroded the hitherto certainties of the BBC and a commercial television monopoly that had originally been dubbed a 'licence to print money' (Thomson 1957).

I was one of a lucky generation of broadcasters who benefited from several decades of non-stop development funded by a boom in the purchase of colour television licences. My career path through BBC local radio and then to Radio 4 was thanks to the opportunities being created by that extra revenue; as the money continued to roll in so did the expansion in output, the launch of Radio 5 Live, the rollout of 24-hour news and the seemingly limitless horizons of a multi-media environment.

But the transformation that started with the arrival of new television services funded by advertising such as Channel 4 (1982), TV AM (1983) and BSkyB (1990), and the corresponding development of new channels on BBC and ITV, required the Corporation's management to come to terms with an unprecedented level of commercial pressure. Such was the rate of growth in both radio and television output that it was not only on-air talent that was in short supply but also production staff, editors and managers. Salaries for many attracted to work in the independent sector far exceeded those in the BBC and so were sown the seeds of what became a growing sense of entitlement among BBC executives whose remuneration had previously been pegged to the going rate in other comparable public services. Although many of these executives had no real intention of ever forsaking the security of the BBC and of taking a leap into the uncertain world of short-term contracts and risky ventures, where frankly some would have struggled to survive, they began to think they deserved pay parity; they started to believe propaganda about their own self worth and then discovered they had the opportunity to rewrite their own terms and conditions.

'I counted them in and I counted them out'

My distaste of the well-funded self aggrandisement of the BBC's 'officer class' (Hall 2013b) is laced with memories of some bruising encounters from my years as an industrial and political correspondent. Line managers came and went, some rising inexorably to positions within a managerial layer that maintained a packed diary of engagements but which seemed remote from the demands being placed on editorial and programme staff. When I reflect on the passage of many of the BBC's executives of my era, I may perhaps be permitted to misquote the unforgettable line from the Falklands War reporting of my former colleague Brian Hanrahan: 'I counted them in and I counted them out.' As they journeyed through the BBC, I experienced at first hand the results of their efforts to make the BBC more cost-effective and competitive; I also saw how with the introduction of a bonus culture bequeathed by Birt they were able to reward themselves handsomely in the process.

Efficiencies were needed and I was a keen supporter, for example, of Birt's push in the early 1990s for BBC journalists to work bi-medially in order to combine the preparation and presentation of editorial output from what until then had been separate newsrooms for radio and television. Indeed, I was the political correspondent chosen to work with the first outside broadcast crew required to report for national news bulletins for both television and radio. But my enthusiasm waned when changes in working practices and pay rates divided the staff and damaged the collective spirit, and yes the pride, of working for the BBC. On more than one occasion I purposely dragged my feet and observed in the process the pained expressions of line managers who I believed were under orders from the top to dismantle long-standing terms and conditions simply to enhance the role of executives, allow them to exercise greater control and earn bonuses for themselves in the process.

Any hint of a reluctance to embrace bi-medial working had career-changing consequences. Newsrooms needed fewer staff once radio and television began to share facilities and resources. Enforced early retirement from the age of 50 became the norm for so many of my erstwhile colleagues; enhanced redundancy terms were on offer; top-up cash payments available in return for a reduced pension entitlement; and for those who resisted, there was the threat of being moved to rotas that involved extra night shifts and additional weekend duty. My willingness to accept the rigours of anti-social working extended my career as a political correspondent for another ten years but not without a fight. I was the last national correspondent at BBC Westminster to relinquish established staff status and instead required to sign a contract. Rather than being paid allowances for nights and weekend working I became eligible for a bonus to be determined by my line manager. Such was the continuing pressure within the BBC to weed out the post-50 survivors that I was called in quite regularly and reminded that new and improved redundancy terms were on offer. Perhaps it was my enthusiasm which won the day because in the event I managed with a few days' grace to see out my last Conservative Party annual conference in 2002, and my 60th birthday, while still a BBC employee.

My pride in becoming a BBC reporter had deep roots; it had taken ten years – and a dozen or so rejection slips – before I finally made it in 1972, and then only because of an unexpected hitch in the final confirmation of the preferred candidate. Family, friends and colleagues considered my appointment as a news producer at BBC Radio Leicester was a step backwards; what had possessed me at the age of thirty to return to provincial journalism as a reporter on a local radio station when after three years in the House of Commons press gallery I had become an established parliamentary and political reporter for *The Times*? The answer was simple: I admired the immediacy and authority of reporting for the BBC and was prepared to take the risk of moving my wife and two children to Leicester in the confident belief that I would eventually get back to London.

Leicester was a successful station with a loyal audience but its reach was small as its transmission area was restricted to the city itself and towns and villages in the immediate vicinity. But we were a truly local station and could fulfil the goal of public service broadcasting. Early each morning during the rota of power cuts enforced by the 1972 miners' strike I read out the name of every school that would have to close that day due to restrictions in the supply of electricity.

Curran's strong commitment to public service broadcasting

At a pep talk some weeks later I remember being impressed by the stance of the then Director-General Charles Curran. He congratulated the local stations for having served licence payers so well at a time when there was so much disruption to daily life. I was struck by the way Curran had defended the principle of a BBC being funded by a fee that had to be paid by every household with a radio receiver or television set; he seemed not only aware but proud of his responsibility to the licence payer.

The strength of Curran's commitment to public service broadcasting had made a lasting impression and I was reminded of his clarity about the BBC's role when Birt launched *Extending Choice*, his expansionist blueprint for the Corporation's future development. In November 1994, I was one of a hundred BBC employees plucked out of a hat and told to attend an *Extending Choice* seminar, followed by an opportunity to ask him questions. Birt had been spewing out glossy reports, position papers and the like at a formidable rate and when he appeared I stood up, holding my two *Extending Choice* workshop brochures, and asked whether he thought there would ever come a day when the BBC might have to concentrate on defending and sustaining what it did best. Could we go on expanding our services, spreading ever more thinly our expertise and resources? He gave me a withering look: 'Of course we must, we can't stand still, we have to embrace each new service, each new channel, and we can't stop innovating.'

Birt went on to become Tony Blair's blue skies thinker and by all accounts produced just as many position papers from his bunker in 10 Downing Street. What happened at the BBC? We lurched into the era of Greg Dyke, staff morale improved and all seemed set fair until his enforced resignation in January 2004 after the publication of the Hutton Report into the death of Dr David Kelly. Nonetheless, I was disappointed by Dyke's stint as Director-General. He failed to deal with management excesses or recognise the fact that the BBC had over-reached itself and faced some hard choices.

At a conference in 2005 organised in response to the government's green paper on the future of the BBC, I gave my account of how I thought Dyke had responded to the verbiage of the Birt era. 'Here it is, his instruction to the staff, Dyke's famous yellow card: "Cut the crap. Make it happen". His bit of plastic is a treasured memento. But while he chased the ratings, and did so very successfully, Dyke failed in my view to define our public service role, to start focusing on and prioritising what the BBC does best' (Jones 2005).

Conclusion: How licence fee payers were taken for a ride

Former employees have not enjoyed spending their retirement reflecting on the failures and fiascos of recent years. We do hope that lessons have been learned and that Tony Hall, can as John Major once said, get back to basics and restore the licence-fee payers' faith in the BBC as an institution and all that it represents. Perhaps a final word should go to Margaret Hodge, Chair of the House of Commons Public Accounts Committee, who has urged Tony Hall and Lord Patten, Chairman of the BBC Trust, to redouble their efforts to establish clearer lines of accountability.

She had her own explanation for the National Audit Office's calculation that in the three years to 2012 the BBC gave severance payments to 150 senior members totalling £25 million, a quarter of the budget of Radio 4 which is a bit over £100 million: 'They failed to understand they were dealing with licence-fee payers' money. There was a culture at the top where people had known each other for years and years. They probably came in together as graduate trainees and it seemed right they should look after each other when they lost their jobs, giving out lots of public money in unacceptably high pay offs' (Hodge 2013). I quite agree: the free-for-all of the Thatcher era and then the bonus culture of the Blair years had encouraged seemingly limitless expansion and profligacy which had combined to exact a terrible toll on the BBC. Hall's recognition that licence-fee payers were taken for a ride is a promising start.

References

Cohen, Danny (2013) BBC Director of Television, speaking at BBC news conference, 5 December

Hall, Tony (2013a) BBC Director-General (Lord Hall of Birkenhead) Speech at BBC Radio Theatre, 8 October

Hall, Tony, (2013b) Speech at Edinburgh International Television Festival, 22 August. See http://www.bbc.co.uk/blogs/aboutthebbc/posts/Edinburgh-TV-Festival-2013-Director-General-Tony-Hall-attends-Festival-session, accessed on 13 December 2013

Hodge, Margaret (2013) Interview, Radio 4 *Today* programme, 16 December

Jones, Nicholas (2005) Speech at conference organised by Campaign for Press and Broadcasting Freedom, on BBC green paper, 5 March

Jones, Nicholas (2008) New Threats to Media Freedom. Speech at conference organised by National Union of Journalists, 26 January

National Audit Office (2013) *Severance payments and wider benefits for senior BBC managers*, 4 September. Available online at http://downloads.bbc.co.uk/bbctrust/assets/files/pdf/review_report_research/severance_benefits/severance_benefits.pdf, accessed on 13 December 2013

Thomson, Roy (1957) Lord Thomson of Fleet speech at launch of Scottish Television

Note on the contributor

Nicholas Jones joined BBC Radio Leicester as a news producer in January 1972. He was promoted to national radio news reporter in 1973; became a labour and industrial correspondent for Radio 4 in 1978; and then a political correspondent in 1988. His books include *Strikes and the Media* (1986), *Soundbites and Spin Doctors* (1995), *Sultans of Spin* (1999), *Trading Information: Leaks, Lies and Tip-offs* (2006) and *The Lost Tribe: Whatever Happened to Fleet Street's Industrial Correspondents?* (2011).

Sweet partings ...

Suzanne Franks examines the saga of the monster pay-offs at the BBC and concludes: 'Even the Corporation's staunchest supporters and friends cannot find words to defend such practices. Indeed, they shake their heads in disbelief'

The saga of the monster pay-offs was one of the most toe curling episodes of the BBC's recent woes. It highlighted the problematic relationship between the BBC Trust and the management, inherent in the way the Trust was established by the previous government and it showed up once again the frequently irresolvable tensions of private enterprise versus public sector. But worse than that was the debilitating effect it had upon internal morale at a critical time for the Corporation.

Rising salaries
In many ways this all goes back to the days of John Birt in the late 1980s. He arrived at the BBC from the well heeled environment of London Weekend Television with expectations about executive remuneration plus associated perks. All previous director generals (barring Lord Reith) had been insiders who had risen up within the culture of the corporation. In the place Birt left behind, senior management were about to reap handsome rewards from golden handcuffs and share options – benefits he had relinquished in his journey to Broadcasting House. So, against this background, Birt (and the BBC governors) viewed it as acceptable that he should not have to join the Corporation's payroll but could, instead, be remunerated in a complicated way as a freelance through a private company. When these unorthodox arrangements came to light after some years there was a rapid readjustment and Mr Birt (as he then was) was forced to become a staff member of the BBC subject to PAYE like lesser mortals – but the outcome was that his pay proportionally was increased so that he did not lose out because of the increased tax liability.

This was the beginning of the collision of private sector and public service expectations. When Alasdair Milne was D-G in the 1980s he was earning the equivalent in today's money of just over £200,000. And until the end of Michael Checkland's period as Director-General, the upper echelons of the BBC were rooted firmly in the values of public service – salaries were less than the commercial sector but there were many associated benefits – generous pensions and of course the sense of being at the apex of the UK establishment with regular invites to Buckingham Palace, access to the best seats of every possible sporting and cultural event etc. But gradually the environment was changing – not least security of tenure was no longer a given – as Milne's brutal exit in 1987 had demonstrated – and private sector habits were starting to intrude and to cause tension.

From Birt onwards, the salaries of the upper echelons were escalating higher into the stratosphere, on the basis that market value had to be considered in attracting such senior talent. The whole question of remuneration was becoming more complicated. Firstly the battle to retain and attract onscreen talent had already injected the idea of an open market into BBC decision-making, with escalating payments being offered in some cases. This process intensified with the arrival of Sky in 1989 and the fierce competition for selected sporting rights. Similar principles were being used to defend the high payments for key staff members who were easily able to demonstrate that they could command more outside the Corporation – in particular roles as such as finance director or heads of commercial operations. Yet at this point there was an elision which started to include all kinds of other roles in the same bracket. Lifetime BBC managers whose roles were not translatable far outside the Corporation were being paid eye-watering salaries on the basis that this was what the market required to retain their talents. But it was never really explained where exactly the temptations might come from to lure away their services.

Two cultures

As a result of these changes a substantial cadre of highly paid managers started to emerge within the BBC. The packages included perks such as private health insurance and up to 30 per cent bonus payments and were being sanctioned by non-executives and sometimes executives more accustomed to private sector remuneration practices. Those who should have known better (i.e. with greater understanding of the principle of the whole licence fee ecology) quietly agreed, partially on the basis that they too might be on the receiving end of such payments in due course, so why rock the boat?

Many of these individuals were not realistically likely to be subject to much market pressure from outside, as their jobs were only available within a public service broadcasting environment. Yet in addition to ever increasing salaries compatible with private sector habits, they were also seamlessly retaining all the benefits, security and comforts of a reliable public service berth –such as the gold-plated pension scheme. So it is this conflation of two cultures which was at the heart of the discontent about payoffs; for if these were roles that lived and died by the market with all the brutal insecurity that entailed, then individuals could argue they were entitled to high salaries as they would be in any private enterprise. Yet different rules should apply if these were in effect public servants who deserved to be looked after if they were eased out after long term tenure on the basis that they could not easily expect to find another job and had given a lifetime to the Corporation on a comparatively modest salary. In the way in which the pay-offs were being applied it looked as if it were a case of 'heads the BBC manager wins and tails the licence payer loses' or for the executives 'have your cake and eat it'.

When Chris Patten became Chair of the BBC Trust he admits to have been shocked at the numbers of senior highly paid managers, and vocally complained that this needed to be addressed. The only salary that the Trust has direct control over is that of the Director-General. It is an open secret that there was little love lost between Mark Thompson and Lord Patten. Once Thompson (whose total package in 2008/9 came to £834,000) departed, the D-G salary was radically cut back. However, for other managers the process was more clumsy. There was an attempt to slim down the manager class – though how it ever grew to such extraordinary proportions full of people with incomprehensible titles has still not been properly explained. But once the decision had been taken to axe swathes of senior managers the argument went that in order to do this as quickly as possible the departing staff were entitled to be given handsome rewards.

In some cases individuals received rather more even than their contractual entitlements, both paid off to the end of their contract and also given redundancy – once again a double whammy to the licence payer. The National Audit Office revealed that the BBC had paid £2 million more than it was contractually obliged to 22 former bosses between 2009-2012 (around £1.4 million in lieu of notice which it was not obliged to pay and a further £510,000 on 'discretionary payments'). Altogether over those three years 150 departing executives were paid £25 million in compensation settlements and ten of the most senior executives accounted for more than £5 million of that sum. The NAO said the BBC not only operated an excessively generous policy on severance payments, but had 'exceeded contractual requirements' in doing so. In a sample, one in four payments was found to have been in excess of contractual requirements.

Several managers left with large pay-outs even though they went almost immediately into other jobs. In fact, some had even lined up a new appointment before they parted from Broadcasting House – but only one of them, Roly Keating, who had been Director of Archive Content, was shamed enough to return the part of the payment deemed excessive, upon starting his new job at the British Library. Others quietly pocketed the takings, sometimes far higher than Keating's reward, and a number of them then moved swiftly on to roles that were also better remunerated than his. A few even continued to receive car allowances, consultancy fees and new IT courtesy of the BBC, to cushion the blow.

John Smith, who headed up BBC Worldwide, received a total remuneration in his final year (2012/13) of £1,396,000. Despite going on to a new job as Chief Operating Officer of Burberry this included six months' notice in lieu of £244,000. His accrued pension pot when he left totalled a around £5 million. In another case which came under scrutiny from the Public Accounts Committee Sharon Baylay the BBC marketing director who departed in 2011 was awarded a package of almost £390,000 – yet she had been at the Corporation less than two years when this was being negotiated, so it was hardly a case of having to compensate a long term employee.

Project Silver

The most high profile case was Mark Byford – a BBC lifer ending up as Deputy D-G – who left with a staggering near £1 million pay-off, plus one of the largest ever public sector pension pots at £3.4 million. Byford is reinventing himself as a writer – but he is still adamant that he was entitled to the full pay-off and will not be giving anything back. His case exemplifies the problem. As a career public service employee he would have been unlikely to have been lured away to a high paid commercial role, but nevertheless was being paid a salary of £474,500 in 2010. When it was time to leave he was awarded a payoff totaling £949,000 – including pay in lieu of notice, even though he stayed on to work out his notice.

It became clear in the hearing before the Public Accounts Committee in September 2013 that Byford who remained in post during his notice was only entitled to half of the total he received but Mark Thompson revealed in his evidence that he felt he had to award him an additional £500k just to make sure Byford 'kept focus' during the period of the Olympics. And the details of Mark Byford's exit negotiations, known to insiders as 'Project Silver' led into a further Alice in Wonderland world. According to the internal email discussions, which were later revealed, the BBC (i.e. the licence fee payers) got off lightly. Apparently Byford could have argued for a payment totaling up to £2.5 million. So his exit was apparently cheap at the price!

Byford's case is the most galling but there are a number of others. The response from those responsible for these decisions is that in the grand scheme of a £3bn income these high level payoffs amounted to chicken feed – no more than a few million. And it had to be achieved quickly to downscale the overall swollen numbers of managers, so it was worth overpaying. Yet this understates not only the impact this issue has had upon politicians and licence fee payers but crucially the effect upon internal BBC attitudes. There are thousands of dedicated programme makers, technicians and assorted others who make the BBC function as the brilliant institution that it is – informing, educating and entertaining us on a daily 24/7 basis. Needless to say their pay and conditions are designed in a parallel universe to the managerial class. But even more galling, when cameramen, designers, engineers or many other are 'let go' after 30 years of service they are unlikely to see anything approaching such levels of generosity. The anger caused by the scale of these senior level pay-offs became a running sore inside the BBC.

Confusion at the top

It is interesting that the succession of pay-offs initially attracted relatively little attention and the story might have gone quietly away. Only after the brief tenure of George Entwistle as D-G in 2012 did they really come into wider public scrutiny. Entwistle was legally entitled to a contractual payment negotiated after his rapid 'resignation' in autumn 2012 and it is a safe bet that he is unlikely to find another senior job in broadcasting. But that prompted the National Audit Office, at the behest of the BBC Trust, to investigate the wider question and to focus attention upon the excesses that had gone before.

Meanwhile, the same conundrums that the payoff saga highlighted have remained unsolved. Tony Hall is employed on roughly half of Mark Thompson's salary (and half the notice period of Entwistle) although he seems well able to keep himself focused on this basis. One of his firm pronouncements has been to announce a cap on any future pay-offs at a comparatively paltry £150k and associated benefits such as private health care payment will no longer be available to incoming senior managers. Lord Hall is determined to get rid of what he calls the 'officer class mentality' within the BBC. But still in the background as the BBC gears up for the next charter renewal there are the rumblings of this same tension. As one observer put it, the organisation is caught between trying to compete within a digital global market place and having to behave like a department of Whitehall.

The other unresolved problem which was highlighted by the successive problem of bloated numbers of managers and managerial pay followed by excessive payoffs is the ambiguous position of the BBC Trust. Its mission on the website and written across the walls of the lobby in Great Portland Street is 'getting the best out of the BBC for licence fee payers'. At face value that would look like the job of a stern regulator concerned to 'follow the money'. Yet in many cases, in particular the question of too many managers paid high salaries or over generous sweeteners, the Trust seemed to be awol, claiming that it simply did not have the authority to impose its will in such matters. The hearings in September 2013 before the Public Accounts Committee made clear this ambiguity and vacuum of authority, with each side (management and Trust) blaming the other.

This tension in the way the Trust functions as an institution between being part regulator and still part champion has yet to be resolved. Even if the Trust model is in future deemed unworkable and the regulatory function is shifted to Ofcom, that would not solve these kinds of problems. What are needed most of all are effective non-executive (and executive) directors who are properly attuned to the sensitivities of a licence fee funded institution.

It is to the Trust's credit that when they realised the scale of greed in the pay offs they were responsible for requesting the National Audit Office to investigate. But when the NAO report appeared in 2013 there was a loud noise of stable doors banging. The report itself makes staggering reading not least because of the sloppy and inadequate management processes it reveals, but running through it is the unmentioned question as to how this scale of excess was ever allowed to happen in the first place. How did the management think they could justify such lavish behaviour and why did the supposed scrutineers let them do it? The report's damning conclusion on value for money was that 'Weak governance arrangements have led to payments that exceeded contractual entitlements and put public trust at risk.'

The painful and painstaking details which the NAO and the PAC reports have revealed naturally give succor to those on the right, starting with the Chairman of the Conservative Party, Grant Shapps, currently sharpening their knives for slicing into the BBC. And it is this extraordinary disregard for the wider public perception that is most damaging of all. Even the BBC's staunchest supporters and friends cannot find words to defend such practices. Indeed, they shake their heads in disbelief. The former BBC Governor and crime writer P. D. James was a guest editor of Radio 4's *Today* programme during this period and observed that the BBC had behaved 'like a very large and unwieldy ship ... recruiting more and more officers, all very comfortably cabined, usually at salaries far greater than their predecessors enjoyed and with a crew somewhat discontented'. Let us hope that Tony Hall will still be able to turn the vessel around successfully.

Note on the contributor

Suzanne Franks is a former BBC TV News and Current Affairs journalist. She is now Professor of Journalism at City University London and has written widely on the history of broadcasting and international reporting. Her two most recent publications are *Famine, Aid, Politics and the Media* (Hurst, 2013) and *Women and Journalism* (I. B. Tauris, 2013).

Section 6:
Songs of Praise: The Reithian 'Holy Trinity' in danger

Richard Lance Keeble

Remember Lord Reith's founding vision for the BBC? It was to 'provide information, entertainment and education': the so-called Holy Trinity. Significantly, George Entwistle on 15 November 2011, while Director of Vision at the BBC (and before his ignominious fall from grace after just 54 days as Director-General a year later) gave a speech in which he repeated the suggestion of Reith's biographer Ian McIntyre (1993) that he had borrowed this mission statement from the American public service broadcaster David Sarnoff. 'If so, at the very least,' Entwistle continued, 'the borrowing was testimony to particularly good taste' (BBC 2011).

Yet, as Fiona Chesterton points out in this section's opening chapter, the BBC's educational output all too often gets far less public attention than either information or entertainment. Significantly even Entwistle in his speech went on to focus on the entertainment remit – and almost totally ignored education.

Chesterton, a former Controller of Adult Learning at the BBC, argues that no broadcaster or other educational publisher has the breadth and depth of the BBC nor the ability to harness famous names in the cause of inspiring learning. Education should be at the heart of the future licence fee discussions. And she concludes:

> Learning may still help make the case for the BBC – it does not necessarily make the case for increased funding, though. It shows what can be done with a relatively small core budget. In its case it might benefit from fewer programmes being commissioned rather than more. Let's include Education then in the public debate about the licence-fee – who cares

about learning? Who values Learning from the BBC? Let them speak out now, where they have been so quiet in the past.

The BBC in Scotland

Kincardineshire-born Lord Reith may well be turning in his grave given the result of a recent survey of Scottish people's views on the BBC which suggests 50 per cent do not think it value for money. As Atholl Duncan comments in 'Grasping the Thistle: Is the BBC still relevant to Scotland?':

> If your customers were telling you that in a private company you would be very concerned about the sustainability of your business. Audience research shows significant concern that that BBC does not provide enough 'programmes and content that cater for Scotland'. A large chunk of the Scottish audience thinks the BBC is not good at portraying 'our nation and culture' to the rest of the UK.

Duncan carefully explores the consequences for broadcasting if the Scots vote either 'Yes' or 'No' for independence on 18 September 2014. He warns:

> What happens if Scotland votes 'Yes'? The SNP's plans for broadcasting in an independent Scotland, outlined in its White Paper *Scotland's Future*, guarantees that Scottish viewers and listeners will pay the same to get access to all the current channels plus double the Scottish output. That sounds too good to be true!

But Duncan, Head of News and Current Affairs for the BBC in Scotland between 2006 and 2011, also outlines a way ahead if there is a 'No' vote. For instance, a new vision needs to emerge in the run-up to the BBC's charter renewal in 2016. Power over broadcasting should be devolved to the Scottish parliament while still regulated by Ofcom. The director-general of the BBC should be made responsible to the Scottish parliament for the performance of the Corporation in Scotland and regularly called to account in person at Holyrood. The UK-wide main television news bulletins should be replaced by high quality, integrated TV bulletins of global, UK and Scottish news. And funding for Scottish programmes must be increased from the current 2.4 per cent of the licence fee. He concludes:

> If the BBC does not adapt it will see a further decline in its standing and perception in Scotland. This path may end in the BBC losing its mandate to be Scotland's public service broadcaster. A paradigm shift in structure, culture, attitude and resource is required for the BBC to remain relevant in Scotland. As a loyal supporter, I can only hope that the Corporation has the leadership, vision and ambition to take swift and decisive action to transform its relationship with audiences in Scotland.

Next, David Lloyd, Visiting Professor of Journalism at City University London and former Head of News and Current Affairs, Channel 4 TV, imagines the thoughts that may have crossed James Harding's mind (and the memos he may well have wanted to send to himself) over his first paper cup of BBC coffee – when starting the somewhat daunting job of Director of News on 12 August 2013. Lloyd's witty, knowing narrative advances like this:

> By now Harding has attempted a croissant and is resisting the temptation to compare its over-solid dough with the consistency of his directorate's output; it occurs to him that, over time, many BBC bulletins on television or radio are not so different from illustrated or sound-described news diaries, aside – of course – from the truly unexpected occurrences of happenstance, at home or abroad, and that-even for a broadcast tyro-this must be surely be to underuse both media.

First Harding memo to self: 'Newsgathering to be less mechanistic – needs restructure.'

Lloyd suggests that, in the future, the government may well require BBC to maintain its World Service coverage no longer out of grant-in-aid but from the licence fee. On the face of it, this could reduce the resources available to journalism as a whole:

> But in truth the funding horse has long since bolted, and the sizeable World Service infrastructure was built on many years of grant-in-aid. Now it is only its running costs which will have to be sustained on whatever share of the licence fee Harding can bid for but as the incumbent, he ought to be in a strong bargaining position, and it is other departments across the BBC which are most likely to feel the chill of a frozen licence fee.

Most urgent Harding memo of all to self: 'Discover how Byzantine funding system actually works before going in to bat, and playing up new boy status; important not to start new job with staff-demoralising defeat.'

Lloyd concludes by noting that, of all news broadcasters with aspirations to be a world player, the BBC is the richest. Harding's challenge is to match the Corporation's impact to its income. 'It will only develop into a crisis if it proves undeliverable.'

BBC 'predominantly white organisation'
In January 2001, Director-General Greg Dyke famously damned the BBC as 'hideously white'. He said: 'I think the BBC is a predominantly white organisation. The figures we have at the moment suggest that quite a lot of people from different ethnic backgrounds that we do attract to the BBC, leave. Maybe they don't feel at home, maybe they don't feel welcome' (Hill 2001). Finally in this section, Farrukh Dhondy, for fourteen years the Multicultural Commissioning Editor of Channel 4, places Dyke's comment in a historical context, critically examining the evolving representations of black and Asian people on our screens.

He suggests that 'multiculture is simply an acceptable, liberal term for an inclusive, wide, but judgemental monoculture'. But at the same time, a snapshot of contemporary BBC programmes 'demonstrates a determination to remedy the hideousness of white reportage'. For instance, there are 'diversity' news presenters and reporters all over the screen. Dhondy continues:

> There are comedy appearances which can be seen as concessional or even abused for being negatively stereotypical – all part of the fun. The *Mr Khan* episodes are a clumsy attempt to cock a snook at positive image and non-stereotype imagery. Then there are plausible black detectives who always get their man or woman and demonstrate compassion for the criminal compelled by his or her fate to unspeakable deeds. Again high marks out of ten, even though the principle could lead to unlikely, say, brain surgeons or black Winston Churchills thrown in.

He ends by looking at the small, independent production companies which emerged after the launch of Channel 4 by Prime Minister Margaret Thatcher, 'the Lenin of the lower-middle-class British revolution', in November 1982. Today, most of them have gone out of business or been absorbed in larger companies. Broadcasting, Dhondy concludes, may not now be 'hideously white' but 'the commissioning landscape, certainly that of the BBC, is now hideously corporate'.

References

BBC (2011) Speech given by George Entwistle at Polis, London School of Economics, 15 November. Available online at http://www.bbc.co.uk/mediacentre/speeches/2011/entwistle_george_lse.html, accessed on 1 February 2014

Hill, Amelia (2001) Dyke: BBC is hideously white, *Observer*, 7 January. Available online at http://www.theguardian.com/media/2001/jan/07/uknews.theobserver1, accessed on 2 February 2014

McIntyre, Ian (1993) *The Expense of Glory: A Life of John Reith*, London: HarperCollins

Who cares about BBC education?

**Fiona Chesterton argues the case for more debate about what the
licence-fee payer expects and receives for its money in educational output**

Introduction

For one of the Holy Trinity of the BBC's founding mission, Education gets
much less public attention than Information and Entertainment. That journalists
write about the BBC's journalism, that most of the BBC's Director-Generals
have come from a News and Current Affairs background, and the sheer scale of
the BBC's biggest department and what its press competitors see as its excessive
market impact, puts Information squarely in the spotlight. Entertainment output,
from *EastEnders* to *Strictly*, fills tabloid pages and has delighted, engaged and
sometimes infuriated viewers throughout the BBC's history. But Education – or
Knowledge and Learning, as the BBC now prefers to call it, what do we hear
about that?

No doubt, most licence-fee payers would agree that there is much of the
BBC's output, which is educational (or strictly speaking, educative), but where is
the public debate, even at a time of licence fee review, about how that part of
the BBC's mission should be fulfilled in the second and into the third decade of
the 21st century? And why was it, that when the BBC just a few years ago, wrote
off more than £100 million of expenditure on BBC Jam, a digital curriculum
project for schoolchildren, and for the first time halted a whole service under
pressure from commercial competitors, there was hardly a peep from press,
politicians, parents or teachers? Did they not care? Or did they not know? We
will try to answer that question later, but it has been a long road back from that
setback – including the whole Learning Department taking the trip up the M6 to
Salford – until today when the BBC's new Director-General has announced a
seemingly ambitious prospectus for BBC Learning as part of his new vision for
the BBC.

Fewer, bigger, better?

When Tony Hall delivered his speech *Where Next?*[1] setting out his vision in October 2013, he committed the Corporation to deliver a big educational project every year for the next three years. These were listed as the World War 1 centenary megablitz in the current year, then in 2015, a digital creativity project to 'get the country coding', and in 2016, the four hundredth anniversary of the death of William Shakespeare, a commitment to digitise the BBC's archive and to make it available free to educational users. You probably did not know that, as, predictably, the press coverage of the speech gave relatively little attention to this, apart from, equally predictably, *The Times* spinning this as the BBC doing 'penance' for past sins.[2]

Now you do know, readers may think – that's good – the sort of thing the BBC should be doing. I have no doubt of Tony Hall's genuine commitment to the educational mission, but forgive me a note of caution. Firstly, grand projects are fine, but we should not ignore the day-to-day bread-and-butter – and question that and how much resource is devoted to it.

We should start with an apparently simple question – how much money does the BBC spend on Learning? It does not have a simple answer. The BBC's annual report does not tell you. That's because the BBC accounts for its spend by service – so by BBC Television, Radio, Online and so on. BBC Learning's core budget is certainly a tiny fraction of, say, BBC One's, although it does not reveal the exact figure. Its Online budget,[3] the only part that it puts in the public domain, is forecast this year to be around £13 million (excluding central management costs). This is down on last year's spend of £16.5 million (apparently because of a focus this year on aggregating rather than new content – see later). Then there's the ring-fenced Learning Fund, which is spent predominantly on Television, but also on Radio, and comes to another £5 million per year. There is further investment beyond this in TV, Radio and on face-to-face learning events. It also excludes some spending in Scotland. Nevertheless, my guesstimate is that the total may amount to the cost of a single big TV entertainment series, such as *The Voice*

Many would argue, however, that to count only the formal BBC Learning budget as a measure of the total educational spend of the BBC is wholly misleading. On this take, we could include most of the budgets of Radio Four, BBC Four, the children's channels, CBeebies and CBBC, hundreds of hours of science, natural history, history, current affairs, arts documentaries, cookery and gardening shows, some of the drama, the list goes on. And maybe it is output and outcomes rather than input that we should consider. Certainly it is the strategy of the current Controller of Learning, Saul Nasse, who aims to harness the output right across the range to maximise educational impact. So inspiring people to throw Star Parties in their gardens off the back of *Stargazing Live*, and using *Doctor Who* to engage children with history and story-telling, are the sort of outcomes that he would point to.

It is a strategy that relies on the co-operation and goodwill of other more powerful colleagues at the BBC, though. In many cases, and cynics would say, especially at licence fee review time, this may be readily given – it is a time, after all, which a former director-general once described to me in an off-the record moment, as when the BBC 'gets Education like old-time religion'. At other times in the past, in my own experience, the pull of sheer entertainment, the perceived uncoolness of education or any hint of didacticism in programmes, readily re-surfaces. Then Learning can find itself seen as a burden, and an afterthought, rather than central to its values. It is all the more difficult when most of the competition is going all out to divert audiences with easily-digestible fare.

I would argue that the only way to keep the BBC honest in this regard is to build in real accountability into its management and governance for Education. It would seem that currently the BBC Trust has no plans to review Learning – as it is not defined as a service. It is also the case that for some years now, there has been no board-level Director for Learning. Instead, the BBC relies on a shared, and so diluted accountability. Is this enough?

Delivering Learning: 'i-Wonder'

It's going to be hard to ignore the first of Tony Hall's mega-initiatives for Learning, the World War 1 Centenary project. There is a four-year assault underway – hundreds of hours of programming on TV and Radio. If we focus though on the educational output, this will be primarily Online – both content for adult informal learners, as they are known (i. e. those learning for their own pleasure and reward) and more formal learning resources for use within schools.

It will be showcased on the new Knowledge and Learning website, just launched as 'i-Wonder'. This has the ambitious aim of bringing together in one easily searchable and navigable place, the wealth of material that the BBC has amassed over the past decade or more across History, Science, Natural History, Arts and Culture and Food (not so surprising, remember Delia started in Education – although its inclusion may ensure more traffic to the site). It is a heroic idea – but it will be dependent for its success and impact on the audience finding it, and using it. It will need marketing, including to specialist audiences, such as teachers.

BBC Education a decade ago had its own dedicated marketing resource, and further ago still had a cadre of education officers whose brief was to communicate with, and understand the needs of schools and colleges. Now BBC Learning has to compete for marketing spend with other bigger departments, so will need to make the case for a big push for 'i-Wonder', and, harder still, for dedicated promotion at educational conferences and direct to teachers.

It may be a long haul to get 'i-Wonder' into the public mind. Will it have its own TV trails? Or will it have to compete in the credits with 'coming up' voiceovers, and the exhortation to go to the Open University's website or to the iPlayer? While researching this chapter, I have come across some evidence, limited and anecdotal, admittedly, that teachers now have less awareness of what the BBC offers them, and are using it less in the classroom than they used to. The BBC stated a couple of years ago that more than half of all the country's schools were still using their resources every year. However, when the BBC Trust did extensive audience research in 2013 on use and attitudes towards BBC Learning Online as part of their general review of the entire BBC Online service,[4] what they found was worrying – there was, it seems, very little awareness of the whole breadth of Knowledge and Learning content.

There was one notable exception – Bitesize, the long-established and hugely-successful learning brand (itself the product of dedicated marketing in the past). Certainly, the aggregation of the content under 'i-Wonder' and improved search and navigation from the Home page which has now been achieved in response to this report, should improve matters. Surely, though, dedicated marketing resource, and over a sustained period, will be needed as well. As the Open University has noted from its own research –'simply making content available will not lead to learning'.

The Open University: A sustainable partnership

When reviewing BBC Learning, you can't ignore its most long-standing partnership. From those lectures by bearded professors broadcast in the small hours forty years ago, to today, it has been remarkably enduring. Now the OU no longer uses BBC airwaves to teach its students but, instead, invests in a range of mainstream BBC programmes which may act as a starting point for a 'learning journey'. The OU claims thousands of students start with them from the inspiration of BBC programmes. It may be an entirely beneficial mutual arrangement but it is surprising that at a time when the OU now has its own YouTube channel with more than 10 million views a year,[5] when many more higher educational institutions than the OU offer online and distance learning and when the OU logo at the end of primetime BBC programmes could be considered of enormous marketing value to just one university in a now highly-competitive environment, that it is not questioned.

Getting the country coding

It sounds like a classic BBC social action initiative – encouraging and inspiring the audience, in particular children, to move from being passive – if ravenous – consumers of digital content, to actually creating their own stuff, by learning the language of computing itself – coding. That's the task that the BBC has set itself for 2015. It will be quite a challenge to translate this into mainstream television programming but maybe there will be an *EastEnders* storyline, *Doctor Who* may come into play and, surely, the rock star physicist, Brian Cox, will be enthusing us. Don't expect a World War I-like barrage of programmes, though.

A key question will be how much the BBC will venture to produce new digital content for use directly in the classroom, or by children at home. This potentially pits it against the educational publishers and software producers who gave the BBC such a hard time over the BBC Jam project. It may explain the very cautious wording in the DG's speech – 'We'll challenge the best creative minds and writers and invite in a range of partners to find the best way of building on the range of initiatives in this area.' Saul Nasse told me the relationship with the commercial sector and with other partners is now transformed from the combative years of BBC Jam. Maybe so, but if we take just one of those former Jam challengers, Espresso Education: they are currently advertising on their website school resources for teaching coding – free, but only to October. Will they really want the BBC offering rival resources free to users from next year?

BBC jam: Getting unstuck

To understand where BBC Learning is now, and the rocks it must still avoid, we have to go back a bit – to around the turn of the century, to 1999. It was a time when broadcasting was beginning to realise the transformative impact that digital technology and the internet were going to have, when the government's mantra was 'Education, Education, Education' and when it believed that it should harness educational television and digital content to improve learning in the classroom. A time when there were hundreds of hours of schools television broadcast every year not just on the BBC but on Channel Four. A time when the new BBC Online department was steaming ahead with pioneering Educational as well as News content. And a time when some engaging characters, called the Teletubbies appeared and showed the potential to engage even two-year-olds for learning in front of a screen.

Internally, the BBC's Education Department was encouraged to move its centre of gravity from TV to Online. All those daytime and overnight hours devoted to educational broadcasting could be useful for more popular fare to improve ratings. So, into this perfect receptive environment, the concept of a BBC digital curriculum for schools was hatched. It was a step-change from what BBC Schools had produced before – a grand project very much in tune with government targets. Maybe it was hubristic, but certainly it failed to take into account the extraordinary commercial opposition that it engendered. An alliance of educational publishers and software producers took the battle all the way to Brussels, claiming distortion of the market by the BBC and unfair state aid. The sorry tale has now been laid out by Maria Michalis, of the University of Westminster,[6] but was barely told at the time in the press, even though, in the end, more than £100 million of licence-fee funded investment went down the drain, a similar sum to the much more-publicised Digital Media Initiative which was axed five years later in 2013.

The BBC would say that this is now all very much a thing of the past, but there are some lessons and unanswered questions. Firstly, I would argue, the Jam project showed what can happen when the BBC fails to win the public's hearts and minds for a project, and relies on more fickle Whitehall support. From the beginning all the debates around the digital curriculum took place behind closed doors. Did the BBC ever really champion the scheme directly to get parents and teachers rooting for it, let alone the children who were the intended beneficiaries? So when the new BBC Trust suspended and then later gave the *coup de grace* to Jam, there was no real public constituency that could be mobilised to stand up for it. Compare this with the later successful campaign to save the digital radio Channel, 6 Music, a service surely much less core to the BBC's mission, but which got a popular bandwagon up and running to save it.

BBC Learning now has far fewer cosy meetings in Whitehall, keeping its distance – and independence – from ministers. The digital coding project may be in line with government ambitions, but it is not directed by them. Michael Gove's department also seems less inclined to concern itself with media projects. Its emphasis would seem to be on letting schools and academies decide what they want for themselves.

What we – and the BBC – should also note, though, is that after Jam was halted, a closure unprecedented in the BBC's history and a major intervention by the BBC Trust , the commercial competitors may have savoured the victory, but they did not rush to deliver the sort of content, that the BBC was developing. Instead, there was an emphasis on providing the 'kit' – the whiteboards, the tablets etc. Was that essential infrastructure or the more profitable area? Would BBC content have helped grow rather than hinder the educational market in this area? Would its commitment to high-quality, UK-produced content commissioned but not necessarily produced in-house have helped an independent production sector flourish in the way that it has for more mainstream output? Would it have helped increase educational attainment, still a huge national need and priority? We shall never know.

BBC learning and the iPlayer

'I prefer to look to the future,' said Saul Nasse, when referring to Jam. Well, the future is clearly the iPlayer. Many commentators see this as the prototype for a post-scheduled, personalised service, delivered to televisions, tablets, phones, and anything else the technology kings of Silicon Valley dream up for us in the coming few years. If the iPlayer is, indeed, the future, then the question of how BBC Learning content is made available on it, and how children and adult learners can access archive content for educational use becomes a central question.

Tony Hall's vision speech laid out the prospect of increasing the seven-day window for viewing BBC programmes to 30 days. He also spoke of a new BBC Store, which seemed to be a platform for purchasing BBC programmes or digital boxsets beyond this window. I am not convinced that such a model will be the right one for education. Firstly, the current iPlayer (unlike the web) apparently has little to offer the adult learner. If you search the Learning section, you will find plenty of programmes for children from two years through to 16 – hours of content from CBBC and CBeebies, with some mainstream output aimed at Secondary schools. When I looked in a randomly chosen week in December 2013 for adult learning, though, I found a single offering: How to Learn Gaelic from BBC Alba. That's partly no doubt because of the seven-day window, but partly a matter of labelling. Does the BBC think that its audience will take fright, thinking a programme to be boring and didactic, if searchable via Learning?

The seven-day and potentially the 30-day window is about allowing producers (many of them independents) to realise the commercial value of their product. Essentially it is too expensive for the BBC to buy out these rights up front. The suggested BBC Store would allow the BBC to bridge that gap, offer viewers the chance to pay to something they had missed, or wished to keep, while giving the producer (whether BBC or indy) an income stream. However, this leaves a gap through which more challenging programmes, including some funded by Learning, might fall. For example, for many years it has been Education which has championed programming and back-up resources around mental health issues. In recent years, this has included the Headroom campaign and in 2013 BBC3's season aimed at young adults, *It's a Mad World*. These excellent – not just educational, but potentially life-saving programmes, are no longer available on the iPlayer or, indeed, on BBC Online. Surely we should not be asking young viewers to pay to access these pure public service programmes after the first 30-day window? Even if it means the BBC committing to commission fewer programmes overall, in order to afford to buy out some rights upfront, that surely is a sacrifice worth making.

To be or not to be? Unlocking the archive

Tackling the iPlayer issue for BBC Learning should mean that the BBC does not find itself in the position it has done with much of its archive. Even though this is a national resource, paid for by the British public, over more than fifty years, much of it is as inaccessible as the treasures that many museums and art galleries had locked in their vaults, until digitisation opened them up. The entire Shakespeare canon that Tony Hall promised to make available free to educational users in 2016 came with a small but significant caveat: 'where rights allow'. We were talking about the rights issue at BBC Education more than a decade ago – and it is still not cracked. It will be wonderful if all those classic Shakespeare plays can be made available, but what about all the other classic dramas – the Dickens, the Austens, the Dennis Potters, the Bleasdales and the Leighs? That's before we start on the landmark factual series – say, Schama's *History of Britain*, which was funded entirely by BBC Education. Whole programmes, not clips – although the treasury of clips available for school use on BBC Online is fantastic. (Oh, and when was that promoted?)

Conclusion

What this comes down to, is how much will BBC Learning help make the case for retaining the licence fee? It is hard for the fundamentalist opponents of the BBC to argue that the market would readily provide or replicate what the BBC has and continues to offer. If we look across at Channel Four, for example, with its public service obligations, it quietly sold off its Learning brand a few years ago. (Who knew? Again the press seemed to miss this.) Now Espresso Education owns the brand, and it in turn has now been taken over by the US giant, Discovery. The Channel Four website is much thinner than the BBC's with the exception of supporting resources aimed primarily at 14 to 19-year-olds. ITV's Granada Learning was also sold some years back, and now specialises in examination assessment materials rather than learning content. No broadcaster or other educational publisher has the breadth and depth of the BBC, or the ability to harness famous names in the cause of inspiring learning.

Learning may still help make the case for the BBC – it does not necessarily make the case for increased funding, though. It shows what can be done with a relatively small core budget. In its case it might benefit from fewer programmes being commissioned rather than more. Let's include Education then in the public debate about the licence-fee – who cares about learning? Who values Learning from the BBC? Let them speak out now, where they have been so quiet in the past.

- The author wishes to thank Saul Nasse, Controller of BBC Learning, whom she interviewed on the telephone on 3 January 2014, and to former colleagues at BBC Learning who provided background information.

Notes

[1] Speech given by Tony Hall, BBC Director-General, at the BBC Radio Theatre in London on 8 October 2013. Available online at www.bbc.co.uk/mediacentre/speeches/2013/tony-hall-vision.html, accessed on 12 December 2013

[2] Hellen, Nicholas (2013) *Times* Social Affairs Editor, 6 October

[3] Figures supplied by the BBC to the author, as presented to invited audience of independent producers at briefing at Media City, Salford, in November 2013

[4] Service review of BBC Online and the Red Button, published 20 May 2013. Available online at www.bbc.co.uk/bbctrust/our_work/online/...reviews/online_redbutton.html, accessed on 13 December 2013

[5] Annual Report, Open University. Available online at www.open.ac.uk/about/main/the-ou-explained, accessed on 13 December 2013

[6] Michalis, M. (2012) Balancing public and private interests in online media: The case of BBC digital curriculum, *Media, Culture and Society*, Vol. 34, No. 8 pp 944-960

Note on the contributor

Fiona Chesterton is a former Controller of Adult Learning at the BBC, and had a long career in television production, commissioning and journalism, mainly at the BBC and Channel 4. In 2008, she was made a Fellow of the Royal Television Society for services to broadcasting. She continues to take an interest in media education and training and writes book reviews for the London School of Economics Review of Books online. Her public Linked In profile is at uk.linkedin.com/pub/fiona-chesterton/10/398/4b.

Grasping the Thistle: Is the BBC still relevant to Scotland?

Atholl Duncan argues that a paradigm shift in structure, culture, ambition, resource and leadership, is required for the BBC to remain relevant in Scotland

The black swans

The BBC has often agonised over what to do about Scotland. Now, with a gale of political change blowing north of the border, the future of the Corporation as a UK-wide public broadcaster is being called into question, once again.

On 18 September 2014, people in Scotland will vote on whether or not to become an independent nation. If the electorate votes 'Yes' – and current opinion polls show momentum swinging to the Nationalists – the BBC, as we know it, will come to an end along with the Union on 24 March 2016. In a newly independent Scotland, the BBC would be replaced by the Scottish Broadcasting Service (SBS).

If the electorate votes 'No', the subsequent constitutional and political changes, which are certain to follow, will mean the BBC can only remain relevant in Scotland through significant structural, financial and cultural change. One or other of these black swan moments is going to happen.

What to do about Scotland?

The Scottish curmudgeon, Lord Reith, is recognised as the father of the mother of broadcasting. However, I have always been more interested in the role played by another Scottish broadcasting pioneer. My mother still remembers her father, Alex Scott, cycling for miles along the banks of the Clyde to see his cousin in Helensburgh. She remembers tales of that cousin's brushes with the law for 'borrowing' equipment from telephone boxes to use in his youthful experiments. That cousin was called John Logie Baird.

So, it is an appropriate coincidence that for the largest part of my working life I was involved in ensuring that every major event and every major story in Scotland was presented through the medium of television to a watching nation.

Every big story; every election; every triumph; every disaster – from Piper Alpha to Lockerbie to Dunblane through devolution to the SNP's historic election victory in 2011. But I wonder how relevant would today's BBC look to Logie Baird were he still viewing from his fireside in Helensburgh?

Challenge from within

When you are a manager and a leader at the BBC it is difficult to admit that things are wrong. I understand that. I was guilty of some of it myself. For insiders, it's easier to focus on how things are improving. Small changes delivered within the current mindset. Outside, the fog clears. It is much easier to see that the paradigm must shift.

The last transformational change in the BBC's service to Scottish audiences came in 1999 when the Scottish parliament was reconvened. Amid a noisy political and media battle, BBC governors rejected the *Scottish Six* and instead proferred pieces of gold to placate the Scottish programme makers. There was money for new studios at *The Tun* in Edinburgh and inside the Scottish parliament. New correspondents, new resources and new programmes were created. Proving that a camel is a horse designed by committee, those new programmes included *Newsnight Scotland*. The ground was laid then for a long-drawn-out and hard-fought campaign by the BBC Scotland leadership for an £188 million investment in Pacific Quay, a new Scottish headquarters on the Clyde.

The story over the past decade has been one of incremental rather than transformational change. Relationships are stronger between Scotland and London. News coverage is more aware of the differences of devolution. Nick Robinson and Brian Taylor stand side by side telling the big Scottish story to audiences around the UK. Network TV spending has crept up towards a much hailed 8.6 per cent target. Creative programming successes are on the show reel. A new, shiny cathedral of broadcasting stands by the river. Those involved can point to improvements at every level. But what is the outcome of all of that as far as the overall perceptions of the Scottish audience are concerned?

Well, today half of the people of Scotland do not think the BBC is value for money. If your customers were telling you that in a private company you would be very concerned about the sustainability of your business. Audience research shows significant concern that that BBC does not provide enough 'programmes and content that cater for Scotland'. A large chunk of the Scottish audience thinks the BBC is not good at portraying 'our nation and culture' to the rest of the UK.

Another strong view in audience research is that the BBC appears to be weak at playing a role 'helping Scottish children and teens with what they learn at school or college'. So, a sizeable group of Scottish licence payers think the BBC is failing to educate, entertain and inform. In short, the BBC underperforms in Scotland across a range of measures, despite the valiant efforts of its committed, hard working staff.

These trends are not new nor have they changed much in recent years. Nor are these customer insights secret. They are available in the dusty recesses of the internet in an 87-page document called *BBC Trust Purpose Remit Study 2011-12 Scotland* carried out by Kantar Media. The BBC may score poorly on these measures in other parts of the UK but it is this under performance in Scotland mixed with a political majority which sees the BBC as an icon of London control to be attacked, challenged and changed, which makes such a potent cocktail.

The need for change
The BBC leadership used to say, when challenged about change, that the Corporation should be in step with devolution not ahead of it. Right now, there is a danger of it falling behind. While the political and constitutional landscape is transforming, is the BBC capable of responding or will it be in denial? Let me illustrate the problem.

The night of the launch of the SNP's White Paper on independence there was excellent coverage on the *Ten O'Clock News* – the nation's main television news bulletin. The best of BBC journalism with Brian Taylor and Nick Robinson giving their analysis and perspectives. Big tick. The next night the Spanish Prime Minister made an important intervention, firing, what the SNP's opponents would regard, as a broadside into the case for an independent Scotland's membership of the European Union.

I switched on the *Ten* to find out more. The first story which lasted for around 10 to 12 minutes concerned David Cameron and actions he may take to stop further immigration to England. Scotland, of course, has a very different story on immigration. The Scottish government seeks to encourage immigration, not limit it. The next political item concerned plans to introduce plain packaging for cigarettes in England. Scotland, of course, has a different story on this, too, having already announced, a while ago, it will forge ahead with such proposals. The rest of the programme contains stories of murders in England and sport in England.

No mention of the big political development in Scotland. As a Scottish licence payer, on this occasion, the BBC's main TV news bulletin had little relevance to me. My argument is that if you don't feel it is relevant now, it is going to become less and less relevant in the immediate future.

One number to remember
When you consider whether or not BBC Scotland has an appropriate level of funding focus on one number to remember. In written evidence to the Scottish parliament, the BBC stated that by 2017 spending on making programmes specifically for the Scottish audience would drop to £86 million. That's 2.4 per cent of the total licence fee income of £3.6 billion. Does that sound about right to you?

Now obviously, in addition to Scottish programmes for Scottish audiences, licence fee payers north of the border are also able to enjoy the whole panoply of delights of all the BBC's network content from *Dr Who* to Radio 4 to BBC Online to *Test Match Special* and their licence fees help to fund all that. Almost 9 per cent of the TV network spending is now invested in programmes such as *Waterloo Road*, made in Scotland, commissioned in London and shown across the UK, creating jobs and economic impact north of the border.

But does 2.4 per cent of the licence fee feel like the right amount of money to be spending on output commissioned in Scotland for Scotland to reflect the current diverse political, cultural and national agenda?

Perfect storm

The perfect storm which is now brewing should give cause for concern at the BBC, no matter the outcome of September's independence referendum. What happens if Scotland votes 'Yes'? The SNPs plans for broadcasting in an independent Scotland, outlined in its White Paper *Scotland's Future*, guarantees that Scottish viewers and listeners will pay the same to get access to all the current channels plus double the Scottish output. That sounds too good to be true!

Let's look at the detail. The Scottish government argues that in 2016 the BBC will spend £175 million in Scotland, while it will raise £320 million in Scotland through the licence fee. Come independence, the SNP says it would fund the Scottish Broadcasting Service (SBS) with that £320 million. It would add an ongoing share of BBC Worldwide's profits and money from Gaelic broadcasting to create a total annual budget of £345 million.

The SBS would continue to make the current level of network TV programming in Scotland for the BBC in London. This is worth around £95 million. In return, through a 'joint venture', Scottish audiences would be able to access all the current channels on BBC radio, TV and online. The SNP argues that this would leave you with double the money that you now spend on Scottish broadcasting and production. But its big assumption is that the BBC would give access to thousands of hours of programmes which cost £3.3 billion to create in return for £95 million of programmes the SBS makes for them. Would anyone in London ever agree to a deal like this?

Nirvana or fantasy?

Comment from the highly regarded media consultants, Enders Analysis, suggests that licence payers in England would baulk at subsidising viewers in a foreign country to what they say would amount to £270 million for BBC1 and BBC2 alone. The SNP would argue that this must be seen as one part of a much wider negotiation about dividing the assets of the UK. Although, I am told privately that senior members of the SNP are aware of the flimsiness of their audacious proposal.

If the 'joint venture' deal was not struck, the more likely scenario is that the SBS would be directed to see BBC Worldwide like any other foreign country. You would negotiate how much it would cost for what you want to buy. At this stage the guarantee of ensuring access to all the current channels would fall by the wayside.

You would cherry pick the best and most popular because what you spend here you can't spend on making Scottish programmes. On the credit side, you would then try and sell your programmes to the BBC and anyone else round the world. Once you know what you want to buy and estimate the level of income from what you might sell, you would then know how much you have left to spend on making programmes in Scotland for Scotland.

Would that be more or less than you have now? Well, that would depend how good you are. My best guess is you would end up with a lot more to spend and a more relevant mix of programmes but you would not be able to access all the you can now from the BBC nor would you double the budget for Scottish programmes as is claimed in the White Paper.

BBC senior managers are incredulous about the SNP's bold assumptions but will remain silent about the proposition for the Corporation post-independence, leaving the voter to decide whether it is nirvana or fantasy. The White Paper also outlines the editorial independence of the SBS from government. This is as obvious as it is essential. Saying it does not mean it will happen.

Amid the euphoria of a referendum victory, it would be tempting, even briefly, for some in the SNP to try to manipulate a national public service broadcaster to be its message carrier and propaganda machine. Such a move would be an affront to democracy and send entirely the wrong signal to the world about what sort of independent country was being created.

Further devolution
Let's look at what will happen if Scotland votes 'No'. The UK parliament has already passed the Scotland Act 2012 which means substantial new powers from 2016. This will mean that the Scottish parliament will take charge of collecting and spending 10p in the pound of income tax raised in Scotland. A Scottish version of HMRC is already being set up to deal with this.

It also hands powers to Scotland on air guns, drink-driving, speeding limits, stamp duty and landfill tax. That's just the start. In the spring of 2014, all three unionist parties will report on their plans for further devolution for Scotland. The news, current affairs, social, political and cultural agendas will grow further and further apart over the coming months and years. This means that the current structure and arrangements for the BBC as relates to its audiences in Scotland will need to change.

One of the confusions for the electorate is that they are not clear what lies in the control of Holyrood and what lies in the control of Westminster. BBC News is in danger of aiding and abetting this confusion and is likely to only exacerbate this further in the future.

How to respond?
If there is a 'No' vote in the referendum, the BBC and both governments must act swiftly to put in place a new broadcasting landscape for Scotland:

- A new vision needs to emerge in the run up to the BBC's charter renewal in 2016. Power over broadcasting should be devolved to the Scottish parliament while still regulated by Ofcom.

- The director-general of the BBC should be made responsible to the Scottish parliament for the performance of the Corporation in Scotland and regularly called to account in person at Holyrood.

- A new digital BBC Scotland TV channel should be created with the complete freedom for decisions to be made in Scotland on scheduling the most relevant output for people in Scotland.

- The UK wide main television news bulletins should be replaced by high quality, integrated TV bulletins of global, UK and Scottish news.

- Funding for Scottish programmes must be increased from the current 2.4 per cent of the licence fee.

The '*Scottish Six*'

I was part of a review of the so-called '*Scottish Six*' in 2009/10, which was led by the then-Head of Journalism at the BBC, Mark Byford. At that time, the audience research told us that nearly half the Scottish audience supported replacing the main TV news bulletins with new programmes covering global, UK and Scottish stories, edited in Scotland. However, many of this group were not viewers of BBC TV news.

The viewers who opposed change were BBC news loyalists. So, the argument was put forward that if you made the change you would risk alienating the majority of loyal viewers, while appeasing people who might never watch your programmes. Many of the London based executives involved at that time agreed on the logic of 'the *Scottish Six*' but argued that its time had not yet come. A few years on, the debate has now passed a point of no return. The editorial case is now compelling.

To continue with the current arrangements would become increasingly unsatisfactory for both viewers in Scotland and viewers in England. Serving each audience with news which is not relevant to them is a lose, lose situation. The *Scottish Six*, the *Scottish Ten* and every other main Scottish TV bulletin needs to be a mix of global, UK and Scotland ordered through the eyes of people in Scotland.

I also believe, the funding of broadcasting in Scotland must be substantially increased to improve the quality and range of the output. Can you really do justice spending only 2.4 per cent of the licence fee on the most relevant content covering the distinct Scottish agenda? It is a paucity of funding which drives ludicrous situations. Scottish education is absolutely central to the political and business debate in the nation, yet as part of its approach to saving money BBC Scotland does not have a dedicated education correspondent. Instead, the brief is shared with local government.

However, the political climate cannot be an excuse for letting up on the drive for efficiency. Working practices at BBC Scotland must continue to be modernised and brought closer to other UK and international broadcasters. BBC Scotland must be shaken and inspired to deliver an exciting, vibrant and ambitious broadcasting vision for Scotland.

Transparency

The BBC's Chairman, Chris Patten, has vowed that the BBC will become more open and transparent. Yet there is little transparency about how it performs and spends its money in Scotland. In researching this article, I have waded through the various public documents produced by BBC Scotland. As pieces of corporate governance they are sadly lacking.

Where are the key performance indicators? Why no mention of the performance gaps, audience dis-satisfaction and value for money measures from the Kantar research? Where's the clarity on how the money is spent in Scotland?

There are plenty of numbers but the key numbers which would really tell the performance story just aren't there.

Gaelic broadcasting

There is only one area where BBC Scotland outperforms the audience's expectations, according to the Kantar research. That's Gaelic. In Scotland, £20 million of public money is spent to serve 50,000 Gaelic speakers. This is a few million pounds more than the entire budget for Scottish news, current affairs and politics on TV, radio and online.

Spending more on one genre for 1 per cent of the population than you do on the most important genre for 100 per cent of the Scottish population does seem a little out of balance. The fact that the 99 per cent of Scots who do not speak Gaelic have to watch much of their rugby and football on BBC Alba with commentaries in Gaelic is a one of the true absurdities of a modern Scotland.

The funding of Gaelic is, of course, a matter which sparks more than a little jealousy and discontent in the ranks at Pacific Quay. The answer is not to reduce what the Gaels have got. The answer is to raise the ambition of BBC Scotland to serve the rest of the audience to the same standard. Much of that is about attitude and application as well as money.

The competition

How does BBC Scotland compare to its main competitor? The current leadership of STV has transformed their company from a basket case into a digital player with relevance, ambition and creativity – all in a relatively short period of time. All with a fraction of the money that has been available to BBC Scotland.

They have created new output such as the *Scotland Tonight* programme as a popular and better-scheduled competitor for *Newsnight Scotland*. BBC Scotland has had to respond by axing *Newsnight* and scheduling a new political programme anchored by Channel 4's Sarah Smith head to head at 10.30. STV's local digital offering is innovative and has great potential. To the outside observer, STV feels as if it is moving forward with pace and purpose while, in comparision, BBC Scotland seems to be treading water.

A good example of where the Scottish audience lies in the priorities of the BBC in London is the approach to mobile broadcast of Scottish output. STV is transforming what it does in this space. As an early adopter of the iPad, I have consumed most of my media on that device for the past three and a half years. London made BBC news and sport programmes and video have been available on the iPad a long time ago.

I have had to wait and wait till recent months before I could access similar, relevant Scottish content on this platform. Why? The truth is that BBC Scotland is not at the head of the queue when innovation rolls out. Instead, it stands in line waiting for London.

Conclusion

If the people of Scotland back a 'Yes' vote on 18 September 2014, the British Broadcasting Corporation will cease to be the UK's public broadcaster. If the majority votes in favour of retaining the Union then that's when the real challenge will begin for the BBC leadership.

The current arrangements for BBC Scotland in the devolution age were created in 1999. Scotland is a very different place now. My challenge in the arguments laid out here is for all the key players – the Scottish government, the UK government and the BBC – to rethink their current positions.

If the BBC does not adapt it will see a further decline in its standing and perception in Scotland. This path may end in the BBC losing its mandate to be Scotland's public service broadcaster. A paradigm shift in structure, culture, attitude and resource is required for the BBC to remain relevant in Scotland. As a loyal supporter, I can only hope that the Corporation has the leadership, vision and ambition to take swift and decisive action to transform its relationship with audiences in Scotland.

This is a time for BBC brave hearts.

Note on the contributor

Atholl Duncan was Head of News and Current Affairs for the BBC in Scotland between 2006 and 2011, responsible for leading a team of 250 journalists working on radio, television and online. He worked for the BBC for more than 25 years leading coverage of every major story in Scotland over that period. He edited *Reporting Scotland*, the BBC's 6.30pm news programme, and played a leading role in covering Lockerbie, Dunblane, Piper Alpha and every major political election over nearly three decades. Atholl was part of the BBC's review of news provision in Scotland in 2010, which ruled out creating integrated international, UK and Scottish TV News bulletins, edited in Scotland.

A clear case of journalistic underperformance: The house that Birt (and Hall) built

David Lloyd ponders the thoughts that may have crossed James Harding's mind (and the memos he may well have wanted to send to himself) over his first paper cup of BBC coffee – on starting the somewhat daunting job of Director of News

I would like to have had a camera at James Harding's shoulder on his first morning in office, documenting his demeanour and teasing out any clues to his detailed prospectus as the incoming Director of BBC News. Did the former editor of *The Times* make straight for the galleys of the newsroom and gaze upon its sheer size to confirm him in his decision to enlist, or did that unwieldy behemoth, and every correspondent, stringer and freelance stretching out beyond it, lead him to ponder, yet again, how it could be that an output not noted for its enterprise – let alone boldness – had shunted his two predecessors sideways out of office in circumstances of some ignominy?

This was clearly his most immediate conundrum – how not to lose his head – but beyond the instinct of simple self-preservation, any experienced and intelligent outsider could surely spot a fundamental flaw of culture, identified by the solipsism of those who had inhabited it for any length of time – and the higher up the ladder, the more self-defensive and damaging it no doubt seemed to him.

Over his first paper cup of BBC coffee there was an opportunity to reflect on the sheer size of public funding that keeps this news and current affairs ship afloat. With his Murdochian hat on, he remembers, no doubt, that the newsroom was designed and paid for, out of public funds, *twice*, installed – first under a certain Tony Hall in an expensively extended Television Centre, before being located, presumably for keeps, at Broadcasting House. Certainly, anyone taking on this mantle would need to study recent broadcasting history, he reflected, particularly if they were new to those media, and – so awesome was the task – perhaps even some illustrative historical parallels as well (*vide* Arrian:

231

Life of Alexander, *Loeb Classical Library for parallel English translation if – disgracefully – possessing* no *Ancient Greek*).

When John Birt was appointed as Deputy Director-General to 'sort out' BBC journalism in the mid-1980s, he lit upon Tony Hall as his most likely and willing lieutenant – let us compare Alexander the Great accompanied by his faithful general Ptolemy looking to topple the 4th century BC Persian empire, which will fall not so much to superior intellect or tactics but from the sheer dysfunction and demoralisation of that empire.

Terminal rows with Thatcher's government

It is customary now to regard what preceded Birt's conquest as something of a barbarian 'dark age' but the more terminal rows with Mrs Thatcher's government had tended to brew in departments other than the then separate BBC satrapies of News and Current Affairs. Indeed, while the News department, in either radio or TV, could hardly be described as the leading edge of broadcast journalism, (TV News had been headed by a succession of unlikely characters, not every one of them able to boast much news pedigree, and the senior figures in the newsroom tended to be long-servers from the days of Alexandra Palace, and almost exclusively male). In old-fashioned style, as on the newspapers of the day, the reporters – many of them notable mavericks – led the journalism, and to them was obeisance paid, yet the system could still deliver notable 'coups' such as Michael Buerk's superb report on the Ethiopian famine in 1984 which not only prompted Bob Geldof's Band Aid but set the tone for the North-South dialogue for a decade.

In short, there were parts of both news and current affairs that truly worked: on Radio 4, the *Today* programme, then as now, set the agenda for the day and was a 'must hear' among politicians and opinion-formers alike. Later at night on BBC 2 *Newsnight* was a new kid on the block but, with the recruitment of Peter Snow and John Tusa and the enlisting of Charles Wheeler and even Joan Bakewell to the colours, had succeeded in forging the first news and current affairs alloy, just in time for distinguished broadcast service in the 1982 Falklands War. Thus equipped, it was giving ITN's *News at Ten*, then the acknowledged 'news leader', a proper run for its money.

At the same time, while the geographically and culturally distinct current affairs department was probably better known for its production skills than its original journalism, *Panorama* retained a high authority and reputation among the audience at large. Even so, *Panorama* was be shoehorned into a new purpose, discussing through documentary film the detail of contemporary policy, rather than follow the proper role of current affairs – to report narrative storylines or arguments that *drive* to a point of policy (it was only under the guidance of the now forgotten and maligned George Entwistle, when Head of TV Current Affairs, that *Panorama* was allowed to re-discover its proper role).

Hall himself had worked on both *Today* and *Newsnight* but they were not to be the blueprint for the original, agenda-setting pro-active news journalism that would speak of a national broadcaster's obligation. For Birt himself had arrived, shrouded in the so-called 'mission to explain', which was at best an elaboration of only one leg in the Reithian triptych to the overshadowing of the others (much education, some information, no entertainment). John Birt now set upon journalism of exposition, and – to a degree – of some analysis, which very quickly came to dominate the mainstream bulletins and, after those, the 24-hour news channel and, later, the news website.

But behind this expository approach lay a particular attitude to its intake of material – a journalism of 'process' rather than enquiry and initiative. As a result, some years into the pursuance of this mission it is common for the BBC's only advancement of a running news story to lie not in further journalistic enquiry but in the excerpting of clips of interviews from the so-called 'news programmes' (those that include interviews, such as *World at One* on Radio 4, or the *Andrew Marr Show* on a Sunday morning). That is 'process' in action, from which in recent years, on a domestic agenda, only Robert Peston – an incomer from the *Financial Times* – has been immune.

News generated by the 'power centres'

Not surprisingly, it took some time for this approach to settle with BBC journalists: at the time of the first Big Storm (the Michael Fish one) they were heard to a man complaining that they were being despatched not to report on the damage done but to discover when was the last time anything comparable had occurred. Over time this caricature came to sophisticate in favour of a more accurate description of the approach as it bedded down but this Birt-ist 'make-over' has never shed a preference for exposition of news stories generated by the 'power centres' of politics, government, business, finance or organised labour than for those discovered through the BBC's own free-standing skill, 'self-start' initiative and resources. And therein has lain a major lacuna, of both coverage and ambition.

By now Harding has attempted a croissant and is resisting the temptation to compare its over-solid dough with the consistency of his directorate's output; it occurs to him that, over time, many BBC bulletins on television or radio are not so different from illustrated or sound-described news diaries, aside – of course – from the truly unexpected occurrences of happenstance, at home or abroad, and that-even for a broadcast tyro-this must be surely be to underuse both media.

First Harding memo to self: 'Newsgathering to be less mechanistic – needs restructure.'

Across the journalism profession as a whole his reasoning will be seen as in no sense idiosyncratic; some years into its conversion the average BBC news day has indeed taken on an undemanding rhythm of simple 'process', where too often the only means of advancing a running news story lies not in inquiry or lateral thinking of any kind but in excerpting brief interview clips garnered from those so-called 'news programmes' (those that contain interviews). It has to be of concern that enlarging a story is so dependent on the preparedness of people to speak on-the-record. And since the mainstream news is the epicentre of any broadcaster's journalism – the most watched and most influential part of its output – that is surely where the focus for change must lie. And that comes from someone who has devoted the majority of his career to Current Affairs!

Before long, word is out that their new director is in the canteen and now, bearing down on his table, is one of the brighter and bolder young journalists of his inheritance. 'There is a rumour around,' she smiles sweetly, 'that you favour more "scoops" in the mainstream news coverage but, if I might suggest, this is a dangerous route, and a chimera: the audience wants to know what's happened of importance, not what we journalists wish to foist upon them as significant – for how do the viewers or listeners know the journalist's agenda? News has to begin from events of acknowledged importance, or the announcements of the powerful or influential, and it is for us to bring our informed analysis and explanation to bear.'

Like any experienced manager, Harding will keep his counsel but, no doubt, reflect on how deeply embedded this culture now sits at the BBC, and among its brightest and most ambitious practitioners – an attitude that you would be unlikely to encounter in any other newsroom, whether at Sky, ITN or indeed *The Times*. But isn't the idea that you can truly strip news down to its purest essentials itself something of a chimera?

Second Harding memo to self: 'Would like to see the audience research that supports this austere approach – need to set something fresh in motion.'

How long this Socratic dialogue can sustain is unclear; had I the opportunity, I would have made the following distinction, which Harding could probably make better than I, but could also quote just a few of the more dynamic broadcast examples which might elude him. And here goes:

Taken at its most basic, news itself can be described – in whatever medium or form it is presented – as a collection of items of information or 'stories' which document how the world is different today from the situation of yesterday, placed in an order of importance suggested by a mix of factors including the number of people affected, the proximity (sadly) of the news provider, the predictable or unexpected nature of the occurrence, and the recognised importance of the people involved.

Class, are you still with me, paying maximum attention?!

Now, if you accept this description – or even if you don't – it follows that those very 'power centres' or institutions of government, politics, finance, business etc. possess enormous leverage in being able to turn the news agenda, and it is how the journalist relates to this leverage that lies at the heart of the BBC's post-Birt approach.

Two distinct traditions of journalism

One could argue that there are two distinct traditions of journalism in a free society – one passive, one active or, if you prefer, reactive and pro-active. The latter looks to respond to the actions or announcements of authority, assessing them fairly at the moment of that authority's choosing; the former expects journalists to enquire of their own volition, assembling evidence from which to construct a storyline or argument, fairly and in the public interest. There is nothing incompatible or irreconcilable about these two traditions, they can and do co-exist in a single news programme or newspaper; what is unusual is to prefer the latter to the near-wholesale exclusion of the former. Certainly, *The Times* could not have survived or prospered for any length of time on such rigidity of input.

An example: we all no doubt remember the murder of Jo Yeates, the young landscape architect student in Bristol in December 2010, for which a Dutch neighbour was finally convicted. Early in their inquiries the Avon and Somerset police would appear to have briefed journalists against her landlord, wrongly, as the prime suspect. This led the ITV news at ITN to run a report questioning the competence of the investigation, in which – of course – the police were given the opportunity to respond but which, in turn, had them banned from the police's press conferences. A single example, but one of many available, of journalists using their instinct and trained method to important effect (*vide David Mannion, then Editor-in-Chief, ITN, on Radio 4's* The Media Show *at that time*).

Now, is it conceivable, one must ask, that such a report – of justified, 'self-start' journalism – fairly conducted and 'duly impartial' to the guidelines of the statutory broadcast regulator, Ofcom, could ever be likely, under the Corporation's current mindset, to have any place in a BBC news bulletin or channel, except perhaps if an MP or someone else of authority were to criticise that investigation? Otherwise, the only opportunity for a news audience to see such a thing would be as a trailer for a forthcoming *Panorama*!

But I am not the only journalist, present or past, who would see such omissions of coverage as, at best, an undershoot, and, at worst, a betrayal of public funds. Another, more recent, example if you need: The BBC has devoted hundreds, perhaps thousands, of hours of radio and television to the 'Lord Rennard Affair' on the justified ground that it goes to the heart of attitudes – even a possible schism – within the Liberal Democrat Party and its credibility and governance. But did anyone think to ask how it was that the mighty cohorts of BBC Westminster, numbers far in excess of any other parliamentary team, failed to break that story in the first place, but that was left to Channel 4 News? (Back in Channel 4 days we used to enjoy a joke that the Beeb's favoured presenter 'lead-in' – 'The BBC has learnt that ...' was a coded euphemism for 'Just how did C4 News discover that ...?')

In Harding's interview with the Director-General for the job (the kind you entertain when you are the only candidate and all internal competitors have somehow fallen away), it is likely that Hall urged him to consider pro-active journalism as more naturally the province of current affairs or hybrid programmes such as *Newsnight*, while Harding urged him to consider the weight of proper journalism being lost to the Corporation under the current approach. Hall countered by asking Harding to reflect on the political damage likely to be done to the corporation by a return to the more eclectic news agenda of the 1980s, but Harding retorted that, as it was, the BBC had been no stranger to that recently!

Perhaps. But we are unlikely to find out, and even a well-framed Freedom of Information request is unlikely to yield this. One day the principals will have to be questioned. However, subsequent correspondence between them ought to be more discoverable, and it is to be expected that Harding raised the role of the Editorial Policy department, also introduced by John Birt and today serving as something of a 'belt and braces' advice service to editors in a quandary. It's likely that Harding regarded this, from his own experience, as strictly unnecessary for any competent editor and may even have suggested that its very existence had led the BBC to appoint less able and authoritative editors. Perhaps a compromise was arrived at, whereby the functions of 'Ed Pol' were to be retained over time, but not as a separate directorate? That, at least, might save staff numbers.

Authority and range of Corporation's international coverage

Of course, one of the things that will have drawn Harding to the job in the first place (well, aside from the fact that he was out of work and available) was an admiration amounting to envy shared among his peers for the authority and range of the Corporation's international coverage; some of its senior on-camera performers are major figures of global journalism and reporters down the line display enormous bravery and courage, especially in war zones. Yet he still has an instinct that, on more everyday, mundane assignments, BBC reporters tend to be less alert to the unexpected within their locations than their rivals at Sky, ITV or Channel 4; he puts this down to an over-oppressive newsgathering desk in London – fine as long as it retains a sense of strategy in the deployment of public funds, not so fine if it stifles reporters' initiative, and the output with it. There is also the canard that he picked up when first enquiring about the job that some of the more senior figures are almost beyond the control of production, travelling and reporting pretty much where they choose.

Third Harding memo to self: 'Need meeting asap with X, Y and Z; sort out bad blood, can't continue.'

It is now some months since Harding's first foray into the BBC canteen when, one must assume, he had finally to be bundled out by security to forestall further, untimely dialogues but let us hope that, now he is beyond his 'honeymoon' phase, even for a novice – he can soon turn to the 'value for public money' equation and liberate the journalism under his command. At least, the early signs of a coming 'Journalism Spring' are encouraging, as a whole new raft of editors and managers has been introduced, even at the risk of over-staffing and a top-heavy management structure (*cf.* Broadcast Magazine, *passim*), whose experience lies – at least in part – outside the BBC and who will be less likely to prove out of their depth, shorn of ideas and bare of background, and cocooned in a 'bubble' if or when the next controversy strikes – as it inevitably will.

The public funding equation is crucial here and one must believe that Harding will address it, if for no other reason than from his background at News International, for consider the probable sums. True, the BBC faces a frozen licence fee but one that has risen exponentially over recent years, yet even that is not the only financial under-pinning for its journalism; its World Service radio and TV operation is now fully integrated with the domestic service available to a British audience, yet it is still funded directly by grant-in-aid from the Foreign Office.

That, at any rate, is the current position at the time of writing (January 2014). However, it's important to point out that, from April 2014, perhaps seizing on this anomaly, the government will require the BBC to maintain its World Service coverage no longer out of grant-in-aid but from the licence fee. On the face of it, this could reduce the resources available to journalism as a whole, but in truth the funding horse has long since bolted, and the sizeable World Service infrastructure was built on many years of grant-in-aid. Now it is only its running costs which will have to be sustained on whatever share of the licence fee Harding can bid for but as the incumbent, he ought to be in a strong bargaining position, and it is other departments across the BBC which are most likely to feel the chill of a frozen licence fee.

Most urgent Harding memo of all to self: 'Discover how Byzantine funding system actually works before going in to bat, and playing up new boy status; important not to start new job with staff-demoralising defeat.'

There is, also, the share of income from BBC Worldwide, reliant on the historic branding of the BBC, even if little Higher Education Funding Council money, arriving through the OU, actually reaches its journalism.

The precise figures are – admittedly – hard to nail down, or fillet from published totals, but I would nonetheless wager that the full resources available to the BBC's journalism far outstrip the wealth of Araby or, more specifically, the market value of natural gas under Qatar which powers al-Jazeera, and certainly dwarf, for sheer dependability and consistency, the income of any broadcaster reliant on the vagaries of the commercial advertising market, in the UK or USA.

Of all news broadcasters with aspirations to be a world player, the BBC must surely be, far and away, the richest. And Harding's challenge is to match the Corporation's impact to its income. It will only develop into a crisis if it proves undeliverable. Or, rather, it may be that the next crisis of BBC journalism will not be political, stretching to Westminster or social media but will be internal, a struggle for the soul of its public mission between Harding and Hall, but one that will define Hall's term as Director-General: is he Tony, Lord Hall, who ran the Royal Opera House with such distinction and took an instinctive and justified chance on Antonio Pappano or is he the faithful Ptolemy?

In the event of a stand-off or stasis between the two men, it would perhaps be for the BBC Trust – assuming it survives – to arbitrate, but I'm not sure I would advise anybody to hold their breath.

Note on the contributor

David Lloyd is Visiting Professor of Journalism, City University London, and former Head of News and Current Affairs, Channel 4 TV.

Still hideously white?

Farrukh Dhondy critically surveys television's coverage of black and Asian lives and issues – and argues that 'multiculture is simply an acceptable, liberal term for an inclusive, wide, but judgemental monoculture'

When Greg Dyke was appointed Director-General of the BBC and was received by the staff of the great Kafkaesque edifice, he was reported as saying that it was 'hideously white'. The liberal elite, especially those who have had a job in Britain's late twentieth century race relations industry, wear their badges of courage and conviction right out there – as proud as the designer labels and vulgar slogans on the T-shirts of the hoi polloi. He obviously saw a lot of female faces and bodies as he surveyed the 'human resources' of the organisation and it would been anathema to announce at the same time that he could discern the sexual orientation of employees and so assess whether the organisation was also 'painfully straight'.

Mr. Dyke (or is he Sir Greg now?) was making a political head-counting statement, one that reflects the concern that in a society whose population is 4 per cent black and brown there ought to be four black and brown people out of every hundred employed by a Corporation which is, perhaps after parliament, the showcase of the nation.

A phrase which adds a severe description to 'white', using the word in a racial sense, is a contention and that contention has a history. Neglecting the fact that there were runaway slaves and adventurers of several sorts from all over the globe in Elizabethan times and that Nehru, Gandhi and others sojourned in Britain as scholars in the era when Western education was deemed the most valuable and progressive in India, mass immigration established itself in Britain several decades after broadcasting.

There are at the time of writing this chapter (January 2014) several BBC programmes featuring black and Asian people. They will as tastes and fashions progress, be short-lived and be replaced in time by others. A critical commentary saying that a current situation comedy called *The Khans* has taken multicultural broadcasting back several decades will carry no conviction, cut no ice, unless the history of British broadcasting featuring ethnic communities is evoked.

Immigration from the ex-colonies

The movement of labour from the ex-colonies to Britain began in earnest in the late fifties and early sixties of the last century. There were no social or political plans, no vision for their integration into British society. They were left to find or form their own ghettos, to work the night shifts and the underground, clean the streets, nurse the sick in hospitals, conduct the buses of the big cities and, in time, set up the mosque-and-mill enclaves of the Midlands and the North and, aided by municipal socialism, the crime-prone vertical slums of London.

The first liberal impulse of the broadcasters was directed towards the Asian peasantry, the Indians and Pakistanis who came in the largest numbers from the Punjab, from Mirpur in what is now Pakistani Kashmir and from Bangladesh, then East Pakistan. The BBC's first instinct was 'integration' – teaching the newcomers to accommodate to British ways and British society – how to get about using the language, how not to bargain at supermarket counters but pay the price that the till rang up and elementary rules of etiquette. They ran programmes with well-intentioned, patronising titles such as *Apnaa Hi Ghar Samajhye* which means *Consider It Your Home* – 'it' meaning Britain. There were other programmes in which white and Asian neighbours befriended each other and cultures rubbed along with pointed explanation, again with the aim of instructing the immigrant to feel at home. A famous programme was *Padosi*, Hindustani for *Neighbours* – years before the Ozzies named their soap.

Television didn't consider that West Indians needed instructional programming to assist the assimilation. Black (or was it 'coloured'?) characters went straight into situation comedies in bit or secondary parts. One or two Asian characters crept into *Newcomers*, a soap whose 'native' writers, unfamiliar with the idiom of the newcomers relied on the uncertain advice of the rare black or Asian RADA-trained actor.

The empire strikes (limps?) back

Settlement gave rise to dissatisfactions, tensions, political formations and demands. There was the paramount question of how temporary was this influx of ex-colonials. Were they here to stay? Was the dream of some of them to live frugally, work hard and earn enough money to return home as relatively rich citizens, capable of buying property and setting themselves up in business in the Punjab or Jamaica defeated by the hand to mouth of immigrant employment and pay? It soon became clear that the road back was paved with yellow bricks — it was a fantasy.

One of the mainly Bangladeshi anti-racist demonstrations in the East End of London, protesting a spate of Paki-bashing and fire-bomb assaults on the estate flats of immigrants was 'Come what may we are here to stay,' though the tones in which it was shouted was loaded with nostalgia and foreboding. Campaigning groups, some in imitation of the rise of the civil rights movement and the Black Panther Party of the USA, began to demand equality in housing, schooling, and employment, in treatment from the police and the courts and in access to public facilities. There was manifest if not universal discrimination towards the new 'coloured' populations in all these fields and the agitation took notice of and opposed them.

There was polite begging for relief but there was also bumptious militancy. The post-colonial era was also the post-war era and while Britain's population looked forward to an acceleration in meritocracy, it also underwent the trauma of revisionist history in which the white man, conqueror, colonialist, imperialist, racist, slave-dealer and owner, composer of nasty nursery rhymes etc. was often portrayed as the natural villain. Britain had just been through the era of the Angry Young Men, the post-war generation of playwrights, novelists and rebels who as the first tide of literary meritocrats saw class as their target. Now here was a new wave of objectors and claimants.

The agitation took to the streets in several instances – in protest, for example, against Enoch Powell's 1968 'Rivers of Blood' speech. In the USA, one could see a link between the civil rights agitation and the new wave of feminist protest. In Britain, the link may not have existed or been clear but together with the movements on immigration and race, feminism and gay rights seem to have been given a fresh breath, one that blew embers into flame.

Joining the big picture

Television was firmly established as a universal demotic medium. Its conscience prompted it to be as inclusive as it dared – 'diversity' was born. *Mind Your Language* and *Love Thy Neighbour* were written to feature Asian, diverse immigrant and West Indian characters. It doesn't matter now that the programmes of the era, mostly situation comedies and the occasional drama featuring black men as crooks, suffered later from accusations of patronisation, 'stereotyping' and racist subtexts. Presence was all..

The battalions of political correctness had not yet laid siege to the public conscience and the writers and producers of these series certainly saw themselves as liberal pioneers of broadcasting. The writers may have misjudged the mood and reviewed today, three or four decades later, their unfamiliarity with the cultures and idiom they sought to dramatise is ludicrously evident. Norman Beaton, working on *Desmond's* in the nineties told me he had to rewrite the lines for himself and other black actors – sometimes on the set.

Probably the true breakthrough in television's dramatic presentation of the new communities came with BBC Pebble Mill's *Empire Road* series, written by Guyanese playwright Michael Abensetts and produced by the team of David Rose and Peter Ansorge. It was 'comedy' only in the sense that the word applies to Shakespeare's work, an exploration of stances and attitudes rather than a gag-fest. The drama kept itself refreshingly free of burning race issues. Not so the

241

programmes that were at the same time, with classically liberal intent invading ITV. There was London Television Weekend's (prop. John Birt) *Skin* which featured in each episode a problem occasioned by race: housing, education, employment, public services, police attitudes etc. This 'etc.' is statistically circular. Once they had done housing, education, employment, police attitudes, public services, they had to start again and do housing, education.... the 'mission to complain' became 'race' TV's mainstay.

So the question being asked was: 'What can TV do for racial minorities?' but not yet 'What can racial minorities do for TV?' The worry of 'hideously white' had not become insistent. The first question was now being answered in one obvious way – put the protest of blacks onto the screen. Protest is one democratic way of winning rights and gaining positions, but is it the substance of TV? For one thing it gets repetitive and boring and begins to sound, as these programmes complaining about racism and asking for concessions inevitably did, like begging in a bullying voice, a bluff that Britain has invariably called through its colonial history.

The new platform

The pressures of British liberalism brought about the conception and reality of Channel 4. There were fresh interests rampant in the population and these would now be represented on a new televisual platform. The channel was conceived under a Labour administration but sanctioned and implemented in the reign of Thatcher. Good Marxist theoretician that she was she and her advisors who gave it their executive imprimatur, realised that Channel 4, while espousing all manner of causes and points of view inimical to Conservatism, would bring the small entrepreneur into the broadcasting market, challenging the large monopolies of the BBC and ITV. It would be the generation of the independent TV producers, the generation of a wedge of small business, hiring and firing its employees, into the union-dominated world of BBC and ITV. The likes of Tariq Ali and Darcus Howe, radical in tooth and claw, would become owners of TV production companies that hired and fired as the processes of commissioning and production demanded.

Ideologically Channel 4 was, by parliamentary remit, the representative of minority interests. Jeremy Isaacs, its first supremo, appointed Sue Woodford, a Trinidadian Brit and an experienced programme producer as the channel's first Multicultural Commissioning Editor. Woodford's programming was revolutionary. She ditched the mission to complain and ran on the channel, among a diversity of offerings, one West Indian and one Asian magazine show, a black arts showcase programme and then a situation comedy called *No Problem*, co-written by veteran Trinidadian playwright Mustafa Matura and myself. The brief to the writers was clear – a situation comedy makes people laugh. It featured five Caribbean siblings living in a house in Willesden, London, each with their own conceits and relationships to Britain. It was funny, it worked, it got audience figures and significantly it was a huge hit amongst the youth of West Indian origin.

In the wake of the series' success I was invited by a Mr Sivanandan, who was the boss of the Institute of Race Relations, to speak to an audience about my TV comedy. I went. Sivanadan was chairing the event. He introduced me, virtually saying that this was a trial of my consciousness. 'No problem is a problem!' he thundered, striking the table. I quickly gathered it was a set up. I was the golden-calf-worshipper of triviality in a Mosaic congregation of anti-racist righteousness. It was a parting of many ways. The sub-text of some of the protest and anti-racist movements of the sixties and seventies was a sort of revolutionary wishful thinking. The Black Panthers in America professed that the demand for rights for black people was tantamount to a demand for a revolution in the United States and black people were the vanguard of that revolution. It was the British counterpart of that argument that led Mr Sivanandan to reject the idea of a black situation comedy on TV. There was no time for frivolity. My own experience, beginning perhaps with the same premise of radical and revolutionary thinking, had brought me to a contrary persuasion.

I had been an active member of a succession of immigrant radical groups one of which ran an agitational newspaper called *Freedom News*. One of the inspirations of the group was the Trinidadian Marxist philosopher C. L. R. James who addressed a meeting of the group on the content of this pamphleteering newssheet. He was of the opinion that an agitational sheet such as ours should first and foremost speak of the experience of its members. 'What is it you do for a living?' was his question to the audience. 'I drive a London Transport bus,' was the first answer. 'Then write about what happens in the garage, your experience in the streets, in the trade union, with the public etc.' Turning eventually to me, a schoolteacher at the time, he said I should write about the conflicts and dramas of the school and the classroom. Surely I had stories to tell.

I did. I wrote these stories week after week and after a few editions was visited by a young man in a pin-striped suit asking for me in the school playground. He wasn't from the police as the pupils whom he accosted thought, but was an editor at the publishing house Macmillan. He said he had found out that I was the writer of the school 'stories' in *Freedom News* and that he would like to commission me to write a book of them. He said, memorably, that the audience for 'multicultural fiction' existed before the books did. I accepted the commission and wrote my first published book and then a second and a third. It was after the third book that Peter Ansorge, the producer of Empire Road at BBC's Pebble Mill approached me and asked if I would transform a set of my stories into TV plays. The series was written and directed by various directors with 'radical' credentials among them John McGrath, Jon Amiel and Horace Ove.

In 1982, a year after the series was broadcast Channel 4 was born. What was its first multicultural editor determined to do? If the Reithian formula of educating and entertaining was generally true for broadcasting then it was true for this specialist programming. Under Sue Woodford the mission to complain was subverted. There were two clear strategic objectives which emerged from Channel 4. More people from the ethnic communities should be making programmes, serving an apprenticeship if necessary. There were, inevitably headcounts of the number of ethnic faces appearing on-screen as newsreaders, reporters, presenters or actors. A fair volume of programming of diverse sorts would ensure or at least begin the assimilation of the new communities into the nation's primary instrument or mirror of self-awareness.

The recruitment of writers, directors, producers and actors from the ethnic minorities assured not only the attrition of hideous whiteness, but perhaps more importantly a familiarity with the culture, the communities and the issues which brought authority and authenticity to the programmes. The problem remains that the word (adjective of 'white', adverb qualifying 'appears'?) 'hideously' is not amenable to statistical exactitude. If the new black and brown communities of Britain constitute 4 per cent of the population, does it mean that there should be only one ethnic newscaster out of every 25? Or one black hero or heroine in 25 series of detective or hospital stories? Wouldn't a strictly statistically representative approach lead to a mass cull of 'diverse' persons from the BBC's output? And one could ask why aren't the successive director-generals crying out for more Polish representation on screen now that there is a considerable Polish working population in the UK?

The impulse to 'diversity' and multiculturalism began with the project of assimilation. It certainly included giving chicken tikka masala the respect it deserves, but was never intended to inculcate a tolerance, for instance, of female genital mutilation, religiously sanctioned polygamy or stoning adulteresses to death on the grounds that these were part of the 'culture' of some new communities. 'Multiculture' is simply an acceptable, liberal term for an inclusive, wide, but judgemental monoculture.

Leave positive imaging to Saatchi and Charles Saatchi (or maybe not)

That doesn't preclude documentaries which tell the truth about the practice of female genital mutilation in the name of religion or culture. The idea that the lives or culture of the new communities should be portrayed by television in 'positive images' is another untenable tenet of liberal thought. It is undoubtedly the first idea that occurs to BBC heads of this or that when they make decisions about 'diversity'. The proposition is untenable because television is not an advertising agency for blacks and any attempt to make it so demeans the intelligence of viewers. There may be a case for the presentation of role models, but there is also a case for inculcating a respect for reality.

A snapshot of contemporary BBC programmes demonstrates a determination to remedy the hideousness of white reportage. There are 'diversity' (I like being called 'a diverse' rather than an Indian person) news presenters and reporters all over the screen. There are comedy appearances which can be seen as concessional or even abused for being negatively stereotypical – all part of the fun. The *Mr Khan* episodes are a clumsy attempt to cock a snook at positive image and non-stereotype imagery. Then there are plausible black detectives who always get their man or woman and demonstrate compassion for the criminal compelled by his or her fate to unspeakable deeds. Again high marks out of ten, even though the principle could lead to unlikely, say, brain surgeons or black Winston Churchills thrown in.

The main failure of the Kafkaesque structure of the BBC in which looking warily over one's shoulder is a necessary survival instinct, is that it prevents editors and commissioners from making the creative associations between 'non-white' and the diverse and vital cultures of the screen. 'Diversity' becomes not a creative but a policing venture.

A brief story featuring the journey towards diversity: I was, from the mid-eighties for several years, the second appointed Commissioning Editor for Multicultural Programmes at Channel 4. Part of the brief I had formulated or accepted was to recruit or encourage a brace of independent production companies with Black and Asian owners, producers, directors researchers etc. Some of the smaller of these companies made a series of investigative, observational and polemically necessary documentaries for the channel. As some of the people making these docs were fairly or absolutely new to the medium, I appointed Bernard Clark, an experienced (white) TV hand to be an executive producer of the series which we called *The Black Bag*.

When the series was about to be transmitted an Asian journalist previewed it and approached me for an interview. He asked a few routine questions and then came out with what seemed a carefully rehearsed question: 'Since you have put a white man in charge of a collection of ethnic producers, what would you say if someone accused you of acting like a typical slave-dealer or a colonial governor?' These parallels had not occurred to me but what did immediately come to mind was a multicultural phrase which I had absorbed from my college days in Poona. I replied: 'I'd say "kiss my cock and call me Charlie!"' He shut his notebook and stormed out of my office. Two hours later I was summoned to the Channel Controller's office to confront two of my bosses, Liz Forgan and John Willis. 'Did you just tell a journalist to kiss your cock and call you Charlie?' asked Liz Forgan with a poker face. I quoted the journalist's question and attempted to justify my answer which I repeated. Neither Liz nor John could now keep a straight face. John nearly fell off his chair. A triumph I thought for multicultural expression.

Conclusion: BBC now 'hideously corporate'

When Margaret Thatcher, the Lenin of the lower middle-class British revolution, and her government set up Channel 4, they structured it to stimulate the existence of small independent production companies. The small companies born out of this venture, some of which, in the early competition that Channel 4 offered the BBC, were commissioned by the Beeb, have all but gone out of business or been absorbed in larger companies.

The BBC never had as its remit the encouragement of small independent companies and very many ethnic producers took employment with larger monoliths or went out of business. As a result the commissioning landscape, certainly that of the BBC, is now hideously corporate.

Note on the contributor

Farrukh Dhondy was born in India, came to Britain on a scholarship to Cambridge University and lives in Britain. He is a writer of fiction, biography, TV, screenplays and journalism and was for fourteen years the Multicultural Commissioning Editor of Channel 4.

Section 7:
The nation's Trust: Trust in the Trust?

Richard Tait

Although it does not always seem like it, public service broadcasting in the UK is in good shape. An international comparison shows Public Service Broadcasting (PSB) in virtually every other part of the world in decline and facing huge problems. In the US, public broadcasting is an impoverished niche: across Western Europe, public television has lost the battle for audiences with nimbler and better resourced commercial competition; in Eastern Europe and the developing world, public broadcasting is often distrusted as state controlled and second-rate.

Although ITV and Channel 4 deserve great credit for the way they have found a way to combine the best values of PSB with commercial success, the fundamental reason the UK is still seen by many as having the best broadcasting in the world is the survival, up to this point, of the BBC as a strong, well-financed broadcaster, independent of the state. The BBC's unique relationship with its audience as the most trusted source of news and the scale and range of its output make it unique – but where once it might have been seen as a model for the rest of the world, it now looks one of a kind.

Of course, this unique position is a doubled-edged sword. For the BBC's critics it is evidence that it is an idea whose time has passed – that if the rest of the world can get along fine without a huge public intervention in broadcasting, so can the UK. For the BBC's supporters, it is wake-up call to protect a crucial part of the British way of life in its contribution to our culture and democracy in a hostile environment.

This section of *Is the BBC in Crisis?* looks at this central argument through the prism of the debates over the two pillars on which the Corporation has been built – its governance system and its funding mechanism – both historically, and currently, independent of direct state or political control. Today, however, the BBC's constitution and the licence fee are in play as never before. How these apparently arcane issues are resolved are the key factors which will determine what sort of BBC we have in the future.

The governors' last stand

The system of governance has only become an issue in the last decade. The concept of a board of governors drawn from civic society (or the great and the good, depending on your point of view) embodying the BBC and supervising its management had seemed archaic long before – when I worked at the BBC in the 1970s and 1980s the board seemed to be appointed according to a Panglossian civil service formula which I am not sure even *Yes Minister* could have parodied – a left-leaning industrialist and a right-leaning trade unionist; a former diplomat/spy to look after the World Service and the Caversham Monitoring Station; a chairman from the governing party, a deputy chairman from the opposition… The only quality which seemed to ensure that you could never be considered as a BBC governor was any direct experience of broadcasting. Michael Grade's appointment as BBC Chairman in the aftermath of Hutton was the first time a seasoned broadcast professional had ever been on the board, let alone in the chairman's seat.

The fact that David Liddiment writes his article 'A Question of Trust' as one of the BBC's longest serving board members, shows how much things have changed. Liddiment is one of commercial broadcasting's biggest figures – he was Director of Television at ITV and is one of the founders and directors of All3Media, the UK's leading independent producer. In his 2001 MacTaggart lecture, he argued for reform of the BBC's governance arrangements. Five years later, he joined the Trust as one of the first members of a new board which included the former chief executive of the Independent Television Commission and (to declare a personal interest) a former editor-in-chief of ITN.

Defending the Trust

Sometimes in broadcasting you have to be careful what you wish for, but Liddiment is still a strong supporter of the Trust – 'disillusionment', he says, 'has not set in'. He confronts, head-on, the issue of executive pay which he believes should have been a triumph for the Trust – who had forced a reluctant executive to cut bonuses, pay rates and executive numbers – but turned into 'a handy stick to beat it with' – as the 'unedifying spectacle at the PAC' revealed the fault lines between the Trust and the executive.

Liddiment believes the new relationship between the two will avoid confusion in the future; that the bigger role for the non-executive directors will help; and that the Trust can then focus on its key responsibilities – value for licence fee payers and assessing performance through its service reviews. But he is suspicious of the current favourite model to replace the Trust – a plc-style board with Ofcom, arguing that 'the idea of a public body spending £4 billion a year of other people's money can be run entirely by its board of management – on-the-ball non-execs and a hawkish NAO and PAC notwithstanding – with no separate body to protect the public interest and public value, is frankly insane'.

Replacing the Trust

On the other side of the argument, Howard Davies, the former Director of the London School of Economics, applies his experience of corporate life at the Financial Services Authority, the Bank of England and the CBI to what he terms 'The BBC's governance problem'. Only the Downing Street cat, he writes, knows the full story of why in 2005 the Blair government rejected both the ideas of the BBC and of its independent advisers (the Burns committee, including Davies himself) for the future governance of the Corporation. But he is no doubt that the outcome was 'a Horlicks'.

Nor does he have much time for the Trust's attempts to make the best of a bad job – 'the system was well understood to be flawed from the start, has failed in exactly the way knowledgeable observers said it would fail and, therefore, must be reformed in a structural way'. He thinks that even before the inevitable committee of the great and the good look at the issue (although Davies himself, after what he terms the 'cavalier' dismissal of the Burns recommendations in 2005 is unlikely to be volunteering) there are already two options on the table. First, there is the original 2005 model of unitary board and a public service broadcasting commission; alternatively, a unitary board and Ofcom. 'Both,' he argues, 'look to be clear improvements on the current system.' He believes the BBC needs now a conventional structure 'with a careful, non-political chair uninterested in his public persona and focused on ensuring that the board does those things which it ought to do and not those things which is ought not to do'.

'Selling the pass' on independence

Whatever governance structure emerges from the next couple of years, it will have failed the public if it does not maintain the BBC's independence from government. As Tim Suter points out, in 'A crisis of independence', it would be unwise to take that independence for granted. Suter is no stranger to the corridors of broadcasting power as a one time Head of Broadcasting Policy at the Culture Department and later an Ofcom partner. He believes that the BBC's independence is being undermined under political pressure.

In particular, he points to two big decisions where he feels the Trust has allowed the principle that the BBC alone is responsible for deciding how its money should be spent – 'a fundamental pillar for BBC independence' – has been quietly, but decisively, broken. Governments of every complexion have tried to nudge the BBC into doing things that suited their agenda or interests – think of Jam, the ill-fated educational project, or even the move to Salford. But Suter's two examples are different and take the pressure and its consequences to a different level.

In 2007, the BBC agreed to fund the digital switchover support scheme. Suter can just about see a defence on the grounds that the switch to digital allowed the BBC better to meet its public purposes. But he sees no such justification for the concessions that were made in the 2010 licence fee settlement. He singles out the BBC helping to fund independent local TV and picking up the tab for S4C as clear evidence that 'the BBC Trust has been forced to sell the pass'. And he sees further risks in the BBC's move toward a more personal relationship with every licence fee payer – the concept of 'My BBC' – exciting and inevitable as it is, runs the risk of undermining collective acceptance of a universal licence fee which pays for programmes you want but also for content you might never watch yourself but under the current system are happy to support.

Suter thinks the BBC needs to seize the initiative back from government or run the risk of the politicians increasingly encroaching on decisions how the licence fee should be spent. If the BBC is not independent, it is no use to anyone – and no system of governance will work unless it makes the BBC's independence non-negotiable.

No future for the licence?

The vulnerability of the licence fee and the growing threats to the BBC's independence are echoed in David Elstein's analysis, 'The licence fee and the question of BBC funding'. Elstein, a former Head of Programmes at Thames and BSkyB as well as the launch Chief Executive of Channel 5, has been one of the BBC's most radical and persistent critics. He is no fan of the licence fee. The switch to colour and the growth in the number of households has funded BBC expansion for half a century – with the licence fee freeze in 2010 the BBC faces for the first time a significant reduction in its spending power. In 2015, the BBC could have more of the same imposed on it, with as an added threat, the possibility that the government might try again to load it with the cost of free licences for the over-75s.

Although Britain's population is again growing and the BBC may gain some benefit from that, Elstein believes the game is up for the licence fee in the medium term, although he expects it to survive this charter renewal process. However, he argues that this will be a missed opportunity and that the BBC would be a stronger and more independent organisation if it now switched to subscription. It would make better programmes if it was freed from the need to make second-rate drama and reality shows to maximise its share; like HBO in the US, it could make more of the sort of must-see quality programmes which have been proved to drive subscriptions; it would insulate the BBC from political interference; and it would enable the BBC to tailor its offering to match what its subscribers actually want and value.

No one knows for sure what would happen if the BBC took the plunge – some research seems to suggest that 40 per cent of viewers would willingly pay twice the current licence fee to keep BBC television – but others would drop out altogether, leaving the BBC with a lower income and/or viewers finding themselves paying far more than they used to pay. But Elstein argues that if the BBC offered targeted packages and took advantage of increased revenue in multi-set homes, it could probably provide its core services more cheaply than at present and offer premium channels as well. Ironically, he points out, one of the reasons the politicians might be cautious about allowing this is they have already loaded so much other public expenditure on to the licence fee (World Service, local TV, S4C) and they do not want those bills to come back to the 'government tab'.

Follow the money

If keeping the politicians' tanks off the BBC's lawn is one key role of any governance system, ensuring value for money is the other. Despite a decade of cost cutting, the BBC still seems a far more complex organisation than it needs to be. Talk (privately) to any independent producer and they will tell of viewing rooms crammed with BBC executives all of whom appear to think they have a say in the final cut. When I joined ITN in 1987 from the BBC I was surprised and exhilarated (and, I have to confess, a little nervous) to discover that in ITN's flat management structure editors were expected to edit with minimal 'referring up'. Your job was to get it right – and you, not your boss, would be held to account if you made a mistake. There has to be something wrong with an approach to editorial responsibility which has resulted in two BBC editors-in-chief walking the plank in the last decade over flawed programmes which they knew nothing about until after transmission.

Bernard Clark was one of the first BBC programme makers to take the plunge as an independent and there is very little he does not know about cost-effective production. In 'When the jacuzzi stops' he argues that only a radical reform of the BBC will ensure that the money goes on screen rather than in unnecessary bureaucracy. He is devastating in his exposure of the insanities of some of the BBC's internal charges – once being asked for £800 for a VHS machine he could buy at Currys for £44.95. His favoured mechanism for reform would be to bring in the National Audit Office (NAO) to supervise a blitz on unnecessary costs (and people), leaving the programme makers more cash and more creative freedom.

Even those who agree with him on the need to make the organisation far less complex might worry about the NAO, as an instrument of government, having even more of a say over what the BBC does. But Clark is confident the benefits would outweigh the risks: 'The trick with the next charter is to ensure a worldly and rigorous balance between policing the internal finances of an overbearing bureaucracy while protecting programmes and editorial from any interference whatsoever.'

'Our best years lie ahead of us'

For much of the last four years, Andrew Scadding, the BBC's Head of Corporate and Public Affairs, has been on the BBC's political frontline, responsible for the Corporation's relationship with politicians as well as other stakeholders. As a former BBC political producer and one-time Head of Broadcasting for the Conservative Party, he understands the delicate interface between politicians and broadcasters. In the run-up to charter renewal, the BBC needs to demonstrate its continuing public value.

In 'The best is yet to come', he sets out what, in practice, Tony Hall's new vision for the BBC means. He accepts that the last eighteen months 'have not been the easiest', but sees a clear strategy for the future. The BBC he describes would be very different from the current organisation in many key areas: 'We are realigning the BBC to be the organisation that we are proud of and that the licence fee payer expects and deserves, delivering robust journalism, promoting creativity and developing talent.'

The big idea is personalisation – creating a direct relationship with each licence fee payer by giving each viewer a more tailored service – 'a public service that is both universal and personal', linked to ambitious partnerships around big themes, such as World War I and Shakespeare and offering much more access to the BBC's unparalleled archive. He argues for the retention of the licence fee and warns that the current settlement means that efficiency savings alone will not balance the budget – 'tough choices on content and services will be necessary'. How the BBC emerges from the forthcoming charter review will depend crucially on ensuring the changes satisfy both the public who pay for the BBC and the politicians who will determine its structure and budget. As the Corporation enters the negotiations for a new charter, the stakes have never been higher.

A question of Trust

BBC Trustee David Liddiment argues for a governance system that builds on the experience of the Trust, maintaining the vital separation of powers on which accountability and future public support for the BBC ultimately depend

'The BBC is Britain's most important cultural institution, one that enjoys extraordinary levels of public support, appreciation and reach for its services, a unique and successful survivor in a revolutionary digital age.'

'The BBC is a scandal-ridden disgrace, an emporium of excess presided over by an over-stuffed executive and guardians who have failed to protect the public's money.'

As was ever thus, in this Tale of Two Corporations we hear much less about its everyday achievements, which we take for granted, than its occasional headline-grabbing failures. Criticism is more newsworthy than celebration particularly when it comes to public institutions. So, despite its success – or, perhaps, because of it – we are now invited to consider the organisation is so dysfunctional that its governance must be rethought from scratch.

I don't underestimate the damage that recent *cause célèbres* have done, but neither do I believe that, singly or cumulatively, they are sufficient reason for urgent or radical overhaul of its governance. In an irony not lost on my eleven colleagues, the one that triggered most 'Trust is bust' headlines – severance pay to senior executives – on closer inspection turns out to be a paradigm of the Trust doing exactly what parliament tasked (and the public expects) it to do. But I shall return to that.

I should say at the outset that I am not necessarily wedded to the status quo and there may be a better way of keeping the BBC honest than the currently constituted Trust. However, I do caution against an over-reaction to the indignations and exclamations triggered by recent events. As one of three original Trustees who will have served eight years under three different chairmen by the time my final term ends in October 2014, I do have the benefit of some inside knowledge and experience. If I had thought at any point that I was wasting my time or the public's money, I wouldn't have stayed on for two terms.

Accountability is key

Before joining the Trust in November 2006 I had argued for some time for change in the BBC's governance. In my 2001 MacTaggart Lecture and through *Guardian* columns I suggested that the Corporation was insufficiently accountable for how it spent large sums of public money and that this structural weakness endangered its public service character and values at a time when commercial competition was growing. Neither the previous charter nor the governors afforded its core values necessary protection in such a dynamic environment. I had no favoured structure or solution but I did advocate a robust guardian of the public interest, clear separation of powers and a much clearer articulation of the BBC's public purposes. And as someone who had spent his career in commercial television (which in hindsight looks regulated to within an inch of its life) it seemed to me that a publicly-funded body of the scale of the BBC needed much tighter definitions of its public services against which performance could be judged.

Why is this accountability so important? First, the BBC is a huge intervention in the media market and commercial players need clarity and transparency around what it does. Furthermore, it must demonstrably add value to what the market on its own can provide. This can be more complicated than it sounds. The BBC is at the centre of UK cultural life but it operates in a commercial environment which means there is an inevitable tension between the drive to provide services that engage with everyone and at the same time ensure that these services are distinctive. When both are achieved together (*Sherlock, Strictly Come Dancing, Who Do You Think You Are?*) the BBC makes an unequivocal case for its existence in the market. This quest for quality that attracts a large following yet also adds something fresh to popular culture should be evident across all BBC services. A couple of other examples: 6Music celebrates the extraordinary impact pop music has made on our society with a playlist that is unlike any other music station yet is the most listened-to digital radio station in the UK; BBC4 discovered and nurtured Nordic noir, boldly broadcast in their original languages with English subtitles, helping to spark the recent international reputational renaissance of television drama over film.

This happy conjunction of quality, popularity and distinctiveness does not happen by chance or come cheap: it is easier to follow the market than to lead it. So the BBC needs a governance structure that ensures that it adds cultural value as well as giving value for money. The hybrid that finally emerged in 2006 – a Trust with added powers and resource backed by a strengthened, more specific charter – seemed to me to put accountability firmly in the frame. A statement of public purposes and the introduction of service licences would, without compromising creativity, for the first time set a clear framework against which delivery in the public interest could be effectively assessed. My main concerns were answered. I bought into the new system and was delighted to be invited to play a part in making it work. Over the years that followed, disillusionment has not set in. There have been frustrations certainly, but on the whole I have found my time on the Trust stimulating and worthwhile.

Reviews improve performance and add value

No-one would claim that it has worked perfectly. For the first time the BBC had a supervisory body with the experience and resource to make an independent assessment of its performance with a clear obligation to represent the interests of licence fee payers. It should surprise nobody that as a consequence there have been spiky moments between the Trust and the executive, particularly early on as we worked out how to make this new system work in practice. Some BBC journalists were unhappy with public criticism of their programmes when the Trust, as the final appeal body for complaints, judged that BBC editorial guidelines had been breached. Aligning the objectives of BBC Worldwide to those of the public service took longer than perhaps it should, and there was something of a turf war over remuneration, a flavour of which emerged at the late 2013 Public Accounts Committee (PAC) hearings. This was the inevitable bedding-in of a new system radically different from the one that went before, and one demanding new behaviours from all participants.

However, the structures introduced with the Trust in 2006 have, I believe, resulted in a more systematic and transparent form of governance than was possible before, with service licence reviews at the heart of the process. Performance can now be properly assessed against requirements set out in service licences, with public consultation allowing licence fee payers and competitors to have their say. This is essential to keep tabs on each service, ensuring distinctiveness and balance across the portfolio and so delivering best value for the public.

Reviews can bring significant results. Radio 2, as well as playing a unique mix of music, now carries distinctive speech elements in peak time whilst consolidating its position as the most listened-to station in the UK. Radio 1 has refocused on its target younger audience, resisting an understandable urge to grow old disgracefully with its listeners. Radio 6 Music has found a distinctive, previously underserved niche, rescuing itself from closure. But this is a dynamic market, audience behaviour is changing with the widespread adoption of digital devices, so in the second round of reviews starting later this year the Trust will be examining all BBC music radio services together.

The service licence and review regime is an important instrument in the UK broadcasting ecology, giving the commercial sector clarity and transparency on what, and what not, to expect from BBC services. Last year's review of Radio 5 Live led to a redrafting of its service licence which toughened its news requirements following an investigation into a complaint from a commercial operator that the station was misclassifying some entertainment and feature material. Furthermore, any significant change to a BBC service is subject to a

Public Value Test enabling the Trust to turn down any proposal whose public value does not outweigh its market impact, as was the case in the proposal for local video online.

The Trust's reviews of BBC Online have highlighted both the core value it offers to licence fee payers – its strong news, sports and iPlayer services – and queried some of the less distinctive elements such as its external web search feature. Under Trust governance, the BBC has developed a much more focused online service which delivers better for audiences – now across hundreds of devices – but with a clear remit.

There are other examples of positive intervention on behalf of the public interest. Notwithstanding the move to Salford and its best efforts, the BBC was born a metropolitan organisation and remains metrocentric at heart. Unlike ITV, which despite wholesale consolidation has regionalism in its DNA because of its federal origins, the BBC has always been run from London and must make conscious efforts to reflect the nations and regions of the United Kingdom on its services. So the Trust ended the anomaly of a lower out-of-London production requirement for BBC television than for commercial PSB channels with the goal of creating sustainable centres of excellence, producing and commissioning programmes for the network which better reflect the UK's full diversity. And to safeguard regionality we intervened to protect regional television current affairs from budget cuts which threatened quality and halted plans to consolidate some local radio services.

Public value, but value for public money?
So there is ample evidence that the Trust has been doing its job of keeping the BBC to its remit of adding value in the public sphere. But what about value for public money in the running of the organisation itself? According to the screaming headlines of late 2013 the Trust let the public down badly here, allowing the squandering of millions and delivering another hammer-blow to public trust in a crisis-prone Corporation.

In fact, regular research shows that public regard for the BBC remains consistently high. It took a knock during the Savile revelations but quickly recovered as the news agenda moved on. The BBC is not in crisis, but waste of public money is always a serious matter and the body responsible – currently the Trust – must account for why more was not done to prevent it. Here I must return briefly to the painful issue of severance pay and explain how what should have been a triumph for the Trust turned into a handy stick to beat it with. The gruesome headlines are familiar enough: tens of millions of licence fee money spent on severance deals for top BBC executives, some of it in excess of contractual obligations and some of it to people who went straight into other highly-paid jobs.

The back-story on the financial side never made the headlines. Why would it? It was just the Trust doing its job of representing the public interest by getting executive pay under control. We had inherited unacceptably inflated senior executive pay in 2007 and identified the potential problem early on. We encountered initial resistance from the executive but by 2008 had agreed a freeze on bonus payments, followed in 2009 by an agreement to freeze executive pay until 2011 and to cut the executive pay bill by 25 per cent by mid-2013, a target date that was subsequently brought forward by 18 months to December 2011.

Cutting a significant proportion of the highest paid executives on that accelerated timescale was never going to come cheap. Between 2006 and 2012 the BBC spent £47.6 million on severance payments to senior managers and, as the National Audit Office (NAO) identified, in a handful of cases people were paid more generously than their contracts required. These overpayments amounted to £3.8 million, an unacceptable figure certainly but dwarfed by the cumulative savings to date of more than £100 million, a very significant reduction over time. This was the supervisory body doing its job of getting executive pay and numbers under control. But that's not the story the public heard.

The Trust and the executive: Roles and responsibilities clarified

Of course it wasn't just about the money. The unedifying spectacle at the PAC and NAO inquiries revealed ambiguities in the relationship between the Trust and the executive board about where responsibility lies when things go wrong – something that the Savile affair also highlighted.

As a result of the painful exposure of this structural fault-line by the NAO and PAC, action has now been taken. By the time this publication appears, the relationship on which the whole governance of the BBC depends will be clarified and strengthened with some important changes. The Trust will concentrate on overall value for licence fee payers and assessing performance through service reviews. There will be fewer Trust committees with greater responsibility devolved to the executive board. This will now have more – and more clearly tasked – non-executives who will be expected to take a more hands-on role in sensitive management decisions to ensure high standards of corporate governance. So the Trust stands a bit further back and entrusts more in the board to ensure that things happen properly and problems are flagged up early. There should be no confusion about respective roles and re-sponsibilities in future.

A better way?

Of course, the BBC must be run efficiently with a keen eye to value for licence fee payers' money. With the Trust, board, non-execs, the NAO and PAC on the case there are now fail-safe checks to ensure this happens. But in the end it is what the BBC *does* that really matters. It is the quality and consistency of the output – programmes and online content – on which the public will judge the BBC and it is that on which any system of governance needs to focus if it is to ensure that the BBC retains broad public support.

I wanted to play a part in making the BBC the best it could be. At the time I joined the Trust I believed it had the tools to do the job and after more than seven years I still believe that. Is the system perfect? No. Will there be crises in future? Certainly: no governance system will prevent errors of judgement. It remains to be seen whether the clarification of roles and the shift of responsibilities from the Trust to a strengthened board this year will reduce the number and frequency of 'BBC in crisis' headlines for the remainder of the current charter. Paradoxically, the changes may well renew calls for a unitary board. After all, if responsibility is shifting further in that direction, what's the point of the Trust?

Clear separation and no 'light touch'

Here's the point: the idea that a public body spending £4 billion a year of other people's money can be run entirely by its board of management – on-the-ball non-execs and a hawkish NAO and PAC notwithstanding – with no separate body to protect the public interest and public value, is frankly insane. The BBC matters too much, and the public investment in it is too great. Whether that body is the Trust, an evolution of the Trust, some form of OfBeeb, or something yet to be imagined, management and the public interest must be kept separate. In fair weather or foul, someone must do the checking and it can't be the people who run the outfit.

The service licence regime is a notable success and deserves to continue in the new charter period. In my view it could even be strengthened. If I have a worry, it is that with talk of a Channel 4-type model with a plc-style board and Ofcom mooted as regulatory back-up, the idea of 'light touch' regulation seems to have gained currency. The last thing the BBC needs is light touch regulation: it is paid for by the public and needs a separate and properly resourced body focused on its content and obligations, not to constrain it but to release it from the inhibitions that come from having to make a living in the marketplace. The BBC must work to higher standards than those of the market and be held to them. That's why a properly enforced service licence regime, backed by a comprehensive complaints apparatus, is so important.

A foundation for the future

I won't be there so I have no axe to grind, but whatever the post-2016 arrangements, the good work started by the Trust must continue. It must ensure that the BBC adds value to the nation's creative life, protects its vital contribution to our democracy and takes the leadership role expected from an organisation privileged to be in our homes and so much part of our lives.

Above all, I would urge those making the decision not to abolish the function of protecting the public interest as a separate and primary responsibility, a function not to be confused with the running of the Corporation. That, I believe, would not only let the public down but would deliver the BBC into a permanent state of genuine crisis.

Note on the contributor

David Liddiment has had a distinguished career in television as a programme maker and broadcaster. He was Director of Programmes for the ITV Network from 1997 to 2002, delivered the MacTaggart lecture in 2001 and was awarded the Royal Television Society Gold Medal in 2003. He is co-founder and non-executive director of independent producer All3media and a BBC Trustee.

Need for clarity at the Corporation on who is responsible for what

Howard Davies examines the BBC's 'governance problem' and concludes that the Corporation needs 'a good, conventional structure, with a careful, non-political chair, uninterested in his public persona and focused on ensuring that the board does those things which it ought to do and not those things which it ought not to do'

Since the financial crisis regulators, academic researchers and assorted consultancies have tried to assess whether governance failures were crucial in those institutions which went belly-up, and what rule changes might make sense to prevent a recurrence. It is easy to say that the boards of Lehman Brothers, Northern Rock or the Royal Bank of Scotland did a poor job, but that does not necessarily help to determine what type of boards we should put in place for the future, unless we can find some common features.

The research – there is a lot of it – does not all point in the same direction, but a few points are clear. Institutions with weak boards with unclear responsibilities did badly. Unconventional governance (think the Co-op or some state-owned Spanish banks) with political interference is a sign of trouble ahead. Boards whose chairs had little experience of the industry failed more comprehensively than those run by bankers – think HBOS, with the good Lord Stevenson at the helm. Looking back, another bad sign was a CEO whose pay accelerated away from the rest of the management, often a sign of a board out of control or in thrall to an apparently heroic leader (Nestor Advisors 2012).

These points sound horribly familiar when applied to the BBC. Of course, the latter's failings, and occasional profligacy, pale into financial insignificance when compared to those of RBS, but any objective assessment of the Corporation's recent travails cannot fail to conclude that they have been made worse by a lack of clarity about who is responsible for what. Otherwise reasonable men have been reduced to undignified public slanging matches as successive parliamentary hearings have tried to get to the bottom of who was responsible for some extravagant payments for failure.

My Lords Patten and Hall – the BBC is long on ermine these days – have struggled in vain to articulate a defence of the current arrangements. That is not surprising: they are indefensible, as the forthcoming governance inquiry by John Whittingdale's select committee will surely conclude. That is easy to say, but a more forensic approach may pay dividends. Three questions are worth asking:

- exactly what is the governance problem today?
- why does that problem exist: in other words 'whodunnit?'
- what could and should be done about it?

What is the BBC's governance problem?

In their review of the extravagant redundancy payments made at the end of the Thompson regime, the Public Accounts Committee concluded last December: 'The BBC's governance is broken' (Public Accounts Committee 2013). They referred specifically to the 'dysfunctional relationship' between the Trust and the executive board, and the lack of clarity about their respective responsibilities. Whatever the rights and wrongs of the payments themselves, which remain heavily disputed, it is undeniable that they exposed a problem of accountability and responsibility.

The current structure was put in place at the last charter review. It first saw the light of day in March 2005, in a paper published by Tessa Jowell when Secretary of State for Culture, Media and Sport (Department of Culture, Media and Sport 2005). 'The BBC's governance,' she said in her introduction, 'needs to be modernised to meet the demands of the modern world.' A bad start, you may think, which puts one in mind of Salisbury's famous expostulation: 'Change? Aren't things bad enough as they are?' After criticising the dual role of the former governors, charged with both directing the BBC and holding it to account, she introduced the notion of a BBC Trust, described as a 'working title', which would be more accountable to licence fee payers, with the BBC run by a formally constituted executive board, accountable to the Trust. 'The functions of the two bodies will be clearly separated, enabling the Trust to judge the management's performance clearly and authoritatively.'

The phrase 'working title' suggested that this was a solution which had not been fully developed before publication. Jowell went on to explain that the Trust was, in fact, not a Trust in the normal sense – 'its legal status would be somewhat different to that of a conventional Trust'. Throughout, the paper struggles to define just what its job will be in relation to the management of the Corporation. For example, a table in the body of the report, which attempts to distinguish between 'delivery', a matter for the executive board, and 'oversight', the business of the Trust, puts 'ensuring efficiency' squarely under the control of the board. Yet the summary of the role of the Trust says it will 'make sure that the BBC … is efficient and provides value-for-money to licence fee payers'. (Connoisseurs of bureaucratese might write PhD theses on the difference between 'ensuring' and 'making sure'.)

The paper was accurate in describing the problem at the heart of the old regime, with a board of governors who had both a leadership and a regulatory role. They could not be cheerleaders and overseers at the same time. But the new system preserved the confusion. The only BBC chairman is the chairman of the Trust, and he is often presented as head and front of the organisation. The executive board is chaired by the director-general. The 2005 paper noted that the BBC's governance model 'is increasingly out of step with best corporate governance practice'. That best practice in the UK, as expressed in the Financial Services Authority Listing rules, now unambiguously requires a non-executive chairman at the head of a board composed of executives and non-executives, with a majority of the latter. The BBC's board is chaired by an executive, with a majority of executives – unless, that is, one regards the Trust as in reality the BBC's board, rather than its regulator.

The confusion of roles enshrined in the Jowell proposals, which were put into effect in the last charter, is at the heart of the problems we have seen. It was an accident waiting to happen. That is not an observation informed by hindsight. When the then-government put these proposals to parliament they were widely derided. Norman Fowler, who chaired the House of Lords Committee which reviewed the draft charter, described them as 'confusing, misguided and unworkable' (House of Lords 2006). Former BBC Chairman Christopher Bland thought they were an uneasy compromise between creating a separate regulatory body and imposing a German-style two-tier form of governance. In an article on the subject in the *Financial Times* in December 2005, I (as a former member of the Burns Committee which prepared advice for the Labour government on the charter review) criticised the structure as one which 'bows in several directions at once' and had not been properly thought through (Davies 2005).

This critical diagnosis is now hardly contested. I am not one of those who thinks that a well-designed governance structure guarantees success: some of the failed banks ticked all the boxes and had every bell and whistle in its proper place. The problem is rather that poor governance makes crises, whether about pay-offs, bizarre and worrying episodes like the Jimmy Savile affair, or rigged Blue Peter phone-ins, very difficult to handle. The problem soon becomes transmogrified into one about who said what to whom, and with whom the buck stops. Without a non-executive chairman, the D-G becomes dangerously exposed. But if the diagnosis is clear, how on earth did we find ourselves in this unhappy position? Whodunnit?

Why does the problem exist?

In one sense, the answer is very simple. Tessa Jowell's signature is on the offending document. While she may have done a good job on the Olympics, this was not her finest hour. But 'the Secretary of State, in her office, with a pen' is not a sufficient answer to the 'whodunnit' question. There were other accessories before the fact. Perhaps only the Downing Street cat knows the full story, but 'sources close to the cat', as they say, suggest that the dirty deed was done in a meeting between Tony Blair and Michael Grade.

The Burns Committee had suggested a quite different structure. It recommended the abolition of the governors and its replacement by, on the one hand, a Public Service Broadcasting Commission to perform the governors' regulatory functions and, on the other hand, a new BBC board constructed on the lines of best-practice corporate governance in the private sector. So there would be an independent chairman and a majority of non-executive directors working with the D-G and his or her top team. Michael Grade did not like the sound of this at all. He did not want another chairman imposed on him. Tony Blair, who was in his debt, as he was the man who had stabilised the Corporation after the Hutton Report, agreed that there would only be one chairman, which heavily conditioned the outcome.

The other piece of the jigsaw was that the government were very reluctant to set up a new regulator. Recall that at the time the Blair government was pursuing a deregulatory agenda. Around that time he argued that the Financial Services Authority was unreasonably restraining the animal spirits of entrepreneurial financiers in the City of London. There was little appetite for a Public Service Broadcasting Commission on the Burns model, and great nervousness in the BBC itself about being put under the aegis of Ofcom, seen as a heavy-handed body which might drive a stake through the Corporation's independence. This cocktail of arguments was shaken, and stirred, and shaken again: the outcome was the Horlicks which Jowell described in her charter review document.

What is to be done?

The Trust itself has tried to apply sticking plaster to the wound. It reviewed the Corporation's governance and published its conclusions in December 2013 (BBC Trust 2013). It noted that 'there is confusion about who is responsible for what in certain key operational areas', and agreed some actions in response. The number of non-executive directors on the executive board has gone up from four to six and some aspirations about the relationship between the board and the trust were described, particularly 'greater separation between the Trust and the executive, with the trust clearly responsible for setting the overall strategic framework for the BBC and the executive responsible for delivering within this (sic)'. Furthermore, 'the Trust will not involve itself in operational decision-making'.

Two points are worth making about this unusual statement. First, it is a stark acknowledgement of just how confused the responsibilities had become. It must mean that the Trust has indeed been involving itself in operational decisions, which betrays a remarkable lack of confidence in the executive. Second, it has no chance of rebuilding external confidence in the structure. A mere undertaking to be good boys and girls in future, and to say please and thank-you to each other, will not do the trick. The system was well understood to be flawed from the start, has failed in exactly the way knowledgeable observers said it would fail, and therefore must be reformed in a structural way.

That, of course, is not in the gift of the Trust or the BBC itself, and will have to wait until the next charter. No doubt the government will do what its predecessors have done in the past, and appoint a committee of the great and the good to examine the issues and make recommendations. That tradition goes back at least to Noel Annan, whose 1977 review was highly influential (Annan Committee 1977). In view of the previous government's cavalier dismissal of Terry Burns' recommendations in 2005, it may be difficult to find someone of similar eminence to serve, but no doubt a worthy group will be assembled. After the usual hearings, consultations, drafts and redrafts, what might they propose?

The Burns model is a starting point. His committee unanimously supported a unitary board model of governance, as is now adopted for all UK listed companies. It would be led by a non-executive chairman, and would contain a majority of independent non-executive directors. The director-general, and a small number of executive directors, would also be members. The chairman would need to be appointed by the government of the day, following the best public appointment rules (which have, in fact, been tightened up in the interim). The other non-executives would be appointed on the recommendation of a committee composed of the chairman, one of the existing non-executives, and another independent person provided by the Civil Service Commission. They would be paid in a way which reflected the size of the BBC, and the complexity of the role.

Of course, it may be argued that the BBC is not a profit-seeking company, so the normal corporate rules may not be wholly appropriate. But this model is widely used for non-profit organisations such as universities, where it typically works well. There is no obvious reason why it should not function effectively in a public broadcaster. So far, so good, our wise men and women might conclude. But what is the role of this board? Is it a recreation of the old governors, clothed in private sector garb? How does it deal with the simultaneous cheerleader and regulator criticism which sank the governors after the Hutton Report? In itself, it does not. So Burns recommended the creation of a Public Service Broadcasting Commission (PSBC) which would be responsible for recommending the appropriate level of the licence fee, providing an independent buffer between the BBC and politicians, satisfying itself that the BBC is acting in the public interest by holding the board to account for its performance against the public interest tests it set. Some of its responsibilities would like rather like the jobs currently performed by the Trust, which appears quite effective in its consultation role, and certainly provides a useful route into the BBC for ordinary licence-fee payers. The difference is that the PSBC would clearly not be a part of the Corporation. Its chairman could not possibly be thought of colloquially as chairman of the BBC, as Patten and Lyons have sometimes been described.

Perhaps unwisely, in retrospect, Burns also noted that 'the new structure would allow for the possibility of allocating part of the licence fee to public service broadcasters other than the BBC, if and when appropriate'. The committee was looking forward to a day when the licence fee might be necessary to support other public service broadcasters, when their terrestrial monopoly power was insufficient to fund their PSB obligation. I think it may well soon be difficult to defend the licence fee in its current form, but a role in allocating funding is not an essential feature of the Burns model. In 2005, the House of Lords Committee liked the Burns governance proposals when it came to the BBC board itself and proposed them to the government. It did not, however, like the idea of a new regulator, which did not fit with the prevailing *zeitgeist* and, instead, argued that the job could go to Ofcom, with a newly strengthened content board, able to address the public interest dimension of BBC regulation. Ofcom would also deal with complaints against the BBC, where complainants are not satisfied by the Corporation's response. Its duties would be those of a Court of Appeal.

So there are two options on the table already, both of which look to be clear improvements on the current model. Perhaps other workable variants may be identified by an imaginative group of the good and the great. What is clear is that any proposal must, at a minimum:

- demonstrate clarity of roles, separating the supporter/advocate role from that of the regulator;
- provide cover and support for the director-general, through an independent chairman who can act as a critical friend;
- generate confidence among a now-sceptical public that the Corporation is well-governed, according to tried and tested best practices.

Arguments based on the BBC's exceptionalism carry far less weight than they once did.

Conclusion

Good governance is no guarantee of successful outcomes. Jimmy Savile would have been an awkward problem for the best-constructed board, endowed with as many distinguished corporate knights and dames as you like. (Though I hazard a guess that the redundancy payment debacle would either not have occurred or, at least, not done such damage to the executives involved. It would have been entirely clear who carried the can.)

What good governance can do is to prevent accidents and events from becoming systemic crises. Corporate history is full of examples of companies with eccentric or unconventional governance doing well for a time, but cracking under stress, as bespoke arrangements fail to respond well to external pressures. What the BBC needs now is a good, conventional structure, with a careful, non-political chair, uninterested in his public persona and focused on ensuring that the board does those things which it ought to do and not those things which it ought not to do. The model for this paragon? David Lees, of the Bank of England. Not heard of him? He has chaired the Bank of England Court for the last five years, managing the bank's response to the financial crisis, providing cover for the last governor, and managing the transition to the new one. He is about to retire. A new challenge in W1, rather than EC4, might not be what he is looking for now. But he has demonstrated how a comparable job can be well done. The fact that he is a mere knight, bereft of ermine, should not be held against him.

References

Annan Committee (1977) *Report on the Future of Broadcasting*, HMSO

BBC Trust (2013) *Review of BBC internal governance*, 11 December. Available online at www.bbc.co.uk/trust, accessed on 21 December 2013

Davies, Howard (2005) This is the wrong way for the BBC to be governed, *Financial Times*, 11 December

Department of Culture, Media and Sport (2005) *Review of the BBC's Royal Charter: A strong BBC, independent of Government*, March

House of Lords (2006) *Select Committee on the BBC Charter Review: First Report*. Available online at www.publications.parliament.uk/pa/ld200506/ldselect/ldbbc, accessed on 21 December 2013

Nestor Advisors (2012) *A comparative analysis of the boards of the largest US and European banks*. Available online at www.nestoradvisors.com, accessed on 21 December 2013

Public Accounts Committee (2013) 33rd report: BBC severance packages, 16 December, Available online at www.publications.parliament.uk/pa/cmselect/cmpublicacc/201314, accessed on 21 December 2013

Note on the contributor

Howard Davies is Chair of the British Government's Airport Policy Review and of Phoenix insurance group. He also is a Professor of Practice at the French School of Political Science in Paris (Sciences Po). He was the Director of the London School of Economics and Political Science from 2003 until May 2011. Before this appointment he was Chairman of the UK Financial Services Authority from 1997 to 2003. From 1995 to 1997 he was Deputy Governor of the Bank of England, after three years as the Director-General of the Confederation of British Industry. Earlier in his career he worked in the Foreign and Commonwealth Office, the Treasury, McKinsey and Co, where he spent five years, and as Controller of the Audit Commission. He has been an independent Director of Morgan Stanley Inc since 2004, and chairs the Risk Committee. He also chairs the Risk Committee at Prudential PLC, whose board he joined in 2010. He is a member of the Regulatory and Compliance Advisory Board of Millennium LLC, a New York-based hedge fund. He has also been a member of the International Advisory Council of the China Banking Regulatory Commission since 2003 and, from 2012, is Chairman of the International Advisory Council of the China Securities Regulatory Commission. In 2006, he edited and introduced *The Chancellor's Tales* (Polity Press) on British economic policy from 1975 to 2000. In 2008 he jointly authored *Global Financial Regulation: The Essential Guide* (Polity Press) with David Green. *Banking on the Future: The Fall and Rise of Central Banking*, on central banks, also by Davies and Green, was published in April 2010 by Princeton University Press. His latest book, *The Financial Crisis: Who is to blame?* was published by Polity Press in July 2010.

A crisis of independence

Tim Suter argues that the recent, high profile disasters that have dominated the BBC headlines should not distract from the more fundamental issue faced by the BBC in its new charter review: how to retain its independence from government when it has been forced to accept increasing levels of government direction over the use of its funding

It's worth casting the mind back to the identical point in the last charter review process. In January 2004, the BBC dramatically lost the fight it had allowed the government to pick with it over Andrew Gilligan's ill-judged two-way on the *Today* programme, with the publication of Lord Hutton's highly damaging report.[1] Both chairman and director-general resigned, and the acting BBC chairman issued an immediate and unreserved apology for shortcomings in its journalism. Serious questions were raised about the quality of BBC governance and oversight, and senior staff were destabilised – and, to some degree, culled – just at the point that the charter review process was gathering pace.

The external environment was unforgiving too. A generous licence fee award secured by John Birt in 1997, allowing it to rise faster than inflation, had funded a serious expansion of the BBC's services – both on-line as well as broadcast – but had also opened it to complaints from market competitors that it was being allowed to get too big, with no serious restraint on its ambitions. Assessment by ministers of the acceptability of new BBC services was cumbersome, and always open to the charge of political interference. Meanwhile, the contrast with a new, converged regulator with a fresh remit and a wide oversight of the rest of the media sector was in danger of making the BBC's approach look at best out of date and at worst self-serving.

Now, that was a crisis. And yet, the BBC survived it pretty well. In Michael Grade, a new, and popular, chairman was swiftly appointed with time to steer a new set of governance arrangements deftly through the charter review process; and in Mark Thompson, a new Director-General arrived with plenty of BBC knowledge (including, crucially, lots of experience in BBC journalism) but just enough time spent outside it to give him much needed perspective. The creative ship was steadied, and the BBC promised that it would in future both demonstrate that it knew what public value was, and more importantly that it would commit to deliver it. The BBC got its new charter,[2] with its independence reinforced: politicians were excluded from any say in whether or not the BBC could launch new services – at the modest, but effective, price of a more rigorous process conducted by the BBC Trust but including an assessment by Ofcom; and the BBC approached the negotiations over the level of the licence fee with its institutional future secured.

How BBC avoided Ofcom oversight

What were the dangers the BBC avoided? The BBC avoided being put any further under the oversight of Ofcom – despite the profound flaws that Hutton had exposed in its editorial oversight. The licence fee survived as the mechanism for funding the BBC. Its services were endorsed and codified via a set of 'service licences' which, while they constrained any unauthorised extension, nevertheless hard-baked the existing scope of the BBC. And its scale was only marginally, and manageably, affected by the clever mechanism of the Window of Creative Competition (WOCC) – the commitment to guarantee only 50 per cent of commissions to its own in-house producers.

You might conclude from this that the timing of any BBC crisis is crucial, and from that perspective the recent consecutive crises of Savile, the Digital Media Initiative (DMI) and executive pay-offs have come at a good time. Once again, a new director-general has been recruited with enough time to sort out the mess, and make a clean break with the past offending behaviour – but sufficiently close to the start of the review for the fruits of his reforms not yet to have become controversial. Costs in the most egregious areas have been capped, and further savings promised. A new chairman (given Lord Patten's decision not to seek reappointment) to steer the BBC through the political process will also be unencumbered by any mistakes of his predecessors.

And there is quite a lot else in favour of the BBC at the moment. The programmes are sound; industry opposition is muted – ITV is in better shape than for many years, and Sky has BT to worry about just as much as the BBC; the iPlayer has ushered in a successful start to an on-demand existence; and the government will not really have a view until after the election – at the moment it will be low on the list of priorities for joined up Tory/Lib Dem thinking – by which time decisions will be needed very quickly. True, the BBC might be taken round the back of the bike shed and given a swift and brutal going-over by the new government, in much the same way that the last licence fee settlement was done: but it is every bit as plausible that, without much time to spend on it, the government will be more inclined to avoid anything too radical.

So history might tempt you to think – crisis? What crisis?

However, I suspect any such complacency is misplaced – and as ever, the issue is around the governance of the BBC, which faces pressures on two separate, but dangerously entangled, fronts:

- the relationship between the supervisory board and the executive management;
- the redefinition of the interests of the licence fee payer – through the new uses that have been made of the public funding that used to be reserved solely to the BBC.

While neither of these pressures is exactly new, they have nevertheless been given particular potency during the current charter period. The line between management and the BBC's supervisory board has always been something of a mystery. The famous dictum that the chairman reads the map while the director-general drives the car was always creaky, and by the early 2000s was no longer a sustainable proposition: the BBC was just too big, the resources available to the BBC governors just too insignificant, and their dependence on the executive BBC just too heavy, for them to exercise an independent judgement about what the map was telling them. Whenever they chafed against their more limited role – for instance, when they insisted on pre-viewing the *Real Lives* programme (in 1985) ahead of transmission, thus inserting themselves directly in the editorial decision making role – they limited their ability to hold the BBC to account for what they had done. But when they remained too distant – for instance, their apparently supine acceptance of the need for Radio 4 Long Wave to be replaced by a rolling news service in the early 1990s – they were criticised for simply failing to oversee the BBC properly.

Governance changes – and journalistic integrity

The governance changes introduced for the current charter were designed to address this – in the cruel light of the Hutton Report, which had criticised the governors for failing properly to hold the BBC accountable for the most important element of their programming, their journalistic integrity. The BBC governors would be replaced by a BBC Trust, bolstered by a proper executive unit of their own and supported by a strict charter requirement that they must be demonstrably separate from the operational management of the BBC.

This has some arcane consequences. Whereas in the past the governors were designated as 'the BBC', Article 9 of the 2006 charter effectively abolishes the corporate BBC: under its terms the members of the BBC are now its Trustees and its executive board, but, since the two boards are forbidden ever to act together, and only ever to do the things that are reserved by the charter to them as separate entities, the notion of 'the BBC' has become, bizarrely and strangely, even more theological than it used to be. This explains the conundrum that, while the Trust chairman is allowed to call himself chairman of the BBC, Article 10 points out that the title is purely honorific and conveys no actual constitutional meaning.

But there are more direct consequences too. The uncompleted process of pulling the two parts of the BBC further apart from each other has resulted in some real confusion over operational control – not just in the public and political mind but demonstrably, and damagingly, within the BBC as well. The BBC Trust has a formal responsibility for stewardship of the licence fee and other BBC resources: but as the Trust acknowledged in their recent review of the arrangements, overlaps have emerged, especially in relation to operational management, that have resulted in confusion at best, and inadequate control at worst.[3]

Putting this right is a task for charter review. The recent reforms announced before Christmas 2013 may patch the current system, but a long-term solution will have to be more radical if it is to address the significantly more fundamental changes that have been quietly introduced during the life of this current charter. The BBC only acquired complete control of the licence fee in 1991. Before that, the government retained a 'precept', mainly to cover the costs of collection. But it was always a point of principle, and a fundamental pillar for BBC independence, that the BBC alone was responsible for deciding how its money should be spent. That principle has been quietly, but decisively, broken.

In 2007, the BBC agreed to set aside a specified amount to fund the costs of digital switch-over support scheme. This may be justifiable on the grounds that a switch to fully digital television transmission is consistent with allowing the BBC better to meet its overall public purposes; but this defence looks shakier in light of the impositions on the licence fee that resulted from the 2010 settlement. Absorbing the funding of the World Service may not damage the BBC's independence; but the other changes look more dangerous. Funding capital costs of independent local TV, as well as committing to purchasing content from the new services; and providing the public funding for S4C out of the licence fee – it's not just at first sight that these look quite distant from the interests of BBC services.

The agreement between the BBC and S4C is an instructive document for the future, since it shows very clearly how the BBC Trust has been forced to sell the pass:[4] to justify taking the licence fee to spend on somebody else's service, which has its own requirements to be independent, the agreement explicitly recognises that the interests of the licence fee payer are broader than simply the services provided by the BBC:

> 2.22 The contribution of the licence fee from the BBC Trust to S4C for the provision of Welsh language programmes and services contributes to the delivery of the BBC's public purposes.

The argument about top-slicing that dominated discussion at the time of Ofcom's last PSB review, fuelled by Channel 4's fears that its long-term future was unsustainable without access to public funding, died down for a time, but it has not gone away. One of the BBC's most senior former executives, Roger Mosey, recently used a column in *The Times* to question whether the BBC should any longer keep the licence fee to itself – linking his comments directly to what he perceives as a dangerous lack of diversity in BBC news output:[5] and ITV, in its submission to the House of Commons DCMS Select Committee,[6] has put its weight behind his argument. When searching for a response, the sentence in the agreement between the Trust and S4C undermines the point of principle they might have relied on.

Need to find new model of governance

So the BBC faces a dangerous combination of two mounting pressures: the need to find a model of governance that will guarantee an appropriate level of internal control and managerial oversight; and a new principle that the interests of the licence fee payer are no longer synonymous with the interests of the BBC's own services, but can – indeed, must – be served by others.

Paradoxically, a further dimension may have been added to this – not least by technology. Tony Hall's first major speech setting out his vision for where the BBC should be heading formulated the proposition that the audience relationship should in future be with 'My BBC'. The iPlayer will be instrumental in delivering this – a new front door to a suite of more personalised services, with the ability to self-schedule, to explore the archive more fully, to be liberated from the shackles of the schedule and the limited creative choices on offer at any one time.

This is an energising and exciting vision, but it leaves a potential gap which is occupied, in a rather old-fashioned and collectivist sort of way, by 'Our BBC' – a BBC that confidently spends resources on content that I, as an individual might never chose but which I, as a member of society, believe should continue to be made. Indeed, years of research by the BBC and Ofcom has demonstrated that audiences recognise the societal value of some kinds of programmes that they do not themselves consume but which they nevertheless believe should continue to be made.

Policy makers, especially of a more radical bent, may well be pondering this gap – if it doesn't exist, then to create it; and if it does, then to widen it. And they may be helped by the fact that the BBC appears to have accepted that, while its own services are necessary to the delivery of public purposes legitimately funded by the licence fee, they may not be sufficient. They may conclude that there are some things that the BBC, however well tuned to its audience needs, will be unlikely to deliver – news, for instance, that is genuinely plural in agenda as well as in treatment; or an institution that can easily form partnerships which put the interests of other providers over the interests of its own services. These demands are often made of the BBC, and the BBC makes a reasonable shift at responding to them – but they are not easy.

The context within which these questions may be asked is one where we have already seen a growing level of engagement by the government – and parliament – more directly into the affairs of the BBC: falling short of overseeing specific content, but getting far too close to determining the way the licence fee should be spent.

Is this a crisis for the BBC? Not necessarily – but it will be unless the BBC seizes the initiative back from government. Surviving Savile, DMI and even executive pay-offs will be hollow if the BBC does not regain control of its destiny.

Notes

[1] See http://webarchive.nationalarchives.gov.uk/20090128221546/http://www.the-hutton-inquiry.org.uk/content/report/chapter02.htm, accessed on 7 January 2014

[2] See
http://downloads.bbc.co.uk/bbctrust/assets/files/pdf/about/how_we_govern/charter.pdf, accessed on 7 January 2014

[3] See
http://downloads.bbc.co.uk/bbctrust/assets/files/pdf/about/how_we_govern/govern ance_review_2013.pdf, accessed on 7 January 2014

[4] See http://www.s4c.co.uk/production/downloads/e_operatingagreement.pdf, accessed on 7 January 2014

[5] See http://www.thetimes.co.uk/tto/opinion/columnists/article3916059.ece, accessed on 21 January 2014

[6] See
http://data.parliament.uk/writtenevidence/WrittenEvidence.svc/EvidenceHtml/4165, accessed on 21 January 2014

Note on the contributor

Tim Suter is the Managing Director of Perspective Associates. A BBC producer, editor and senior manager between 1985 and 1999, he was Head of Broadcasting Policy at the DCMS during the passage of the Communications Bill in 2003, and the founding Ofcom Partner for Content and Standards, overseeing all of Ofcom's regulation of broadcasting content.

The licence fee and the question of BBC funding

David Elstein examines the arguments for and against the BBC's current funding arrangements and argues that 'converting to subscription would allow the BBC to break free of the inexorable dumbing-down effect of the licence fee, as audience fragmentation forces a greater reliance on soaps in drama and so-called reality in factual programmes'

The BBC has been funded primarily by a licence fee since its inception. For the decades when the BBC enjoyed a monopoly on radio and television broadcasts, the licence fee was essentially a household subscription, with separate fees for radio and television. After the monopoly was broken (in television in 1955, in radio in 1973), licence fees became a household charge in relation to equipment being used. Reports commissioned by both Conservative and Labour governments have recommended replacing the licence fee, but the BBC has persuaded successive broadcasting ministers to reject those reports. The case for replacement is no less strong today, but the likelihood is that the licence fee will survive the current renewal process for the BBC charter and agreement, as it has survived all others.

Principle and practice
There are two ways of approaching the issue of the licence fee: what is the best way of funding the BBC in principle, and what in practice? There are four possible main sources of revenue for the BBC – the licence fee, a government grant, advertising and subscription. These are all combinable with each other. In addition, all public broadcasters attempt to emulate the BBC's success in generating revenue through the sale of rights and of content, and from operating commercial businesses alongside its public service offering.

Actually, the BBC is not currently purely financed by the licence fee. Some 30 per cent of its total income is earned by BBC Worldwide, though the net benefit of that £1.5 billion after expenses is only about £150 million. BBC Worldwide's income includes the BBC's share of subscription and advertising revenue from commercial channels, including UKTV in the UK. Some 20 per cent of BBC income currently comes from government payments – £600 million for those aged over-75, who are granted free licences, and £270 million from the Foreign Office for World Service radio (though that will be paid for out of the licence fee from 2015).

Other public broadcasters

In fact, there are very few public broadcasters who rely almost exclusively on a licence fee: just those in the Czech Republic and in part of Scandinavia. Even in Scandinavia, the licence fee is not safe. Sweden is mulling over a recommendation from an expert committee that, on grounds of social fairness and efficiency, a surcharge on income tax should replace the licence fee. Finland replaced the licence fee in 2013 with just such a means-tested ring-fenced tax on individuals and companies in 2013. The fee has been abandoned by Australia, New Zealand, the Netherlands, Hungary, Flemish Belgium, Portugal, Singapore, Malta, Cyprus, Gibraltar, India, Malaysia and Bulgaria. Countries which never had a licence fee include Spain, Luxembourg, Latvia, Lithuania, Estonia, Liechtenstein, Andorra and Monaco – and, of course, the USA.

For many of these countries, it was the disproportionate cost of collection which led to the dropping of the licence fee. For others, it was the scale of evasion. Countries which still have the licence fee include Italy (with a 40 per cent evasion rate), Poland (65 per cent) and Serbia (45 per cent). Licence fee levels are very variable. The Scandinavians, Switzerland, Austria, Wallonia in Belgium and Germany charge more – in some cases, much more – than the UK's £145.50. France and Italy are well below the UK level, and allow their public broadcasters to take advertisements. All the smaller countries in Europe apart from Slovenia charge on average £40 a year. To control costs and limit evasion, fees are collected through electricity or telephone bills in Greece, Turkey and Bosnia.

The case for the licence fee

Why does it matter whether the licence fee survives or not? The first argument offered in support of the licence fee is that this funding mechanism offers purity that cannot apply to others. What is that purity? At least in the UK, there are no advertisements on BBC public service channels. However, there are advertisements on the domestic commercial channels it part-owns and fully controls in operating terms.

Moreover, many BBC programmes are made with 'natural breaks' and shorter lengths than would be needed to fill BBC slots, so as to allow for subsequent deployment on commercial channels. When it broadcasts these programmes itself, the BBC fills the gaps with promotions. The gaps can be quite large in a co-production such as *Blue Planet*: though broadcast by the BBC in a 60-minute slot, it is made to an international 50-minute running time, with the balance of the hour being filled in the UK by 'how we made this programme' snippets.

A guarantee of quality

The second argument in terms of purity is that the licence fee allows the BBC to concentrate on quality, not ratings. Sadly, the overwhelming evidence is that the opposite applies. The BBC monitors audience share and reach very closely, not least because it feels that any weakening of performance might put the licence fee in jeopardy: a paradoxical result of licence fee funding. In point of fact, the only method of funding which appears to allow a broadcaster to ignore ratings, audience share and advertisers is pure subscription, as with HBO and similar pay-TV channels in the US, which spend their content budgets on a limited number of high-ambition programmes, in the hope that people will renew their subscriptions so as to retain access to the likes of *Game of Thrones* and *Mad Men*, even if those are the only actual programmes watched on the services providing them.

In contrast with those examples, the BBC chooses to offer high volumes of middle-of-the-road or populist output, most of which is indistinguishable from that of the commercial sector in the UK. A good 50 per cent of radio output, and arguably 90 per cent of television output lacks real distinctiveness, let alone the independence of market share measures that the purity of licence fee funding is meant to allow. Of course, the BBC continues to provide many excellent programmes – with £3.6 billion of licence fee revenue guaranteed, anything else would be unforgiveable. But as even Mark Thompson, until recently Director-General, has observed, for the highest quality drama and comedy available on UK screens, one has to rely upon US imports.

Independence

The third argument for licence fee purity is in terms of political independence. To be any more dependent on government grants than it already is might undermine the BBC's ability to stand up to government. Yet we saw only three years ago that the licence fee offered no defence as a determined government forced the BBC to use the licence fee to fund a range of government projects: the completion of digital switchover (including a subsidy to Channel 4), World Service radio, S4C, BBC monitoring, broadband rollout and local TV provided by third parties.

Does the licence fee allow the BBC to ignore government pressure editorially? There have been a number of well-publicised battles, of which the most recent was the bitter dispute over a mis-spoken live contribution from a Radio 4 journalist early one morning in relation to the Iraq War dossier. The BBC stood its ground to the very last, until an adverse verdict from a judge-led inquiry led the chairman of the BBC governors to resign, his deputy to issue a formal apology, and the rest of the governors to force the resignation of the director-general. In some ways, the scars from these battles can be interpreted as evidence both that the BBC fights hard for its independence, but that the struggle for it is open-ended. This is scarcely a ringing endorsement of the value of the licence fee as a shield.

There is reason to believe that the status of the BBC, together with its dominant position in news supply, exposes the BBC to far greater political scrutiny than any other broadcaster. Not long ago, we had the odd spectacle of the BBC director-general himself turning up at Downing Street to explain to ministers and spin doctors how the BBC would cover the proposed health service reforms: unthinkable for ITN or Sky News. In any event, the track record of commercial broadcasters in the UK in terms of political independence is at least as strong as that of the BBC: and I write as the broadcaster who commissioned and transmitted *Death on the Rock*. Channel 4 – almost entirely funded by advertising – is further evidence that public ownership, public service output and editorial forthrightness are not dependent on licence fee funding.

A moral purpose

A further argument of principle that attaches to the licence fee is that it gives the BBC a moral purpose. In theory, that might be true, but in practice that moral purpose is often very hard to find. The BBC prides itself on its six public purposes, but the truth is that the vast majority of its television output fulfils those purposes in the most nominal fashion. *The Weakest Link* may be 'informative', as a former BBC executive notoriously argued: but it is also a vapid quiz which is simply a schedule-filler and a poor justification for a compulsory levy.

Ofcom's tests of what constitutes public service broadcasting are equally unsatisfactory. When asked to name a single BBC programme that failed all the tests, Ofcom chose not to reply.

Fairness

The final two arguments of principle are two sides of the same coin. Finland's decision to change the way it funded its public broadcaster is an important clue. A licence fee can be seen as a fair way to pay for a public broadcaster, as all owners of television sets have equal access to its output. However, it can also be seen as unfair, as rich and poor, single-set homes and multi-set homes, all pay the same, whereas most other 'public goods' – health services, education, the police, defence, libraries and most of the arts – are paid for out of national or local tax revenues (where the poorest pay nothing and the richest pay the great majority of the cost).

Even the concession of free licences for those aged 75 and over has paradoxical outcomes. Many over-75s can easily afford the cost of a television licence; and the contrary is also true – millions of people aged over 65, but under 75, and who are reliant on the state pension, find allocating 2 per cent of their gross income to the BBC a stretch. The theory is that we all benefit from the BBC, so we should all pay for it, irrespective of income. Moreover, because the BBC – thanks to the licence fee – is free at the point of use, the BBC can fulfil the objective of universal availability.

As it happens, most people do indeed consume BBC output. However, you do not have to pay for a licence to listen to BBC radio or click on to BBC online (the radio-only licence was abolished decades ago when the cost of collecting it came close to exceeding the actual revenue). Moreover, the 1.5 million households that evade the licence fee also have full access to BBC TV, just like the law-abiding households that pay up. As for universality, ITV and Channel 4 are also free at the point of use: does that give them a high moral purpose? And, of course, the BBC is absolutely no different from Sky Television: once you have paid your licence fee or subscription, you can consume as much as you like. Free at the point of use is a piece of political rhetoric.

Value for money

Another attractive phrase is 'good value for money', as if anything can be so described where you have absolutely no choice as to what you are paying (other than to pay nothing and do without all television, not just BBC television). In fact, the cost per hour for viewing non-BBC programmes on Sky is lower than the cost per hour of viewing BBC programmes, once you measure actual hours consumed and actual payments made. And, of course, you cannot watch Sky until you have paid for the BBC.

The BBC is fond of citing the wider range of services it now provides, as compared with twenty years ago, for an annual cost slightly less than then (allowing for inflation). The problem with this approach is that there is considerable evidence of money being spread more thinly so as to achieve this effect. The television channels BBC3 and BBC4 are on air for barely a third of the day, and are substantially dependent on repeats. At the same time, BBC2 has been denuded of original programmes in daytime, so is effectively also a part-channel. When BBC1 deploys a +1 channel (as promised by the director-general), television broadcast hours will increase by some 20 per cent, but there will be no increase in new programmes (indeed, their number might reduce to pay for the additional transmission costs).

Universality

As for universality, this is a late arrival in the rhetorical stakes. For the first 33 years of its existence, the licence fee was a payment made by people who wanted to receive BBC content and were within reach of its transmitters – there was no compulsion, and certainly no universality. The Annan Committee in 1976 was opposed to the licence fee funding local radio, on the grounds that not all licence fee payers would be within range of local stations (its advice was ignored). Another Committee of Inquiry, in 1999, chaired by Gavyn Davies (who was subsequently appointed chairman of the BBC), recommended that BBC digital services should be paid for by a separate digital licence fee. The BBC and its sponsoring Department accepted this argument, but commercial interests persuaded Downing Street to over-rule Davies, and for more than a decade all licence fee payers shared the costs of these service, even though only a minority could actually receive them.

Indeed, the only universality is the compulsion to pay. The BBC is the only organisation allowed to convert a civil debt into a criminal conviction, as more than 150,000 people find every year. The vast majority of these – as we know from the magistrates who rubber-stamp their convictions – are too poor or disorganised to manage full-year or even staged payments of the licence fee. These 150,000 prosecutions constitute 30 per cent of the non-indictable offences that crowd our magistrates' courts – a cost borne by the taxpayer, not the BBC. There is no defence to a charge of non-payment if you have any equipment that can be used to receive live television pictures: a definition that includes laptops, tablets and mobile phones, though the BBC has not yet steeled itself to prosecute anyone other than the owner of a television for this offence. The money raised by these prosecutions is trivial: it is a tactic designed to send a signal to others (though in point of fact, 18 per cent of all households not paying by direct debit, and not having their licence paid by the government, successfully evade paying the licence fee every year). It now appears that, to remove the unwelcome burden of these prosecutions on the court system, ministers are contemplating allowing the BBC to obtain a conviction simply by presenting evidence of evasion, without any actual hearing.

TV licensing methods

Another revenue-generating BBC idea is to allow new annual licences only to run to the last day of the month previous to the date of the licence. If you take out a new licence on any day of the month other than the last, you would pay for 12 months, but be legally covered for only eleven full months and part of the twelfth. By the way, the BBC is that rare organisation which feels able to charge an extra £5 a year for payments by quarterly direct debit: nearly all other providers of services offer a discount for paying by direct debit.

TV Licensing – a wholly owned subsidiary of the BBC – sends out 23 million warning letters a year to homes without a TV licence: letters of increasingly threatening nature, which have been denounced as unacceptable by successive chairmen of the Commons Culture, Media and Sport Select Committee. TV Licensing also makes 3.5 million unannounced home visits every year: most of which have no outcome other than to frighten or anger law-abiding people. It is hard to spot the high moral purpose in the machinery underpinning this funding mechanism.

Alternatives to the licence fee

But is there any alternative? This is the practical question. Advertising, except at the margin, has been rejected by virtually every committee of inquiry, on the grounds that any benefit to the BBC would severely damage commercially-funded broadcasters, and eliminate any public service content they currently provide. Nor is there any expectation of replacing the current level of BBC income by that means. Of course, a government grant could easily fulfil that function, and would certainly be more equitable than a flat-rate, regressive household tax. Moreover, there has never been any doubt about the editorial independence of the World Service, despite being wholly financed by the Foreign Office.

One alternative would be to replace the licence fee with Treasury funding only to the extent that a pure public service broadcasting fund be established that would be contestable, in the sense of allowing all broadcasters and producers to apply, including the BBC. However, even a modest increase in public expenditure would go against the grain of current policy. One way of squaring that particular circle would be to allow the BBC to replace the licence fee with a subscription system, thus delivering a new flow of VAT revenue which would be sufficient to fund a wide range of public service content, provided by multiple suppliers, including no doubt the BBC for such offerings as Radio 3 and Radio 4.

Arguments against subscription

Subscription has been opposed by supporters of the licence fee for two reasons. The first is that it allows people to avoid paying for the BBC altogether, if they so choose. That way, they might end up losing out on valuable content. Yet the time when the mandarin in Whitehall knew best is surely long past: why should people be forced to pay for something that might be good for them, when there is no mechanism to force them to view it? In any case, the bulk of what 'might be good for them' should – under a subscription mechanism – still be available for free, including all TV news and current affairs and BBC radio, as public service content would always need to be unencrypted (as will radio for the foreseeable future).

Welfare loss

The second reason takes us back to practicality. Many studies have been provided – some even funded by the BBC – to show that subscription would either leave the BBC with lower income (implying a loss in consumer welfare amongst subscribers compared with the present situation) or that prices would have to be set at a level above the present licence fee (implying that subscribers would have to pay more for the same, as well as excluding some who would have been happy to continue at the level of the licence fee, but would now drop out – evidence, it is claimed, of further welfare loss).

Even if the underlying argument were true, that the BBC adopts it – as it has in its evidence to the 2014 Commons CMS Committee's hearings into the future of the Corporation – reveals how brazenly the BBC takes its income for granted. Only by treating choice, and the right to opt out of the BBC's services, as having no welfare value whatever, could it be argued that people who prefer to do without BBC TV, and not pay the licence fee, should be compelled to pay nonetheless, in order to keep down the cost of BBC TV to those who are happy to pay for it (especially as the BBC's research shows that 40 per cent of viewers would be prepared to pay double the licence fee to keep BBC television).

In any event, the problem with these flat-rate calculations is that they fail to reflect the way in which subscription systems work – with different options for viewers at different prices – or that they miss the most important driver for subscription revenues: the fact that the average number of television sets per home is nearly three, and that, under a subscription system, each set that the householder wanted enabled to receive BBC channels would need its own smart-card.

The benefits of subscription

This means that even though many households might choose – at least initially – to do without BBC TV channels, the total number of subscriptions (in the jargon of cable and satellite, revenue generating units) would almost certainly exceed the current number of television licences. This means that the cost to a single-set household of keeping just BBC1 and BBC2 could be a good deal less than the current licence fee, that the full array of BBC channels could be provided for probably £20 less than the current licence fee, and that for the first time the BBC could offer premium channels – such as arts, sport and documentaries – to specialist audiences.

As both Greg Dyke and John Birt have said in the past, the likelihood is that the BBC would thrive under a subscription system, which would also have the major side benefit of ending the prosecution of so-called evaders (non-payers would simply not be able to see BBC channels, unless these were showing unencrypted public service content). A huge benefit of switching to subscription would be to end government involvement in the way the BBC was funded, and create a true model of accountability – to consumers – to replace the artificial and unconvincing structures that currently prevail.

The prospect of joining the most dynamic of revenue mechanisms is all the more important for the BBC, in that it otherwise faces, not just steady decline in real-terms spending power as a result of its acquiescence in the coalition's licence fee policy, but even greater relative decline, as Sky ratchets up its budget for UK origination – already out-running Channel 4, about to overtake BBC2, and with both ITV and BBC1 in its sights.

The drivers of licence fee revenue

The truth about the licence fee's success is little understood. Essentially, the BBC has benefited from two extraordinary bursts of revenue dynamism – colour TV and household growth – which have either completely or largely run out of steam. The original radio BBC licence in 1922 had been ten shillings, which remained unchanged for many years, with rapid take-up of wireless sets allowing the BBC greatly to expand its income. Twenty five years later, the fee was still only £1. In 1946, a television licence was introduced, at £2. Both fees were, of course, subscriptions – if you paid for a service, you could legally receive it. There was no notion of universality; indeed, in many parts of the UK, TV was not even available.

At first, the costs of TV exceeded the revenues – BBC TV had to 'borrow' money from radio. But the launch of ITV in 1955 led to a surge in TV licence revenues, relegating radio to junior status. By 1971, the costs of collecting a separate radio licence were such that it was abandoned. Thereafter, radio would be free, funded out of the TV licences that well over 90 per cent of homes by then had taken out. Of course, the deal whereby the BBC monopoly was broken also broke the subscription link between the BBC and its customers. Now, the licence fee was required to watch any television, not just the BBC.

In 1968 came a huge advance: colour television. The colour television premium was set at £5, over and above the monochrome £6. That £11 total is roughly equivalent to the current £145.50: index-linking has protected the value of the fee, but the massive take-up of colour has generated revenue far exceeding the marginal additional cost of broadcasting in colour.

In the early 1980s, the combined revenues of ITV and Channel 4 had been double those of the BBC. Today, the licence fee provides the BBC with twice as much income as ITV and Channel 4 combined. This has enabled a huge expansion in TV and radio channels, and online. A much less obvious contributor to the BBC's remarkable growth has been a change in the UK's demographic structure. Natural population increase and immigration have pushed the UK's population to above the 60 million mark. But what has helped the BBC has been the surge in single person households. In 1961, there were 16.3 million households, with an average size of 3.1 persons. By 2001, there were over 22 million, with the number forecast to grow to over 25 million by 2021. In fact, that number was reached long before – the current figure is 25.5 million households, with an average size of 2.4 persons.

The proportion of single person households – all requiring a television licence – has soared from 12 per cent to 29 per cent: and this increase is almost entirely accounted for by the 40-65 age range. The 50 per cent rise in the number of households since 1961, with the licence fee essentially index-linked, and no additional costs required to reach the extra households, has been an enormous bonanza for the BBC. But that phenomenon has almost run its course. Average household size is unchanged in a decade. At the same time, colour penetration is nearly 100 per cent. There are only 11,000 monochrome licences in issue, and the monochrome licence was allowed to drop to one-third of a colour licence decades ago.

The licence fee freeze
What makes all this of even greater concern is that the coalition's licence fee settlement has carved 16 per cent of spending power out of the BBC. The freeze on the licence fee level until 2017 will further erode that spending power – for the first time in the BBC's 90-year existence. By relying on the licence fee, the BBC is not only shutting itself off from the dynamism of the subscription market, but also from that market's ability to add on new products that imitate the colour and household phenomena of the past. Sky and Virgin Media vigorously market high definition, 3-D, premium services, video on demand and multi-room, all requiring additional fees.

Converting to subscription would also allow the BBC to break free of the inexorable dumbing-down effect of the licence fee, as audience fragmentation forces a greater reliance on soaps in drama and so-called reality in factual programmes. The essence of the subscription model – as HBO has shown – is the opposite of the licence fee: emphasising the very highest quality, which commands subscriber loyalty. Subscription is certainly compatible with continued public ownership of the BBC and would give a solid underpinning of consumer satisfaction to whatever new accountability measures might emerge from a likely re-design of the BBC's governance structure. Arguably, having to engage directly with its audience would teach the modern generation of BBC managers the meaning of an important word: choice – without which, all kinds of bureaucratic error and bad habits can flourish.

Prospects for the licence fee

Yet there are several reasons why the licence fee might survive the pending negotiation over the BBC's future. First, population growth has resumed, and is forecast to accelerate. Although the BBC might feel nervous about being one of the few public bodies with a vested interest in mass immigration, the connection between that phenomenon and BBC revenues is little understood amongst the general public.

Secondly, politicians continue to have a vested interest in maintaining some degree of leverage over the BBC, in being able to vary the level of the licence fee. The BBC provides exposure for individual politicians, year in year out, across its various services, and as the overwhelmingly largest source of news consumption – and one with a constitutional commitment to impartiality – is the most important news organisation that politicians believe can be subject to some kind of pressure.

Thirdly, as the former BBC Finance Director, Zarin Patel, told the BBC Pension Fund trustees two years ago (in a letter obtained from a reluctant BBC under a Freedom of Information Act application), the BBC can draw some kind of perverse sense of security over licence fee funding by the sheer scale of expenditure that has been transferred to the BBC from government departments. In that connection, even if the BBC itself concluded that it might be better off giving up the compulsory licence fee, it might meet resistance from ministers, who would not want those hundreds of millions of pounds of expenditure (on S4C, the World Service, broadband roll-out, local TV and BBC monitoring) returned to the government tab.

Indeed, when Tessa Jowell, as Secretary of State at the time the BBC was seeking to re-develop Broadcasting House in Central London, was asked by the landlords for assurance that the BBC would be sufficiently securely funded for decades ahead to pay rent on the new building, she secretly gave a guarantee to that effect, which could only be underpinned by the licence fee lasting in perpetuity – or the government itself taking over the obligation. A similar guarantee might be sought by the BBC pension trustees in relation to the billion pound deficit in the fund if there were talk of replacing the licence fee with another mechanism.

Of course, these are not insuperable obstacles, but they are substantial. The BBC might hope for a change of government before its new charter and funding are finalised, but the chances are that the coalition will push for a settlement before the election. If so, there is a real risk that yet another swathe of public expenditure – perhaps the growing annual cost of free television licences for the over-75s (currently £600 millions) – will be loaded on to a frozen licence fee. In that event, the BBC might grasp the nettle which ministers have so studiously avoided and refuse to refund the licence fee to any of the over-75s unless they can demonstrate need: for instance, by showing that their council tax charge is below – say – £300 a year. That would reduce the impact on the BBC of such a transfer of responsibilities, but at a certain cost to its popularity amongst those who view television the most. The likelihood is that the licence fee will survive: but that the BBC will find such survival a bitter pill to swallow.

Note on the contributor
David Elstein is a former Chief Executive of Channel 5, Head of Programming at BSkyB, Director of Programmes at Thames TV, and managing director of Brook Productions Ltd and Primetime Productions Ltd. He has been Chairman of the British Screen Advisory Council, the National Film and Television School and the Commercial Radio Companies Association. He has been a Visiting Professor at the Universities of Oxford, Stirling and Westminster. He was the lead author of *Beyond the Charter*, published by the Broadcasting Policy Group (which he chairs) in 2004.

When the jacuzzi stops

Bernard Clark recommends the setting up of a semi-autonomous cash business *inside* the BBC. Moreover, an outside body with real teeth has to take the financial administration apart, put it back together in a wholly different way, and then police it

The BBC is a rich organisation – both creatively and financially. Mark Thompson wasn't wrong when, from the Chief Executive's chair at Channel 4, he described the BBC as 'wallowing in a jacuzzi of cash'. Oh, how he must have regretted that memorable phrase when he took over as Director-General and had to plead straightened times to government and parliament. It's clear they did not believe him, and don't believe the BBC now when it talks of poverty, and rightly so. It may no longer be a jacuzzi, but the cash flows very nicely into the BBC; it's far, far wealthier than the people who bankroll it – the licence fee payer.

Take redundancy, for instance, or what I call hyper-redundancy. A BBC staffer is guaranteed four weeks' pay for every year they have worked for the corporation, that's way more generous than the population of the UK as a whole, who have to foot the bill. Ditto holidays; ditto all kinds of allowances, and ditto – with a very big D – pensions. If only the workers and pensioners across Britain, who scrimp and save to pay their £145 each year had similar terms. And all this internal largesse is possible because at present there is no mechanism to stop it. So, if those jolly nice bosses want to over-reward trendy staff or, inexplicably, pay for half a dozen orchestras, or pay for a score or more foreign language services, out of money taken compulsorily from old ladies in Rochdale – too bad for the ladies.

Personally, I do not begrudge the BBC its money. The licence fee is a brilliant instrument for financing broadcasting, and the BBC has been consistently wise in making sure it serves the whole population, the folk who pay for it, rather than the elites it employs. As a result, very few, and I do mean very few, licence fee payers resent what they pay, certainly when compared to the energy companies, the banks or local authorities. Not least because it seems, and actually is, great value for money, which is the genius of the mechanism. Because we all have to pay, we all pay really very little, and what we get in return is a wonderland of programmes, channels, radio stations, web pages, the iPlayer, news and more.

The approaching apocalypse: Financial accountability

So far so good. However, there's not so much a cloud on the horizon, but an approaching apocalypse. It is called financial accountability, one thing the BBC has been very short of under the Trust and, indeed, throughout its history, which parliament is now on to, with significant support from the public. In a phrase; we love the programmes, abhor the extravagances, even if we know they are exaggerated by most of the press who always bash the BBC. Whatever we defenders of the Corporation say, we know something has to change pretty radically, that the *laissez-faire*, aka the bubbling jacuzzi, has to stop.

I have a hunch that with the next charter the governance of the BBC, broadly, will be split into two – Content to Ofcom and Finance (essentially supervision of the income from the license fee) to the National Audit Office (NAO). Paradoxically, so long as editorial freedom is protected and guaranteed, this could lead to the programming bosses genuinely deciding how to spend the money, rather than internal BBC bean-counters, which will be good for the BBC and, therefore, the viewer and listener. The key is the way the BBC's editorial bosses deal with the NAO, a less-than-sparkling organisation itself. It must be wholly on the BBC's terms, in particular, that the directors and controllers of television and radio and news decide how the money is spent.

Surely, you will say, that's how it works at the moment. Think again. If Director of Television Danny Cohen and Controller of BBC One Charlotte Moore really have the freedom to decide how to spend even a quarter of BBC1's £1.5 billion a year I would be surprised, because there are so many layers (I once counted nine) of administration and bureaucracy between commissioning decisions and audience, many of them just in the way. In fact, it was a former MD of Television, Aubrey Singer, who said to me: 'Programmes get made in spite of the BBC, not because of it.' So this friction between the commissioners and the organisation is nothing new. But it certainly has got worse.

When I last worked in Television Centre, about seven years ago, on the way to my office I would pass the main meeting room for the News Department, a long room with a single glass corridor window. Many times it was full of perhaps twenty to thirty people passively listening to a couple of bosses – bosses of what I do not know – pontificating, while writing on a white board or referring to single-spaced typed documents. Occasionally, I knew a couple of the attendees, who would raise their eyebrows with the desperation of the truly bored, dutifully going through corporate purgatory. As an ex-trainee cost accountant, I calculated the cost of such meetings. Presuming twenty-five people, at an average of £15 per hour, with overhead, establishment costs and depreciation, it worked out at about £3,000 for a two-hour meeting (some were much longer). That's a small street-worth of annual licence fees gone up in waffle. Being a curious sort of character, I once asked what the meetings were for. Staffing, internal communications, I learned: that sort of thing. One was about new office seats, which I later discovered were £295 each, with special orthopaedic support.

Obviously, the greater the grip an organisation has on the way it spends its money, the more that money is spent on its core purposes which, in the case of the BBC, is running television channels, local and national radio, news and internet services. If oversight from outside, whether the NAO or others, can get the BBC to focus its cash and creativity in the right direction – what it broadcasts – it will lead to something akin to a renaissance in what is a good institution, but one which is suffering under a self-imposed straitjacket.

The irony at present is that many well-intentioned and otherwise smart administrators in the BBC know that the organisation has a kind of bloat, but can do very little about it because it is in the nature of bureaucrats that they never see themselves as the problem. It's always someone else who is 'in the way' and should go, so you get a kind of pass-the-parcel staffing structure. A few years ago I ran into an old current affairs colleague in the canteen and he mentioned that he was spending the day commentating for News 24 on the latest round of BBC job cuts, said by the BBC to be about 2,000 over two years. 'This is the third such announcement I've covered in five years,' he said resignedly, 'but it's amazing how the Corporation always ends up the same size, about 23,000. It's because they get rid of the Indians, the producers and reporters, and have to hire them back, rather than the non-programme-making bosses, who have grown roots. Not that I'll say that on air, old chap. Wouldn't go down well.'

If you look closely at what the BBC spends its money on the problem is clear. Depending on how you classify Worldwide, the overall income is around £4.5 billion, of which more than a billion – 25 per cent – goes on training, marketing, property, finance and policy, none of which is directly about making programmes. And of the remaining three-quarters, I estimate that something like 40 per cent goes on administration, which means that less than half of the BBC's money is spent on actual broadcasting or new media, and it might be considerably less. I don't think there are any villains involved in this – on the contrary, the BBC is full of fine people, but they are trapped within inflexible structures, hierarchies and a management stranglehold. So how do we release them, and the generally benign corporation they work for?

Free up the money

In a phrase, free up the money. Literally, begin a process of allowing the directors of various broadcasting services and their controllers, to have as much freedom as possible, and cash-like control, over how every single pound is spent. Elsewhere in this book, Michael Grade argues that the BBC should become a commissioner broadcaster, and how if that were to happen it would in theory lead to the people who commission the various channels being free to spend as they wish. But my guess is that, although it would help, the commissioners would end up being sidetracked by the same old wily bean-counters who have been stacking the system for several decades.

I would like to go further, to actually create a semi-autonomous cash business *inside* the BBC. For instance, give Danny Cohen £2.5 billion in cash so he can dole it out to his controllers. OK, I don't actually mean in £20 notes, but if we begin from there, it's astounding where we reach. Let's invent a currency, we'll call them 'Beebs'. Danny sits at home one weekend and allocates the next year's Beebs to Charlotte Moore, B1 billion, B500 million to Janice Hadlow, former Controller BBC2, and so on, being careful to keep a few hundred million for Salford. Meanwhile, Charlotte and co are required to spend a certain proportion in the regions, on diversity and a few other compulsory nods to special interest groups, but otherwise they can dispense their dosh to whomever they feel will provide the content their audience wants, while taking full account of their public service obligations. Meanwhile, James Harding at News does the same, while saying he's not going to pay for any meetings attended by more than four people.

Guess who would immediately find they got no money? The very same people who at the moment control the corporations purse strings. So not only would Danny and Radio's Helen Boaden and even Peter Horrocks in Global News get to spend their full, true budget, but the folk who have stood in the way for oh-so-long would be out of a job. Hundreds, probably thousands of them, and all their wages and overheads and human resources and buddy-mentors and pension costs could end up, instead, on air. If a channel controller wants a bean-counter they could have one, and pay for them just as they would a producer, but I'd wager they would end up with one or two rather than half an army.

The funny thing is I am not the first person to come up with this plan. That great technocrat and misunderstood Director-General, John Birt, had much the same thought with 'Producer Choice', but even he, no slouch when it comes to bureaucratic in-fighting, got nobbled. At that time my independent production company was renting an office in the Television Centre and we had many a run-in with BBC Supply, BBC Buildings, BBC Engineering, BBC Communications and BBC Central Services. We have all heard about the cost of replacing a light bulb – £24 – yes, it was true. So we did it ourselves for 65p. We wanted desks – £115 per year for ones that cost less than that to buy, so we went out and bought them.

Then there was the VHS machine. The BBC had a rule that you could not have any electrical device (defined as anything with a plug) in the building unless it was supplied/certified by BBC Engineering. They wanted £800 for the same machine we could get down the road at Curry's for £44.95. So, employing the spirit of Producer Choice, if not the letter of BBC Regulations, we smuggled it in. And finally my favourite: when we needed to refurbish the room, basically a small voice-over booth, half a dozen shelves, a few monitors put up and a lick of paint, the Building Department wanted £88,000. My own builder, a reliable Welshman, offered to do it for £11,000, including VAT. When I told the BBC building boss and cited Producer Choice he said we would not be able to use my builder's men because they didn't have BBC passes, hadn't been vetted by BBC building staff or checked by HR, wouldn't be allowed to bring any equipment in, wouldn't be able to park, might be security risks, and weren't members of the BBC Club. I compromised on £21,000 – but he made me promise not to tell anyone, especially any BBC production staff, 'or everyone will be at it'. I was left with the abiding thought that if a director-general as powerful and determined as John Birt could not create an effective market inside the BBC, no one ever could.

The crucial role of the National Audit Office

In that experience, multiplied every week by a hundred or a thousand across the BBC, there are clues about why schemes such as Producer Choice, or any fair pricing mechanism, continue to be denied at the BBC, and why an outside body with real teeth has to take the financial administration apart, put it back together in a wholly different way, and then police it. Which is where the National Audit Office comes in.

I once met an engaging woman from the NAO who could recite the name of every Liverpool FC manager since the Second World War, and she was not the kind of person to mess with. If she sat in an office next to Danny Cohen or Charlotte Moore, I guarantee no one would pull the wool over their eyes about what something cost, or tie them in knots with bureaucratic gobbledegook. It would be the financial equivalent of the barley loaves and fish: almost overnight BBC1 would have all the cash it needed for what it does best: content. If the creative hub was allowed to have true financial control this will come quickly, and perversely that's the discipline an outside body would bring.

I am not saying the BBC is the only public organisation to suffer from exorbitant internal costs, I know it isn't, but it's the one I am most committed to, the one I would most like to see throw off internal constraints and fully open its doors to the competitive external world. But it won't do this willingly, so, sadly, parliament and the DCMS will have to act through the new charter to impose real financial discipline and market forces from the outside. Sad, but also exhilarating, because proper accountability, from wherever it comes, will ensure the licence payers' money is spent where it should be. The trick with the next charter is to ensure a worldly and rigorous balance between policing the internal finances of an overbearing bureaucracy while protecting programmes and editorial from any interference whatsoever. Given the existing overwhelming support of the public for the editorial independence of the BBC, I think it can be done.

It is a risk, certainly. But the greater risk is to do nothing and let the world's greatest cultural institution be pulled down by its own civil service. It's time to put the 'creatives' back in charge and make the organisation serve them, rather than the other way round.

Note on the contributor
Since leaving the BBC, Bernard Clark has been an independent producer for thirty years.

The best is yet to come

The BBC may have had a tough time over the last 18 months but Andrew Scadding believes it has begun to set a clear and ambitious vision for the future – the best really is yet to come

Everyone knows the last 18 months have not been the easiest for the BBC. We have got things wrong – and have rightly been held to account – but we have also got many things right. Throughout this period the BBC has continued to deliver and often excel in its central role of giving the nation fantastic, enlivening, thought provoking programmes. If the BBC had failed in that, then our future would be in doubt. I believe the BBC is now more relevant today than it has ever been. But to continue into the future, there are issues that need to be addressed.

When Director-General Tony Hall outlined his vision in autumn 2013, he announced his intention for the BBC to be 'well managed, robustly but with simplicity and with directness'. Addressing severance pay and the Digital Media Initiative head-on demonstrates our commitment to this new approach, proactively tackling poor practice. Thoroughly investigating the failures in the historic culture that allowed Savile to operate unchecked and the mistakes made in the aftermath of the revelations was the only proper response and the BBC has taken strong corrective measures – re-evaluating and strengthening child protection and bullying and harassment procedures as well as implementing changes to governance and reporting.

But through this period, the BBC delivered: in 2013, 17.3 million people watched Andy Murray win Wimbledon; eight of the top ten watched programmes at Christmas were on the BBC; there were 3 billion iPlayer requests; more people than ever listened to radio with record-breaking Q4 RAJAR results and we broadcast great British dramas including *Sherlock*, *Doctor Who*, the award-winning *Top of the Lake* and *Luther*. The BBC has secured rights to the FA Cup for the next four seasons and strengthened our commitment to women's sport, including extensive coverage of the 2013 Women's European Championships.

We have moved 6,000 staff into world-class facilities at Broadcasting House, bringing together network and global services in Television, Radio, News and Online and providing the most advanced digital broadcast and production centre in the world. We reached our target to audio-describe 20 per cent of our programmes a year early and, in November 2013, we raised more than £31 million for Children in Need, supporting 2,600 UK projects. Mishal Husain joined Radio 4's *Today* programme and Marin Alsop was the first woman to conduct the *Last Night of the Proms*. Radio 1's Academy gave hundreds of young adults in Derry/Londonderry the opportunity to learn practical production skills and the Young Ambassadors programme in Salford continues to provide work placements to school-leavers.

Audience trust and approval have risen in the current charter period and have at all times been higher than 2007 levels. We have focused on growing reach, quality and value and been successful in achieving an increase in each. There have been serious failings but it would be a mistake to shy away from the investigative reporting and technological innovation that are the BBC's trademarks. We are realigning the BBC to be the organisation we are proud of and that the licence fee payer expects and deserves, delivering robust journalism, promoting creativity and developing talent.

Where next?

The BBC has always been at the forefront of technological change: the first public television service in 1936, Europe's first colour TV service on BBC Two in 1967, Ceefax in 1971, the red button in 1999 and iPlayer in 2007. This has been made possible by a combination of our R. and D. expertise, long-term perspective and access to stable funding. We can be an early-mover where commercial risks may be too high for others, and can help in coordinating the industry to achieve collaborative initiatives and open standards – as, for example, our pan-industry work developing standards with groups such as the Digital Video Broadcasting Project (DVB). We are always looking at new ways of delivering the content – via mobile apps, via social media and via web-connected TVs. We are developing products that are more responsive, more prone to personalisation, more adaptable to any device. It is this sort of innovation and creativity that the public want to see the BBC focusing on.

In his speech in the autumn 2013, the Director-General said the BBC needed to evolve from an organisation that speaks to everyone at the same time, to one that also has direct relationships with individual licence fee payers. We want to create a public service which is both universal and personal. We want people to be able to easily find the content they enjoy, but we also want to surprise them – a world of 'you like this … but you might never have thought you would like this'. With this in mind, we have announced a range of dynamic new services, personalising the audience's experience of the BBC. Already people are tagging and downloading music favourites from BBC radio with Playlister, which was launched in October 2013 and, crucially, done in partnership with the music industry. In the summer of 2014, we will re-launch the Space, the online partnership between Arts Council England and the BBC, showcasing new talent and new content, allowing artists and audiences to access digital art, live, free and on demand. Building on the unparalleled success of iPlayer, the BBC, working with PACT and others, propose to extend the period that programmes are available to watch for free from seven days to 30. We know that people want to see and re-watch older programmes so we plan to launch BBC Store, a commercial venture allowing the UK public to buy a wide range of programming – classics as well as recent ones they might have missed – which they can keep forever. In addition, Tony Hall committed to some major educational initiatives – again based on the principle of the BBC as the body that can help curate and lead, using our own content and linking to that of others – for computer coding in 2015 and Shakespeare in 2016. This is an ambitious and innovative time for the BBC.

These ambitions cost money. The licence fee has been frozen since 2010 and like many organisations in recent years, the BBC has had to make tough choices about what we can afford and what we prioritise. As part of the current licence fee settlement, by 2016, we have to deliver £700 million of annual savings. We are committed to investing as much of the licence fee as possible in programme making and technology development, so there has been a focus on streamlining infrastructure and the amount we spend on running the BBC. We have a strong track record of delivering annual efficiency savings – 3.7 per cent of our cost base each year since 2008/9. That's £580 million by 2012/3. We have reduced staffing levels and marketing spend as well as rationalising our property portfolio, with the exit from Television Centre and other London sites. Unfortunately, the scale of the savings challenge we face can not be met by efficiency alone – tough choices on content and services will be necessary. They may also be controversial.

What should the BBC be?

That people still so actively debate the BBC, and everyone has a view, demonstrates its significance, relevance and central position in British culture. Critics have always said that the Corporation is too big, too wasteful, too left-wing, too right-wing, too monolithic, too insensitive, too white, too male, too old, but still 96 per cent of the population consume some BBC output every week.[1] Harriet Harman summarised it in her speech to the Oxford Media Convention in 2013:

> It's impossible to describe – without sounding gushing – the centrality of the BBC in the life of this country. We think we bring up our own children – but Auntie is there alongside us as we do it. The BBC news is most trusted not just here – but around the world. The sheer scale of the BBC – the world's biggest broadcasting organisation – means that it is able to be, and is, a massive centre of gravity for our creative industries. Under its

wings, there flourish an eco-system of trainees and independent production companies.[2]

The benefits to Britain of the BBC go far beyond the programming, events and partnerships that the audience sees. In 2011/12, the BBC's total expenditure in the UK was £4,341 million. This generated a Gross Value Added of £8,323 million for the UK economy, equivalent to £2 of economic value for 1£ of the licence fee. The BBC supports the creative sector by investing in skills and technology innovations. The scale and scope of our commissioning of content from the independent production sector and the support for exports of UK content create jobs and investment. Speaking at MediaCityUK in May 2013, Chancellor George Osborne used the Brian Redhead Lecture to argue that the BBC 'has been catalyst for what is now the biggest creative digital hub in Europe outside of London'.[3] By that time, the BBC's move to Salford had already added 1,500 jobs to the creative sector in the North West. The BBC shares its knowledge and expertise with the wider creative sector by training BBC staff and others working in the creative sector, encouraging the development of creative clusters, and joint ventures and partnerships. Following on from a similar event in Birmingham, we worked with local and national partners to host 'Digital Bristol' and 'Digital Cardiff' weeks in 2013, aimed at boosting the creative economy. In a multitude of ways, we set the industry standard for broadcasting and the creative sector – hardware design for Digital Terrestrial Television (DTT), interactive services, local radio apprenticeships, provision of access services, blind casting.

The Prime Minister also advocated a robust and diverse BBC: 'It should be independent of government. It should not be privatised … You have to allow the BBC to have popular shows as well as high quality public news and affairs. You can't have BBC One without *Strictly* and *EastEnders*; you have to have a mix of making the popular good, and the good popular.' And there are tangible results from the good becoming popular: John Lewis reported that sales of telescopes has risen 136 per cent 'thanks to prime time TV shows' such as *Stargazing*[4] and a similar increase was reported by a number of retailers in response to the *Great British Bake-Off*.[5]

Plurality in the media industry has also been under particular scrutiny recently. Critics claim the BBC has strayed too far from its core purpose and is becoming too dominant, particularly in provision of online news. These concerns are not new. Before the BBC was even launched in October 1922, 'some anxiety had been expressed by the press as to whether the Broadcasting Company would be allowed to broadcast news' but there was 'hope that they would be able to come to a friendly arrangement'.[6] The BBC has a smaller TV and radio market share than 20 years ago despite providing more services. In fact, the BBC today takes a smaller share of UK broadcast revenues than at any other time in its history.[7] The market is becoming ever more competitive and the resources of the new international players, including Google, Lovefilm (Amazon) and Netflix, dwarf those of the BBC. Both domestically and abroad, a wider range of companies are beginning to invest in content, but strong public broadcasting spurs a 'race to the top' between public and commercial media, raising overall standards across the industry. There is a positive correlation between expenditure of content and programming by a public broadcaster and its commercial competitors – a 'competition for quality'. Countries in which the main public service broadcaster shows a diverse range of genres and content, particularly the UK, Germany and Denmark, tend to have commercial channels that also broadcast wide-ranging content.[8] Despite the increasing competition globally, the BBC is a news powerhouse and we want to reach half a billion people worldwide with our current affairs output by 2022. Internationally, the BBC's reputation is undiminished and is a great ambassador for Britain abroad. We outperform all international rivals too, with BBC One rated highest on quality out of 66 major TV channels examined globally and BBC Two in third place.[9] Famously, Aung San Suu Kyi said of her detention: 'Everywhere I have been, the BBC has been with me.'[10] For many, the BBC is their only source of impartial information. In April 2014, funding for the World Service transfers from the Foreign and Commonwealth Office to the licence fee and this gives us the opportunity for further investment – an increase of £5 million for 2014 has already been announced by the BBC Trust.

A number of the contributions in this book have concluded that the licence fee has had its day, that it is regressive, unpopular and poor value-for-money. We do not believe that is a view shared by the majority of those who pay their 40p a day, for content they have consumed more and enjoyed more than they did 20 years ago.

The principles of universal access, shared investment and ownership by the public, not only enables economies of scale, it allows the BBC to be a national cultural mission. The main alternatives would mean more expensive services enjoyed by fewer people. Adopting a subscription model would remove that universality, excluding those who can not afford to pay, and would turn the BBC into a commercial operator with an incentive to provide services that maximise revenues and/or profits. The evidence suggests that a subscription model would be likely to reduce the payment base, increasing costs for consumers who remain.[11] Both subscription and introducing advertising could jeopardise the BBC's impartiality. It is notable that audiences report the lack of advertising on our services as a key characteristic they value about the BBC. An advertiser-funded BBC would also have significant consequences for commercial broadcasters, splitting those finite income streams between more providers, and the revenue available for investment in content. Funding through direct taxation would leave the BBC exposed to fluctuations in government spending and priorities as well as threatening our independence. In the modern world, awash with opinion, that independent voice is ever more important.

The BBC is in the middle of a period of genuine creative success, from the Olympics to *Dr Who*, from *In Our Time* to promoting emerging talent on Radio 1.

Is the BBC in crisis? No. Has it had setbacks? Yes. Is it developing a clear and ambitious vision for the future? Unapologetically. The BBC has already embarked on its biggest ever season of programming and events, commemorating World War 1 over the four years of the centenary. This is the BBC doing what it does best. As the Director-General said when he took over the BBC: our best years lie ahead of us.

Notes

[1] Cross-Media Insight Survey by GfK for the BBC, c6,000 UK adults per quarter, FY 2012/13

[2] Harriet Harman speech to the Oxford Media Convention, 25 January 2012. Available online at http://www.labour.org.uk/harriet-harman-speech-to-oxford-media-convention, accessed on 10 February 2014

[3] George Osborne's Brian Redhead Lecture, 24 May 2013. Available online at: http://www.bbc.co.uk/blogs/aboutthebbc/posts/Brian-Redhead-Lecture-2013, accessed on 10 February 2014

[4] John Lewis Press Centre (2013) Sales of telescopes up 136% at John Lewis, 11 March. Available online at http://www.johnlewispresscentre.com/Press-Releases/Sales-of-telescopes-up-136-at-John-Lewis-146b.aspx, accessed on 10 February 2014

[5] *Daily Telegraph* (2013) How the *Great British Bake-Off* changed Britain, 12 March. Available online at http://www.telegraph.co.uk/foodanddrink/10370144/How-the-Great-British-Bake-Off-changed-Britain.html, accessed on 10 February 2014

[6] *The Times* (1922) Broadcasting 'an a week or two', 13 October

[7] All BARB-measured news provision (i.e. the PSB channels including BBC News Channel, Sky News, Euronews and Fox News) for H1 2012. Excluding the smallest of these in 2010, Fox News and Euronews, the BBC accounts for 52 per cent of TV news minutes broadcast (but 72 per cent of viewing)

[8] BBC Report (2013) Public and Private Broadcasters across the World: The Race to the Top. Available online at http://www.bbc.co.uk/blogs/aboutthebbc/posts/Public-and-Private-Broadcasters-across-the-world-The-race-to-the-top, accessed on 6 February 2014

[9] Populus for the BBC, October 2013: 14 countries (UK, UAE, USA, Netherlands, Australia, Brazil, Sweden, Portugal, Denmark, Germany, France, Italy, Japan and Spain), 500 adults per country rated the quality of TV overall and the quality of each of the biggest channels in their country

[10] BBC News (2012) Aung San Suu Kyi visits her BBC 'family', *Ariel*, 19 June, Available online at http://www.bbc.co.uk/ariel/18508549, accessed on 10 February 2014

[11] Based on analysis by Terrington and Company/Ipsos MORI 2012. Ipsos MORI for BBC, 2,078 adults 15+, 2012

Note on the contributor

Andrew Scadding has been Head of Public Affairs for the BBC since 2003 and is now Head of Corporate Affairs, leading the BBC's engagement with the political world. He was Head of Broadcasting for the Conservative Party from 1999-2003 and before that worked as a producer in BBC News and Current Affairs, including at *On the Record*, producing interviews for John Humphrys and in elections coverage.

Lightning Source UK Ltd.
Milton Keynes UK
UKOW06f0013270515

252346UK00001B/5/P